How to Do Everything with the Internet

How to Do Everything with

the Internet

About the Author

Dennis Jones has taught introductory computer courses at adult-education and college level, and has been a professional writer for over twenty years. In non-fiction, he is co-author of Que's *Special Edition Using Microsoft FrontPage 2000,* and has contributed to several other books related to Windows and the Internet, including Que's *Platinum Edition Using Windows 98* and *Using HTML 4.*

In his fiction career he has written ten internationally published novels, and at present is working on the third volume of a fantasy trilogy entitled *The House of the Pandragore.* The trilogy's first volume, *The Stone and the Maiden,* was recently published in Canada and the US by HarperCollins, and the second volume, *The Mask and the Sorceress,* is scheduled for release in early 2001. Dennis lives with his wife Sandi in a log farmhouse near Ottawa, in Canada.

About the Contributing Author

Sandra Jones is a painter, editor, and Internet researcher. She provided most of the background material for *How to Do Everything with the Internet,* in addition to giving editorial input to keep the book as user-friendly as possible. She is deeply involved in the local artistic community, and is currently working on an extensive project to catalogue and record the works of the Canadian painter William Caldwell. She lives near Ottawa, Canada, with her husband Dennis.

About the Tech Reviewer

Bill Bruns is currently the Assistant Director for Business Systems at the University of Illinois' College of Medicine.

Originally wanting to work in television production, he became interested in computers while working on an undergraduate internship at Square One TV, a children's mathematics and problem-solving show produced by the Children's Television Workshop.

Bill has been a technical editor for five years and has recently started tech editing for Osborne/McGraw-Hill.

Recently, he and his partners have started Jacob Marlie Financial, Inc. (www.jacobmarlie.com). Jacob Marlie is an Internet company that provides professional invoicing and collection services to college fraternities and sororities.

Previously, he built the computer network at the University of Illinois' Illini Student Union, and he ran administrative computing at New York University's Tisch School of the Arts. Bill holds bachelors degrees in Telecommunications and English Literature from Indiana University, a Masters of Public Administration from New York University, and is a Certified Netware Engineer.

How to Do Everything with the Internet

the Internet

Dennis Jones

Osborne/**McGraw-Hill**

Berkeley   New York   St. Louis   San Francisco
Auckland   Bogotá   Hamburg   London
Madrid   Mexico City   Milan   Montreal   New Delhi
Panama City   Paris   São Paulo
Singapore   Sydney   Tokyo   Toronto

Osborne/**McGraw-Hill**
2600 Tenth Street
Berkeley, California 94710
U.S.A.

For information on translations or book distributors outside the U.S.A., or to arrange bulk purchase discounts for sales promotions, premiums, or fund-raisers, please contact Osborne/**McGraw-Hill** at the above address.

How to Do Everything with the Internet

1234567890 CUS CUS 01987654321

ISBN 0-07-213028-8

Publisher	Brandon A. Nordin
Vice President & Associate Publisher	Scott Rogers
Senior Acquisitions Editor	Jane Brownlow
Project Editor	Monika Faltiss
Acquisitions Coordinator	Cindy Wathen
Technical Editor	Bill Bruns
Copy Editor	Claire Splan
Proofreader	Stefany Otis
Indexer	Claire Splan
Computer Designers	E. A. Pauw, Elizabeth Jang, Melinda Moore Lytle
Illustrators	Robert Hansen, Michael Mueller, Beth E. Young
Series Design	Michelle Galicia
Cover Design	Albert Leggett, Tom Willis

This book was composed with Corel VENTURA™ Publisher.

Contents at a Glance

Contents

Acknowledgments

A lot of friends contributed their ideas for what should go into this book, and I'd like to thank them for their invaluable help: Carolyn Acorn, Rob Acorn, Debby Baker, Debbie Broughton, Carol Fragiskos, Marie Hamilton, Bob Higham, Kieran Jones, Philip Jones, Robert A. Jones, Peter Leliveld, Margaret McClintock, Bob McCook, and Marny McCook.

I'd also like to thank Jane Brownlow for thinking of me when this project came up; and my thanks also go to Cindy Wathen, Monika Faltiss, and the rest of the editorial and production team at Osborne/McGraw-Hill, for their sterling work in making the whole project run so smoothly from beginning to end.

Dennis Jones

Introduction

Over the past few years, literally millions of people in North America and elsewhere have gotten themselves hooked up to the Internet. This book is intended to help those users, both the novices and the knowledgeable, to get the most out of the vast array of services and resources that this extraordinary communications tool provides.

The book begins at the beginning, and assumes you have some basic understanding of how to use a Windows-based or Macintosh computer. The first essential is to actually get connected, so Part I, "Explore the Internet," starts by telling you how to obtain basic Internet services. From there it goes on to teach you how to surf the Web with a Web browser like Netscape Navigator or Internet Explorer, and covers the key skill of using search engines to locate the information and resources you need.

Part II, "Keep and Use What You've Found," shows you how to get your computer to save the information you find on the Internet, and tells you how you can download and install computer software to your own machine. It also explores the ways in which you can enjoy the music and video available on the Web.

In Part III, "Communicate on the Internet," you'll learn the essential skills of e-mail, including using attachments and dealing with spam. In this section also, you'll find out about newsgroups, chat rooms, online gaming, and buying and selling online.

Since not all is sweetness and light in this world, the subject of Part IV is "Your Security and the Internet". These chapters cover the issues of your personal privacy and the possible threats to it, the dangers of computer viruses and the methods of dealing with them, and ways you should protect yourself and your family from the less savory corners of the Net.

Finally, in Part V, we cover the basics of creating your own Web site, including how to acquire and use a Web page editor and how to select a hosting service that will present your site to the world.

Like the other books in the How to Do Everything series, *How to Do Everything with the Internet* has special elements to help you get the most out of it. Some of these are:

- ■ **How To**   These text boxes contain techniques or procedures that will help you carry out useful supplemental tasks.

- ■ **Notes**   These provide extra information to round out the matter being discussed in the main text. They're sort of like footnotes.

■ **Cautions**   These warn you of possible unwanted consequences of some action or condition.

■ **Tips**   These are small tidbits to make your current activities a little easier.

■ **Did you know?**   These text boxes give extra background information on the matter being discussed in the main text.

I'd like to say in closing that this book was a pleasure (usually) to write. When it wasn't a pleasure, it was generally because of my very slow, rural Internet connection. In fact, you may rest assured that if *I* could get something to work with my scratchy old phone line, then no matter how bad your connection is, *you* should be able to get it to work, too. Enjoy the book.

Part I

Explore the Internet

Chapter 1

The Very Basic Basics

How To . . .

- ■ Understand dial-up and high-speed Internet services
- ■ Decipher modem speed ratings
- ■ Understand the difference between online services and Internet Service Providers
- ■ Evaluate available services and decide which is best for you
- ■ Set up a dial-up connection in Windows
- ■ Monitor your Internet connection
- ■ Carry out advanced dial-up connection setups
- ■ Fine-tune your dial-up modem
- ■ Understand high-speed connection setup
- ■ Understand shared Internet connections

If you've leafed through other books about the Internet, you've likely noticed how many of them begin with a detailed account of the Internet phenomenon and how it developed. This, however, is not one of those books.

Why not? Well, when you're lost and you open up a road map, you don't want to be greeted by a history of road maps. You just want to use the thing to get un-lost. If you're buying shoes, you don't want to have to listen to a history of footwear before you can even try on a pair. You just want the shoes.

So let's get right into it, shall we?

What Is the Internet?

Here's all you need to know about the Internet, for the moment:

- ■ The Internet is a huge, worldwide collection of computers that are connected by various types of communications links, including the telephone system. Together, these linked computers store an immense quantity of information about everything under the sun.

- ■ Such a collection of computers is called a *network* (that's the "net" part of "Internet"). Computer networks are very common in business and government establishments, but the one we call the Internet is different from all the others for two reasons. First, it's the biggest network on the planet; second, it's freely accessible to the public.

- ■ You can connect your computer to this enormous network. Then you can get your hands on almost any of the information contained there, and store that information for your own use, again using your own computer.

Those are the essentials. (However, if you *do* want to read a history of the Internet, there's one at the end of this book, in Appendix A.)

The Internet can provide you with access to many useful services. E-mail is one such service and the World Wide Web ("the Web") is another, but there are plenty more. This book will help you explore all of them.

Understand the Types of Internet Connections

If you're reading these words you're probably already connected to the Internet, or you're thinking about getting yourself connected. But if you're a computer novice, or even a moderately experienced computer user, the whole issue of getting started may be somewhat intimidating. This feeling can be made worse by the fact that *everybody else* seems to find getting on the Internet no big deal—or at least it looks that way to you.

In fact, getting connected isn't quite as easy as mowing a lawn, but it's not neurosurgery, either. Actually, you may find it's less of a problem than the legendary one of trying to program your VCR.

But how to begin? Apart from a computer and a phone line, the main thing you need is an Internet service company that can set you up with your connection to the Internet. However, even before you can figure out which company to pick, you have to find out what types of connections are available to you, and then decide which of these types you want. Armed with that knowledge, you can then go looking for the right organization to sell it to you.

At the moment, there are two basic kinds of Internet connections. There are low-speed connections, and there are high-speed connections. Actually, there's only one kind of low-speed connection. It's called a dial-up connection, because it uses the regular phone lines, and because it actually does dial a phone number to connect you to the Internet.

Understand Dial-Up Connections

At the moment, most North Americans who use the Internet are linked to it using a dial-up connection. Here's what you need to join them:

- ■ A computer. If you bought it within the last two years, it's almost certainly adequate for a dial-up connection.

- ■ A modem. This is a piece of hardware that allows you to connect your computer to the phone jack in your wall. Modems can be internal (inside the computer case) or external (a small box connected to the computer by various wires). Computers of recent manufacture often have modems already installed. If you're not sure whether you've got one, check the documentation that came with your machine or contact the vendor.

- ■ An account with an organization that provides Internet connections. There's nothing mysterious about such an account. You simply pay a monthly fee for your connection.

- ■ A telephone line.

Those four items are all that's required. Once the dial-up connection is installed, here's how it works in everyday use.

1. You make a couple of mouse clicks to tell your computer to dial the phone number your service provider gave you.

2. The provider's computer answers the phone call. The two machines warble at each other for a few seconds, which you can hear from your modem unless the modem sound is turned off.

3. The warble stops and the connection is complete. Depending on how your connection is set up, you may be asked at this point for your username and password; this is called *login authentication.*

4. To disconnect, you use a mouse click or two to tell your computer to hang up the phone.

That's all there is to it. Where the complications begin—somewhat—is with the hardware, specifically with the modem.

Modems and Dial-Up Connections

Almost all Internet providers supply what's called a "56K connection" or "56K dial-up account," or something like that. The 56K is the important bit. It refers to the speed with which the information from the Internet can travel down the phone line into your computer, so you can look at that information on the screen.

Currently, 56K is the highest dial-up speed available. However, to take advantage of this speed, you have to use what's called a "56K modem." Almost all modems manufactured now are 56K modems. In the case of a modem, the "56K" refers to the maximum amount of information the device can receive and process in one second, under ideal conditions. However, your actual connection speed will be affected by the quality of the telephone system itself. Some telephone company switches limit the speed to 28.8K, and lines with a lot of static on them will also slow things down. The result is this: the slower your connection, the longer the information will take to appear fully on your monitor screen. A poor-quality phone line may also cause the connection to be broken off at unpredictable intervals, and you then have to reconnect.

You should be aware, too, that even 56K modems will not handle information at their maximum rated speed. This is a technical limitation imposed by current phone line technology. Even with very good, modern phone lines, your 56K modem will actually connect at maximum speeds between 42K and 48K.

Modems manufactured prior to the 56K devices connected at speeds between 14.4K and 33.6K, which is pretty slow. If you've got one of these, you might consider replacing it; quality 56K modems from well-known manufacturers have become fairly inexpensive these days. You'll enjoy the faster responses you get, assuming your phone line is capable of the higher speed.

If you don't have a modem or if you want to upgrade, you'll obviously need to acquire and install the hardware. The details of modem installation and setup depend on the particular make and model of the device, and unfortunately there are far too many modem types to allow covering them here. You should refer to the modem documentation for details on how to carry out the installation.

Understand High-Speed Connections

High-speed connections allow information to travel quickly from the Internet into your computer, much more quickly than a dial-up connection permits. In practice, this means that you don't have to wait so long for images and text to appear on your screen. With dial-up connections, a picture appears sloooowly on your monitor. With a high-speed connection, it's there in a flash. Lots of Internet services work better at higher speeds: music, radio, video, voice, downloads. It's a more pleasant experience all around.

There are four basic types of high-speed connections, but not all are available in all areas, and in some regions none are available at all. Also, not all the bugs have been worked out of these technologies yet, and some subscribers report service outages and unexplained glitches. These presumably will diminish as the technology matures and the providers gain experience. We'll examine each of the four technologies in the following sections.

Digital Subscriber Lines (DSL)

DSL is also called ADSL, the "A" meaning "Asymmetric," which doesn't matter for our present purposes. DSL cleverly uses existing phone lines to carry the Internet service so that you can talk on your telephone while you're still connected to the Internet. In fact, with DSL, you're *always* connected to the Internet—you don't connect and disconnect, as you do with dial-up. Connection speeds vary, and you pay more to get a faster connection. DSL is not available everywhere, though. To find out if you can get it, contact your telephone company.

NOTE

Sooner or later you'll come across the phrase "broadband access." This buzzword refers to a connection, either wired or wireless, that can carry a large amount of information in a short time. High-speed Internet connections, as discussed here, are an example of broadband access.

Cable

The Internet signal here is carried on the TV cable network (it doesn't interfere with the TV signal). As with DSL, you're always connected. It's fast, but there have been reports of slower service when a lot of subscribers are using the service at the same time.

Satellite

This is just edging above the horizon, so to speak. Its great advantage is that it is available wherever there's a line of sight to an appropriate satellite, even in rural areas (like the authors') that are beyond the reach of cable or DSL. As yet, however, the technology has some way to go. So far you still need a phone line to send information out, even though you're receiving data at high speed from the satellite. It's slower than cable or DSL, and is considerably more expensive. However, improvements in these areas are on the way and satellite Internet services may eventually become competitive with DSL and cable.

Integrated Services Digital Network (ISDN)

ISDN may be available from your phone company, provided you live in an urban area. It has formerly been a business-oriented technology, and residential ISDN isn't all that common. It has a reputation for being difficult to set up and maintain, and it can be quite expensive even if you can get it. It's also not all that much faster than dial-up—about three times as fast, generally.

Make the Decision

Having absorbed all the information just presented, you now have to decide whether you want a dial-up service or one of the high-speed services. Of course the decision may be made for you if dial-up is the only service available where you live.

Let's suppose you settle on dial-up, for whatever reason. Now, how do you pick a provider? Unfortunately, you have yet another decision to make, between two major classes of service provider. These are:

- ■ Online services
- ■ Everybody else

At present there are only two major online services in North America. The best known of these is America Online (AOL). CompuServe used to be another one, but it is no longer an independent since AOL bought it; it's still available, though not very widely used. The other major online service is MSN, an acronym for the Microsoft Network.

"Everybody else," which is the second choice, refers to the enormous number of national, regional, and local companies that provide Internet access. The generic term for these organizations is Internet Service Providers (ISPs).

Of course, the online services like MSN are also in a sense ISPs, in that they provide access to the Internet. However, while the true ISPs furnish mainly the basics (which are pretty impressive in themselves), the online services add some extras that are only available to members, such as (in the case of AOL) proprietary newsgroups, parental controls, and members-only chat rooms.

If you decide on an online service, there's not much deciding to do; you're stuck with AOL or MSN. And if you're a Mac user, there's no decision at all. MSN can only be used by PCs running Windows, so it's AOL for Mac users and that's that.

If you don't want AOL or MSN, you must then choose an ISP. Unlike the online services, ISPs are plentiful and you won't have much difficulty locating lots to choose from. They come in all sizes, too, from small local and regional services to others that work at a national level. The problem is, how do you know which one to sign up with?

I'd begin by asking people I know who are already connected which ISP they use and how they like it. You might be able to make a decision on that basis, but such anecdotal evidence is more of a beginning than an end. To be on the safe side, you really should supplement it with some research. Here's a checklist of things to find out:

■ Are you a Macintosh user? If so, your first question to the ISP should be whether they support Macs. Some of them don't.

■ Is there a local number you can use for your dial-up access? You don't want to incur long-distance charges for your time online. Note that an 800 number, supplied for long-distance access by the ISP, may not be free. Also, in some areas an ISP will charge for what they call a "local long-distance" call. Avoid these if possible.

■ Does the ISP provide adequate software to get you up and running, along with suitable documentation? There should be a step-by-step procedure to help you set up your connection, along with a recent version of a browser and e-mail software.

> NOTE *A browser, or Web browser, is a computer program that retrieves information from the Internet and displays it for you on your monitor. You'll discover plenty more about browsers as you go along in this book.*

■ Does the ISP furnish adequate technical support? This is very important, obviously, if you're a novice to the details of getting connected.

■ Is the technical support free? Is it available 24 hours a day, seven days a week?

■ Does the ISP have a reputation for reliability?

■ Can the ISP handle its customers at peak times, or are there a lot of busy signals when people try to connect? You can check this by getting their dial-up number and calling it from a regular phone at busy periods; one of these is just after the dinner hour when people are checking their e-mail at home. If you get continual busy signals, that's a bad sign. If, instead, you hear screeching and warbling, that's their computer answering your call. That's a good sign.

■ If you travel a lot and need to use your e-mail while you're on the road, is the ISP large enough to provide this service? In other words, does it provide local connection numbers in the regions you intend to visit? If it doesn't, you'll have to dial long distance and foot the bill. This is where a nationally available ISP may be preferable to a local or regional one, especially if you're on the road a lot.

■ Will the ISP keep up to date with technology? For example, if it doesn't offer DSL, does it intend to do so at a later date? This is where the local ISPs may be less attractive than regional or national ones. These small companies may be unable to find the capital for upgrading or replacing their hardware. Also, they have a larger chance of going under and leaving you scrambling to replace the service.

■ Does the ISP allow simultaneous connections? That is, if you have two phone lines and two computers, can both connect to the ISP at the same time? If the ISP allows it, how are such connections billed?

■ How many mailboxes (for e-mail) are supplied with the account? If you want more, how much is the additional charge per box?

■ How much does the service cost? Much of the industry is moving to dial-up accounts that give you unlimited connect time for around $20 per month, regardless of the time of day. With others, you pay a monthly fee for a set number of hours of connect time per month, and if you use more hours in a month than specified, you're charged additionally. These "overlimit" rates can be steep, as much as $2 per hour of extra connect time, so be sure to find out about them. Note that if you use *fewer* than the specified number of hours in a month, you don't carry the surplus over to the next month; it's "use it or lose it." Also, see if the ISP gives a discount if you pay for several months in advance.

■ Is there a trial period available? If not, do they have what's called "block hours"? This is when you buy a certain number of hours that you use over a specified period. If you don't like the service, you can decline to buy more and look for another ISP.

■ Do they have a privacy policy? Do they sell their subscriber lists to businesses?

■ What Internet services do you get with your subscription? You should expect at least one e-mail address, browser software (probably Netscape) to get you started, a provision for you to put your own Web page on their computers if you want to, newsgroups, telnet, and access to FTP and the World Wide Web. (Don't worry if you don't understand what some of these services are for. You'll learn about them later in the book). Actually, the chances of any ISP *not* offering these services nowadays are remote, but it's best to verify.

That's quite an extensive list, but if you get the right answers, chances are that you'll be satisfied with the dial-up service.

Once you've decided on an ISP, phone them and sign up. You will be expected to specify a *username* to identify yourself when you're connecting to the ISP's service. People usually compose their username from their own names, for example, cdickens. If the ISP has already assigned that username, you'll have to pick another one.

At sign-up time you'll also have to give the ISP the password you want to use when you're making your connection. Note that your username is not the same as your password. There's nothing secret about your username, but you should keep your password to yourself.

There are some generally accepted guidelines about composing passwords. Do *not* use the names of your nearest and dearest, or easily determined numbers like your birthday, anniversary, or phone number. The best passwords are random strings of numbers and letters, at least six characters long and preferably longer, such as ty5sv5tw. The drawback is that such passwords are hard to memorize and remember. Worse, you're not even supposed to write them down. Human nature being what it is, though, people frequently break this rule. Try not to be among them; one trick is to pick a password that means something to you but will mean nothing to anyone else, such as stringing together the initial letters of each word of some quotation you know. And whatever you do, *don't* leave a list of passwords on a Post-It® note stuck to your monitor. (You'd be surprised at how many people actually do this.) If you eventually find yourself doing online banking, you don't want to give a snooper the combination to the vault.

> **NOTE** *Larger ISPs may assign your username and password to you, instead of letting you choose them. However, you should be able to change your password at will without involving their technical support.*

Once your username and password have been settled, it won't take more than a day, sometimes less, to establish the account. You will also receive, in some fashion, a package with instructions for setting up your computer for dial-up to their system. These instructions will vary with the ISP, but a generic description of the process for a Windows machine is given in the next section. Macintosh users should consult the package provided by their ISP, which should include a Mac TCP/IP modem program. Macs with System 7 or above should already have the Open Transport TCP/IP program on them, and late models also usually have modem software already installed.

Set Up Dial-Up Connections in Windows

One thing you should do is verify that your computer has something called "Dial-Up Networking" (DUN) installed in it. This is software that allows your modem to connect to the phone lines and therefore to the ISP. If your machine has a modem, DUN is normally installed automatically when you install Windows 98, 98 Second Edition, or Millennium, but it's preferable not to assume things. With Windows 95, even if you have a modem, DUN is not automatically installed. To make the check, double-click the My Computer icon on the desktop.

> **NOTE** *The "desktop" is merely the screen you see when Windows starts up—the green or blue background with icons on it. It's called a desktop because you can move things around on it and open them up.*

When the My Computer window opens, look in it to see if there is an icon labeled "Dial-Up Networking." If there is, DUN is indeed installed and you're in business. If it doesn't appear, you have to install it (but if you use Windows Millennium, be sure to read the next Caution). To do so, choose My Computer | Control Panel | Add/Remove Programs | Windows Setup and install Dial-Up Networking from the Windows CD-ROM.

> **CAUTION** *In Windows Millennium (ME), the DUN icon has been moved to a new location. Windows ME users must choose My Computer | Control Panel and look in the Control Panel window to locate the DUN icon.*

Once DUN is installed, you may want to check your modem. Windows has a diagnostic program to help you do this. To use it:

1. Choose My Computer | Control Panel | Modems.

2. In the Modems dialog box, choose the Diagnostics tab. This opens a window that should show, among other things, the name of your modem.

NOTE *These various windows that open to allow you to interact with the computer are called* dialog boxes. *In this book they will often be referred to simply as* dialogs.

3. Select the modem, then click More Info. If it's working properly, you'll see a bunch of technical information in a window labeled "More Info." If this doesn't happen, the device hasn't been correctly installed, and you'll get an error message.

4. Once you've determined that the modem is (or isn't) working, you can close the window. If it isn't working, you'll have to consult the modem documentation and fix the problem before you can proceed.

So far, so good. Now we get to the actual stage of setting up the connection.

Begin by seeing if you have an icon on your desktop that is labeled "Connect to the Internet." If so, double-click it. If you don't see the icon, choose Start | Programs | Accessories | Internet Tools | Internet Connection Wizard. This starts the wizard that helps you set up your connection.

NOTE *The illustrations and figures in this book are taken from a PC running Windows 98 Second Edition (Win98SE). If you're using Windows 95 or Windows Millennium, or if you've modified your Windows settings, what you see on your display may differ from what's here in the book.*

In the first screen of the wizard, you get three choices:

■ "I Want to Sign Up for a New Internet Account." This connects you to the Microsoft Internet Referral Service, which helps you locate ISPs in your area. These will be the major providers, including online services like AOL and, of course, MSN. Since we're assuming you've already selected an ISP and have the sign-up package, ignore this choice.

■ "I Want to Transfer My Existing Internet Account to This Computer." This works only if you already have an account with one of the major providers. Since you're setting up a new account, ignore this choice.

■ The third choice is the one you want: "I Want to Set Up My Internet Connection Manually." Select it, and choose the Next button to make the second wizard screen appear.

The rest of the procedure goes like this:

1. In the second screen, the wizard asks if you connect through a phone line and modem or through a Local Area Network (LAN). We assume here that your computer is not hooked up to a network, so choose the first option, Phone Line and Modem. Click Next.

2. In the next screen you can enter the area code and phone number of your ISP, and select the country it's in. If it's only a local call to your ISP number, rather than long distance, you can uncheck the Dial Using the Area Code and Country Code check box. Click Next.

3. In the next screen you enter the username and password that your ISP assigned you or that you chose. Asterisks will appear when you type your password; this is a security measure to keep onlookers from reading it as you type. Click Next.

4. In the next screen you get to choose a name for the connection. It can be anything you like, such as MyISP. Click Next.

5. In the next screen you're asked if you want to set up an Internet mail account. You could do it here, but to keep things simple, choose No and then Next.

6. The next screen is the final one. To see if the connection works, click the check box labeled "To Connect to the Internet Immediately Select This Box" and click Finish.

7. Now the Dial-up Connection dialog box appears, as shown in the following illustration. Your username and password (as asterisks) are already entered. If you want your PC to record the password so you don't have to type it in every time you connect, check the Save Password check box. However, if your machine isn't set up with networking capabilities, the Save Password check box may be grayed out. If so, you'll have to type the password every time you log on. This may seem a nuisance, but is actually preferable from a security point of view.

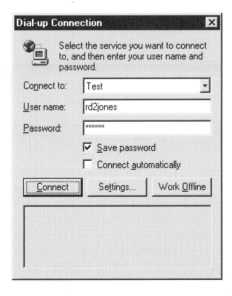

8. If you want to connect automatically, so that you don't see this dialog every time you start your browser, check the Connect Automatically check box. Don't worry about the Settings and Work Offline buttons for the moment; their functions will be covered later in the book. For now, just click the Connect button.

9. Assuming your modem sound is turned on, you'll hear warbling and buzzing from your computer as the modem attempts to connect to your ISP. As soon as the connection is made, the Dial-up Connection dialog vanishes and is replaced by a small icon (called the DUN connectoid) down in the System Tray. In another few seconds Microsoft Internet Explorer (the built-in Web browser that comes with Windows) starts up. In another few seconds the browser will display the MSN (Microsoft Network) page. You are now connected to the Internet, specifically to the Microsoft Network Web site.

10. That's as far as we'll go for the moment. Close the browser and the Auto Disconnect dialog box pops up, asking if you want to close your connection.

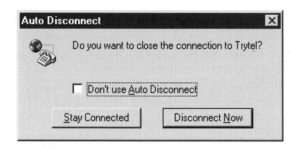

11. In this dialog, you could choose the Disconnect Now button and the connection would be shut down. However, to learn how to close your connection manually, we'll choose the Stay Connected button. This closes the dialog box. (If you don't want to use Auto Disconnect at all, check the check box in the dialog before closing it.)

Monitor Your Connection and Close It Manually

After you close the Auto Disconnect dialog box, there's nothing very obvious on your screen to show that you're still connected. However, if you look down at the System Tray (the small box at the far-right end of the Windows Task Bar, which runs along the bottom of your screen) you will see an icon of two tiny computer monitors. This icon is the DUN connectoid mentioned earlier, and appears only when your Internet connection is active. If you see it, you're connected. In addition, the icon also tells you when data is being received or transmitted. The little monitors flash bright green as the information comes and goes.

Now right-click on the connection icon. A pop-up menu appears with two choices: Status and Disconnect. To close your connection immediately, you would choose Disconnect. If you want to see what your connection is doing, choose Status to open the status window.

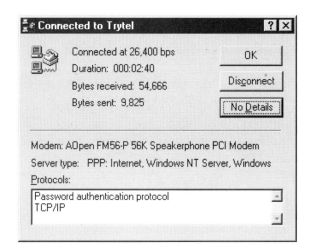

This window tells you how fast your connection is, how long you've been connected in this session, and how much data has been received and transmitted. Choosing the Details button, as has already been done for this illustration, gives you some technical data about your connection type. Finally, if you choose the Disconnect button, you (obviously) disconnect. Go ahead and disconnect now. In a few seconds the dialog box and the connection icon will both disappear, and you're no longer hooked up to the Internet.

Start Your Connection Manually

With the setup just described, you initiate your dial-up connection to your ISP whenever you start your browser. But what if you want to establish that connection *without* starting your browser? You can do so quite easily, as shown next.

The process of connecting to any network, including connecting to the Internet, is called *logging onto the network*. It is also, more succinctly, called the *login* or the *logon*. You can create a shortcut icon on your desktop that will let you log on manually. Do this:

1. Choose My Computer | Dial-Up Networking. In the Dial-Up Networking window, you will see the name of the connection you created earlier with the Internet Connection Wizard (you did this in step 4, to be precise).

Windows Millennium users must choose My Computer | Control Panel | Dial-Up Networking.

2. Right-click on this connection. From the pop-up menu, choose Create Shortcut. A question box appears, asking if you want the shortcut placed on the desktop. Choose Yes.

3. Close the various windows you just opened. You'll see the shortcut on the desktop. Double-click it and a connection dialog box appears.

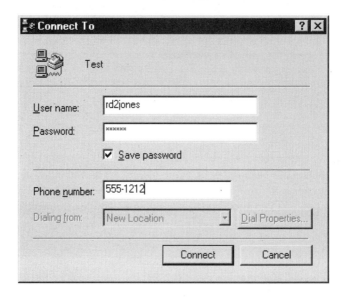

4. If the password box is blank, type in your password. If your machine isn't set up with networking capabilities, the Save Password check box may be grayed out and you'll have to type the password every time you log on.

5. Click Connect. The modem will warble, and you'll see a progress report of your login. When the connection succeeds and you're logged onto your ISP, a Connection Established box appears. If you don't want this box to appear every time you log on, check the appropriate check box. The More Information button in this dialog will open a small Help screen telling you what you can do next. Read it if you like, then close it and click the Close button to dismiss the Connection Established box.

To disconnect after making such a connection, use the manual disconnection method you learned earlier. Note that if you connect manually using dial-up, you aren't asked if you want to close the connection when you close your browser.

Advanced Dial-Up Connection Setup

You don't need to refer to this section unless your connection isn't working properly, or unless you want to delve into some of the technical details of dial-ups. Practically speaking, though, if you know the stuff discussed here, you can set up a dial-up connection without resorting to the Internet Connection Wizard.

Create a Connection

To avoid messing up your existing connection, we'll create a new one you can experiment with. Here's how:

1. Choose My Computer | Dial-Up Networking. In the Dial-Up Networking window, you will see the name of the connection you created.

> **CAUTION**
>
> *Windows Millennium users must choose My Computer | Control Panel | Dial-Up Networking.*

2. Double-click the Make New Connection icon. A dialog box appears with a text box labeled "Type a Name for the Computer You Are Dialing." This is just the connection name, and can be anything you like—unoriginally, I called it "Test." Go ahead and type the name you prefer into the text box.

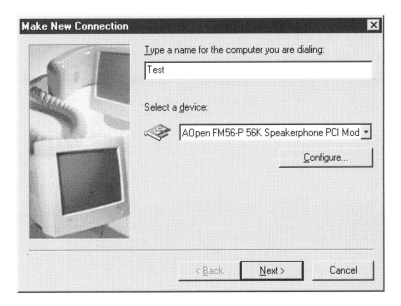

3. This dialog also has a list box labeled "Select a Device," which shows an entry for your modem. You likely only have one installed modem, so leave it as it is and click Next.

4. In the next box you type your ISP's area code, telephone number, and select the name of the country where the ISP is located. When you're finished, click Next.

5. The last dialog box appears. All you can do here is click Finish, so do so. The dialog vanishes.

Configure a Connection

You've now created the basic connection. The next step is to set it up the way you want it. This is called *configuring the connection.* Do this:

1. As you did in step 1 of the previous procedure, open the Dial-Up Networking window. The connection you just created is now listed. Right-click on it, and from the pop-up menu, choose Properties.

2. The configuration dialog for this connection appears. It has several tabs. Choose the General tab.

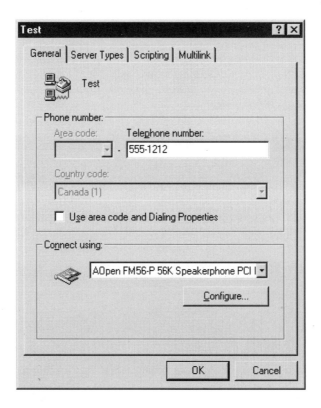

3. Assuming it's a local call to reach your ISP, clear the check box labeled "Use Area Code and Dialing Properties."

4. Choose the Server Types tab to open the Server Types sheet. Your ISP may have given you values to put into the check boxes in the Advanced Options section. If they didn't, uncheck everything except Enable Software Compression.

5. If, and only if, your machine is *not* on a corporate network, clear the NetBEUI and IPX/SPX Compatible boxes in the Allowed Network Protocols section. Note that you *must* leave the TCP/IP box with a check in it. If you *are* on a corporate network, you should check with your network administrator about exactly what options to select.

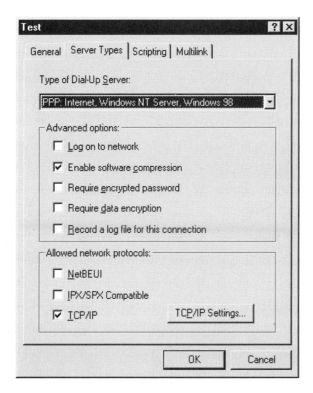

6. Your ISP may have given you a pair of DNS addresses, also called Name Server addresses. Each address is four numbers separated by periods, such as 192.168.0.23, and there will likely be a primary one and a secondary one. If they did give you such numbers, click the button labeled TCP/IP Settings on the Server Types tab. This opens the TCP/IP Settings sheet.

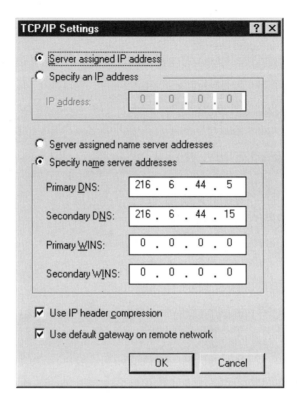

7. In the middle section of this sheet, click the Specify Name Server Addresses option button. Then, in the Primary DNS box, type in the primary number the ISP gave you, and the secondary number in the Secondary DNS box. Leave everything else as it is, and click OK.

8. Back in the original configuration dialog, ignore the Scripting and Multilink tabs and click OK.

9. To test the connection, double-click on its name in the Dial-Up Networking window. This is a manual logon, exactly as described in the earlier section. If it doesn't work, repeat the previous steps, making especially sure that the TCP/IP check box is checked in the Allowed Network Protocols section. Make sure too that you got the DNS addresses right. If it still doesn't work, your ISP may require a different configuration from that given. Consult the documentation you received.

10. To remove a connection, right-click on its name in the Dial-Up Networking window and click Delete.

Did you know?

If you remain connected for a long period of time but don't actually use the connection (if you forgot about it, for example) your ISP may disconnect you since there was no activity from your computer. However, if your phone line is of marginal quality, you may get accidentally disconnected from time to time even when you're actively using the Internet. When this happens, you'll see a message to the effect that you "have been disconnected from the network." Rest assured that your ISP didn't do this because they were annoyed at you for something you did. The cause is bad phone lines or a poor connection to them. You might want to check your phone jack if it happens a lot. If the jack doesn't seem to be the problem, complain to the phone company.

Fine-Tune Your Modem

This too is advanced stuff that you needn't mess with, unless you want to. In this section we'll look at a few adjustments you can make to the configuration of a modem in a dial-up connection.

Begin by opening the Dial-Up Networking window as you did earlier. Right-click on the name of the connection you want to work with, and choose Properties from the pop-up menu. Then do this:

1. When the Properties dialog appears, click the Configure button on the General sheet. This opens the configuration dialog for your modem. Depending on the make and model of your modem, the dialog may have more or fewer sheets than shown here.

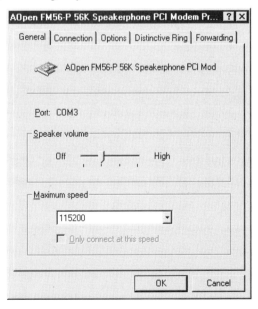

2. If you have a 56K modem and good phone lines, make sure the Maximum Speed list box is set to 115200. If your computer is an older model and won't support this speed, this number won't be available. In such a case, choose the highest number listed. You can also set the modem speaker volume here.

3. Choose the Connection tab. If you want to automatically disconnect from the Internet after a certain amount of idle time (in other words if you walk away and forget you're connected) click the third check box and enter the desired idle time in the text box. The Cancel the Call If Not Connected option is intended to terminate the call if the ISP doesn't answer for a specified period of time.

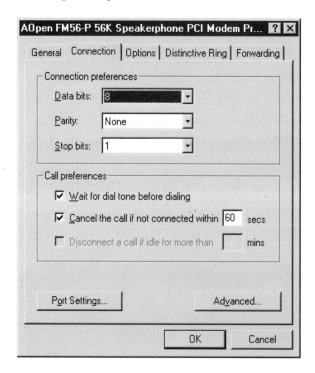

4. If your phone lines are poor and you keep losing your connection, click the Port Settings button to open the Advanced Port Settings dialog. Move the buffer sliders all the way to the left. Click OK and leave them there for a day or so to see if it helps. If it does, keep moving them one stop to the right until the problem recurs. Then move them back to the last good position and leave them there.

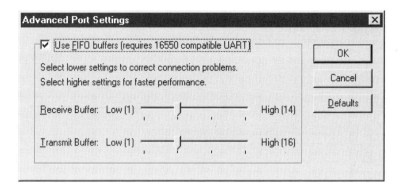

5. Back on the Connection sheet again, click the Advanced button to open the Advanced Connection Settings dialog. Make sure the Use Error Control check box is marked, and clear the check box labeled Compress Data. (You're already using software compression, specified in your Server Types setup. Hardware compression is less effective, so you should turn it off.)

6. Leave everything else as it is, and click OK until all the dialogs you opened are closed.

 These modem dialog boxes are also available by choosing My Computer | Control Panel | Modems. However, changes made there will not modify the modem settings for an already created dial-up connection. Such changes will be applied only to new connections.

Set Up High-Speed Connections

When you establish a connection using ISDN, DSL, or cable, you're essentially making your computer into part of a large network. This network consists of your machine, plus all the other machines that have an Internet account with your ISP, plus the computers run by the ISP. In fact, through this smaller network, your machine becomes part of the Internet itself.

To use high-speed services, you need a special modem: an ISDN modem, a cable modem, a wireless modem for satellites, or a DSL modem, depending on the service you get. Normally you don't need to buy one of these modems, which are quite expensive; instead, your ISP will rent the appropriate device to you when you subscribe to the service. You will also need a device called a *networking card,* which is a piece of hardware installed inside your computer. A wire runs from this networking card to the high-speed modem, and hooks your machine up to the high-speed line.

There are two ways of getting your end of the high-speed service set up. If you don't want to do it yourself, the ISP will send a technician who will install a networking card, hook up the modem, and set up the software so that everything works properly. This full installation option usually costs about $100-$150, including a small surcharge of $10-$20 for the network card.

The second way is the do-it-yourself option, which most ISPs will permit. If you're knowledgeable about computers and can install a network card and set up the required TCP/IP networking software, you may be able to obtain the modem and its cables from the ISP and get the service running by yourself.

Unfortunately, network cards and networking can be a real headache for the inexperienced, so unless you really do know what you're doing, let your ISP handle the setup of your high-speed connection. Then, if something later goes wrong with it, they can't blame you for an inept installation.

Share an Internet Connection

This is for people who have two or more computers under the same roof. Sooner or later, two or more people under that roof will want to connect to the Internet at the same time. How do they do this?

The least satisfactory way is to have a separate phone line for each computer, and an ISP that allows simultaneous user connections (many don't). It's also the most expensive. But there's a better way—you can have all the computers share the same Internet connection. This, by the way, does not count as a simultaneous connection.

If you want to achieve this happy state, the first thing you do is set up one of the computers to connect to the Internet. Then you connect the other computer(s) to that machine (the various methods of doing this are described next). This is called *setting up a computer network,* or *networking your computers.* Computers on a network can transfer information from one machine to another, including information flowing from a single Internet connection.

Telling you exactly how to establish a network is way beyond the scope of this book, but here's some information to get you started. The following are the basic methods of networking your computers:

■ You can wire them together using special cables similar to phone wires, but thicker. This is called an Ethernet connection. An Ethernet network card must be installed in each networked computer, but these cards are relatively inexpensive and readily available from many manufacturers. If you want a package deal, several companies, such as D-Link and 3Com, supply home networking kits that contain everything you need to connect two computers. Many of these kits sell for under $100. The downside of Ethernet is that if the computers are in different rooms, the cables have to wander through your residence or office, and your significant other(s) may not want you to drill holes in the walls to achieve this.

■ You can wire the computers together using the telephone lines and phone jacks already in your residence or office. This method gives adequate speed and you don't have to run more wiring, assuming you have enough telephone jacks in each room. Again, D-Link and 3Com supply phone-line networking kits that include the required special network cards, wiring, and software. Prices at the time of writing ranged between $70-$170 to wire up two computers.

■ You can use a wireless network. This technology is new and the computers will communicate quite slowly compared to Ethernet or the better phone-line systems. Again, some hardware installation is involved and the kits (at the moment) are more expensive than the two types just described.

■ You can use the AC power lines in your house, the ones you plug lamps into. This is the least desirable solution, being very slow and supported by only one company, Intelogis. The phone-line systems are a better bet.

Note that only one computer on the network needs to be connected directly to the Internet, so you only need one modem—phone, DSL, or whatever. The other computers communicate with this computer through the network cables, so people at these other machines can use its Internet connection.

If you use Windows 98 Second Edition or Windows Millennium, the easiest method of setting up a shared connection is to use the built-in Internet Connection Sharing (ICS) software. It's fairly simple, and the Windows Help systems will tell you how to install it. Unfortunately, ICS didn't come with Windows 95 or the first edition of Windows 98, and Microsoft doesn't offer it as a free download. Consequently, if you want Microsoft ICS you'll have to buy the Windows 98 Second Edition upgrade or the Windows Millennium upgrade to get it.

An alternative to Microsoft's ICS is some version of proxy software. A *proxy* is simply a computer program that allows networked machines to use a single Internet connection. In fact, Microsoft ICS itself is a proxy program, but there are lots of others, and some are free. If you don't want to pay to upgrade to Windows 98SE, one of these programs may be exactly what you're looking for.

One last word about connection sharing: It works better if you have a high-speed connection. A slow dial-up line will be even slower if two people are using it at the same time. However, connection sharing, even on a dial-up, has the advantage of needing only one phone line, one set of connection hardware, and one ISP account to serve two or even more computers. And there's no speed penalty if only one person's online at a time, as might often be the case. That alone makes it worth it.

Where to Find It

Web Site	Address	What's There
D-Link	www.dlink.com	Network hardware
Homepclan	www.homepclan.com	Networking guides
ISPS	www.isps.com	ISP directories
Spoonproxy	www.pi-soft.com	Proxy software
3Com	www.3com.com	Network hardware, modems
Vsocks Light	www.pscs.co.uk	Proxy software
Winproxy	www.winproxy.com	Proxy software

Chapter 2

Installing and Using Web Browsers

How To . . .

- Understand and obtain browsers
- Understand the World Wide Web
- Use Netscape Navigator's supplied Web site lists
- Use Microsoft Internet Explorer's supplied Web site lists
- Learn the basics of Web browsing
- Create and organize Favorites in Internet Explorer
- Create and organize Bookmarks in Navigator
- Navigate with Internet Explorer and Navigator History lists
- Understand slow Internet connections and Internet error messages

In Chapter 1 you learned how to make the actual electronic connection to the Internet. However, just making the connection is like picking up the phone and then merely listening to the dial tone—it's not very interesting. To actually *do* something, you need a communications tool. In the case of the phone system, that tool is the telephone itself. In the case of your Internet connection, the tool is a computer program called a *Web browser*.

Here's one thing to be aware of before we continue. The World Wide Web, which is what you explore with a Web browser, is not identical to the Internet, which is why we have the two different names. The differences between the Web and the Net will be explained later in this chapter.

Which Browser Should I Use?

There's nothing very mysterious about Web browsers. Once you're connected to the Internet, a browser simply allows you to summon information from the Net to your computer so you can look at it. This information is displayed on your screen in what are called "Web pages." You can do other things with browsers, too, but displaying Web pages on your monitor is their most basic function.

There are two browsers in common use today: Microsoft's Internet Explorer and Netscape's Navigator. The most recent version of Internet Explorer is version 5, usually abbreviated to IE 5. The most recent version of Navigator is version 4.73. Earlier versions of both browsers are also still in use, especially IE version 4 (IE 4) and Netscape Navigator version 3.

NOTE *The earlier versions of the Netscape product were called "Navigator" but incorporated other tools, such as e-mail, along with the browser. When version 4 came out, Netscape Corporation renamed this suite of programs "Communicator," thus introducing a certain amount of confusion among users. In this book I'll refer to the version 4 suite, as a whole, as "Communicator," and to the browser component of it as "Navigator."*

2

Microsoft Internet Explorer has recently become the browser used by the majority of the people who frequent the Web. However, this doesn't necessarily mean that IE is a better browser than Navigator. In fact, lots of Navigator users detest the thought of switching to IE, and adamantly refuse to contemplate doing so.

The fact of the matter is that both browsers are pretty good at what they do. On the negative side, each has its own set of quirks and bugs, which cause them to malfunction from time to time. Which one to use is really a matter of personal preference. The best way to decide is to try each of them for a while and see which one gives you less trouble and more preferred features. This is easy to do, since both browsers can be installed and used on the same machine.

All screen illustrations and figures of browsers in this book are of Internet Explorer version 5.0 or of Netscape Navigator version 4.73. Users of earlier versions may notice some differences between their browser displays and those in the book.

Obtain a Browser

If you're running Windows 95 or later, you've already got some version of Internet Explorer on your PC. Therefore you don't need to worry about obtaining or installing the program, though you might want to upgrade to a later version, as described in Chapter 8 in the section called "Use Windows Update." Also, if you use a Macintosh, there is a version of IE 5 available for that system, though you may have to obtain it from the Microsoft Web site if your ISP can't provide it when you sign up. As for Netscape Communicator, it comes in versions for Windows, Mac, Linux, and Unix.

It is almost certain that the account sign-up package you received from your ISP includes a CD-ROM with a recent version of the Communicator suite for your Mac or Windows machine, and possibly the Mac version of IE if you use a Macintosh. If your ISP didn't supply the versions you want, contact them and ask for the appropriate software.

If you want to try something different, there's also a third browser called Opera. You can download a trial version of it from the Opera company at **www.opera.com** and use it for 30 days, which don't need to be consecutive. But if you want to keep using it after that, you have to pay them $35, or $18 if you get the educational price. (The other browsers, in case you were wondering, are free). It's a fast and capable browser and some users swear by it. It also takes up much less disk space than the Big Two; so little space, in fact, that it fits on a floppy. If you need a floppy-portable browser, Opera is the only choice.

Install and Start the Netscape Communicator Suite

The Communicator installation process is simple, and is followed by a stage in which you set up a "profile" that tells the software how you prefer it to operate. This section assumes that you have a functional Internet connection, set up as described in Chapter 1.

Assuming you have a CD-ROM from your ISP, insert it into the drive. There may be an auto-start program that puts an installation menu on the screen without your needing to do anything. If this happens, find the menu choice that installs Netscape Communicator, and choose it. If no menu shows up, consult your ISP's sign-up package to find out how they want you to install the browser, and follow the instructions.

Eventually, you'll see the Communicator installation screen. While the onscreen directions are fairly straightforward, here are some tips to make the process go more smoothly:

- When asked if you want a Typical or Custom installation, choose Typical. Later in the book you'll see how to customize the software.

- If you're told that the Netscape directory doesn't exist and are asked if you want to create it, choose Yes. If you choose No, you can't proceed with the installation.

- There's a list of three check boxes that specifies whether you want Navigator to be your default browser, whether to make Netscape Netcenter your home page, and whether you want to use Netcenter to search the Web. Leave the boxes checked for the moment; these choices can be changed later.

- After you see these check boxes, just keep clicking Next buttons until the installation process actually starts. You'll see its progress in a Setup window at the bottom of your screen, and some other messages may appear.

- At the end of the process, you're asked whether you want to view the README file. Do so if you like, but at this stage it's not necessary. Answer Yes or No as you prefer.

After all this is over, you get a message saying the installation is complete. Click OK. Then you're told that you have to restart your computer to complete the installation. Select the Yes, I Want to Restart option and click OK.

After the computer restarts, you'll see a new icon labeled Netscape Communicator on your desktop. An AOL Instant Messenger icon and a Realplayer G2 icon may also be present, and maybe a Winamp icon. Ignore these for now; their functions will be covered later in the chapters on multimedia and chat.

The next step is to double-click the Communicator icon so you can create a profile for yourself. A *profile* is simply a record of the way you like to use the software, which Communicator stores for future reference. Here's how to do it:

1. The first screen that appears after you double-click the Communicator icon is called "Creating a New Profile" and tells you what profiles are all about. After you've read it, click Next.

2. Now you get to enter your name and e-mail address. Your ISP assigned you the e-mail address and it will appear somewhere in your sign-up package. However, if you aren't

planning to use Netscape Messenger for e-mail or for posting messages to newsgroups, leave these boxes empty. Filling them in allows Web sites that you visit to obtain your name and e-mail address without your knowledge, and you may not want this to happen. Click Next.

3. Next you can give the profile a name, in case there will be other profiles created on this machine. This might be done if two different people use Communicator on it, and each has his or her own preferences. Leave the storage directory entry as it is and click Next.

4. In the next screen you can begin setting up an e-mail account, but we won't do this right now. Click Finish.

The dialog closes and Communicator automatically starts up with the Navigator browser running. This can be a bit confusing so I'll clarify.

Remember that Communicator is a suite (collection) of programs that includes the Navigator Web browser. When you launch Communicator, it in turn launches Navigator. So launching Communicator and launching Navigator amount to the same thing in practice, though technically speaking there's a difference.

Anyway, once Navigator appears, one of three things will happen next:

■ If you have a high-speed connection, which as you remember is always on, the Netscape Netcenter page will almost immediately appear in the browser window ("window" refers to the area in which the page is displayed).

■ If you have a dial-up connection and you're already connected to your ISP, the same thing will happen, but more slowly.

■ If you have a dial-up connection and it's not connected at the moment, the connection dialog box you saw in Chapter 1 will appear. Use the dialog to establish the connection, and in a few seconds the Netscape Netcenter page will appear.

The Netcenter page will resemble Figure 2-1, although since Netscape changes the page occasionally, the match may not be exact. There is also a *floating toolbar* (a collection of buttons you can drag around the screen for convenient placement) hanging over the view. To get rid of it, click the Close button in its top-right corner. You'll learn how to get it back when we discuss browser customization in Chapter 3.

NOTE   *If you close the dial-up connection dialog without connecting, Navigator will tell you it's "unable to locate the server home.netscape.com." Despite the technical jargon, it's merely telling you, in its roundabout way, that you're not connected.*

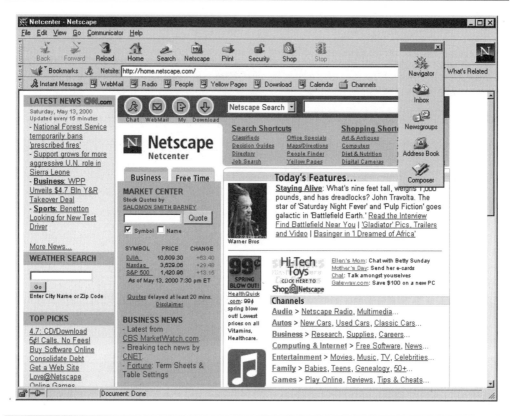

FIGURE 2-1
Navigator opens automatically to the Netcenter page if you're online

Start Internet Explorer

This should be simplicity itself, but it isn't, because of the bitter corporate rivalry between Netscape and Microsoft. So, if you've installed Communicator as described in the previous section, you'll find there's been dirty work at the crossroads when you try to use IE.

What happens is this: When you start IE by double-clicking its desktop icon (assuming you're connected to the Internet) the page that opens in the browser window is not the Microsoft Network (MSN) page, as it should be. Instead, it's the Netscape Netcenter page. This is happening because the Communicator installation program has changed IE's startup behavior. Here's how to switch IE back to the way it was intended to behave.

NOTE *Other versions of the Netscape browser may not exhibit this behavior. If they leave IE alone when they install, the MSN page will open, as it should.*

From the IE Tools menu, choose Internet Options to open the Internet Options dialog. Click the Programs tab, as shown in the following illustration, then click the Reset Web Settings button. This restores IE's startup behavior.

NOTE *If you are using IE 4 instead of IE 5, the Internet Options choice is in the View menu.*

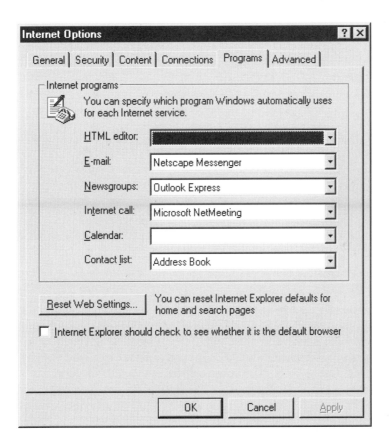

Close IE and double-click on its icon to launch it again (*launch* is just another word for "start"). Assuming you're connected, the MSN page will now appear in the IE browser window.

There's one further complication. To see what it is, close IE and launch Communicator again. You'll see the dialog box illustrated next, which asks if you want Navigator to be your *default browser*. This question is being asked because you actually made IE your default browser when you clicked the Reset Web Settings button earlier. But what does this mean?

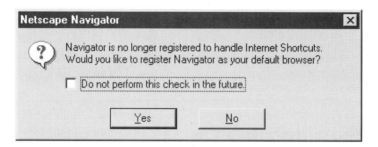

Simply put, it means that whenever you ask the computer to carry out an action that involves a browser, such as viewing a Web page stored on your computer, Windows will automatically launch the default browser rather than the non-default one. Which browser you make the default boils down to your personal preferences. For the moment, we'll arbitrarily decide to leave IE as the default. To do this, and to keep Communicator from asking the question every time you launch it, mark the check box labeled Do Not Perform This Check in the Future and choose No. Navigator opens to the Netcenter page as before.

Congratulations! You've successfully joined the Internet and the World Wide Web. The next section presents some background information on the Net, the Web, and the two major browsers. You may want to use some of it to impress your friends. If the subject doesn't interest you at the moment, feel free to skip to the next practical bit, which is called "Get the Hang of Browsing."

Understand the World Wide Web

The terms "the Web" and "the Internet" are often used interchangeably, but in fact they're not the same beast. As was noted in Chapter 1, the Internet is a vast network of computers, spanning the planet, that are connected to each other through telephone lines, satellite relays, microwave transmission, optical-fiber cables, and so on. All those connections, together with the computers they link, make up the Internet's hardware, the stuff you can walk up to and kick. This hardware is used to store uncountable billions of pieces of information, in the same way that you store documents on your own computer. The Internet's computers also run a myriad of programs that keep them talking both to each other and to the machines of people like you. The end result is that the Internet can provide anybody hooked up to it with a variety of information and communications services.

What sort of services are these? Well, if you've used e-mail, that's a communications service. Another example would be copying documents to your own machine from another computer "out there" on the Internet. That's an information retrieval service.

What the Web Is

But, you're probably muttering, what *is* the World Wide Web, then?

The answer is that the Web, to give it its common name, is just another service available on the Internet. This Web service gives you access to a very large collection of documents, called *Web pages*, which are stored on the Internet's various computers. "Gives you access" simply means that while you're connected to the Internet, you can make any Web document, stored anywhere on the Internet, visible on your computer's monitor. To do this, as you've already figured out, you use your Web browser.

But Web pages have a special feature that sets them apart from paper documents. Almost every Web page available on the Internet has *links* to other Web pages, and these other pages can be stored on any computer, anywhere on the Internet. You can see these links on the Web page that bears them, and you can identify the links in various ways. The most basic kind of link is some underlined text, with both the underline and the text in a color different from that of the page's normal text.

What Links Are

To understand a link, think of it as a road sign pointing to a destination. That destination is another Web page, a page stored in an Internet computer somewhere. When you click your mouse on the link, that destination page will appear in your browser, replacing the page with the link you just clicked. The new page will also have links on it, and you can use one of these to open yet another Web page, which in turn... you get the picture. You can keep going, and going, and going.

This process of moving pages in and out of your browser is often referred to as "navigating the Web" or "Web Browsing" or "Web surfing." These phrases are a bit of a misnomer since *you* don't actually go anywhere; you actually bring the contents of the Web to *you*. People also speak of "surfing the Net" but usually they mean that they're doing so on the Web.

So that's what the World Wide Web service of the Internet is—a collection of linked Web pages, among which you can navigate using a Web browser. Technically speaking, it's a hypertext system residing on the Internet. "Hypertext" simply means that the pages are linked to each other; in fact, the precise term for these links is "hyperlink." But if you just say "link," everybody will know what you're talking about.

What Web Sites Are

You've also heard the term "Web site" and may have wondered exactly what such a thing is. Basically, a Web site is a collection of linked Web pages that are stored on a single computer, and which have been created to represent a particular organization or individual. So another way to think of the Web is to picture it as a very large collection of linked Web sites—a web that has been woven, so to speak, by connecting a multitude of individual sites. You can have your own Web site, too, if you want one. Chapters 20 and 21 give you the basics of getting one set up.

One final note: The Web happens to be the most glamorous and razzle-dazzle of all the Internet services, but in fact it's not the most widely used of them. Your humble, everyday e-mail service has that distinction.

How Web Browsers Work

Here's a much-simplified account of what goes on behind the scenes when you're Web surfing. Let's assume you're looking at a Web page in the browser window. When you click a link on that page, it sets in motion the following chain of events:

1. Though the mechanics aren't visible to the user, the link "points to" a page stored on another computer on the Internet. Clicking the link makes your browser send a message to that second computer, which is called the *remote computer*. The message asks this remote computer to send a copy of the Web page back to the originating browser.

2. The remote computer receives the request. It responds by transmitting a copy of the requested page down the phone or cable lines to your computer.

3. Your browser receives the information, converts it into a form readable to humans, and displays it on your monitor.

That's all there is to it, in principle. If you're wondering how the computers know where to find each other, there's an Internet addressing method that allows them to do this. The nuts and bolts of how the addressing works is more involved than we need to consider here.

Understand Browser Versions

Netscape, as you know, is the name of the company that produces the Communicator suite, which contains the Navigator browser. People who use the Navigator browsers often refer to them simply as "Netscape," but what they're really referring to is Navigator.

The latest finished version of the Communicator suite, at the time of writing, was Communicator 4.73. An unfinished version, called Netscape 6, was at this writing in what's called public beta release, which means that it's still full of bugs and you use it at your own risk. There is no version 5, in case you were wondering.

When the Web first came into widespread public use, Navigator seemed to be the only game in town, having very capable versions for both the Macintosh and Windows operating systems. It was also the first widely used "graphical" browser—that is, one that could display images as well as text. For some time it seemed that the Netscape browsers would become the dominant, standard-setting Web browser software.

Then Microsoft's leaders abruptly noticed the Internet and brought out their own browser, Internet Explorer 3, just as fast as they could. Because Internet Explorer 3 was bundled and automatically installed with the Windows operating system, you got it whether you wanted it or not. This was and still is a source of intense irritation to many people, including, of late, the U.S. Department of Justice. Consequently, the integration of IE and Windows has led to monumental and complicated legal battles that will likely go on for years. Whatever the eventual outcome, it's probably safe to say that the two browsers and their parent companies will remain locked in bitter competition for the foreseeable future.

As I write, the most advanced version of the Microsoft browser is Internet Explorer 5, which is the one used in the IE examples in this book. Many people are still using IE 4, but most of what applies to IE 5 also applies to IE 4. You'll find out how to upgrade from IE 4 to IE 5, if you feel you need to, in the "Use Windows Update" section of Chapter 8.

> **TIP** *You can easily tell what browser version you're using. For IE, launch the browser and from the menu bar choose Help | About Internet Explorer. A window will open, showing the version number. For Navigator or Communicator, launch the browser and choose Help | About Navigator (or Communicator). A window opens to show the version number.*

Get the Hang of Browsing

Browsing is a fundamentally straightforward activity, but there are some basic techniques and tricks that will make it easier and more pleasant. To learn them, we'll take a ready-made browsing situation and work within it. This is possible because both IE and Navigator automatically install a set of links to a selection of interesting Web sites.

Basic Web Sites Supplied by Your Browser

In both IE and Navigator you can keep records of Web sites you visit often, so that you can go to these sites with a couple of mouse clicks. Navigator refers to these records as "Bookmarks." In IE, they're called "Favorites." "Bookmark" has become the generic term for these records, however, so IE's Favorites and Navigator's Bookmarks are all bookmarks. We also refer to the act of making such a record as *bookmarking a page* or *bookmarking a site*.

To see what preset Web sites are available in Navigator, launch the browser. This will immediately open the Netcenter page (from now on we'll assume, unless it's otherwise specified, that you're connected to the Internet). Now click the Bookmarks button in the upper left of the browser screen. In the list that appears, you'll see two kinds of icons: purple folders and skinny green rectangles with a fork at one end. The green rectangles are the actual bookmarks, while the purple folders are containers for collections of bookmarks.

Did you
know?

The bars across the top of the browser displays are called *menu bars* if they drop a menu down when you click an entry. The entry can be a word or an icon, or both. If the bar has buttons that make something happen immediately (that is, you don't get a menu) the bar is called a *toolbar* or occasionally a *button bar*.

To see how these purple folders work, move the mouse pointer so it's on top of the folder labeled "Directories." Another menu appears. This one has the green bookmarks in it only, and has no folders.

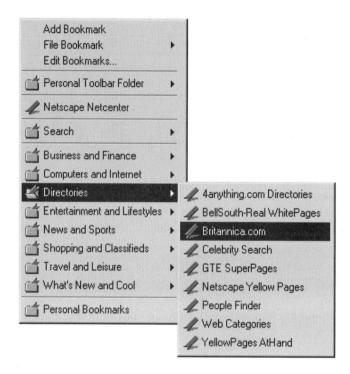

Now slide the mouse pointer onto the second list so it's on top of the "Britannica.com" and click the mouse. In moments, the home page of the Encyclopedia Britannica Web site opens in your browser.

NOTE *Home page, in this context, refers to the entry page of a Web site, a page designed to provide easy and organized access to all the other pages of the site. As other examples, the Netcenter page that opens in Navigator is the home page of the Netcenter Web site, and IE's MSN page is the home page of the Microsoft Network Web site.*

Now close Navigator and try the same thing with IE. Launch the browser, then click on Favorites in the menu bar. A list appears, containing yellow folders and small IE icons (a blue "e" on a white rectangle). As in Navigator, the folders are containers for collections of bookmarks, while the IE icons are the bookmarks themselves.

Slide the mouse pointer to rest on top of the folder labeled "Media." A second list opens, this one containing exclusively bookmarks.

2

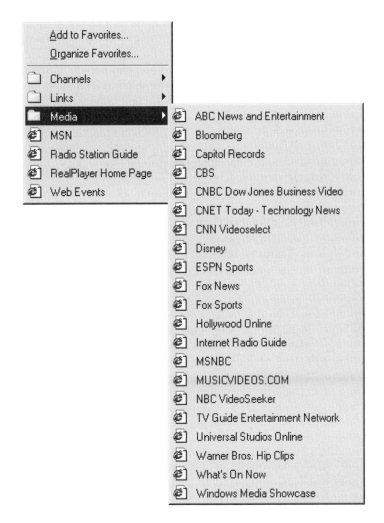

Now slide the mouse pointer onto this second list so it's on top of the bookmark labeled "Disney." Click the mouse and the home page of the Disney site opens in your browser.

The supplied IE bookmark collection isn't as rich as Navigator's, but don't reject the use of IE on that basis alone. As time passes and you become an accomplished Web traveler, you'll amass a large set of your own bookmarks anyway, so the disparity between the two browsers likely won't be much of an issue.

Work with the Basic Browser Controls

Here's where you learn the fundamentals of using your browser. For this section, you'll start off from one of the preset bookmarks in Navigator.

Close Navigator if it's still open so you can start with a clean slate. Then launch the browser, which will, of course, open the Netcenter home page again. Now open the bookmark list. Slide the mouse pointer on top of the News and Sports folder, and in the second list click the News and Media Directory icon. The page for this bookmark now opens in the browser window. Note that the content of this page can vary, so it may not look exactly like the one in Figure 2-2.

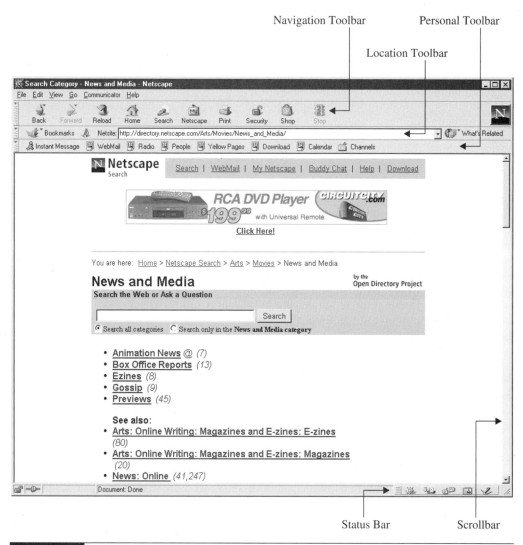

FIGURE 2-2   You use the links on a Web page to "travel" to other pages

2

Here you see various bits of underlined text, such as "Animation News." These are links to other Web pages; it's common for *text links,* as these are called, to be underlined. If they are embedded in other text, text links will often be of a contrasting color, as well.

There's another way you can tell that "Animation News" is a link. Move the mouse pointer on top of the text, and you'll see the pointer turn from an arrow to a hand with a pointing finger. Whenever the pointer looks like this, it's resting over a link. If you click on it, the Web page the link points to will open in your browser window.

NOTE   *Usually people speak of the link taking them somewhere. So if you click the Animation News link, you will be "taken to" the Animation News page.*

The text link is one of the two main categories of links. The other major category is the image-based link; with these, you click on an image in order to be taken to the link's destination. Image-based links fall into several subcategories, such as buttons, photographs, line art or drawings, and toolbars, which are collections of buttons glued together. In Figure 2-2, the small "N" icon to the left of the words "Netscape Search" (top-left corner of the browser window) is a button-type link. You can verify this by putting the mouse pointer on top and seeing that the arrow changes to a hand.

At the right edge of the browser window in Figure 2-2, there is a vertical scroll bar. This tells you that the Web page runs farther downward, past the bottom of the browser window. You can scroll up and down through the page by using the mouse to drag this bar up and down, or by pressing the PAGE DOWN and PAGE UP keys.

Using either of these methods, scroll down the page a few lines until you see a list of text links. Click on one of these links; for the sake of illustration, I chose the one called "BBC News and Entertainment." After a few moments (more than a few, if you're on a slow dial-up connection) the BBC page will appear, as in Figure 2-3.

Let's now say you've seen all you want of the BBC page, and you'd like to return to the News and Media Directory page so you can select another link. But how do you do this? There's no link on the BBC page that will take you back.

However, if you look at the topmost row of icons on the Navigator screen, you'll see an icon labeled "Back" (see Figure 2-3). The icons on this row are usually called "buttons," so this is the *Back button.* Click it and the page you just came from will reappear in the browser. In fact, if you've passed through a lot of pages, you can just keep clicking the Back button to retrace your steps, until you reach the page you started with.

Next, find the BBC link that you used earlier. You'll see that it has changed color, if only slightly. This is because it has now become a *visited link.* The color change is there to tell you that you have already used this link. Being able to identify visited links is useful if you're working your way through a long list of links. It's an example of what's called a *navigational aid*—assistance in keeping track of where you've been.

Now suppose, having returned to the directory page, that you change your mind suddenly and want to see the BBC page again. You could click the BBC link to go there, but there's an alternate way. Just click the Forward button, which is next to the Back button, and the BBC page will open again.

Back Button   Home Button

Forward Button

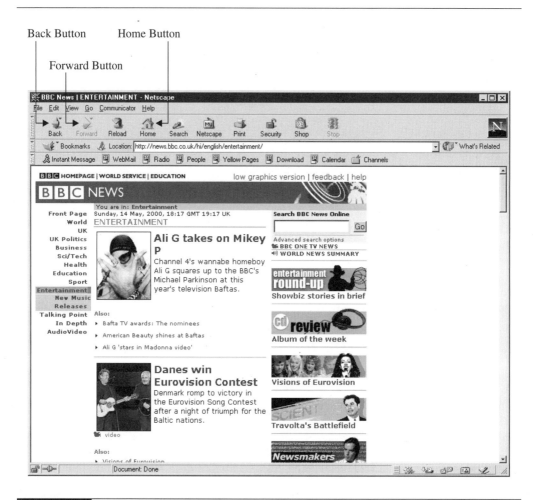

You reach the BBC page by clicking on a link in the previously displayed page

While you're looking at the BBC page this second time, you'll see that the Forward button is now "grayed out," which means it's nonfunctional. This is because the BBC page is the farthest one you've traveled to so far. There's no longer any "forward" to go to.

Now suppose that you've gone through a lot of pages, and you decide you want to return to the Netcenter home page, which is where you began when you launched Navigator. You *could* click the Back button till you got there, but that would be inefficient and clumsy, to say the least. Instead, click the Home button, which is in the same row as the Forward and Back buttons (see Figure 2-3). The Netcenter home page reappears. These are the basics of browsing: text and image links, Back and Forward controls, and the Home button. To demonstrate that IE works exactly the same way, let's take a fast look at it.

Close Navigator and open IE. Click Favorites, slide the mouse pointer down to Media, and click Disney from the second list. Using what you've just learned, find a link on the Disney page and click it. When the next page opens, click a link on that one. When *that* page opens, use the Back and Forward buttons to move around a bit. Then click the Home button to return to the MSN home page.

Understand Home Pages and Start Pages

An earlier Note told you that *home page* refers to the entry page of a Web site. Home page has a second meaning as well, which we're using in this section: It also refers to the page that opens automatically in your browser as soon as you launch it. This automatically appearing page is also sometimes called the *start page*, because it's where you start.

As you already know, the preset home pages in IE and Navigator are, respectively, MSN and Netcenter. You're not stuck with what IE and Navigator give you, however. You can customize each browser to open with a page of your own selection or, if you prefer, to open with a completely blank page. Making these changes will be covered in Chapter 3.

Browse on Your Own

The preset Web sites provided in IE and Navigator are fine to begin with, but you won't likely want to be restricted to them. Finding useful Web sites on your own can be much more interesting and fruitful. But how do you get to them?

One method you may have heard of is *search engines*. These tools will search for information for you, rather like a somewhat undiscriminating reference librarian. Search engines will be examined in detail in Chapter 4, but for the moment we'll restrict our ambitions and examine some of the other things you can do with your browser.

Understand Links as Internet Addresses

We noted earlier that a link contains an *Internet address,* which tells your browser which Internet computer it should contact to retrieve the page. Actually, you've already seen these addresses in the Location or Address box of your browser, perhaps without realizing what they were.

For an example, let's say that you're looking at a Web page with a text link that says *Click Here for Encyclopedia Britannica*. This link contains an Internet address, though you can't see it. A simple address might look like this:

http://www.eb.com

This address happens to be a real one. To fit the example, it points to the Encyclopedia Britannica Web site. The *http://* refers to the communications method the Web site uses, a technical issue that doesn't concern us here. The *www* means the site is part of the World Wide Web. The *eb* refers to Encyclopedia Britannica, and the *com* means the site is classed as a commercial site. The periods between the *www, eb,* and *com* are just separators. In practice, the *http://* is often omitted from the address, since your browser will automatically add it if it isn't there.

This simple string of characters is all your browser needs to go out on the Internet and get you the information you want. A lot goes on behind the scenes to allow it to do so, of course, but this is what it boils down to.

 You may come across the acronym URL. *This stands for* Uniform Resource Locator. *For our purposes, URL is just a complicated way of saying "Internet address."*

Type Internet Addresses into Your Browser

One advantage of understanding such Internet addresses is that they let you bypass search engines, bookmarks, and long spells of link-following. If you know the address, you can just tell it to your browser, and the browser will take you to the site. Here's how you do it in IE, using the Encyclopedia Britannica address as an example.

Launch IE. Look in the upper part of the browser screen, and you'll see a long text box labeled Address. If IE is displaying the MSN home page, the entry in this box will read **http://www.msn.com**.

Click in the Address box to put the text cursor (the blinking vertical line) there, and erase all the text from the box using the BACKSPACE and/or DELETE keys. Then type in **www.eb.com** but be sure not to put a period after the *com.* Then press the ENTER key. After a few moments, the Britannica home page appears. That's all there is to it.

 If the address is incorrect, such as having a period at the end of it, the browser will display an error message. If this happens, type the corrected address into the Address text box, and try again. Some Internet addresses are quite long and lend themselves to typing errors.

There's a second way to get an Internet address into the Address box. Suppose you are looking at a document on your screen that has such an address in it, and this is a long address, such as www.somesite.com/installation/docs/version3.html (or even worse). You could, of course, open your browser and laboriously type it all in. The easier way, though, is to use Windows' cut-and paste method: Select the text of the address, then copy it to the Windows Clipboard using the CTRL-C key combination. Next, switch to your browser, erase everything in the Address box, and use the CTRL-V key combination to paste the address into the box. Check it for accuracy, then press ENTER to open the page.

 *In fact, clicking once in the Address box automatically selects the entire address contained in it. As long as the old address is fully selected, you can simply press* CTRL-V *to paste the new one right over it, without having to delete the old address at all.*

The preceding assumed you were using IE, but Navigator works the same way. The only difference between the two browsers, in this context, is that the text box you use in Navigator is labeled "Location" instead of "Address."

Stop a Page from Downloading

"Downloading" refers to the process whereby the information from the Internet travels into your computer, where the browser turns it into something humans can understand, and then displays it on the monitor. This is also sometimes called "loading a page." With a slow connection, or a large Web page with a lot of information contained in it, a download can get tedious and you may want to stop it. To let you do this, both IE and Navigator provide stop buttons on their menu bars. Click the stop button and the download will end.

Create and Organize Favorites Lists in IE (Bookmarking)

The unfortunate fact is that the bookmarking methods of the two major browsers are so different that you can't use Navigator's bookmarks directly in IE, and vice versa. There are programs that will convert the bookmarks from one type to the other, but it remains an awkward incompatibility if you like using both browsers. This is one factor that helps push people toward using one of them to the exclusion of the other.

Given their differences, we'll examine them separately, beginning with IE.

Add a Favorite in IE

Assume you've been surfing around on the Web and you've found a page that you know you'll want to visit again. While the page is displayed in the browser, choose Favorites | Add to Favorites (remember that IE refers to its bookmarks as "Favorites"). The Add Favorite dialog appears.

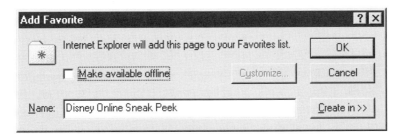

The Name text box already contains a suggested name for the page. If you don't like it, click in the text box to put the text cursor there, and retype the name. Then click OK.

To see what happened, choose Favorites again. You will see an IE icon and next to it, the name of the page you bookmarked. To return to this page in the future, all you have to do is click on that bookmark.

Delete a Favorite in IE

If you want to remove a Favorite from the list, right-click on its entry. A pop-up menu appears. Fourth from the bottom is the Delete option. Left-click on Delete, and Windows will ask if you want to send the entry to the Recycle Bin. Click Yes, and the entry will be removed from the Favorites list.

Rearrange Favorites in IE

The trouble is, once you've added a lot of bookmarks in this manner, the Favorites list will get disorganized and unwieldy. As a stopgap, you can manage it by dragging entries from one place to another so as to group them into categories. Do this:

1. Choose Favorites to open the list.

2. Place the mouse pointer on the entry you want to move. Hold the left mouse button down and drag the entry. A solid black line shows where it will be placed when you release the mouse button.

3. Release the mouse button when the black line is at the desired spot and the entry will move there.

Eventually, however, this will be unsatisfactory and you'll need a better method such as the following.

Organize Favorites in IE

The better method is to organize your bookmarks into folders of related information. To do this, you create the folders and then move existing bookmarks into them. If you add a new Favorite, you can specify its folder at the time of addition. If the new Favorite requires a new folder, as it might if you're starting a new category of information, you can create this new folder at the same time you add the new Favorite.

Move an Existing Favorite into an Existing Folder   Let's begin by organizing some Favorites into some existing folders. We'll use the preset ones to test things out. Do this:

1. Choose Favorites | Organize Favorites. The Organize Favorites dialog appears (see Figure 2-4).

2. Now we'll move the Favorite labeled "Radio Station Guide" into the folder labeled "Media." Select Radio Station Guide, then click the Move to Folder button. A dialog labeled Browse for Folder appears, displaying all the folders in your Favorites list. Select the desired folder (Media in this example) and click OK. The Favorite has now been moved to the desired folder.

3. Choose Close to exit the Organize Favorites dialog. Repeat the procedure to complete your organization.

TIP   *You can also drag an existing bookmark onto an existing folder to move it there. Make sure the folder is highlighted and the solid black positioning line has disappeared, before you release the mouse button.*

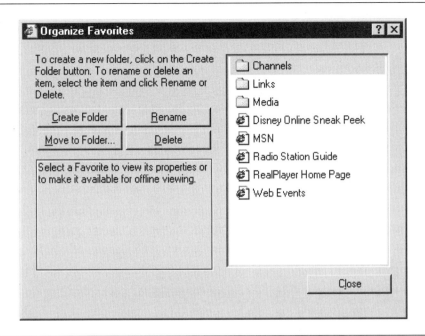

FIGURE 2-4   You use the Organize Favorites dialog to put your bookmarks into folder-based categories

Move an Existing Favorite into a New Folder   In this procedure, you'll create a new folder and move an existing Favorite into it. Do this:

1. Choose Favorites | Organize Favorites again to open the desired dialog (see Figure 2-4). Click the Create Folder button.

2. A New Folder text box appears in the dialog window. Type a name for it (I chose Entertainment) and press ENTER. This creates and names the folder. If you get the name wrong, select the folder, click Rename, retype the name, and press ENTER.

3. Select the Favorite you want to move. Click the Move to Folder button. The Browse for Folder dialog appears, as it did in the previous procedure.

4. Select the new folder and click OK. The selected Favorite is transferred to the new folder.

TIP   *At any time, you can rename either a Favorite or a folder by selecting it and clicking the Rename button.*

Add a New Favorite to an Existing Folder   Now let's examine how you add a brand new Favorite to an existing folder. Do this:

1. Open a Web page in IE, and let's assume you've decided to save it in an existing folder, the Links folder, for example.

2. Choose Favorites | Add to Favorites. The Add Favorite dialog appears, with a suggested name in the Name text box. Change the name if you like.

3. However, if you simply click OK at this point, the new Favorite will be placed straight into the Favorites list. It won't be in the Links folder where you want it.

4. To avoid this, click the Create In button to make a list of available Favorites folders appear, as in Figure 2-5. Select the desired folder (Links, in this example) and click OK. The new Favorite is saved in the selected folder.

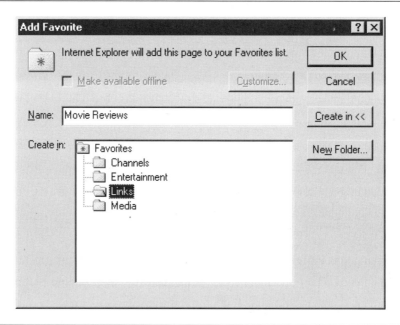

FIGURE 2-5   You can store Favorites in any desired folder in the Favorites list

2

Add a New Favorite in a New Folder   If you want to save a new Favorite and create a new folder for it at the same time, you use a combination of the previous procedures.

1. Open a Web page in IE, and let's assume you want to bookmark it as a Favorite. However, you also want to create a new folder to contain this category of information.

2. Choose Favorites | Add to Favorites to open the Add Favorite dialog. Click Create In to expand the dialog (see Figure 2-5).

3. Select the folder labeled Favorites to ensure that the new folder is created at the top level of the Favorites list. "Top level" simply means that this folder will be immediately visible when you open that list. If you select a different folder at this point, your new folder will end up being created inside the selected folder—the new one will be a *subfolder* of that folder.

4. Still with the Favorites folder selected, click New Folder. A Create New Folder dialog opens. Type the desired name of the new folder into the Folder Name text box, and click OK.

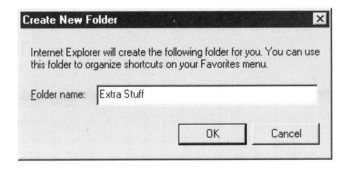

5. Now you'll see the new folder in the expanded Add Favorite dialog, and you'll also see that this folder is highlighted to show that it's been automatically selected.

6. Click OK. The new Favorite is added to the new folder you just created. (Remember, if you accidentally select a different folder, the Favorite will be added to that one.)

Use Subfolders to Organize Your Favorites   Organizing your Favorites can sometimes be made easier and more effective if you use *subfolders*. As noted briefly earlier, a subfolder is a folder contained in another folder. It's exactly like taking a paper file folder and slipping it into a second one.

For example, you might have an Entertainment folder that's getting unwieldy. To make it more manageable, you could split its contents into subfolders, such as Books, Movies, TV, and so on.

NOTE *People with a computer background sometimes refer to folders and subfolders as directories and subdirectories. They mean exactly the same thing.*

To create a subfolder of another folder, do this:

1. Choose Favorites | Organize Favorites to open the Organize Favorites dialog.

2. Expand the folder that will contain the new subfolder. "Expand" means open the folder so its contained Favorites are visible, as in the following illustration, where the contents of the Media folder are displayed. If the contained Favorites aren't visible, click on the folder.

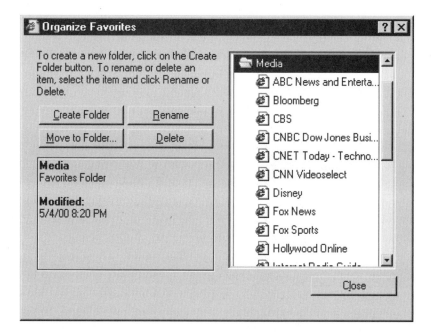

3. Click Create Folder. A New Folder entry will appear in the dialog list box. Type the name you want and press ENTER.

4. The new folder is created as a subfolder of the currently open folder.

CAUTION *The Organize Favorites dialog has a quirk: You can't expand a folder that has no Favorites in it, so you can't create a subfolder of that folder. If you try to, the new folder gets created at the top level of the Favorites list, not as a subfolder. The fix is to add a Favorite temporarily to the empty folder, create the desired subfolder, and then delete or move the temporary Favorite.*

2

Incidentally, if you have a folder and you want it to become a subfolder of another one, it's easy using the Organize Favorites dialog. Select the subfolder-to-be, then click Move to Folder. When the Browse to Folder dialog appears, select the destination folder and click OK. The new subfolder moves, taking with it all its Favorites. Or you can simply drag one folder into another one, as described in the earlier tip about dragging Favorites into folders.

Use the IE History List

IE's History list is a navigational aid: a tool to find a previously visited Web page that you didn't bookmark. The list is automatically maintained to record all pages visited in the last 20 days, though this can be customized. It's just the sort of tool you need when you find yourself muttering, "Where *was* that page I saw on making Tibetan yak butter?"

To use the list, open IE, click the History button, and the History window opens at the left of the browser display. You'll see major headings like Today, Monday, Tuesday, Last Week, and so on, depending on how much surfing you've done recently. This is because the list starts off organized by date. Assuming you can remember when you might have visited the site in question, click on the appropriate day or week. A list will appear, made up of yellow folder icons that represent Web sites. If you can identify the site you want, click on that folder. The folder will expand to show all the pages you visited at that site. Identify the one you want and click on it. IE will go and get it for you, as in Figure 2-6, where the Disney Online Sneak Peek page has been summoned by using the History list.

However, if your memory is as bad as the authors', you won't likely remember the day on which you saw the page in question. To help us out, IE lets you arrange the History list by Date (the way it opens), by Site, by Most Visited, and by Order Visited Today. To make this happen, choose View from the History window menu bar. Using these arrangements is pretty self-explanatory, so we'll leave it at that.

If all else fails, you can resort to Search, also on the History menu bar. Choose Search and a text box opens where you can type in your search term. The search is done on the words of the Web page titles in the History list, so "yak" or "butter" would have to be included in one of these for a search on "yak butter" to be successful. If it is, a list appears giving all the pages that have the search words in their title. Then you can click on each of them to go to the corresponding page. (Actually, perhaps Search should be the first thing you try.)

Create and Organize Bookmark Lists in Navigator

Navigator, as noted earlier, handles bookmarking differently from IE, but it does everything IE does. We'll examine Navigator's methods in detail in the following sections.

Add a Navigator Bookmark

This is much like the technique in IE. Navigate to the desired Web page (*navigate* just means "go there") and choose Bookmarks | Add Bookmark. Choose Bookmarks again and you'll see the new bookmark down at the bottom, right after the entry labeled Personal Bookmarks. What

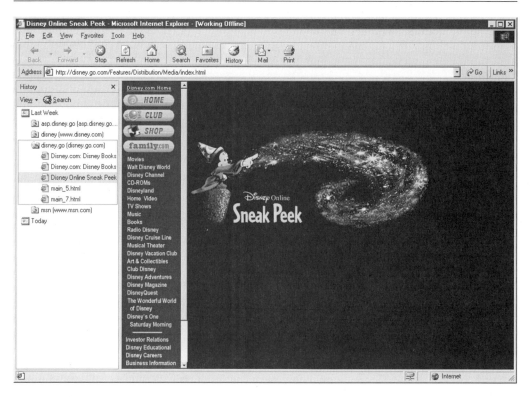

FIGURE 2-6   You use the history list to return to pages you've visited in earlier browsing sessions

Navigator doesn't do, and IE does, is allow you to choose your own name for the bookmark at the time you add it. You *can* change bookmark names in Navigator, but in a more roundabout way, which will be examined later.

Add a Bookmark to an Existing Navigator Folder

Navigate to the Web page. Choose Bookmarks | File Bookmark to open the list of existing bookmark folders, as in the illustration. Click the desired destination folder, and the bookmark will be added to it.

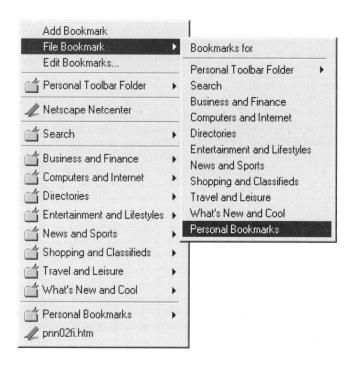

Edit Navigator Bookmarks

Navigator has an editing window where you do most of your bookmark maintenance and organization. It corresponds more or less to IE's Organize Favorites dialog. With it, you can rearrange, rename, delete, and organize your bookmarks.

Rearrange and Organize Bookmarks in Navigator   Choose Bookmarks | Edit Bookmarks to open the Bookmarks editing window (see Figure 2-7). The window opens with all folders fully expanded, that is, you can see all the bookmarks contained in them. To collapse a folder's contents (*collapse* means "hide the contents"), click the minus-sign (–) icon next to the folder icon. To expand a collapsed folder, click the plus-sign (+) icon next to the folder icon.

If you want to move a bookmark from one place to another, all you need do is drag it to the place you want. A gray line shows where it will be placed when you release the mouse button. If you drag a bookmark onto a collapsed purple folder, it will be placed as the first bookmark within that folder. If you want precise placement, expand the destination folder first and then drag the bookmark to the desired position.

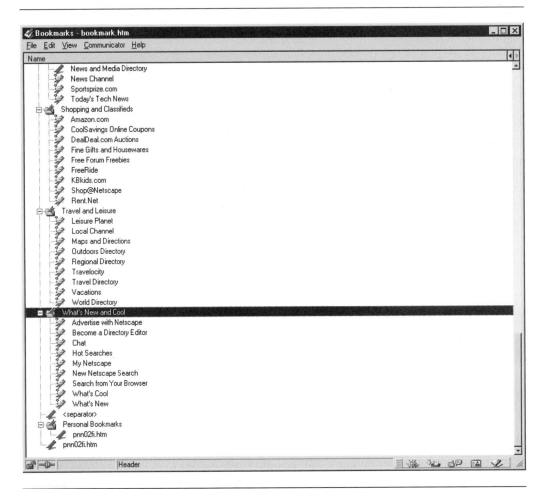

FIGURE 2-7 You use the Bookmarks editing window to maintain and organize your bookmark lists

Rename Bookmarks in Navigator To rename a bookmark or folder, first select it in the Bookmarks editing window. Then choose Edit | Bookmark Properties. The Bookmark Properties dialog opens. In the Name text box, type the name you want, then click OK to rename the bookmark or folder.

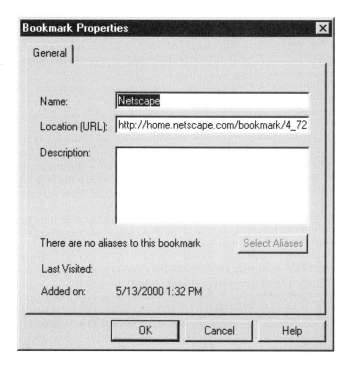

Delete Bookmarks in Navigator   In the Bookmarks editing window, select the bookmark, then choose Edit | Delete, or simply press the DELETE key. Note that Navigator does not issue a warning, it simply deletes the bookmark. Furthermore, it doesn't send the deletion to the Recycle Bin. Furthermore, if you select a folder and press the DELETE key, the folder and *all its contained bookmarks* are deleted without warning. If you accidentally do this, your only hope is to immediately choose Edit | Undo. So be careful when deleting bookmarks.

Create New Folders in Navigator   This is very simple. If you want to create a new folder at the top level of the list, select the very top entry, which is labeled Bookmarks For. Then choose File | New Folder. The Bookmark Properties dialog appears. Type a name for the folder into the Name text box and click OK. The folder appears with the desired name. Note that it isn't inserted alphabetically into the list. You have to drag it to the desired location.

If you want to create a subfolder, first select the folder that is to contain the subfolder. Then choose File | New Folder. Again, the Bookmark Properties dialog appears. Type a name for the subfolder into the Name text box, and click OK to create it.

As an alternative method of placement, select the entry (bookmark or folder) that is to appear just above the new folder. Then create the folder.

Create a New Bookmark in a New Folder   You recollect that in IE there's a way to create a new bookmark and a new folder for it at the same time. Here's how it's done in Navigator:

1. Navigate to the desired Web page. Choose Bookmarks | Edit Bookmarks.

2. When the Edit window opens, choose File | New Folder and create the new folder. Close the Edit window.

3. Choose Bookmarks | File Bookmark. Then find the entry for the new folder, and select it. The new bookmark will be stored in the new folder.

Search Navigator Bookmarks   You can search the bookmark list for a specific bookmark. Open the editing window and choose Edit | Find in Bookmarks. In the Find Bookmark dialog, type the word you're looking for into the Find box, and click OK. You can search either on the bookmark name, or on the Internet address it refers to, or both. An example of a Internet address, as you remember from our previous discussion, is **www.eb.com**.

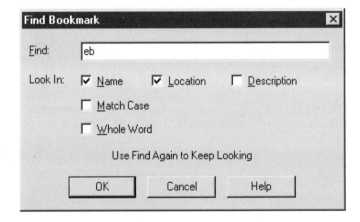

Use the Navigator History List

In Navigator as in IE, you can examine the history of your Web browsing. Choose Navigator | Tools | History (or press CTRL-H) and the History window opens.

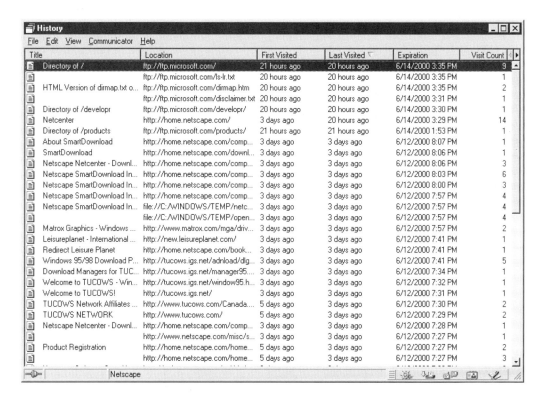

You can sort the various columns by clicking on the Title button at the column's top. If you choose Edit | Search History List, you can search the list for specific words in the history records. To go to a page in the list, double-click its entry and Netscape will take you there.

Bookmark Pages in Frames

Some Web sites make use of frames. This means that the browser displays more than one page on the screen at a time: a main page, plus at least one other page that appears in a kind of window within the main page. This type of window is called a *frame*, and the page within it a *framed page*. You can tell when you're looking at one because when you click a link, part of the browser display changes while another part remains static. The part that remains is often some kind of advertisement, menu, or navigation tool.

While frames are useful to Web designers, framed pages can be awkward to bookmark successfully. In both browsers, if you use the bookmarking techniques described earlier, what you will usually bookmark is the main page that contains the other page(s). If what you wanted to bookmark was the *framed* page all by itself, that is, the one within the window of the main page, this doesn't happen. You get the whole works, main page and all.

There's a way around this, however. In Figure 2-8, there are two frames in the IE window: the main frame with an advertising bar across the top, and the framed page about koalas within it.

If you simply choose Favorites | Add Favorite, the new Favorite will point to the main page, and when you use the bookmark again you'll get both that and the framed page, as indicated earlier. But suppose you just wanted to bookmark the page about koalas?

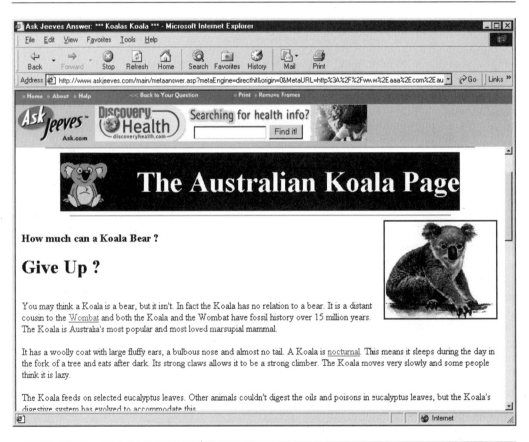

FIGURE 2-8 This framed page requires special techniques to bookmark it

In IE, do this: right-click on the framed page (the one you want to bookmark) and from the pop-up menu, choose Add to Favorites. The normal Add Favorite dialog appears. Save the Favorite and when you use it later, the browser will display only the page that was in the frame— just the page on Koalas, in the example.

In Navigator, you follow the same procedure, opening the pop-up menu by right-clicking on the framed page. In Navigator's pop-up menu, you choose Add Bookmark to bookmark the framed page by itself.

Find Text in Long Pages

Information on the Web is still largely textual information, and some pages are fairly long and run well off the bottom of your screen. To find a particular word or phrase in such a page, in IE choose Edit | Find on This Page. A search dialog opens where you can type in the desired text. Choose Find Next to carry out the search.

In Navigator, choose Edit | Find in Page. This opens a dialog similar to the one in IE.

Follow Links to Images and Documents

Links on Web pages don't always take you to other Web pages. Sometimes they are links to other kinds of information, like images, non-Web documents, and multimedia. Multimedia deserves a whole chapter to itself, so at this point we'll restrict ourselves to images and non-Web documents.

View Images

Some Web sites don't put their images right on the Web page, but instead provide links to them. This is because images need more time to transmit than text, so keeping large pictures off a page lets the page appear faster in the user's browser. Then the user can decide for himself or herself whether to call up the images.

There are two main types of links. The first is a text link, usually being the name of the picture. Click the link, the Web page vanishes from the browser window, and the image replaces it. To return to the page with the link, merely click the browser's Back button. If the Web site is using frames, the picture may appear in a smaller window within the main window.

The other common link is a small version of the actual picture, produced by some kind of image processing software. This is called a *thumbnail*, for obvious reasons. Being small, thumbnails load into a browser quickly and give the viewer some idea of what the bigger picture looks like. When clicked, a thumbnail link behaves exactly like the text link just described.

View Word Processor and Text Documents

Some Web pages have text documents that were produced by non-Web software, such as word processors or text editors. If you click on such a link, what you see depends on what programs are installed on your computer. If the document is a Microsoft Word document, for example, you'll only be able to read it if Word is on your machine.

Fortunately, this situation isn't all that common, and in any case most Web managers make alternate types of documents available. One example of what you may run across is the plain old text document. You can often tell such a document by its link, because the link will actually show the name of the document. An example could be STUFF.TXT, where the TXT after the period means that this is a plain-vanilla text document. Your browser will be able to display a text document without difficulty.

View PDF Documents

A type of document commonly used on the Web, especially for user guides and software manuals, is the PDF (Portable Document Format) document. To view these, you need to install a special reader called Adobe Acrobat. Acrobat is free, and can be downloaded from the Adobe Web site at **www.adobe.com**. It's also often included on CD-ROM with purchased software as a way to provide the purchaser with electronic documentation (*documentation* just means "information and instructions"). You'll learn how to download and install such useful software in Chapter 6.

Understand Security Warnings

When you navigate to some Web sites, you may get pop-up security notifications when you click a link. This most often happens, and certainly *should* happen, when you're entering the part of a Web site where you can buy things. For example, the security alert at PowerQuest Corporation's site reassures you that you are entering a secure Web site and that the information you exchange with it can't be observed by anyone else on the Web. This is, of course, to protect sensitive information like your credit card numbers and your purchasing habits.

Other security alerts just warn you that you're about to transmit information across the Web and ask if you want to proceed. Often these warnings are associated with registration forms, for example, when you're registering to download some free software. Such forms often ask for your e-mail address, your name, and similar stuff. If it isn't truly sensitive information in your view, you can probably go ahead without concern. For more information about security on the Internet, see Part IV of this book.

Why Your Connection May Be Slow

Dial-up is slow by nature, but even high-speed connections may seem sluggish from time to time. Here are some of the reasons this may be happening.

Phone-Line Quality

This is related to dial-up connections and was covered earlier in Chapter 1, but it bears repeating here. Not all phone lines are created equal; some are of poor quality and your modem spends a lot of time asking for data to be re-sent because it detected a transmission error. Older phone company switches may limit your line speed to 28.8K or worse, even if you're using a 56K modem.

Internet Traffic Jams

The information-carrying capacity of the Internet is not infinite. When a lot of people are logged onto the Internet, there can be slowdowns as parts of it experience congestion from heavy signal traffic. This will affect the speed with which pages appear in your browser, even if you have a fast connection. As well, cable connections can become slower when a lot of the ISP's subscribers are logged onto the cable system at once (DSL does not have this drawback).

Also, Web sites have a limit to the traffic they can handle. A site can be overwhelmed by a sudden interest in its content, as the NASA sites sometimes are when a space mission is in headline news. But even without such surges of interest, widely popular Web sites may be slow, especially at certain times of the day.

Your ISP's Technology

Smaller ISPs may not have the capital needed for upgrades of hardware and software, which can cause problems for their subscribers. Your ultimate connection speed also depends on what service is providing your ISP with its feed to the Internet. ISPs use even larger service providers to give them access to what's called an Internet *backbone*, and some backbones carry information faster than others. If your ISP seems to be getting slower and slower and if you can determine that it's because they're losing technological ground, you might consider switching to another service.

About Internet Speed-Up Software

You can obtain, usually by download from the Web, software packages that claim to speed up your Internet connection. These programs are directed to dial-up users who may be getting poor results even on a good phone line. They work by adjusting some internal Windows settings to allow data to flow more quickly between your machine and the line. In some cases they can help, though they won't work the miracle of turning your dial-up connection into DSL. Many such packages have trial versions, so you can try before you buy. However, they do assume technical expertise on the part of the user.

Diagnose a Connection with Ping

You can check your Internet connection with a Windows utility called Ping (a *utility* is the common name for a small program that does one useful thing and does it well). Ping sends a signal to a Web site you select, and listens for the Web site to answer. It's sort of like calling "hello?" into the dark and hoping for a response.

Ping is a DOS program, so you have to open what's called a *DOS session,* which you do by choosing Start | Programs | MS-DOS Prompt. In the DOS window that appears, type **ping** followed by a space and the Internet address of the desired site: for example, **ping www.eb.com**. Ping sends four "hellos" and within a few seconds you should receive four replies from the target Web site. If instead you see "Request timed out" four times, it means the site exists but isn't answering for some reason. If you see "Unknown host" it means there is no record on the Internet of that Web site.

If Ping does get an answer, you know your Internet connection is working and that the pinged Web site is alive and well.

To open a DOS session, Windows Millennium users must choose Start | Programs | Accessories | MS-DOS Prompt.

Why Sites Don't Respond

Sometimes you click on a link or a bookmark and nothing happens for a long, long time. Eventually, however, you get an error message. Usually, it tells you the Web page is currently unavailable and may give technical-sounding reasons for this. This may mean that the computer containing the site is down, or that the communication link to it is broken for some reason (phone system outages, dead satellites, microwave tower collapse, hurricane, tornado—you'll likely never know). It may also mean that the Web site has been permanently closed down by its owner, or has moved to another computer without leaving a forwarding address. Or it may mean that your phone line, if you're using one, is behaving badly, or your ISP may be having software or hardware problems. The best thing to do is try again in a while; sites are sometimes down for maintenance or repairs and reappear as mysteriously as they vanished. Also, you might try the Ping utility as described in the previous section to make sure your connection really is intact. Another program that might help is Tracert, which you use from a DOS prompt like Ping. It displays a list of the various computers and networks through which the connection is being attempted, and may give you an idea of where on the Internet the problem really is.

If the problem affects only one Web site, it's not likely your connection or your ISP. But if you can't get to any Web sites at all, first make sure that your phone line is working, assuming you're on one. If it is, there's something else wrong, and you should contact your ISP to see if they've identified a problem or are experiencing one.

Where to Find It

Web Site	Address	What's There
Adobe	http://www.adobe.com/products/acrobat/readstep.html	Adobe Acrobat PDF reader
Opera Software	www.opera.com	Opera browser

Chapter 3

Customizing Your Browser

How To . . .

- Change your browser's home page
- Understand and use portal pages
- Deal with the browser's temporary cache files
- Manage History lists
- Customize your browser's fonts and colors
- Adjust toolbar views
- Customize a dial-up connection
- Prevent unwanted image and multimedia downloads
- Safeguard your bookmarks by backing them up
- Learn about bookmark conversion programs

Both IE and Navigator can be extensively customized to meet your preferences. So many adjustments can be made, in fact, that a complete treatment of all of them is beyond the scope of this book. Instead, we'll examine the settings you're most likely to want to change. The browsers' online help will assist you in understanding the more exotic customizations.

Change Your Start or Home Page

IE 5 and Navigator 4.73 both refer to a browser home page, meaning the page that opens automatically in your browser when you launch it. Somewhat confusingly, such a page is also sometimes called a start page. To be consistent with the usage of IE and Navigator's latest versions, we'll refer to the page that automatically opens as the home page. If you see "start page" somewhere on the Web or elsewhere, just translate.

Specify a Home Page in IE

In IE, choose Tools | Internet Options (IE 4 users: choose View | Internet Options). This opens the Internet Options dialog with the General sheet displayed (see Figure 3-1).

As installed and without customization, the Home Page section of this sheet specifies the home page's address as **http://www.msn.com**. This is the Web site address of the Microsoft Network, as you know. But if you prefer a simple life and want a blank page when you launch IE, click the Use Blank button and click OK. When you next launch IE, it will open with a blank page in the browser window.

However, you may eventually discover a favorite Web site that you want to appear whenever you start IE. To make this happen, determine the Internet address of the page. Then open the Internet Options dialog as just described, and type that Internet address into the Address text box of the General sheet. Then click OK. From then on, whenever IE is launched, the browser will download and display that page.

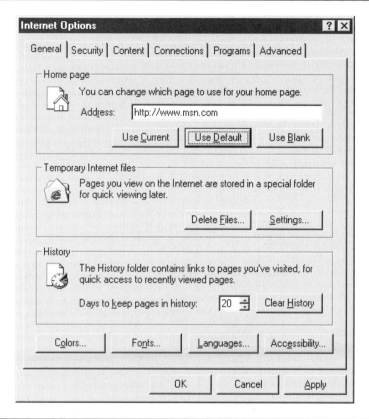

FIGURE 3-1   IE customization is mostly done through the Internet Options dialog

However, there's an easier way. Simply navigate to the desired Web page, then open the Internet Options dialog as before. On the General sheet, click the Use Current button. The Address box will immediately display the address of the desired Web page. Click OK and this page becomes your home page.

If at any time you want to make the Microsoft Network site your home page again, click the Use Default button. This resets the Address box to **http://www.msn.com**. Click OK to complete the change.

TIP   *You've probably noticed the Home button on the IE toolbar. Assuming you're online, clicking this button will take you to whatever home page you specified in the Internet Options dialog.*

Specify a Home Page in Navigator

To choose among home page options in Navigator, choose Edit | Preferences to open the Preferences dialog. Select the Navigator entry from the Category list if it isn't already selected (see Figure 3-2).

In the section labeled Navigator Starts With, you have four choices:

■ Blank Page sets the home page blank, as in IE.

■ If you want a particular Web page as your home page, navigate to it, open the Preferences dialog, and click the Use Current Page button. Also make sure the Home Page button in the upper section is selected before clicking OK. The desired page is now your home page, and whenever you click the Home button on the Navigator toolbar, you'll be taken there.

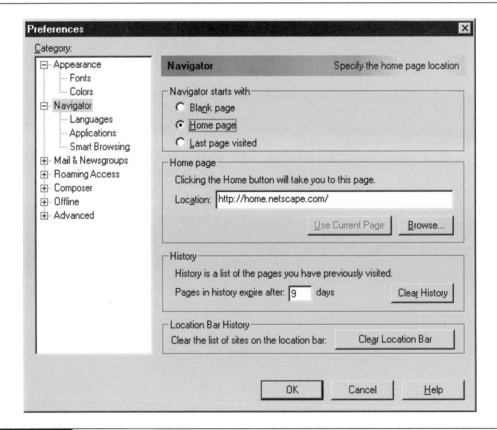

FIGURE 3-2 You can set a desired home page in Navigator's Preferences dialog

- A further option is to make the most recently visited page the (temporary) home page. This is useful for picking up where you left off in an earlier browsing session.

- If you have a Web page stored on your computer and want that as your home page, you can use the Browse button to locate it and place its filename in the Location text box. Then select the Home Page option button and click OK.

Use Portal Pages

While you can choose any page on the Web to be your home page, you may want to pick one that gives you a variety of resources, such as weather, news, search tools, and so on. Such pages are available, and in fact are specialized to be home pages for browsers. You don't have to shell out money for them, either, because the purveyors of such pages pay their way by displaying advertisements. If you don't mind ads, a portal page may be for you.

Your own ISP's home page may be a portal, offering some useful services. Netscape's Netcenter, the default home page in Navigator, is a type of portal as well, and so is MSN. But if you don't want these, there are lots of other possibilities, so many that we can't possibly examine them all. But a representative portal, and a popular one, is Yahoo!.

To look at it, start your browser and navigate to the Yahoo! Web site by typing **www.yahoo.com** into the browser's Address or Location box and pressing ENTER. The page appears, resembling Figure 3-3.

Here you can sign up for free e-mail, read news, go shopping, check the weather, look at TV schedules and movie reviews, search for information... the list goes on and on.

The only drawback may be that there is too *much* on offer. To get more selective, you can use Yahoo! to set up a personalized portal. Click the My Yahoo! link from the set of links just under the Search button (Yahoo! may have changed its page layout by the time you read this, but keep looking) and you'll be taken to the My Yahoo! portal site. Here you can create a personalized page to serve as your home page. To do so, however, you must register with Yahoo!, and set up a username and password so you can log onto the page. This is necessary from a technical point of view, since the portal has to know what page to give you when you ask for it, and also because you probably don't want other people looking at your home page. Registering, of course, also gives Yahoo! an opportunity to send you merchandising e-mail, which is what pays for the service.

Anyway, after you've decided on a portal site, and possibly registered for a personalized home page, use the procedures described earlier to make it the home page of your browser. Some more portal sites are listed at the end of the chapter.

The My Netscape button on the Navigator toolbar (immediately to the right of the Search button) takes you to the My Netscape portal site. You can set up a personalized home page here, just as you can in Yahoo!.

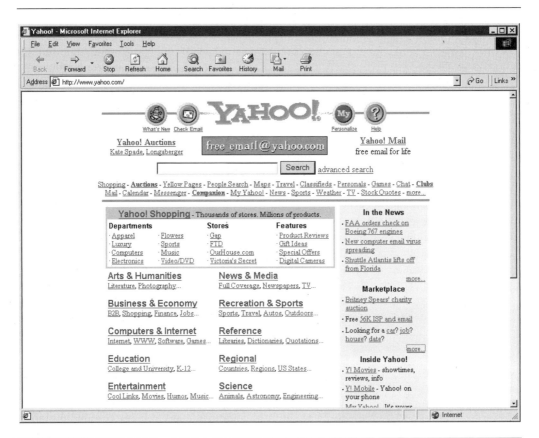

The Yahoo! main page is a good example of a portal page

Customize Basic Browser Settings

Your home page is probably the most important factor in personalizing your browser, but as mentioned earlier, there are other modifications you may want to make. The next sections will help you understand how to do it.

Display Toolbars

You can turn on or off various toolbars in both browsers. In Navigator, choose View | Show to reveal a menu of four toolbars, including the floating toolbar that appeared when you first installed Communicator. Check or uncheck these toolbars to hide or reveal them.

In IE, choose View | Toolbars. This displays a menu of various toolbars you can turn on or off. If you need a specialized toolbar you can design it yourself by choosing the Custom entry to open a customization dialog. Here you can add buttons to or remove buttons from the browser's main toolbar.

Understand Temporary Internet Files

Both browsers maintain a set of temporary records about the browsing you've done over the past while. These records are actually data files, and their precise name is *cache files.* They are contained on your computer in a set of folders referred to collectively as a *cache.*

But what are the cache and its files used for, and where do they come from? Well, the whole idea is to speed up your browsing experience. As you browse the Web, the browser stores a temporary copy of each page you open in a cache file. Now, suppose you leave that page and go on to others, but at some later time in the current browsing session, you want to see that page again. When you request it (for example, by clicking on a bookmark) the browser doesn't immediately look for it out on the Web. Instead, it checks its cache to see if a copy of the page is already stored there. If it is, the browser uses that copy, instead of going to the Web for it. This way, the time required to display the page is much shortened, because it's much faster to load a page from the cache than it is to get it from a remote computer.

But what if the original page has been changed while you weren't looking? Then the cache copy would be an old version, not the most current version. This is what IE's Refresh button and Navigator's Reload button are for. (They're up on the browser toolbars, under the menu bar.) Despite the different names, they do exactly the same thing: click them, and they force the browser to get the most recent version of the currently displayed Web page from the Web site where it lives. This is how you can make sure you're looking at the newest version of the page.

The basic cache behavior in both browsers can be adjusted as follows.

Cache Settings in IE

From the IE menu, choose Tools | Internet Options (IE 4 users: choose View | Internet Options). The Internet Options dialog opens with the General sheet displayed (see Figure 3-1). From the

Temporary Internet Files section of this sheet, click the Settings button to bring up the Settings dialog, as shown in the illustration here.

In this Settings dialog you can specify that IE check for new page versions as follows:

■ Every time you open the page, whether you just had it open or not. This will slow things down because the browser never uses its cached pages.

■ Every time you start IE. This means that in any single session (that is, as long as you don't close IE) a page will only be checked the first time you open it in that session.

■ Automatically. This is the *default setting* (see the Did You Know? box that follows to find out what this means). This behaves much like the previous choice, but checks less often over time, if the page rarely changes. Unless you have a specific reason to do otherwise, leave this setting selected.

■ Never. IE never checks for a new version of the page. If a lot of pages seem out of date, see if this setting has been selected by accident.

You can also adjust the amount of hard disk space reserved for the cache files. Leave this setting as is unless you're really low on disk space. When the cache is full, the oldest entries are automatically discarded to make room for new ones.

Did you know?

Computer and software manuals use the word "default" a lot. A *default setting* refers to how the software set itself up when it was installed, previous to any changes made to that setting by a human. More generally, a default is what the computer will resort to doing if you don't tell it to do something different. As another example, "leave the settings at their defaults" means "don't make any changes to them."

When you click OK, you return to the General sheet. Here you can also click the Delete Files button to erase all the cache files from your hard disk. When you start browsing again, IE will begin creating a new set. You'd probably do this only if you were low on disk space.

Cache Settings in Navigator

To adjust the cache settings, choose Edit | Preferences to open the Preferences dialog (see Figure 3-2). From the Category menu, choose Advanced | Cache. Here you can adjust the amount of hard disk space reserved for the cache files, and also the amount of system memory reserved for them. You can clear both these caches, too. Normally, you won't need to change these settings.

Navigator has three choices for page checking, similar to IE's. Once Per Session checks only once for each browsing session, Every Time checks the page every time you go to it no matter what, and Never (guess what?) never checks at all.

Manage Your History List

Still on the General sheet of IE's Internet Options dialog (see Figure 3-1), you'll find a History section. You can do two things here: erase the history list with the Clear History button, or specify how many days' worth of history IE maintains. You might want to reduce this if you don't like searching through long History lists, or if you don't want other people to look at the sites you've visited.

Navigator has a similar tool. Open its Preferences dialog as before (see Figure 3-2) and from the Category list choose Navigator. In the right panel of this dialog is the History section. You can set the expiry number to discard any history entries older than a certain number of days. As well, you can erase the History list with the Clear History button.

Modify the Browser Display

You can change some of the cosmetics of the two browsers' displays, particularly fonts and screen colors. You can also modify settings for accessibility by people with disabilities.

Customize Screen Colors and Fonts

After opening the General sheet of IE's Internet Options dialog (refer to Figure 3-1, if necessary), click the Colors button to open the Colors dialog. To set your own text and background colors, clear the Use Windows Colors check box and use the Text button and the Background button, respectively, to customize those colors. You can also change the colors of visited and unvisited text links. Finally, you can specify what the hover color will be for a *hover button* (a button that changes color when the mouse pointer is on top of it).

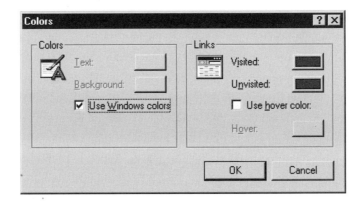

In Navigator, you open the Preferences dialog and choose Appearance | Colors from the Category list. Here you have the same options as in IE, except that the hover color option is replaced by an option to underline or not underline text links. As well, you can specify that your selected colors will appear no matter what colors the Web page has by selecting the check box in this section.

While you're still in Navigator, you can experiment with font settings by clicking on the Fonts entry under the Appearance entry of the Category list. Disregard the box labeled "For the Encoding," since we won't change our language setting to a non-English one.

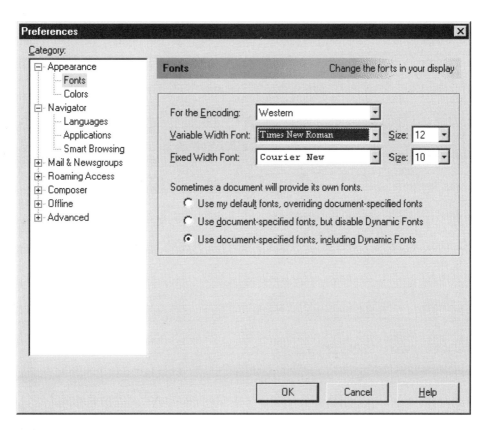

By clicking the arrow button at the right end of the Variable Width font box, you can specify which of the fonts installed on your computer will be used to display the text in Web pages. For example, the body text in Web pages is usually Times, but if you prefer body text to always appear in Arial, you'd set this box to display Arial. *Variable width* means that the characters occupy different amounts of space; for example, the "i" takes up less lateral space than the "m."

There is also a box for a Fixed Width font. The characters of a fixed width font all take up the same lateral space, which makes this font useful for filling in forms. Unless you have a compelling reason to change from its setting of Courier New, leave it as it is.

To make similar font changes in IE, you open the Fonts dialog by clicking the Fonts button on the General sheet of IE's Internet Options dialog. The Web Page Font setting serves the same purpose as Navigator's Variable Width font, and the Plain Text font is the same as Navigator's

Fixed Width font. Leave the Language Script box as it is unless you're customizing the browser for a different language.

Customize Accessibility Options

Back on IE's General sheet again, you'll see a button labeled "Accessibility." Click it, and you get a dialog that lets you manage the browser display for people with disabilities. Some Web pages specify their own fonts and colors, and these may not be suitable if, for example, a user is visually impaired and wants the font to remain set at his or her personal preferences. Selecting the top three radio buttons for colors, font styles, and font sizes forces the browser to display the page according to the user's font and color settings, overriding any that are specified by the page.

You can achieve a similar result in Navigator, using the Preferences dialog as in the previous sections. From the Appearance category, choose Fonts, and select the Use My Default Fonts option. Then choose Colors and select the check box labeled Always Use My Colors. Your settings will now override any that are given by a Web page.

Customize Your Dial-Up Connection

As you're aware, both IE and Navigator automatically open a connection dialog if you launch them before you make your dial-up connection (this doesn't apply to high-speed connections, since they're always on). Some people, however, prefer to make their connection manually without the browser's intervention.

To keep IE from trying to open the connection when it starts, do the following. First launch IE. Then choose Tools | Internet Options (IE 4 users: choose View | Internet Options) and select the Connections sheet, as in the next illustration.

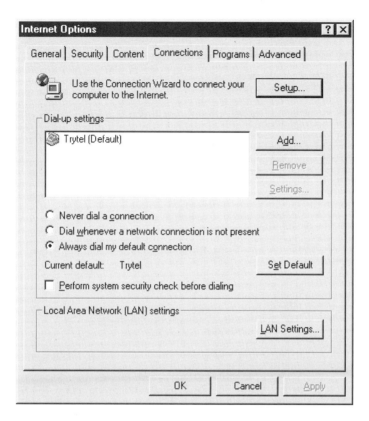

3

Look about halfway down the sheet and you'll see an option button labeled Always Dial My Default Connection. If the button is marked with a black dot, then the browser will always try to open the dial-up connection for you. To change this behavior, select the button labeled Never Dial a Connection by clicking on it. Then click OK and close IE. Launch it again, and the connection dialog will not appear.

What *will* happen, though, is that the browser will try to open your start page anyway, and since it can't do so without a connection, it will eventually give up in despair and issue an error message. The only way to prevent this from happening is to set the start page to be a blank page, as was explained earlier in this chapter.

This change of settings will also be applied automatically to Navigator the next time you launch it. As with IE, you won't see the connection dialog, but you will see Navigator trying to connect to your start page. Ultimately, it will give you an error message saying it can't locate the server. Again, to prevent this, set the Navigator start page to be a blank page as explained earlier in this chapter.

Specify Which Program to Use for a Service

A browser does not work entirely on its own. Both IE and Navigator set up internal connections to other programs on your computer. IE makes changing some of these connections relatively easy; Navigator is much less friendly about it.

Specify Programs in IE

You might, for example, need to tell IE that when you want to use an e-mail link on a Web page, it should not try to launch Outlook Express (the e-mail program included with Windows) but instead should start a different e-mail program for you.

NOTE *An e-mail link on a Web page is a kind of shortcut. If you want to send an e-mail to that address (often it's the address of the person or organization who runs the Web site), all you have to do is click the link and the browser will open your e-mail program with the correct address already filled in. This is so you don't have to leave the browser, open your e-mail program, and laboriously type the address into it.*

To make this and similar changes, choose Tools | Internet Options to open the Internet Options dialog (IE 4 users: choose View | Internet Options). Then click the Programs sheet of the dialog.

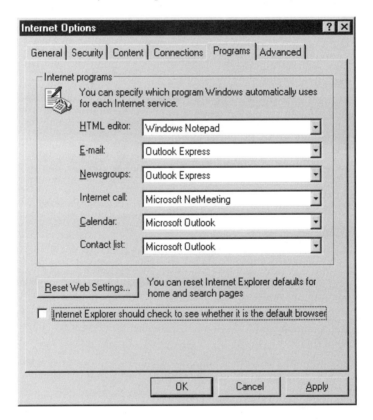

As you can see in the example illustration, the selected e-mail program is indeed Outlook Express. Since this machine has Navigator installed, however, you can instead use Netscape's e-mail program, which is called Messenger. Click the button at the right of the E-mail text box, select Netscape Messenger, and click OK. Now when you click an e-mail link on a Web page, Messenger will launch instead of Outlook Express.

There are other choices also, such as which newsgroup reader to use. The programs available will depend on what's installed on your computer, naturally.

This Programs sheet has two other tools. One is the Reset Web Settings button, which returns your IE home and search pages to their original settings as first installed. This is useful if you want to start with a clean slate, so to speak.

The other tool is the check box labeled "Internet Explorer Should Check to See Whether It Is the Default Browser." This is quite a mouthful. What does it mean in practice, if you check this box?

It's not all that mysterious, in fact. You may know from using Windows that you can sometimes double-click a filename in order to open the file and display its content. The program that was used to create the file actually displays the content: a file named STUFF.TXT, for example, will open in Windows Notepad. Similarly, Web-type documents, including pages and pictures, will be displayed in the default browser when their filenames are double-clicked.

Suppose Navigator is the default browser. To change the default to IE, check the box labeled "Internet Explorer Should Check to See Whether It Is the Default Browser." Then click OK and shut down IE and all other programs. Restart your computer and launch IE again. IE will look around to see if another browser (Navigator in this example) has been set to be the default. If this is the case, IE will ask if you want to make IE the default browser. If you choose Yes, Navigator is in effect demoted and IE becomes the system's principal browser.

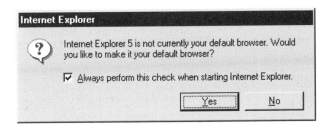

As a rule of thumb, you should set your default browser to be the one you use most frequently for browsing the Web.

Specify Programs in Navigator

As indicated earlier, specifying the programs that Navigator uses for certain purposes is not at all user-friendly, and is much more complex than we can deal with here. There isn't much real reason to do it unless you're of a technical bent, and are prepared to cope with MIME types and other esoteric subjects.

There is no speedy button to make Navigator the default browser once it has lost that status. There is a manual procedure for doing so, which you can read about at the Netscape Web site at **home.netscape.com/download/win32_instructions.html**. However, it involves editing one of Netscape's configuration files, and you may be very unwilling to get into this sort of thing.

A much easier way is simply to reinstall Communicator, while making sure that the Make Netscape Navigator My Default Browser option is checked when you get to the Netscape Desktop Preference Options install dialog. After finishing the install, restart your machine and launch Communicator.

Navigator is again the default browser. However, Communicator will also have reset the IE home page to the Netscape Netcenter. To change this, don't use the Reset Web Settings button on the Programs sheet of IE's Internet Options, or you'll make IE the default browser again. Instead, use the General sheet and insert the desired home page address into the Address text box, using the procedures described earlier in this chapter.

Prevent Image and Multimedia Downloads

Pictures, audio, and video all contain a lot of information, and downloading them takes much more time than downloading text. This is a particular issue if you're on dial-up, which is slow to begin with and which can really bog down if it's coping with big multimedia or image files.

To speed up the appearance of the pages' text, you can stop the browser from trying to download these items. In IE, go to the Internet Options dialog and choose the Advanced sheet. Scroll down until you find the Multimedia section. Then check or uncheck the boxes for playing animation, sounds, or showing pictures. If they're unchecked, the item won't show up. However, if you turn off pictures, you may want to mark the Show Image Download Placeholders check box. If you do this, a marker will appear on the page to show where the item will go. If you decide you want to see it, right-click the marker and choose Show Picture from the pop-up menu.

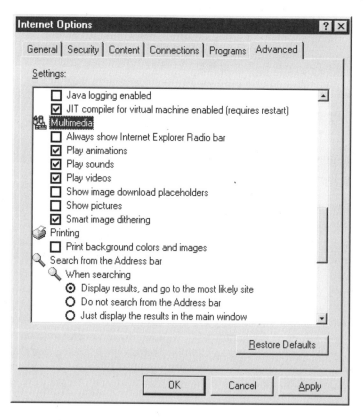

To achieve a similar result in Navigator, go to the Preferences dialog again and choose the Advanced category. Uncheck the check box labeled Automatically Load Images. Since Navigator uses a different technique from IE to handle video and sound, there is no provision here for preventing such downloads.

You may be wondering why we don't deal with IE's Content and Security sheets in these sections. It's because they fit better into the chapters on viruses and Net slums respectively, and so will be dealt with there.

3

Safeguard Your Bookmarks and Favorites

Once you've been on the Web for any time at all, you'll probably have built up quite a collection of bookmarks. Reassembling it, if it got lost, would be difficult, but what do you do if you get a new computer and you want to move your bookmarks over to it? Or if you have to reinstall Windows from scratch, which involves erasing everything from your hard drive?

Fortunately, if you know even a little about file management in Windows, it's not difficult to back up your bookmarks (*back up* means make copies for safekeeping). Unless you have vast numbers of bookmarks, the files involved are relatively small and should fit comfortably on a floppy disk. All you need is the files' location on your computer, so you can copy them.

For IE, use Windows Explorer to go to the C:\WINDOWS\FAVORITES folder. All your Favorites are stored here. To back them up, copy the Favorites folder from the Windows folder to your floppy disk.

For Navigator, there is one bookmark file for each Communicator profile. Use Windows Explorer to go to C:\PROGRAM FILES\COMMUNICATOR\USERS. In the Users folder you'll see a folder for each user profile. (Recollect that you created a profile when you first installed Communicator; if no one else has created others since then, that profile will be the only one present.) To back up all profiles at once, just copy the Users folder to a floppy disk. The bookmark filename itself is always BOOKMARK.HTM or BOOKMARK.HTML.

When you want to restore either type of bookmark file(s), simply copy them from the floppy disk back to their original locations on the C: drive.

Transfer Bookmarks Between Browsers

Suppose you've accumulated a lot of bookmarks in Navigator, but now you want them available on IE, or vice versa. Unfortunately, neither browser gives you a way to transfer Favorites to Bookmarks, or the reverse. However, there are programs that will allow you to do this. Examples of such converters are Bookmark Converter and Bookmark Magic. They're not difficult to use, and will save you time and energy.

Before you do such conversions, however, you should first back up your Bookmark and Favorites files using the techniques described in the previous section.

Where to Find It

Web Site	Address	What's There
AOL	www.aol.com	Portal site
Cybermatrix	www.cyber-matrix.com	Bookmark converter
Excite	www.excite.com	Portal site
Lycos	www.lycos.com	Portal site
Magnus Brading	www.magnusbrading.com	Bookmark converter
Yahoo!	www.yahoo.com	Portal site

Chapter 4

Finding Information on the Internet

How To . . .

- Understand the varieties of search tools available
- Use a search engine for basic searches
- Use a directory for basic searches
- Carry out advanced searches
- Understand and use metasearches
- Use expert sites
- Search with IE's and Navigator's built-in search tools
- Get the most out of specialized directories
- Find and use reference resources like news portals and encyclopedias

As we've said at least once, the Internet is a vast and rich repository of every sort of information under the sun. The trouble is that it's somewhat of an embarrassment of riches. Locating and identifying a particular piece of information so that you can extract it from this enormous labyrinth can be a daunting task. There are literally *billions* of Web pages and other documents stored on the Internet. Nobody knows how many there are, nor ever will, for the number grows with every second.

Just as with traditional libraries, however, various tools have been developed to help people find what they're after. These tools are not yet as discriminating as users might like; they often give you far more hits than you can possibly use. (A *hit* is when the search tool finds an item it thinks you want, and displays a link to that item.) But some of these tools are uncannily good at locating information for you, and without them the Internet would be far less useful than it is.

About Search Tools and Their Varieties

There are two broad classes of search tools: directories and search engines. Directories work in a hierarchical way: that is, they start you off with a list of major categories, each of which is divided into subcategories. The subcategories are again subdivided, and so on down through the hierarchy. Each layer of subdivision provides more specific and narrower references until, ideally, you end up with a small number of sites and/or documents that meet your needs.

Web sites that provide such directories are often called *search sites*. Search sites also invariably include the second type of search tool with their directories, so that you can dig through several categories at once if you wish. This second type of tool is called a *search engine*. A search engine is a program that takes one or more *search terms,* and then goes looking for Web sites or pages that have those terms in them. A search term is the word or phrase you're looking for, such as "pigeons" or "Caribbean resorts."

Search engines also exist independently of directory-type search sites. They dispense with directories altogether, so that you just use search terms to go looking for what you want.

Some directories are specialized for particular purposes. For example, phone directories are for locating people or businesses. Other directories are general-purpose ones, like Yahoo!, and cover just about everything you could ever want to know. Since there are so many different variations within the main classes of directories and search engines, it's hard to figure out at first which will be most suitable for your purposes. The best thing to do is experiment with a range of them; eventually you'll end up with a selection that works best for you.

Carry Out Basic Searches Using a Search Engine

The simplest search possible is to have a search engine use a one-word search term. This example uses Google, one of the more effective engines currently available.

To try it out, launch your browser and navigate to the Google site, **www.google.com**. The opening screen is very simple, consisting of a box where you type your search term, along with two buttons, one of which is labeled "Google Search."

Click in the text box to place the blinking text cursor there, and type the search term. For an example, I typed **crocodile**, then clicked the Google Search button. In a few seconds the search results were displayed, as shown in Figure 4-1.

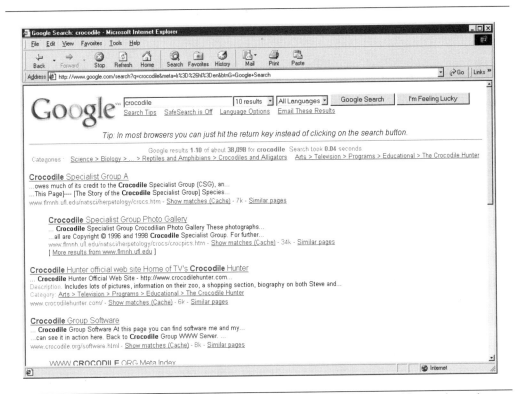

You can use a search engine like Google to search for specific words, such as "crocodile"

Each search engine displays its results in its own way, but most return a list that resembles the Google results pages. (*Return* in this context means "retrieve and display.") The Google results page, for example, returns 10 hits per page, with the best matches listed first and less precise ones bringing up the rear. Each hit includes an underlined text link to the relevant page, and if you click on this link, you will be taken to that page.

Depending on what you've searched for, the engine may return tens, hundreds, or even thousands of hits. Consequently, at the bottom of each results page there will be a link that takes you to the next page.

My crocodile search returned 38,098 results, far too many for easy examination. But that can be narrowed down. Let's say I want to know about a particular type of crocodile, the Nile crocodile. Scroll down to the bottom of the page and you'll see another Google Search button and to its right, a text link that says *Search Within Results?* Click this and a new search page opens, with its own text box and its own Google Search button. I typed **Nile** into the box and when I clicked the button I got 3,519 hits. This is still a lot, but since Google ranks its results according to the best match, the ten hits on the first result page were all highly relevant.

Suppose, however, that you didn't want to go through the stage of searching within results? Well, obviously you wouldn't have to if you'd searched on *Nile crocodile* in the first place.

However, if you type **Nile crocodile** into Google's text box, what you'll get is all the Web pages that contain both the word "Nile" and the word "crocodile" in them. The two words don't have to be together as a phrase; the page could refer to the Nile Hilton Hotel and the availability of crocodile-leather shoes in Cairo, and have nothing to do with Nile crocodiles at all. This, in fact, is how the search in the previous example worked; it was Google's cleverness at ranking that gave us the ten good results on the first page.

So let's try another tack. I typed **"Nile crocodile"** into the text box, *including* the quotation marks as shown. The quotation marks tell Google to search on the words together, not separately. When the results came back, I got 815 hits. This is obviously much more manageable than the 3,519 returned with the previous search.

You can enclose more than two words in quotation marks, of course, and search for "Duesenberg Torpedo Roadster" if you're an antique car buff.

This doesn't mean that it's pointless to search within the results of another search, however. If you're interested in the spice called saffron and use Google to search on **saffron**, you get a lot of references to the English town called Saffron Walden. However, if you search within these results using the search term *spice*, you get a much better set of results.

You could also have used **saffron spice**, without quotation marks, as the initial search term. That would give the same results as the search within a search, but wording the search term that way might not have occurred to you (it didn't to me).

So, to boil down what we've covered so far:

■ You can search on one word alone (*crocodile*).

■ You can search within the results of a search (*Nile* within the *crocodile* results).

■ You can search on a phrase (*"Nile crocodile"*) that is identified as such by being enclosed in quotation marks.

■ You can search on two or more words that must both be contained in the hit page, though the words do not need to be together (*saffron spice*).

These patterns work with Google, but apply to the other search engines too. With some engines you can specify that you're searching on a phrase so that you don't need to type in the quotation marks. HotBot and FastSearch both have this phrase option.

TIP   *When you're learning to use a search engine, be sure to look for a link to its instruction page. This page will give you exact information not only about advanced searches, but also about details such as how the engine deals with capitalization and phrases. The link to the Google instruction page, for example, is on the Google opening page and is labeled "About Google."*

4

Carry Out Basic Searches Using a Directory

Among the best known and most widely used of the directory-type search sites is Yahoo! (**www.yahoo.com**), whose home page is shown in Figure 4-2.

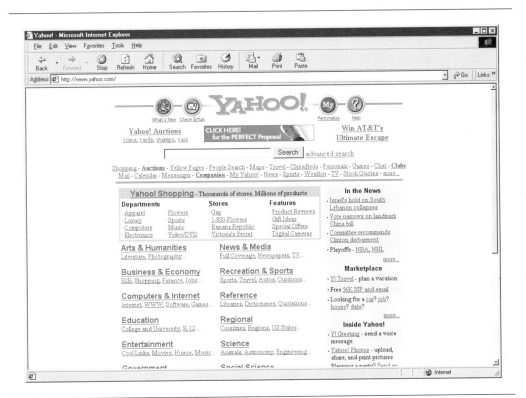

FIGURE 4-2   Yahoo! provides a very capable directory search tool

As you can see from the figure, Yahoo! presents more than a dozen top-level categories for you to start with. One of these broad divisions likely contains a subcategory that contains the information you need, so you can just keep "drilling down" through the subcategories until you find the one that looks most likely. At that point you use Yahoo!'s search engine to let you specify a search term or phrase, and then you let Yahoo! go looking.

For example, suppose you want information about particular types of diets. This seems like a candidate for the Health category, so click the Health link. This opens a page with a lot of subcategories, among them one called Weight Issues. This looks likely, so click on Weight Issues to open the page for that subcategory. On that page are links to further subcategories, among them nutrition, obesity, and weight loss. This looks even likelier, so this Weight Issues page is a good place to use the Yahoo! search engine.

At the top of the page are a text box and a Search button, and next to these are two option buttons. One is labeled all of Yahoo!, and the other Just This Category. Select Just This Category, type **diet** into the text box, and click the Search button. You get a page listing category matches and site matches, with links to each of them, as in Figure 4-3. What has happened is that the Yahoo! search engine has searched through the Weight Issues category *and* all its subcategories, and returned the results for your inspection.

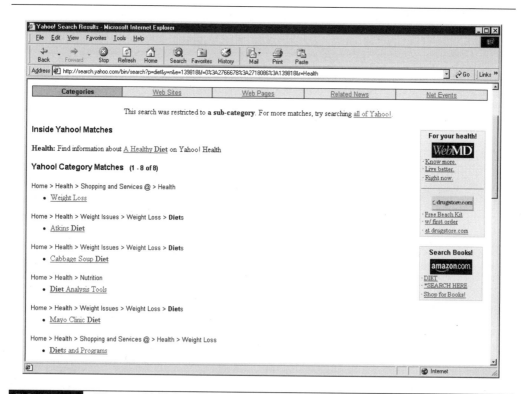

FIGURE 4-3 You can "drill down" through Yahoo!'s categories to narrow your search

If you had selected the option all of Yahoo!, of course, the search would have looked through every category that Yahoo! has to offer. So, if your searches in subcategories aren't getting results, you can instead try searching all Yahoo!. The hits you get may give you a better idea as to what category or categories you should really be searching in. Alternatively, you can take the shotgun approach and use Yahoo! just as a search engine, entering your search term(s) on the home page and not bothering with the categories at all.

These basic search techniques will take you a long way, and in fact may be all you'll need most of the time. However, search engines also provide more advanced tools that may help you get even better results.

> **TIP**
> *There are directories of search engines themselves. An example is at **http://websearch.about.com/internet/websearch/** where the menu has a link to an A-Z listing of search engines.*

Advanced Searches

To explore advanced searches, we'll look at the AltaVista search engine. Navigate to **www.altavista.com** and when the page opens, click the Advanced Search tab. This opens the Advanced Search page, as shown in Figure 4-4. On this page you can use the text boxes to specify the sort order of the results, the language in which the information is written, and the date range that must contain the information.

You will also see a box labeled Boolean Query, and though it's just a text box, this is the most important and powerful of AltaVista's advanced search options. Moreover, while search engines vary somewhat in their other options, they can *all* do Boolean queries. Consequently, once you know how these queries work, you can use them with any search engine (though some may use slightly different wordings for their queries).

> **NOTE**
> *In case you're wondering why it's called a Boolean query, it's named after George Boole, the mathematician who developed this specialized logic.*

Boolean queries are not difficult; they're just a method of restricting your search to get the results you want. You type the query into a text box, like the one on the AltaVista page, and click the Search button. The queries work by using the words AND, OR, AND NOT, and NEAR, as follows (they must be typed in capitals so the search engine will recognize them as Boolean terms):

- To find documents containing all the specified words, use AND, for example: Beethoven AND symphony. This finds documents that have the words "Beethoven" and "symphony" in them, though not necessarily in that order or next to each other.

- To find documents containing at least one of the specified words, use OR, for example: Beethoven OR symphony. This finds documents that have either "Beethoven" in them, or "symphony" in them. It will also find documents that have both words in them.

■ To exclude words, use AND NOT, for example: Beethoven AND NOT symphony. This will find all documents with "Beethoven" in them but will reject any that contain "symphony"—useful if you had already found all the symphony pages you needed.

■ To find documents containing the words near each other (within ten words in AltaVista), use NEAR, for example: Beethoven NEAR symphony.

That's how Boolean searches work. With these as a basis, plus the other tools provided by the various search sites, you can do very precise and fruitful searches. Incidentally, the AND option is understood if you use two or more search terms, so you usually don't need to type the AND. That is, typing **Nile crocodile leather** into the search box is the same as typing **Nile AND crocodile AND leather**.

TIP

Some of the search sites also have popularity engines, which supplement your search with a list of the most visited sites that are related to that search. Lycos is an example; its results page leads off with a list of such sites. These can save you a lot of time.

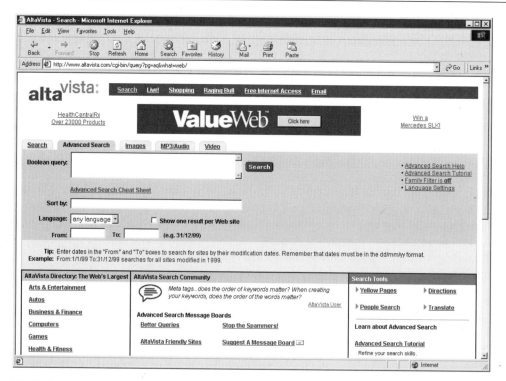

FIGURE 4-4   The AltaVista advanced search tools provide more elaborate search specifications

Use Metasearches

A *metasearch* is a search of the results of other searches. What this means in practice is that a metasearch engine goes to several regular search engines at once, runs your search on all of them, and then compiles the results from all the other engines into some organized arrangement. Metasearch engines often also do some filtering of the accumulated results, so potentially useful hits may be discarded before they reach you. However, they can be a good place to start, since their results should help you identify which of the regular search engines gave the best answers.

There are not as many metasearch engines as there are search engines. The one we'll take as an example is MetaCrawler. Navigate to **www.metacrawler.com** and you'll see a page that looks much like an everyday directory-oriented search site. However, when you click the Customize tab, you get another page that shows you which search engines are being consulted by MetaCrawler for you (see Figure 4-5).

4

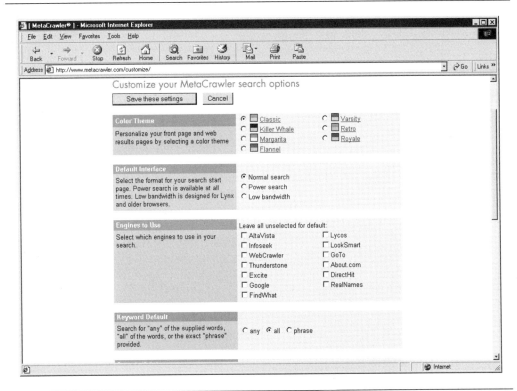

FIGURE 4-5   MetaCrawler is an example of a metasearch engine, which consults multiple ordinary search engines for you

You can specify which engines to use in your metasearch by following the instructions in the Engines to Use section. For my example, I left all the engines selected, returned to the MetaCrawler home page, and searched on **Nile crocodile** again. I marked the third option button under the text box to specify that the two words were to be treated as a phrase, and when the results came in I used the View By Relevance line (immediately above the first result) to sort them by source, that is, according to the search engine that found them. Figure 4-6 shows a part of what I got. Note that the Source Index line gives you a summary of how successful the regular search engines were at finding the phrase.

Some other metasearch engines you might want to investigate are Dogpile (yes, that's its name) and Mamma ("the mother of all search engines").

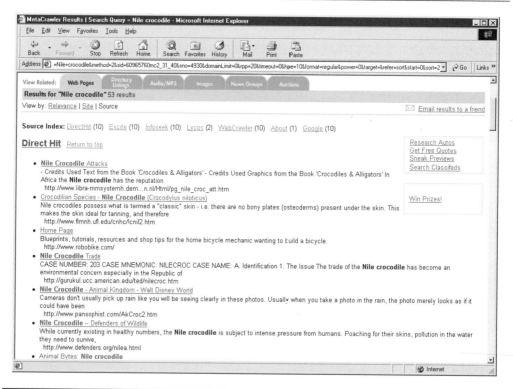

FIGURE 4-6   A metasearch engine returns results from several search engines, as listed in the Source Index line

Use Expert Sites

An *expert site* is a specialized form of metasearch engine. These sites are characterized by an ability to do what are called natural-language searches; in other words, you can type **How do I make butter** into the text box and the engine will understand what you want.

The best known of the expert sites is probably Ask Jeeves. Navigate to **www.askjeeves.com** and you'll go directly to the search page. It has two boxes, a small upper one and a large lower one. The lower one shows questions most recently asked on various subjects, if you're interested. The upper box is the one you use; type your query into it and click the red Ask button. In a few seconds a results page appears, giving links to sites with the answers you need. Figure 4-7 shows the results page for the query **How do I make butter?**

Natural-language queries are easy and give useful results, but if you're doing exhaustive research you should supplement expert sites with the regular search engines.

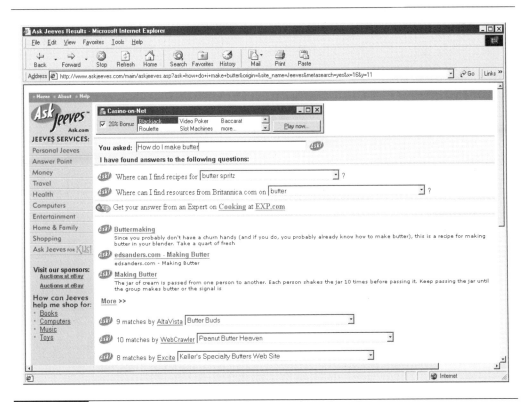

FIGURE 4-7   Ask Jeeves is an example of an expert search engine

Use IE and Navigator Searches

Both IE and Navigator provide search facilities built right into the browser. These facilities allow you to search by using several search engines in turn, but they aren't metasearch engines because they don't compile the results into one list. However, they're useful because they put the major search engines in one place for you.

To use IE search, click the Search button on the toolbar. This opens a simple search window at the left of the browser display. You can, of course, use it as is, but to find out what it's really up to, click the Customize button.

As in the following illustration, you'll see that IE is using several search engines, and you can check them on or off as you wish; they are consulted in the order appearing in the box to the left of the list. The results of your search show up in the Search window.

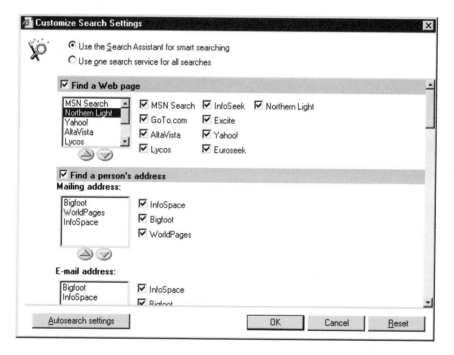

Note that you get separate lists of results from each search engine; the results aren't cumulated into one list. The first engine, for example, is MSN search, and you click the next>> and <<previous links below its results list to move back and forth in the list.

TIP

At default, only the links to the relevant Web pages appear in the list of hits in the Search window. To make summaries appear as well, select the Show Result Summaries check box just above the hit list.

To get the results from the next selected search engine—GoTo, in IE 5's default list—you click the button labeled Next, which you'll find up on the Search window toolbar. (Don't confuse this with the next>> link down at the bottom of the results; it's an easy assumption to make, but they don't do the same things.) The new engine runs the search and as before, its results appear in the Search window.

In Navigator, you click the Search button on the toolbar. This opens the Net Search page, as in Figure 4-8.

At the left of the search box is a list of search engines. To select one, click on it. Then type your search term(s) into the text box and click Search. The results appear in a page produced by the selected search engine. To search the same term(s) in another engine, click the Back button, select a new engine, and click the Search button again.

4

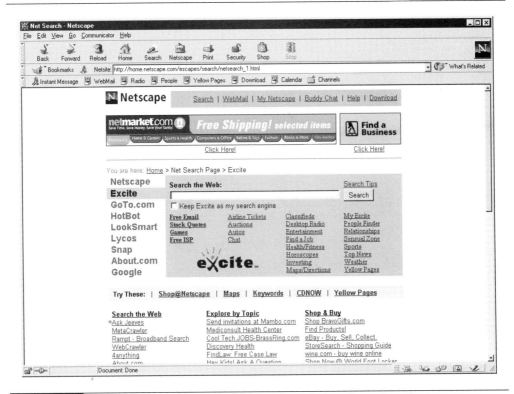

FIGURE 4-8   Netscape's Net Search page gives you a choice of search engines

If you want one of the engines to be the default engine so you don't have to choose it every time you go to the Netscape search page, first select the desired engine. Then select the check box labeled Keep [*search engine name*] As My Search Engine.

Use Specialized Directories

The Internet provides not only the general-purpose search and directory services described so far in this chapter, but also specialized ones. These range from **www.123world.com** (oriented to business travel) to **www.zinezone.com** (oriented to music and entertainment). You can find a good directory of these specialized sites in Yahoo! by starting on Yahoo!'s home page and drilling down from Computers and Internet, to Internet, to Word Wide Web, to Searching the Web, to Web Directories.

Two commonly used types of specialized directories are those that help you locate people or businesses. Both IE and Navigator provide people finders and business finders, but there are also Web sites dedicated to these purposes. One is WorldPages, whose main search page appears in Figure 4-9.

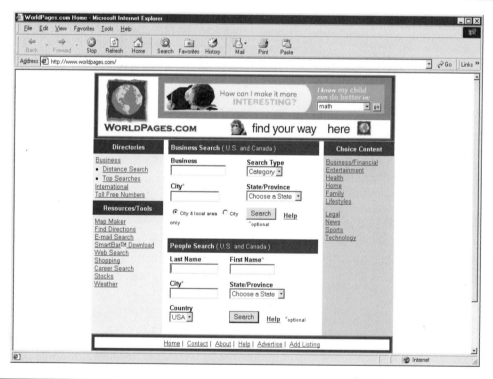

FIGURE 4-9 WorldPages specializes in finding people and businesses

A form of directory (sort of) that is unique to the Web is the *Web ring*. This is a collection of sites that provide similar resources or information. What makes it a ring is that the member Web sites are all linked to each other, and you can link to any of them from any member site. This form of directory is not yet all that common on the Web, however.

Here you can type in various bits of information, click the Search button, and the software will try to find the person. If it succeeds, it will display a small map with a red star marking the person's street address. A further menu above the map lets you get the e-mail address, and also allows you to generate a map of how to get there from another address, complete with driving instructions. Finally, you can do a distance search to look for businesses within a specified distance of the target address.

If you don't find your person or business with the first search service you use, try another one. Depending on their information sources, they don't all give the same results. Yahoo! has a service like WorldPages (click the People Search link on the Yahoo! home page), including the mapping and direction tools, though it seems aimed more at residential addresses than at businesses. Another is Anywho, which resembles WorldPages. A really massive resource is Telephone Directories on the Web, which is a comprehensive index of online phone books.

For Canadian addresses, both residential and business, Canada411 is a good search tool, though it does not include the mapping abilities.

Use Reference Resources

You will also find on the Web a very rich assortment of reference sites and tools. There are libraries, newspaper collections, encyclopedias, dictionaries, and thesauri, to name just a few. In the following sections we'll examine some of them.

Library and News Portals

A lot of these Web sites are in fact specialized directory sites, which serve as portals to a large collection of resources. An example is Reference Desk, at **www.refdesk.com**. You can see the home page of this library portal in Figure 4-10.

From the Reference Resources section of this page you can link to an extraordinary number of sites that probably hold just about anything you're likely to look for.

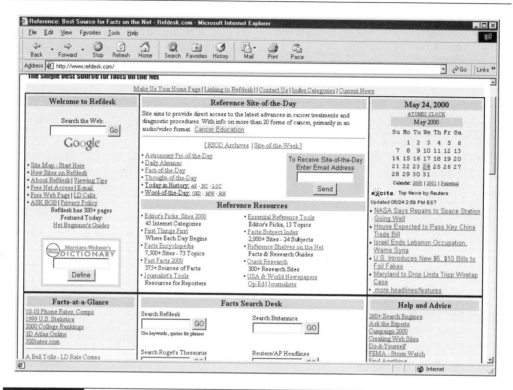

FIGURE 4-10   Reference Desk is a sample of a library portal site

News portals are a second kind of reference site. At News Resource at **www.newo.com**, you'll find links to traditional newspapers, radio and TV news services, and online news, all organized by geographical area and searchable by location and keyword. Figure 4-11 shows part of the page that opens from the Asia/Oceania link.

Encyclopedias

Probably the best known encyclopedia in the English-speaking world is the Encyclopedia Britannica, and its full text is available on the Web, believe it or not. (*Ripley's Believe It or Not* is also on the Web, at **www.ripleys.com**. I couldn't resist mentioning that.)

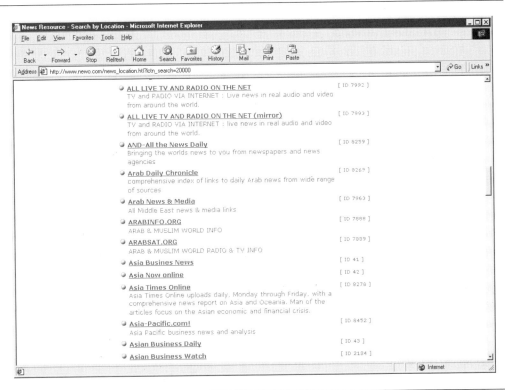

FIGURE 4-11   Another kind of reference site is the news portal, like News Resource

When you open the Britannica page at **www.britannica.com**, you can either select subjects from the menu bar or click the Advanced Search tab and search on the full text of the encyclopedia, complete with images. The home page also provides links to news and other topics of current interest.

Another online encyclopedia is Microsoft's Encarta Online. Like the Britannica, it not only has categories within which you can search, but also a search engine for the encyclopedia itself. It is not as comprehensive as the Britannica (what is?) but it is certainly a useful online reference.

A third online encyclopedia is the Concise Columbia Encyclopedia, at **www.encyclopedia.com**. While the entries are brief, as the site's home page itself admits, this is a good place to look for the essentials.

Where to Find It

Web Site	Address	What's There
AltaVista	www.altavista.com	Directory search
Anywho	www.anywho.com	People finder
Ask Jeeves	www.askjeeves.com	Expert search
Canada411	www.canada411.com	People and business finder
Concise Columbia Encyclopedia	www.encyclopedia.com	Encyclopedia
Dogpile	www.dogpile.com	Metasearch engine
Encyclopedia Britannica	www.britannica.com	Encyclopedia (complete)
FastSearch	www.ussc.alltheweb.com	Search engine
Google	www.google.com	Search engine
Mamma	www.mamma.com	Metasearch engine
MetaCrawler	www.metacrawler.com	Metasearch engine
Microsoft Encarta Online	encarta.msn.com	Encyclopedia
News Resource	www.newo.com	News portal
Reference Desk	www.refdesk.com	Reference library portal
Telephone Directories on the Web	www.teldir.com	Index to all phone directories on the Web
WorldPages	www.newo.com	People and business finder
Yahoo!	www.yahoo.com	Directory search

Part II

Keep and Use What You've Found

Chapter 5

Save Text, Images, Web Pages, and Web Sites

How To . . .

- Understand and create folders to store files
- Save whole or partial Web pages with your browser
- Print whole or partial Web pages
- Understand and work with framed pages
- Display what you've saved
- Save Web pages for offline browsing

If you're already familiar with Windows file management, the next two sections may be of minor interest only. However, if you're uncertain about things like files and folders, working through the material here may help you. This is because one key to having a happy relationship with your computer is keeping its content organized. It's very frustrating to save a program or document, from the Internet or anywhere else, and then be unable to figure out where on your computer it ended up.

Understand Files and Folders

One basic thing to remember is that Windows (and Macs) store information in packages called *files*. "File" is a generic term; just about anything stored on a computer is a file of one kind or another. However, even small computers and their users tend to accumulate *very* large numbers of files. If there were no way of organizing these files, finding a particular one would be just about impossible.

This is why we have *folders* (occasionally they're called *directories* but there's no difference). Folders are simply a method of organizing information, no more and no less; just as the folders in an office filing cabinet contain sheets of paper, the folders on your computer contain files. If there's a difference between the office folders and the ones on your computer, it's merely this: the office folders usually just have papers in them, while computer folders frequently contain not only files but other folders. These contained folders are called *subfolders*.

Where do folders come from? Well, some are created automatically when you install Windows or Windows programs. If you're running Windows 95 or later, for example, there's always a folder called My Documents on your C: hard drive (unless somebody deleted it).

Other folders are ones you create yourself, for your own purposes. Except for some rules about composing folder names, there are no particular restrictions on what folders you can or can't create, nor where you're allowed to put them. You pretty much have free run of your computer's hard drive. But you do need to exert some effort towards keeping things organized, which means putting your own folders in places where you can find them later.

A complete examination of file management is way beyond the scope of this chapter, so for more advanced topics you should consult your Windows documentation. To get us started however, we'll take a fast look at how you create a folder in Windows.

Create Folders

As emphasized earlier, you're going to need folders in which to store the information you collect from the Internet. But where should you put these folders?

Well, a simple and reasonable thing to do is create them as subfolders within the My Documents folder. That way you'll be certain to know where they are. Here's how you do it:

5

1. Choose Start | Programs | Windows Explorer. (Millennium users: choose Start | Programs | Accessories | Windows Explorer.) This opens Windows Explorer, the file manager.

2. In the left pane of the display, look for the My Documents folder under the C: drive. If it isn't visible, click the plus sign (+) next to the C: drive to display the drive's contents.

3. Still in the left pane of the display, click once on the My Documents icon to select it. Then, from the Windows Explorer menu bar, choose File | New | Folder.

4. In the right pane of the display, a new folder appears with the name New Folder selected. Since that's not a very informative name, type one that reflects the intended content of the folder, and then press ENTER (or click anywhere outside the folder's name box). If you make a mistake and need to rename the folder again, right-click on it and choose Rename from the pop-up menu, then retype the name.

NOTE   *Here is one basic thing you need to know about folders and subfolders: When you select a folder in the left pane of Windows Explorer, any folders you then create will be subfolders of that selected folder.*

Now you have a known location in which to save the desired information. If you need to delete a folder, all you have to do is click on it to select it, then press the DELETE key. The folder and its contents (and *all* its subfolders and *their* contents, by the way) will be sent to the Recycle Bin.

Use Your Browser to Save Information

There are a couple of basic ways to preserve information you've found on the Internet. The first is to save it as a file. The second is to turn it into hard copy, that is print it out. The next few sections will show you how to do both.

You may not be aware of this, but copyright law applies to documents, software, and images on the Internet, just as it does to books, magazines, commercially available software, and the other traditional forms of publication. Saving such information for private purposes won't get you into trouble, but using it for public or commercial purposes might involve you in a lawsuit. It would be very ill advised, for example, to create a public Web site and festoon it with images of Disney characters.

Save a Whole Web Page

IE and Navigator have slightly different options for saving entire Web pages. But before you save the page, be sure that it has loaded completely. If it has, IE will display the word "Done" in the status bar at the bottom of the browser display. Navigator will display the words "Document Done" in its status bar.

TIP *If the status bar isn't visible in IE, choose View | Status Bar to turn it on. In Navigator the status bar is always visible.*

Save a Whole Web Page with IE

Begin by launching your browser and navigating to the page you want to save. Then, if you're using IE, choose File | Save As. The Save Web Page dialog opens, as shown in the next illustration.

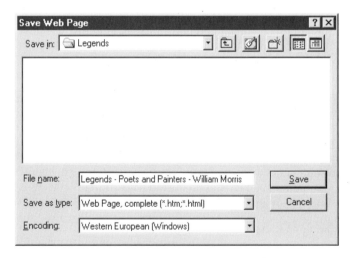

Now look at the text box labeled Save In. This must display the name of the folder in which you want to save the page, or you'll end up storing the page in the wrong place. So, if the desired folder isn't visible there, click the arrow button at the right end of the box to open the dialog's miniature file manager, and navigate to the appropriate folder. In the example just illustrated, the folder is named Legends, and is a subfolder of the My Documents folder.

Next, look at the File Name text box. It displays the name originally assigned to the page. If you want to change this name, type the new one into the box.

Now you have to decide the form in which you want to save the page. To see what options are available, click the arrow button at the right end of the box labeled Save As Type. This gives you four possibilities:

- ■ **Web Page, Complete:** This saves all the files required to display the page fully, including any frames. It also saves the graphics and images visible on the page, although if the page links to such items, instead of displaying them directly, it does not save the linked items.

- ■ **Web Archive:** This creates a single file of all the information needed to display the Web page completely. In essence, it's a snapshot of the page. This is useful for e-mailing as an attachment, which you'll learn about in the chapters on e-mail. Note that the option appears only if Outlook Express 5 or later is installed on the machine.

- ■ **Web Page, HTML Only:** This saves only the text information of the page, along with a few other types of Web page elements like horizontal lines and text color, but discards graphics.

- ■ **Text Only:** This saves just the Web page's text information, as an ordinary text file. No Web page elements at all are saved, and no graphics.

For quick saves when you don't need graphics, choose either the Web Page HTML or the Text Only option. If you need the graphics, then either Web Page Complete or Web Archive (if available) is what you want. Select the desired option and click the Save button. Now the page is safely inside the desired folder.

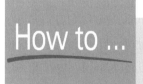

How to ... Create a Folder on the Fly

If you want to save a page but don't have a folder for it yet, you can create one on the fly from the Save Web Page dialog. Somewhat to the right of the Save In text box, there is a folder icon with a star on it. Click this icon to create a new folder that you can name as desired.

Note that this new folder will be a subfolder of whatever folder appears in the Save In text box. If you want it to be a subfolder of a different folder, first navigate to the desired one by opening the dialog's miniature file manager (click the down arrow button at the right end of the Save In text box). Then create the new subfolder.

Save a Whole Web Page with Navigator

To do this, navigate to the desired Web page and choose File | Save As. This opens the Save As dialog, which works the same as the corresponding one in IE. However, Navigator has fewer options in its Save As Type list. You can save the page as HTML Files, which is the same as IE's Web Page HTML Only option. Or you can save it as Plain Text, which is the same as IE's Text Only option. There is no way to save the page's graphics from this dialog.

Save Part of a Web Page

Again, the two browsers have slightly different ways of handling this task. There are two basic situations: first, when you save a selected part of a page and second, when you save a page that appears within a frame of the main page.

Save Part of a Page in IE

If you want to save a selection of a Web page's text in IE, you need to turn it into a file first, and then save it. To do this, you can use any word processor or a text editor such as Windows Notepad. For the following example we'll assume you're going to use a word processor, and that you've already navigated to the desired Web page. Do this:

1. In the Web page, drag the mouse pointer across the desired text to select it, just as you'd do with your word processor. Choose Edit | Copy. This will copy the desired test to the Window's Clipboard.

NOTE *If the desired text selection runs off the screen, the dragging technique may be difficult. Instead, select the first few characters of the desired selection. Then use the scroll bar (not the PAGE DOWN or cursor keys) to scroll down to the end of the desired text. Hold down the SHIFT key, place the mouse pointer at the end of the desired text, and click once. This will select all the required text. With the text selected, choose Edit | Copy to copy it to the Windows Clipboard.*

2. Launch your word processor and open or create the word processor document where you want to store the text.

3. Place the insertion point where you want the text to begin. From the word processor's menu bar, choose Edit | Paste to insert the text.

That's all there is to it. If you've used a word processor at all, you'll recognize this as a very common copy-paste operation.

Saving an image from a page is somewhat simpler, because the image doesn't need to be turned into a file since it already is one. Right-click on the image to open the pop-up menu. From this menu, choose Save Picture As to open the Save Picture dialog (see next illustration).

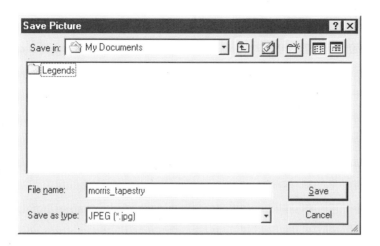

You use this dialog just as you used IE's Save Web Page dialog, except that you have only two options in the Save As Type box: JPEG and Bitmap. Unless you have reason to do otherwise, leave the selection at its default of JPEG. Click the Save button to save the image to the folder specified in the Save In text box.

Did you know?

Mac users are pretty much unconcerned with file types, but in Windows they are important. File types, also called *file formats,* tell the computer how it should display or process the file. There are many, many different file types, but on the Internet the following are most common: HTML (Web pages), JPEG or GIF (images), EXE (programs), TXT (plain text), PDF (portable document files), and ZIP (compressed files). For those readers who like knowing filename extensions, use these respectively: .HTM, .JPG, .GIF, .EXE, .TXT, .PDF, and .ZIP. Also common are video file types, notably MPEG (.MPG), AVI (.AVI), and RealMedia (.RM). Widespread sound file types are MP3 (.MP3), RealAudio (.RA), MIDI (.MID), and WAV (.WAV).

Save Part of a Page in Navigator

Not much is different here. To save text selections in Navigator, you use exactly the same copy-and-paste method as you do in IE. Saving an image is similar, too; right-click on the image and from the pop-up menu choose Save Image As. The Save As dialog opens and you proceed as with any save.

Save a Framed Page in IE

As you may recollect from Chapter 2, some Web sites use frames. These consist of a main page, plus at least one other page that appears in a kind of window (the frame) within the main page. This subsidiary page within the main page, as you may also remember, is called a *framed page*.

Framed pages can be tricky to save; if you're not careful you'll get either just the main page or the entire collection. There are a couple of techniques you can use.

First, see if the framed page you want has a link to it. You often will find such a link in a navigation or menu bar of the main page. If you do, right-click on the link to open the pop-up menu. Choose Save Target As, and the regular Windows Save As dialog will open. Navigate to the folder in which you want to save the page, rename the page if necessary using the File Name box, and click Save. Then the target of the link, that is, the framed page you want, gets saved in the desired folder. This, however, does not save any of the page's graphics. These will be represented by placeholders when the page is redisplayed later from the saved file.

TIP   *You can also use the Save Target As technique for pages that are not frames. The technique works with any link at all, including links to images.*

Second, you can right-click on the link and choose Open in New Window. This launches a new copy of IE (the first one remains open, too) and the framed page appears in the new browser window. The advantage of doing this is that you can save the page using the Web Page Complete option, so that any images on the page are saved as well.

If there's no detectable link for you to use, right-click on the desired framed page. From the pop-up menu, choose Add to Favorites. You can then use this Favorite to open the framed page in its own separate copy of IE, and proceed from there to save it as needed. Delete the Favorite afterward if desired.

Save a Framed Page in Navigator

Navigator is much friendlier than IE in this regard. Simply click in the frame you want, and then choose File | Save Frame As. This opens the Save As dialog, where you can proceed as you did for saving a whole page in Navigator. Again, however, you don't have the option of saving the images along with the page.

Get at What You've Saved

Now that you've saved the information in neatly organized folders, what's the best way to retrieve it?

One case is simple. If you saved selections of Web page text into a word processor document, you just launch the word processor and open the document.

However, what you'll mostly save is Web pages. Later versions of Microsoft Word (Word 97, Word 2000) will display Web page files, but Web pages are really designed to be seen in a browser, and of course not everybody has Word.

So the best viewing tools are IE and Navigator. One of these two will be your default browser, something you learned about in Chapter 2. This makes our first viewing technique quite straightforward. Do this:

1. Open Windows Explorer and navigate to the folder where the desired Web pages are stored.

2. Select and open this folder so you can see the names of the pages.

3. Now you can open them in the default browser simply by double-clicking on them. The same goes for any images you've saved; double-click on their names and they'll open.

NOTE   *If you've installed a graphics viewer like Windows Imaging, or a graphics program such as PaintShop Pro, the images may open in that program instead of in the browser.*

The other method is to open the page or image through the browser itself. In Navigator, choose File | Open Page and the Open Page dialog appears (see next illustration). Then follow the following procedure.

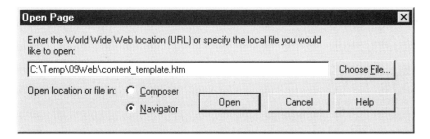

1. Make sure the option button labeled Navigator is selected (selecting Composer opens the file for editing, quite a different task).

2. Click the Choose File button and the Open dialog appears.

3. Use the Open dialog to navigate to the Web page file or image file you want. Select it and choose Open. The dialog vanishes.

4. Choose Open again, in Navigator's Open Page dialog, and the page appears in the browser window.

In IE the technique is similar. Choose File | Open and IE's Open dialog appears, as in the following illustration.

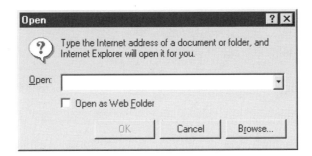

Leave the Open As Web Folder check box blank. Click the Browse button and a file manager dialog opens. Navigate to the desired Web page file and click OK. The page opens in the browser window.

Print Web Pages

There are hundreds of kinds of printers in use these days, and they vary enormously in capabilities. However, with most of them you should be able to carry out the tasks described in the next sections. Just as with saving pages, there are two major options: printing the whole page, or part of it.

Print the Whole Page

Web pages tend to have a lot of color on them these days. However, if you have an old dot-matrix printer, a black-only inkjet printer, or a monochrome laser printer, you will, of course, be printing in black, white, and gray.

With IE, once the page is fully loaded, choose File | Print to make the Print dialog for your printer appear. The illustration shows the dialog for a LaserJet Series II.

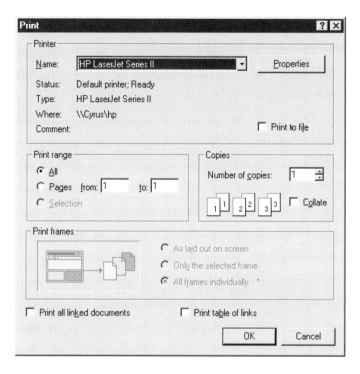

If you click the Print icon on the IE toolbar, the page will be sent directly to the printer and you won't see this print dialog at all.

CAUTION

Some of your choices in the Print dialog will depend on the printer you have. However, the Print Range will always run from 1 to 1. This is because you are only dealing with a single Web page, even though it may eventually print out on several sheets of paper. If you use IE, there are also check boxes for printing all documents linked to the current document, and/or a table of links. Be wary of selecting the former unless you know what you're asking for; a lot of links to long pages will mean a lot of printing. The table of links might be handy, however. When you're satisfied, click OK and the page will print.

Now we come to color printing. With inkjets, color printing is much more expensive than black and white printing, and it is also a lot slower. To help you out on this, IE ignores any background images or background colors when printing. However, anything else that is colored will be printed in color, which is often not necessary.

To get around this, see if you can set your printer so that it always prints in black and white unless you specify otherwise. If you click the Properties button beside the printer's name in the Print dialog, you may be able to set this option from there. Of course, when you do want color, you'll have to change the setting and then remember to change it back to black and white afterward. Other than that, printing with a color printer works the same as printing from a monochrome printer.

In IE, you can determine the page setup by choosing File | Page Setup, and specifying margins, paper size, and whether you want portrait orientation (the page in its usual orientation) or landscape orientation (the page turned on its side).

NOTE   *If you are running Windows Millennium, you have the latest update of IE 5 (IE 5.5, to be precise), which gives you a Print Preview choice on the File menu. By the time you read this, the finished IE 5.5 version may also be available for download from the Microsoft update site, so that users of older Windows versions can also obtain it.*

In Navigator, you choose File | Print to open the print dialog. This is the same dialog as the one you get with IE, except that you can't print linked documents or a list of links. You also can choose File | Print Preview to see what the printed pages will look like; this also tells you how many pages will be printed. Finally, File | Page Setup presents you with some options for modifying the appearance of the page.

TIP   *The first thing you might do when you want to print a Web page is look for a link that says something like "printer-friendly version." These files are specially set up to print quickly and efficiently.*

Print Part of a Page

Again, the techniques for printing parts of pages differ somewhat between IE and Navigator. The next two sections cover the various methods.

Print Part of a Page in IE

Printing selected text is simple in IE. Navigate to the desired Web page, select the text in the framed page (as described earlier in this chapter) and choose File | Print to open the Print dialog. In the Print Range section, mark the option button labeled Selection and click OK. The printer will print the selected text.

If an image appears on a page and you want to print it, you must first save the image as described earlier, by using the right-click menu and selecting Save Picture. Then display the image in IE with the File | Open command (or in any other suitable program) and print it from there.

However, if you can find a link to the image, you don't need to save it in order to print it. Right-click the link, and from the pop-up menu choose Print Target. The familiar Print dialog appears and allows you to print the image. (Print Target works with any link, incidentally, but you'd best look at what the link points to before using the command.)

Print Part of a Page in Navigator

Oddly, if you select text in Navigator and then choose File | Print, the Selection option in the Print dialog is grayed out, indicating that you can't print selections. To get around this, you'll have to save the text in a word processor or similar program, and print it from there. Perhaps Navigator 6, when it's finished, will remove this annoyance.

As if to make up for this problem, printing an image is easy. Right-click it, then choose View Image from the pop-up menu. This opens the image by itself in a new window. Select File | Print to print it.

Print Framed Pages in IE

In IE, it's actually less difficult to print a framed page than it is to save it. Click on the framed page you want to print, then choose File | Print. The print dialog opens, but this time the Print Frames section is active, as you can see at the bottom of the illustration.

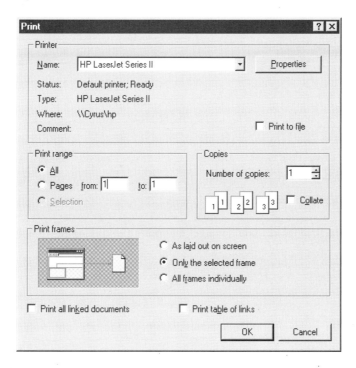

Here you have three option buttons. If you mark the top one, the entire browser display will be printed. If you mark the middle option, only the frame you clicked on will be printed. If you mark the bottom button, all the framed pages will be printed separately. Choose the option you want, then click OK to carry out the printing.

Print Framed Pages in Navigator

This is very straightforward. Click in the desired frame to select it. Then choose File | Print Frame to open the Print dialog and print the selected frame.

Browse Offline

Browsing offline is an IE 5 technique whereby you save several pages from a Web site at once; if it is a reasonably small site, you might even save the whole thing. Once this is done you can browse through it at your leisure, even if you're not connected to the Internet. This is particularly useful with dial-up connections; you can download and save a large number of pages while you're doing something else, then close the connection to save on connect time charges. With high-speed connections that are always on, this isn't a factor, but you may still want to preserve the pages in case the Web site vanishes or the site management changes them.

This kind of offline browsing is only possible with IE 5 and later. IE 4 has offline browsing of cached pages, but this is not as well developed as it is in IE 5. Navigator has offline tools but they are only for e-mail and newsgroup use, not Web page browsing. This may change with the complete version of Navigator 6.

Save Sites or Parts of Sites

The process is somewhat lengthy, so we'll break it into parts. To get started, navigate to the Web page that you want to begin with. Then do this:

1. Choose Favorites | Add To Favorites to open the Add Favorites dialog.

2. Check the Make Available Offline check box, then type an appropriate name into the Name text box.

3. Click OK. The Synchronizing information window appears as the page is downloaded, then vanishes. So does the Add Favorite dialog.

At this point we've merely saved a single page for offline browsing. However, we might want several more pages from that Web site. Here's how to get them:

1. Choose Favorites | Organize Favorites to open the Organize Favorites dialog (see next illustration).

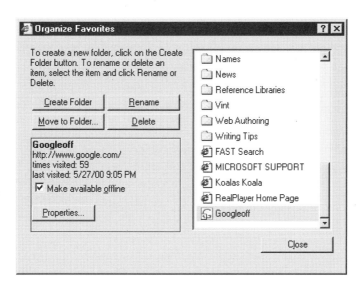

2. In the Favorites list, select the offline Favorite you just created. Click the Properties button to open the Properties dialog for the favorite and then select the Download tab (see next illustration).

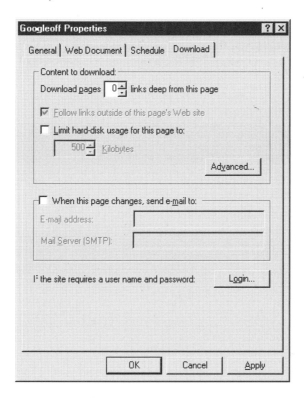

3. The text box labeled Download Pages *x* Links Deep From This Page has 0 as the default. This number specifies how many levels of links (maximum 3) you want to save. One level saves the original page and all the pages it links to. Two levels saves that, plus all the pages to which *those* pages link. Three levels saves all the pages linked to by pages at the previous level. This can amount to a lot of pages, so you should perhaps start with a level of 1 and see how it goes.

4. If the link depth is 1 or greater, the check box labeled Follow Links Outside of This Page's Web Site becomes active and is checked on. If you leave it on, pages from other Web sites that are linked to by the pages in this one are also downloaded. That also could be a lot of pages, so clear the check box.

5. If you want to limit the disk space taken by these offline pages, mark the appropriate check box and type the desired storage allocation in the text box.

6. Click OK, then close the Organize Favorites dialog.

At this point, the additional pages have not yet been downloaded. To do this, your offline pages must be synchronized with the Web site itself. This is described in the next section.

Synchronize Offline Web Pages to a Web Site

Open IE's Tools menu and choose Synchronize. The Items to Synchronize dialog opens, as in the next illustration.

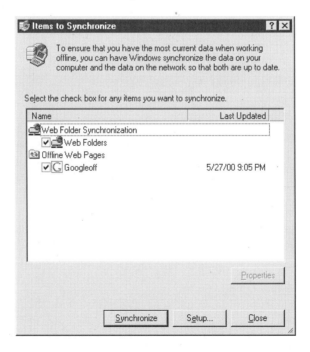

Mark the check box next to the item you want to synchronize (that is, what you want to download, in this context). Then click the Synchronize button. The Synchronizing information box opens and tracks the progress of the synchronization download. When it's done, the box closes.

To test the offline functions, choose File | Work Offline from the IE menu bar. Then open the Favorites menu and choose the offline favorite you created. That page and the pages linked to it at the specified link level will open as if you were online.

With this, we've finished our examination of saving Web pages to the computer. However, you may be wondering about all the other things that people get from the Internet: video files, programs, MP3 music, and so on. We'll deal with obtaining and using these in the next few chapters.

5

Chapter 6

Download Software with Your Browser

How To . . .

- ■ Understand the concept of downloading
- ■ Understand trialware, shareware, freeware, and adware
- ■ Find out where you can locate downloadable software
- ■ Organize your downloads
- ■ Download and install an essential program called WinZip

Not only is there lots of useful information on the Internet, there's also lots of useful computer software. Need a program to print business cards? There's one out there somewhere. Need a program to organize the digital photos you've been taking with your new digital camera? It's out there, too. But not only computer programs are available. The Internet has games, music, video … the list goes on and on. This chapter gives you a start at getting your hands on such useful and entertaining items.

Understand Downloading and Downloadable Software

Downloading is simply the process of copying a file from the remote computer where it is stored, to a folder on your own computer. In other words, you end up with your own copy of the original file. Since a computer program is simply another kind of file, this is an easy way to get your hands on a program. In fact, some companies distribute their software (*computer software* is just another name for *computer program*) only through the Internet, and don't provide physical copies at all.

There are lots of Web sites that make software available for download. However, the software varies in how you can obtain and use it, as discussed in the next sections.

Commercial Software

This is an obvious one. You can often purchase commercial software from the Web site of the company that manufactures it. A typical example would be the PowerQuest Web site, where you can purchase their Partition Magic program by filling out a form and submitting a credit card number. Once the purchase is approved, which takes only a minute or two, you can download the software and use it freely. Often a physical copy of the software that is shipped to you as part of the purchase will supplement the download.

Trialware and Demoware

Trial and demo software (trialware and demoware) is generally commercial software whose use is limited in some fashion. It is intended to be downloaded so that you can use it enough to decide whether you want to purchase the fully functioning version—a "try before you buy" arrangement. Usually it is time-limited and it will stop working after thirty days or so (and if you uninstall and reinstall it, it still won't work). In other cases some part of it will be disabled as well, such as the ability to save any work done with it. Usually, you have to register with the company before you can download the software.

Shareware

Shareware is software that is made available by its developer(s) for free, but if you continue to use it past the end of an evaluation period, you're expected to pay a fee and register your copy. Ordinarily, shareware isn't expensive; prices are usually well under $100, depending on what the software does. Sometimes you have to fill out a registration form before you download, and re-register later on if you decide to keep using the software legitimately. Despite its modest cost, a lot of shareware is very good, and well worth the registration fee. Indeed, some of it is of commercial quality and astonishing at the price.

Most shareware attempts to persuade you to pay for it by presenting you with *nag screens*, messages that pop up when you start the program or during your use of it, reminding you to register. At the time you register and pay the registration fee, which you usually do online by using a credit card, you get a registration key or serial number that stops the nag screens and may unlock some further functions of the program. Alternatively, after you register you may be permitted to download a full-featured version of the program without the nag screens.

While a lot of shareware will continue to work after the evaluation period expires, some is strictly time-limited. Such programs stop functioning entirely as soon as the evaluation period ends.

If you ignore the nag screens and continue using the software after the evaluation period expires, you won't get into legal trouble, or at least it's very, very unlikely. Any trouble is between you and your conscience.

Freeware

This is what it sounds like. You download the software and can use it freely, without ever having to pay for it. There are no evaluation periods and no nag screens. The creator is making it available just because he or she wants to. You may be asked to register before you download, but not always.

You might think that because it's free, freeware isn't likely to be much good. This isn't the case. Some of it may have a few rough edges, like not being particularly user-friendly, but much of it is very effective at doing one or two things well.

Some companies produce two versions of their software, a full-featured one that you can purchase, and another with just the basics. The basic one they make available as freeware, in the hope that you will eventually want to buy the full version.

Adware

This is a new phenomenon. Adware software is software that you use on the Internet, such as an e-mail program or a newsgroup reader. You can use it freely, but while you use it, the program downloads small ads from the supplier's Web site and displays them in a corner of the screen. Sometimes if you register and pay for the program, you get a software key that turns the ads off.

What About Copyright?

As was pointed out in the previous chapter, just about everything that is on the Internet is owned, and therefore copyrighted, by *somebody*. With commercial software, for example, the owner wants to be paid for his product and doesn't want people to make illegitimate copies of it. The same usually goes for adware and shareware, though shareware authors don't usually mind if people copy the unregistered version of the program for friends—the friend might buy it himself, after all.

With freeware, even though there's no charge for the software, the author of the program still owns the rights to it. He or she doesn't care if people copy it for other people, but it's still illegal to charge money for it, or try to pass it off as one's own.

There's generally a legal statement or usage agreement accompanying any software you might download from the Internet. Often this document is on the Web page or in the registration form, and frequently appears during the installation process. It will tell you what you can and can't do with the software after you download it.

Where to Get the Software

As you'll have gathered previously, many software manufacturers and creators of shareware and freeware programs make their programs available through their Web sites. If you're looking for a specific program and you know who makes it, their Web site is the obvious place to go.

However, there are also Web sites that offer large collections of software for download. One of these is the TUCOWS site, which specializes in Internet-related software but also has other stuff like graphics viewers and image processing programs. The collection includes shareware, trialware, freeware, and some adware. Other sites providing software collections are Winfiles, ZDNet, and C|net.

Did you know?

Occasionally, you'll come across something called *beta software* or a *beta version* of a downloadable program. *Betas,* as they're often called, are versions of a program that are still under development. Such programs have bugs in them and may be unstable, meaning that they may freeze when you're using them or exhibit other unpredictable and unwanted behavior. The program developer makes a beta available so that those people who don't mind playing with unfinished software can try the program out, and then let the developer know what doesn't work. It's a common method of real-world software testing. However, if you use a beta, you do so at your own risk. It won't perform as reliably as a completed program.

Organize Your Downloads

In Chapter 5 we discussed folders and files, and where to create them. When you're making a collection of software for yourself, it's obviously important to keep it organized so you'll know where you put things. And if I might offer one piece of advice from hard-earned experience, it's this: store each program you download in its own folder, and don't put other programs into the folder with it. This is because the installation process for some programs generates new files within the folder. So, if you have two such programs in one folder and install both, you'll end up with a hodgepodge of files for both programs and won't be able to tell which is which. As your collection grows, the bit of extra work in creating a unique folder for each program will pay for itself several times over.

6

Download and Install a Program: WinZip

For the rest of this chapter we're going to work through the process of downloading our example program, WinZip, and installing it on the computer. WinZip is a *utility program*, which is a type of program designed to do just a few useful things and do them very well.

But, you may ask, why should I bother learning to download a boring utility program, when I can skip ahead in the book and maybe learn to download the interesting stuff, like games and music?

A good question. There are two answers. First, you *need* WinZip. If you don't get it now, you'll have to get it later, because a whole lot of files and programs on the Internet can only be used after you've installed WinZip on your machine.

Second, WinZip provides a solid, basic example of the download process. Once you've learned how to download it, you're well on your way to knowing how to download anything.

Also, it doesn't take all that much time to install the program once it's been downloaded. Excluding the actual downloading time, you can likely go from not having WinZip to having it in about fifteen minutes. If someone has already installed WinZip on your computer, you might want to go through the process for yourself, anyway. Doing so will also ensure that you have the most up-to-date version of the program.

 Downloading and installing aren't the same thing. Downloading *merely copies the program file from the remote computer to your machine.* Installing *is the process of using the downloaded file to set up the program so that it will run on your computer.*

Understand WinZip

As noted earlier, WinZip is utility software. More specifically, it is a file *compressor* and *decompressor*, also called an *archive program*. Here's why having such a program on your machine is so essential.

Many files on the Internet, both programs and non-programs, are *compressed* files. This means that they have been cleverly shrunk in size so that they can be downloaded more quickly by users, and also so that the remote computer needs to spend less of its valuable time in sending them. Some files, like text files, compress a lot, so that the squashed version is only half the size of the unsquashed version. Program files don't compress so much, but many are sent out in compressed form anyway. Of course, once the user has downloaded the compressed file, he or she needs a way to restore it to its original form—to decompress it, in other words. This is what WinZip is for: It decompresses files (and will compress them, too).

WinZip is one of the most widely used Windows utility programs in existence; accordingly, compressed files are often referred to by the generic name of *ZIP files*. You can tell a file is a ZIP file if you see the .ZIP extension at the end of the file's name; MYFILE.ZIP would be an example of this.

WinZip has other talents as well. It can take a single file and compress it into a smaller ZIP file. Better than that, it can also take several files and store them all within a single compressed file, called an *archive file*. (This is why WinZip is also called an *archive program*.) Conversely, it can take an archive file, decompress it, and restore all the contained files to their original state. Archive files are extremely useful for putting several files into one neat package that can be handled with a minimum of fuss.

Now you can see why WinZip is such a key utility program. Without it, you can't do anything with ZIP or archive files, and there are a lot of both on the Internet.

NOTE *WinZip isn't the only file compressor/decompressor/archive program around. It happens to be the most widely used by consumers since it was designed to work with Windows. Another Windows archiving program is WinRar, but it's in less common use. Unix and Linux users have their own archiving software (tar and gzip), as does the Mac (Stuffit Expander).*

Locate and Download WinZip with IE

You can get WinZip from a lot of places but we'll go to the source at the WinZip Web site (**www.winzip.com**) for it. Navigate to the page and look for a link that takes you to the WinZip download page. At the time of writing, this link was prominent and said Click Here For the New Version - WinZip 8.

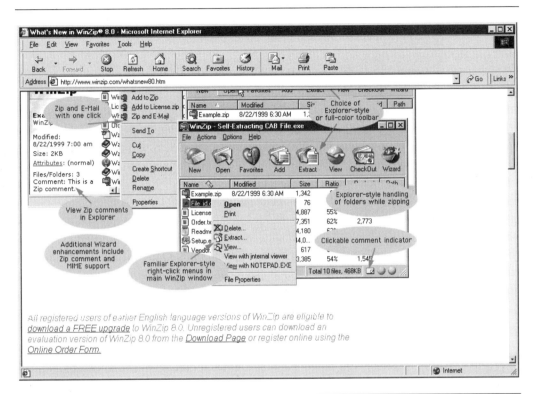

FIGURE 6-1   The WinZip What's New page gives you up-to-date information on the latest version of the software

Clicking this link opens a What's New page. This gives some background on the new and changed features of the current WinZip version (see Figure 6-1). Scrolling down the page reveals a link to the actual download page.

Click the download link to go to the next stage of the process. This page tells you that you can download an evaluation version of the software; to do so, you use the text link that says Download and Run WinZip. Click this link to go to the next stage.

At the time of writing, WinZip didn't ask you to register, as some shareware distribution sites do. So, within a few seconds, the next page opens to start the download and a File Download dialog opens, as in the next illustration. Follow the procedure after to save the file to your machine.

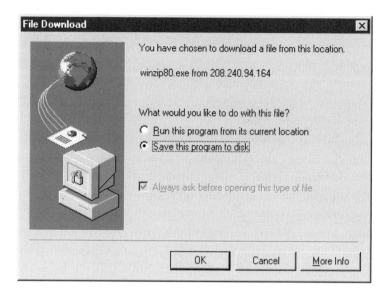

1. In the File Download dialog you have two options: Run This Program From Its Current Location and Save This Program To Disk. Make sure the second option is selected and click OK.

2. The Save As dialog opens. Use the dialog, as you learned in the previous chapter, to navigate to the desired folder and display its name in the Save In box. You can rename the file if you wish in the File Name box, but I myself don't usually bother. Click OK.

3. The download starts, and displays an information window so you can monitor the progress of the download. With a 28.8K dial-up connection, it will take about 15-20 minutes. When the download ends, the information window will either close automatically, or remain open and show a Close button. Click the button if needed, and you're done.

CAUTION   *You've no doubt heard about the dreadful things viruses can do to your computer, and you may have heard that you can get a virus from downloading and running a program. This is true, and you should always keep an anti-virus program operating on your computer. However, programs downloaded from reputable sites like the WinZip site are very unlikely to contain viruses, so if you don't have an anti-virus program at this point, you're in little danger (or at least not from WinZip). Chapter 18 tells you about viruses and how to defend against them.*

Download WinZip with Navigator

As in the preceding procedure, navigate to the WinZip download page and click the download link. In a few seconds you get an Unknown File Type dialog with four buttons:

More Info, Pick App, Save File, and Cancel. Don't be alarmed; this is perfectly normal. Click the Save File button and the Save File dialog appears. Navigate to the desired storage folder and click Save. A Saving Location info box appears to tell you how the download is going. When it's finished, the info box vanishes and your download is complete.

Install WinZip

Once downloaded, WinZip is easy to install. Do this:

1. Open Windows Explorer and navigate to the folder where you stored the downloaded file. You should see the filename there; for WinZip version 8 it's WINZIP80.EXE. This is called an *EXE file*. All files with an .EXE extension are programs. This one isn't the WinZip program itself; it's a program which, when you run it, installs the actual WinZip utility for you.

2. Double-click on the filename. The installation process begins with an introduction screen. In this screen, click Setup.

3. In the next screen you can select the folder into which you want to install WinZip. In Windows, most programs automatically install themselves into subfolders of the C:\PROGRAM FILES folder.

NOTE   *The C:\PROGRAM FILES folder is automatically created when Windows installs, so you don't need to do it. However, since the installation folder for a program usually doesn't exist before the install, you may be asked if you want to create this folder during the install process. Normally this is what you want, so answer yes.*

4. Let's see where WinZip intends to install itself. Look at the Install To box in the WinZip Setup dialog, as shown in the next illustration. Here you can see that the program will be installed to C:\PROGRAM FILES\WINZIP unless you specify differently. There is no good reason to use a different folder, so click OK.

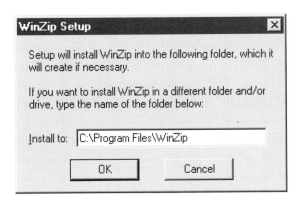

A progress indicator appears as the program installs, then vanishes. Now you get into the setup process, as the following procedure describes.

1. The first screen of the WinZip Setup dialog is just introductory. Click Next.

2. In the next screen you get the legalese governing the use of the program. Read it if you like, then click Yes to indicate that you agree to the terms. (If you click No, the program will not be installed.)

3. The next setup screen allows you to print or view a Quick Start guide. This has a lot of useful information in it, so at least scan it. After doing so, click Next.

4. In the next screen you have two option buttons: to use the WinZip Wizard to work with zipped files, or to use WinZip Classic. The Classic version is powerful and easy to use, so choose the Classic option. Then click Next.

5. In the next screen you can choose between Express and Custom Setup option buttons. Express is fast and effective, so choose it and then click Next.

6. In the next screen you let WinZip determine what kind of archive or compressed files it will work with. This can be customized with the Associations button, but at this point there is no good reason to do so. Leave it alone and click Next.

7. In the final screen, you click the Finish button to end the install procedure. WinZip opens as shown in the next illustration, with the Tip of the Day window open. We'll explore the use of WinZip in the next chapter, so for now close the Tip window and then exit the WinZip program.

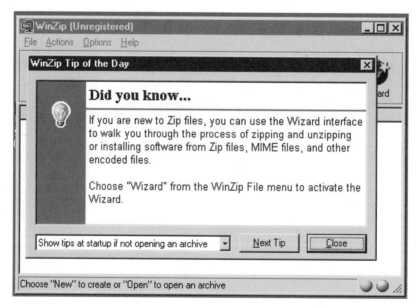

Note that a small window with various WinZip icons will remain visible; you can close this as well. Also, a WinZip icon has been automatically placed on your desktop. You can delete it, if you want to, without affecting the operation of the program.

Congratulations! You've completed a very important and useful task—you've learned how to locate, download, and install a program from the Internet. Of course, while there are general similarities in the installation procedure for all programs, they do differ depending on their complexity and the installation options available. Consequently, you won't see the same installation screens in every case. We'll examine some of the various types of installation in the next chapter.

Where to Find It

6

Web Site	Address	What's There
C|net	www.cnet.com/downloads	Software collection
TUCOWS	www.tucows.com	Huge software collection for Win 95, 98, 2000, NT, Mac, Linux, Unix, BeOS
Winfiles	www.windows95.com	Software collection
WinZip	www.winzip.com	ZIP file utility
ZDNet	www.zdnet.com/downloads	Software collection

Chapter 7

Installing Downloaded Software

How To . . .

- Run an install program from its location on the remote computer
- Install programs from self-extracting files
- Unzip zipped archives
- Install programs from unzipped archives
- Install programs directly from WinZip
- Uninstall unwanted programs
- Understand the threat of program-borne viruses

Installing software, once you've downloaded it, can be a fairly simple process. Much of the trepidation new users feel about this arises because they're unsure of what they're doing, and don't know exactly what will happen if they try. This chapter, I hope, will dispel some of the anxiety.

Save to Disk or Run from Location

Back in Chapter 6 we encountered the IE File Download dialog, as shown in the illustration here. At that time we used the second option to save the program to the hard disk. But what happens if you select the first choice, Run This Program From Its Current Location?

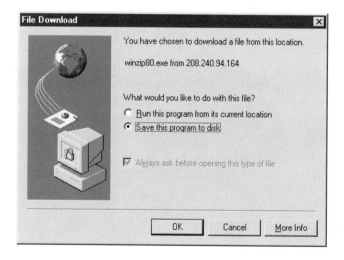

Well, remember that the file you were downloading was actually the installation program for WinZip. Choosing the Run option downloads a temporary copy of the program to your hard disk, and this temporary copy is then used to install WinZip automatically, without your intervention. When the installation is complete, the temporary file is deleted from your hard disk.

This procedure is useful if you're short on disk space to store software, or if you simply can't be bothered saving a permanent copy of the program to a folder. However, if you later need to reinstall the program, you'll have to go through the process again. If you have a high-speed connection this may not be much of an issue to you, but if you're on a slow dial-up connection it's probably better to save the program to a folder so you can use it again as needed.

Install Programs from EXE or Self-Extracting Files

When you installed WinZip as described in Chapter 6, you were actually installing it from an EXE file. Files with an EXE filename extension (the *filename extension* is the three characters after the period) are always program files; the EXE stands for "executable," in case you were wondering. As you discovered in Chapter 6, the simplest way to install any program from its EXE file is to locate that file in Windows Explorer and double-click the filename.

However, not all EXE files install the program directly. Some EXE files are what are called *self-extracting files*, and installing such programs requires an intermediate step. You can't tell by looking at a filename if the file is a self-extractor, but the download page from which you obtain it may tell you. Download pages also often have a link to installation instructions, or have them right on the page, so look for these as well. In Windows, these self-extracting files are usually based on WinZip technology.

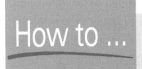 **Display Filename Extensions**

If you can't see the extensions in Windows Explorer (Win 98 or 98SE), open Windows Explorer and choose View | Folder Options. Then click the View tab to display a list of check boxes. Clear the one labeled Hide Extensions for Known File Types. This applies the change to the currently selected folder. If you want the change to apply to all folders, click the Like Current Folder button. Click OK to complete the changes. Millennium users must choose Tools | Folder Options and then click the View tab. Macs don't use extensions, so if you're a Mac person, you can ignore the issue.

Suppose you've downloaded such a file to a folder on your machine. To begin the installation, use Windows Explorer to locate the file, then double-click its name. The self-extracting file immediately displays a WinZip Self-Extractor dialog resembling that in the following illustration.

```
WinZip Self-Extractor [1677_411.EXE]                    [X]

To unzip all files in 1677_411.EXE to the specified          [ Unzip ]
folder press the Unzip button.

Unzip To Folder:                                          [ Run WinZip ]

[C:\WINDOWS\TEMP                              ]
                                                          [ Close ]
[✓] Overwrite Files Without Prompting

                                                          [ About ]

                                                          [ Help ]

            © Nico Mak Computing, Inc.        www.winzip.com
```

As you could easily guess from the dialog title, a self-extractor is actually a form of ZIP file; it's an archive file, in fact, which as you may recollect is a file with a bunch of other compressed files tucked away inside it. All you have to do to turn them into usable files is *extract* them, which means decompress each one and copy it to a folder as a normal file.

Before you do that, though, check the entry in the Unzip To Folder text box. It reads C:\WINDOWS\TEMP, which means that it will place the extracted files in the WINDOWS\TEMP folder on the C: drive. If you want them to go somewhere else, you must type the destination into the text box manually, since there's no file manager facility. But the WINDOWS\TEMP folder isn't all that good a choice, since it tends to get cluttered with temporary files put there by Windows. I generally extract the files to a temporary storage folder that I create and which I know is empty (such as C:\UNZIPS), and then erase them after completing the installation. The original self-extracting file, of course, I keep for later use (extracting the files does not actually remove them from the self-extracting file, it just copies them).

When you've decided where to extract the files, click the Unzip button (*unzip* means extract and/or decompress a file). You see a progress indicator and then an info box that tells you the files have unzipped successfully. Click Close to close the extraction dialog.

Now open Windows Explorer and navigate to the folder where you stored the extracted files. There may be a lot of them, but one of them will be the installation program. It's often called SETUP.EXE, much less often INSTALL.EXE, and sometimes it's just an EXE file with a name resembling that of the actual program. If you can see just one EXE file and can't see a SETUP.EXE or INSTALL.EXE file, then that single EXE file is almost certainly the one you want. Double-click it, or whatever file is applicable, and the installation procedure will begin. As suggested earlier, you can delete the extracted files from the temporary folder after you complete the installation.

> **TIP** *You can also run any program, including setup programs, by choosing Start | Run to open the Run dialog and then clicking the Browse button to navigate to the desired program file.*

Use Zipped Software

ZIP files are a common packaging medium for files and collections of files, of all types—images, text documents, audio, and so on. Program installation software also comes in ordinary ZIP files, as well as in the self-extracting type of ZIP described earlier. These ordinary ZIP files are also archives, and one of the files within the archive will be the installation program.

The next section will show you how to unzip such files manually. The best part is that once you've learned how to unzip a program archive, you've learned how to unzip anything.

How to Unzip

Let's assume that you've downloaded a zipped file to a folder, preferably one created especially for it. Open Windows Explorer and navigate to the folder, where you'll see the downloaded file. It will have a .ZIP extension. If the extension isn't visible you can still identify a ZIP file by its standard icon of a tiny clamp around a file folder.

To begin the extraction, double-click on the filename. The main WinZip window opens (see the next illustration). In this window are the names of all the files in the archive.

Name	Modified	Size	Ratio	Packed	Path
pdspadn.mva	7/3/98 2:54 PM	1,943	10%	1,747	
inst_eng.dll	7/3/98 1:13 PM	17,920	76%	4,236	
inst_fre.dll	7/3/98 1:14 PM	19,968	77%	4,512	
inst_ger.dll	7/3/98 1:15 PM	19,456	77%	4,544	
inst_ita.dll	7/3/98 1:15 PM	19,456	77%	4,510	
inst_spa.dll	7/3/98 1:18 PM	18,944	76%	4,462	
mga.ini	7/2/98 5:50 PM	3,257	69%	1,013	
mgallx64.dll	7/13/98 1:35 PM	170,752	57%	73,525	
mgapdx64.drv	7/13/98 1:36 PM	222,720	63%	82,321	
mgapdx64.inf	7/10/98 3:18 PM	5,063	77%	1,141	
mgapdx64.vxd	7/13/98 1:36 PM	79,118	85%	12,057	
mgaxdd.drv	7/13/98 1:33 PM	36,032	57%	15,502	
mgaxdd.vxd	7/13/98 1:36 PM	15,990	59%	6,531	
mgaxdd32.dll	7/13/98 1:35 PM	345,088	60%	138,193	
pd_color.mva	7/3/98 2:54 PM	68,364	1%	67,907	
pd_color.mvb	7/3/98 2:54 PM	3,201	0%	3,201	
pd_dnav.mva	7/3/98 2:54 PM	38,453	1%	38,214	
pd_eng.mva	7/3/98 2:54 PM	68,143	4%	65,601	
pd_fre.mva	7/3/98 2:54 PM	70,882	4%	68,313	
pd_ger.mva	7/3/98 2:54 PM	73,091	3%	70,565	

Selected 0 files, 0 bytes   Total 50 files, 2,428KB

By the way, you don't have to extract all the files merely because they're there. You can instead use the normal Windows selection methods to select one or a few of the files, and extract only those (see the following How To box for details). For example, with an archive of documents or pictures, you might want only four out of a dozen, so you'd select those four and then extract them.

When installing programs, however, all the files will be needed, so select all of them (a quick method is to choose Actions | Select All). Now choose Actions | Extract or click the Extract button. The Extract dialog opens as shown in the illustration here.

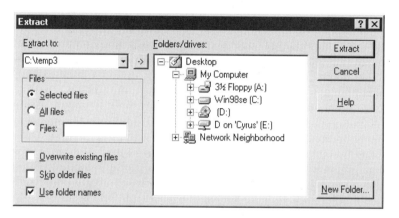

This dialog is pretty well self-explanatory. You can specify the folder where the files will be extracted by using the Folders/Drives list box to navigate to it, and selecting that folder. The name of the folder will then appear in the Extract To text box. Once the folder name is correctly displayed, click Extract, and WinZip will extract and decompress the files to the folder. When the green light appears at the bottom-right corner of the WinZip dialog, the process is complete and you can close WinZip.

Select Files

The methods of selecting files in Windows are these: to select one file, click on it; to select a continuous range of files, click the first one in the range, hold down the SHIFT key, then click the last one in the range; to select scattered files, hold down the CTRL key and click the desired files. Whatever files are highlighted are the selected ones.

What to Do When You've Unzipped

We noted in the section on self-extracting files that the installation program is usually SETUP.EXE, or another EXE file with a name resembling that of the actual program. The same applies to the results of unzipping an archive. Navigate to the folder containing the extracted files and look for the SETUP.EXE or other installation file. Double-click it to start the installation. Once installation is complete you may delete the extracted files. If you need them again you can just re-extract them from their ZIP file.

Install Directly from WinZip

The preceding procedure is the manual method for installing a program from a ZIP file. There is a useful shortcut, however.

Open the ZIP file in WinZip, as described earlier, by double-clicking on it. Then choose Actions | Install or click the Install button. An Install dialog opens, saying that WinZip will extract all files to a temporary folder and then run the setup program. Click OK. The program installs, and the temporary files are automatically deleted.

Note that the Install option appears only if there is a SETUP.EXE or an INSTALL.EXE file in the archive.

Remove Programs You Don't Want

One of the questions beginning users have about downloading and installing software is: What will I do if I install a program and then decide I don't want it? Another such question is: Is the program likely to break my computer if I do install it?

To answer the second one first: No, it's unlikely to mess up your computer, though some programs can change certain settings, such as which is the default program for viewing images. If a program does make such changes, it should reverse them when it's uninstalled. Most do, but a few don't. Generally, however, software from reputable providers like WinZip will not cause you any trouble.

The answer to the first question is that if you don't like the program, you can uninstall it. You uninstall most Windows programs by choosing Start | Settings | Control Panel and double-clicking the Add/Remove Programs icon. This opens a dialog showing the programs installed on your machine. Select the one you want to remove, and click the Add/Remove button.

Sometimes a program supplies its own uninstall program. You'll likely find this by choosing Start | Programs and navigating to the menu entry for that program.

Lastly, a few programs don't need an uninstall program because of the way they're constructed. If you don't see an entry for the program in the Add/Remove Programs dialog, and if you can find no uninstall utility accompanying the program itself, it may be one of these. Navigate to the folder where the program is stored, and delete the folder with its contents. If this seems to cause problems, you can restore it from the Recycle Bin.

7

A Quick Look at Computer Viruses

At this point you may be wondering if it's wise to download programs for another reason: the threat of viruses. This subject is treated at length later in the book, but a brief word about them is appropriate here.

Understand the Virus Peril

The most widely spread and publicized virus problems lately have been from e-mail viruses like Melissa and ILoveYou. However, the older type, the viruses that infect computer programs, are still around and still pose a threat.

But first, a word about the dimensions of the program-virus danger. While the danger is real, it isn't as pervasive as the threat from the e-mail types, and in fact you're unlikely to encounter a program virus if you take reasonable precautions, such as running a virus scanner and not installing software from doubtful sources. Doubtful sources aren't just the Internet, by the way; they include things like floppy disks brought home from school by students in the family, or handed to you by a co-worker because there are some neat games on them. As an Internet example, files made available through newsgroups should be automatically suspect.

All this said, the danger from program-borne viruses is relatively small. With a virus scanner and a few safe-computing precautions, you're reasonably well protected.

About Anti-Virus Software

When you install anti-virus software, you can set it up so that a virus scanner runs in the *background*. This means that the scanner is always operating, but that you can use the computer normally while it's going about its business.

As data flows between your computer and the Internet, the scanner looks for the telltale patterns of virus activity. If it detects any, it immediately isolates the suspect file, sounds an alarm, and displays the name of the file. You can then decide how you want to deal with the problem. For more details, refer to Chapter 18.

Chapter 8

Advanced Software Downloading

How To . . .

- Understand software updating from downloads
- Update Windows and Microsoft Office software from downloads
- Update old versions of programs with new ones
- Understand driver software and update it
- Do online updating of Windows, Office, and Netscape
- Use smart download tools

Back in the pre-Internet days, nobody thought much about updating the software on their computers. You bought your machine with MS-DOS or Windows on it, installed Word or WordPerfect or whatever else you needed, and proceeded to use it. Once in a while an improved version of the software would appear, and you could either buy a copy of it or go on using the old one.

The Internet changed all that. Pretty soon you could download updates for Windows 95 that got rid of some of its bugs and added new features. If you bought a game, the game company's Web site probably had an update (read "bug fix") for it by the time you got home. Soon after Windows 98 came out, the Microsoft Web site sprouted a whole subsite devoted to Windows 98 updates. Today, if you download the Eudora mail program or the RealPlayer media program, there'll likely be updates of each within a month or two.

It's all rather dizzying, and you may feel anxious about keeping up. (If it's any consolation, computer professionals feel the same anxiety, only on a larger scale.) So it's natural to wonder, uneasily, about what may happen to your computer if you don't get the latest Windows 98 or Millennium update.

The honest answer is, probably not much. If your system is working well and you don't feel an overwhelming need for the latest version of every piece of software on your machine, you can upgrade when it's convenient, or even not at all. The only exceptions to this are security fixes to protect your system from evils such as the recent ILoveYou e-mail virus.

That said, let's examine how you might update your machine, when you finally decide you can't avoid it any longer. We're talking here, of course, about updating the software on it, not about updating its hardware. Hardware upgrades are a subject for another whole book, or several.

Understand Updating with Downloads

Essentially, software updates do two main things: They fix bugs in earlier versions of the program, and they add features or improve the operation of features already present. They fall into two broad classes, the first being updates for the computer's operating system, the second being updates for applications.

Did you know?

Computer software falls into two main categories: operating systems and applications. An *operating system* is the complex piece of software that controls the computer's hardware, and therefore is the essential package that makes the computer do things like respond to the keyboard and save files to the hard disk. Windows 98 is an example of an operating system, and so is Mac System 9.

Applications, which most people simply call computer programs, are what you use for work or entertainment. Microsoft Word is an application; so is the game Doom. To put it another way, if you have an operating system but no applications, you can still run your computer, though you can't do much with it. If you have applications but no operating system, on the other hand, your computer is merely an expensive boat anchor.

8

One simple way of updating any software on your machine, either the operating system or an application, is to download a program that will do the job for you. These are sometimes called *patches,* although many companies use the term *update* instead, no doubt because they don't want people to think their software has holes in it (even if it does). Other companies call them *maintenance releases*. Microsoft sometimes uses the term "patches," but for heavy-duty updates prefers *service packs*. But no matter what the name, they all do much the same things, so the rest of this chapter will refer to them as updates.

Use Downloaded Updates

The first issue in updating your software is to find out whether there are, in fact, any updates. This information is usually somewhere on the manufacturer's Web site; look for a link that resembles "technical support," "patches and updates," or even just "downloads." When you arrive at the update page, you may have to look around to see if there is an update for the software in question, especially if the manufacturer produces a lot of different programs. If there appears to be one, read any information about it *carefully*. As well as describing exactly what version of the software the update is for, there may be instructions for using it, and a description of the changes and/or improvements the update makes. You might want to print these out for use when applying the update, and for future reference.

Once you've identified the update file, download it to a folder on your computer. Then follow the update's instructions for applying it. Since an update usually comes in the form of a program, or as a ZIP file containing the program, applying the update is usually just like installing any other piece of software. Use the methods you learned in Chapter 7 to do this.

If the update is an EXE file and not a WinZip file, and if you're using IE, you will see the Run This Program From Its Current Location option when downloading. You learned about this in Chapter 7, and we noted that this option doesn't save a permanent copy of the program to your hard disk. So, if you want to preserve the update file, be sure to use the Save This Program To Disk option.

Use Microsoft Downloads to Update Windows Software

Microsoft issues a lot of updates for the various versions of its Windows operating system and associated programs, as well as for its large collection of applications and games. While you can use the online method to obtain and install updates for Windows itself, as described later in this chapter, many other types of updates can be had as downloads.

To see what's available, navigate to the Windows download site at **www.microsoft.com/downloads**; you then see a search screen similar to the one in Figure 8-1.

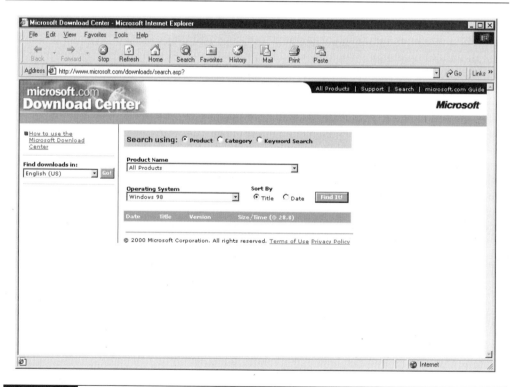

FIGURE 8-1   You use the Microsoft Download Center search tool to look for updates for your software

Here you can search for an update according to product name, product category, or keyword, and according to the operating system you're using. As an example, let's assume that you have the Encarta 98 Encyclopedia installed on a machine that uses the Windows 98 Second Edition operating system. To look for an update, click the arrow button at the end of the upper list box and scroll down the list until you see Encarta Encyclopedia 98. Click this to select it.

Next, use the lower box in the same way to select the operating system your computer uses; there's no separate entry for Windows 98 Second Edition, so choose Windows 98. When both boxes show the appropriate entries, click the Find It button. In a few moments, the results appear (see Figure 8-2).

TIP

If you want to know exactly what version of Windows you have, choose Start | Settings | Control Panel and double-click the System icon to open the System Properties dialog. The General sheet will tell you which version is installed.

There are two updates in the example, beginning with the date each was issued, followed by its name, its version, and how long it will take to download with a 28.8K dial-up connection.

8

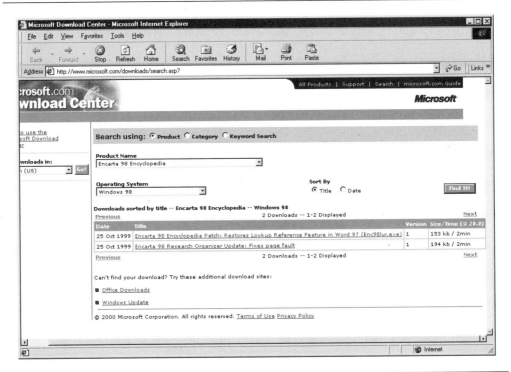

FIGURE 8-2   A search for an Encarta 98 update returns two relevant results

The update name is actually a link. Click it, and you'll be taken to another page where you get a description of the problem the update fixes, how the update fixes it, and a link for downloading the update. Read over the page, download the update (assuming it's what you want), and install it.

NOTE   *The results listed on the Microsoft download site do not always point to software updates. You may find links to technical documents and to workarounds for problems, as well.*

Use Downloads to Update Microsoft Office

The Microsoft Office suite has so many programs in it that there is a whole update site devoted to it alone. If you own one or more of Word, Excel, PowerPoint, Outlook, Access, or FrontPage, there may be updates here you can use.

Begin by navigating to **www.officeupdate.microsoft.com** to open the Office Update page. On the page's left side you'll see a list of the various Office programs. Click one of them and a new page opens, where you can select the version for which you want the updates. In the example in Figure 8-3, I picked first Word and then the Word 97 version by selecting the Word 97 Downloads option button.

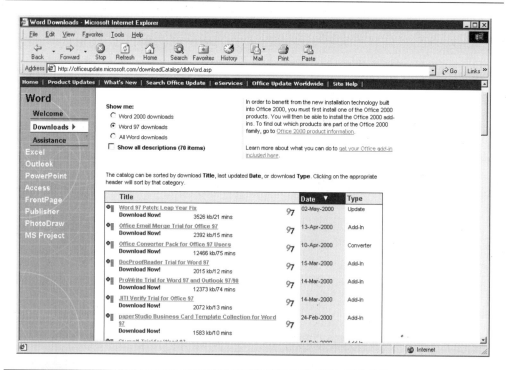

FIGURE 8-3   The Office Update site provides updates for all versions of the Office suite; shown here are updates for Word 97

As you'll see if you follow this example, there are add-ins and converters available for Word 97, as well as updates.

Update with a New Version of a Program

The majority of updates are just fixes and minor enhancements, and not a full copy of the program. In other words, if you don't already have the program installed on your machine, the update won't install it for you. Sometimes, however, the program manufacturer comes out with an upgrade that is so comprehensive that it's a whole new version of the program. This kind of update can be downloaded and installed even if you don't already have the actual software on your computer.

NOTE   *Usually you can't download a new version of a commercial program unless you already own the older version, and can prove ownership by means of a serial number or some other verification method.*

An example of both minor and major updates would be the Eudora Pro e-mail program. Version 3.0 was updated several times, running from 3.01 to 3.05. Each of these updates, when applied, removed bugs and polished some of the features, but you couldn't install the program from them. Then, the company came out with Eudora Pro version 4. This update is actually the full program, which you can download and install even if Eudora isn't already on your machine. And version 4 has now been improved just as version 3 was, the most recent update being 4.3.2. Eudora, by the way, is an example of a product that calls its updates "maintenance releases."

If you already have an older version of a program and you download a new one, you have two choices. First, you can uninstall the old one and then do a fresh install of the new one. Second, you can install the new version "on top of " the old. There's no hard and fast rule as to which you should do; it really depends on the program. Installing on top of the old version usually ensures that any customizations remain in effect, while an uninstall may remove them. The instructions with some programs, on the other hand, recommend that you remove the old version before installing the new one. This is another good reason for reading the manual.

Once you decide how to approach the installation, though, you proceed as for installing any other program. You'll almost certainly be starting from a WinZip or EXE file, just as you learned in Chapter 7.

Update Driver Software

A phrase you may hear if your computer is misbehaving, especially if new hardware has recently been installed in it, is "did you update your drivers?"

You can be forgiven for having no idea of what this means. Here's the explanation.

Your computer contains various bits of hardware. An example is a *video card*, also called a *display adapter*, which is a flat thing about the size of your palm that plugs into a slot inside the computer's case. Your monitor cable in turn is plugged into the video card, and the idea is that the video card sends the pictures to the monitor so you can look at them. But to do this, more than just the hardware is needed; the video card requires a small software program to tell it *how* to send the pictures.

This program is called a *driver*, or in this particular case a *video driver* or *display driver*, since it works with your video card. Driver software, though, is written by programmers, who are human and fallible. Consequently, they don't always foresee all of the situations the driver and card will have to work with. In some of these situations, the driver fails to display the pictures properly. Sometimes the company finds this out for itself, and sometimes it does so by getting a lot of complaints from its customers. In both cases, the company will usually rewrite the driver and make it available as an update.

Since the companies that make the hardware usually also supply the drivers for it, you'll likely find driver updates at the company Web site. Because installing drivers can be an arcane process, there may well be instructions on the page about doing so; be sure to read them.

Drivers often come as ZIP files, and installation directions may be included in a text file within the zipped archive. Read the directions if they're available and follow them carefully. Basically, though, drivers are programs, and since you've already learned how to install software, the process shouldn't give you much trouble.

I wouldn't be too quick to obtain and install a new driver, or any other kind of update for that matter, just as soon as it's available. It's uncommon, but not unheard of, for an update to fix one problem but introduce another (or several). In these cases the update is usually withdrawn or superseded by a later one. Wait a week or two and then, if the driver's still on the Web site, go ahead and use it.

Do Online Updating

Online updating means installing the update while your machine is connected to the supplier's Web site. The simplest method is one you've already been told about, choosing the Run From Location option in IE's Download dialog. However, more sophisticated methods of online updating are now available.

Use Windows Update

Microsoft periodically issues updates and bug fixes for the Windows 98 and the Windows Millennium operating systems, most of which you can obtain via the Internet through the Windows Update site. As this can be a rather intimidating place for novice users, we'll do some exploration in an attempt to demystify it.

To go there, ensure that you're connected to the Internet. Then, assuming you're using Windows 98, Windows 98 Second Edition, or Windows Millennium, choose Start | Windows Update. Eventually the Windows Update Web page appears, as in Figure 8-4.

NOTE   *Poor old Windows 95 doesn't do online updating, so if you need a patch, you'll have to get it manually from the Windows Download site. Also, the Windows Update site only updates the Windows 98/Millennium operating systems, along with their associated programs like IE. It does not update applications such as Microsoft Office, or games.*

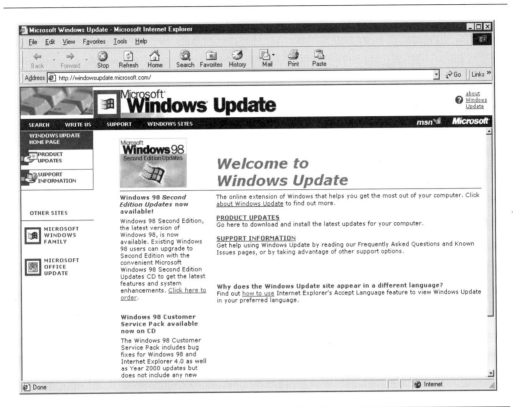

FIGURE 8-4   The Windows Update site provides online updating services for Windows 98, 98SE, and Millennium

The link you want in our context is the one that says Product Updates. Click it, and a Please Wait message appears. As it informs you, the update software is checking your Windows installation to see which updates you don't have. When it has determined this, it presents a list of all the updates available for your Windows version (see Figure 8-5).

It may be a long list, and you do *not* have to take all, or even any, of the updates. The category labeled Critical Updates does bear consideration, though, especially the ones related to security. For the rest, though, you can decide for yourself which ones you need.

When you decide to download an update, click the appropriate check box to select it. After making all your selections, click the large Download button near the top of the page. This takes you to a summary page, where you see all the items to be downloaded, plus the download times for them. If you want, you can also view an instruction page for all the items. Printing the instructions out, as the summary suggests, might be a good idea, but first check how much there is to print—it may be lengthy.

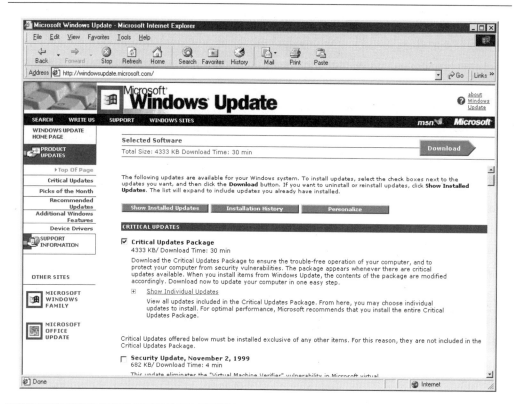

FIGURE 8-5   The Windows Update site provides a list of updates customized for your particular Windows installation

When you're satisfied, click the Start Download button. A screen of legalese appears, asking if you really want to do this. Assuming you still do, click Yes. The download begins, and a progress meter shows each item being downloaded. What's happening now is that the various installation files are being copied to a temporary folder on your machine.

Once all the update software has been copied to your computer, the updates will be installed automatically and the temporary files will be erased. Depending on what you installed, you may be asked to restart the machine. Doing so will complete the installation process.

Use Office 2000 Update

As you learned earlier, the Office Update site offers updates to the various components of Microsoft Office, including Office 2000. However, you can also do online updating of Office 2000, just as you can with Windows 98 and Millennium. One note before we begin:

If you haven't any Office 2000 components installed, there's no point in attempting this, because all you'll get is an error message.

To get started, navigate to **www.officeupdate.microsoft.com** as before, but this time click the Auto Update button. If this is the first time you've used Auto Update, you'll immediately get a security warning, as illustrated here.

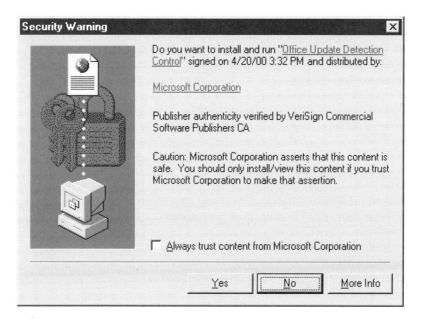

This isn't as alarming as it may appear. The dialog is asking if you want to install and run the Office Update Detection Control, but unfortunately it doesn't tell you why, so I will.

Not many people have all the various Office programs installed on their machine. The Update Detection Control is a small program that is installed on your computer to figure out what bits of Office you do have, and thereby work out which updates the Update Web site should suggest to you. The security warning and certificate are present to assure you that the program is a genuine one from Microsoft and not a host for some appalling virus. You can click the More Info button to find out more.

If you do want to download the updates, you have to install the control; otherwise the whole process stops. Assuming you do, click Yes.

You next see a message saying that the update catalog is being customized. When that's finished, you'll see a list of available items. Check the ones you want, as with the Windows online update site, and click Start Installation. A Confirm Selections window opens, where you can check what you've chosen and view installation instructions.

When you're satisfied that everything's okay, click Install Now. A window of legalese appears; read it if you're so inclined, then click Accept to go ahead with the process. The software is downloaded, installed, and the temporary files erased.

Do Online Updating with Netscape SmartUpdate

Netscape SmartUpdate allows you to update Communicator online, rather as the Microsoft Update site does for Windows. These updates are not only to the components of Communicator itself (Navigator, Messenger, and Composer) but also to the various auxiliary programs Communicator uses. To demonstrate its use, let's assume you're using Communicator 4.72 and you want to update to version 4.73. Here's what you do.

Navigate to **www.home.netscape.com**. Find the Download link near the top of the page, and click it. The Download and Upgrade Page opens; somewhere on it you'll see a link for SmartUpdate. Click that, and you're on the SmartUpdate page, where you use four big green numbered buttons to download and install the updates. Now do this:

1. Click the green #1 button, labeled Click Here to Select Software.

2. A second page opens that tells you what your current version is, and lists the updates available in the Netscape software category (see Figure 8-6). Other kinds of updates are available as well; you can click on the links under the large red button to view them. For now we'll just do a couple of sample updates.

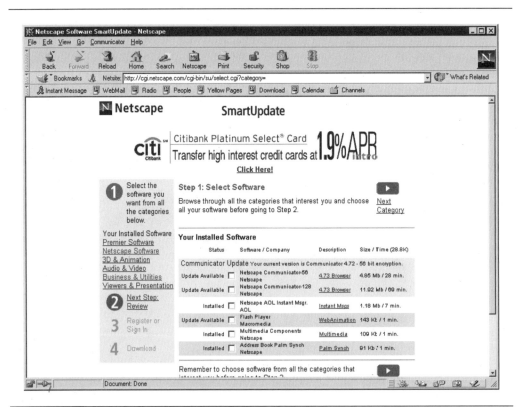

FIGURE 8-6   You select your desired software updates from the checklist that appears on the second SmartUpdate page

3. There are two check boxes for the Communicator update; select the one that has the same number (56 or 128) as your currently installed version. Then, of the remaining check boxes, mark only the ones that say Update Available.

NOTE *The difference between the 56-bit and the 128-bit versions is the encryption level each employs. Encryption is used to encode sensitive information that you may send to a secured Web site, such as credit card numbers for a purchase. The encryption level indicates how difficult it would be to break this encoding, with 128-bit being more difficult and therefore more secure than 56-bit. Software with 128-bit encryption cannot be legally sent outside the United States, so if you're in the U.S. and you try to update your 56-bit version to 128-bit, you'll have to state that you will not export it before you're allowed to download it.*

4. Click the green #2 button labeled Next Step: Review. This takes you to a page where you can check a list of what you're downloading.

5. If the list is okay, click the green #3 button labeled Next Step: Register or Sign In, and you'll go to the registration procedure. You have to fill out at least some of this in order to proceed, although if you've already registered, all you need do is sign in with username and password. As this is not a secured connection, don't re-use a username and password you employ to protect truly sensitive information. When finished, click Next.

6. A security warning now appears, which is why I made the suggestion about passwords in the previous step. Assuming you want to go on, click the Continue button.

NOTE *If you don't want to register but still want to update, the best thing to do is simply download a full and current version of Communicator from the Netscape download page at **www.netscape.com/computing/download/**.*

7. You now get a confirmation message. It has stuff about free e-mail in it, but disregard this and click Next.

8. And finally, in the next screen, you get to start the download. Click each link to download and install each component, following the instructions that appear with the Download Manager window.

9. When you're done, click the text link labeled Click Here After You Have Downloaded All Your Software, and you'll return to a Thank You page. You're finished.

Use Smart Download Tools

One of the perennial problems in downloading, especially with dial-up, is dropped connections. Losing a connection stops the download process and forces you to start it all over again from the beginning. If you've been waiting two hours for a long download to finish, and it breaks off three minutes from completion, it's nothing short of infuriating. The solution comes with smart download programs, which can pick up an interrupted download at the point it was broken off.

Use Netscape SmartDownload

A simple and easily obtainable program of this type is Netscape's SmartDownload. Before you decide to use it, though, you should know a few things.

First, SmartDownload only works with Navigator running on Windows; if you're an IE user or a Mac person, it won't help you. Second, while it's running it displays a window with advertising in it, which you may not find pleasing. You can minimize the advertising window, although you can't close it without canceling the download.

Third, not all Web sites support pause-and-resume downloading. If you lose a connection to one of these, you'll have to start again from the beginning. This isn't SmartDownload's fault; it's a characteristic of these Web sites. However, with those sites that do support it, the program works well.

To obtain it, navigate to Netscape at **home.netscape.com** and click the Download link. On the download page, at the time of writing, there was a text link labeled SmartDownload; if you can't find that or something similar, use the Netscape Search tools on the Netcenter page to search for the term "SmartDownload" and go from there.

Eventually, you'll find your way to the SmartDownload page. Follow the instructions there to download the installer program, which is called SMARTDOWNLOAD.EXE. When you've got it, stay connected and double-click on it to do the install. It's very brief, but it will ask if you want to add the smart download feature to your browser. Answer Yes.

Now try it out. Launch Navigator and navigate to a site where there's downloadable software. Pick something and begin downloading it. You'll see the ad window mentioned earlier, plus the control dialog. The latter appears in the next illustration.

Not only will the program pick up an interrupted download from the sites that support the service, you can also use the Pause and Resume buttons to stop the download and restart it. This is handy if you're on dial-up and want to shut down your connection in the middle of a long download so you can make a phone call. However, if you try to pause a download from a site that doesn't support the service, the program will warn you about it.

You can also close Navigator and the download will continue quite happily, or you can go on Web surfing with Navigator during the download. On a dial-up connection, though, this will be painfully slow, since the connection is doing two jobs at once.

The program can be customized to a degree. Click the Advanced button and you get the dialog shown in the next illustration. Note that the My Download Files folder, the default download folder, is created automatically on the C: drive when you run the program for the first time. You can leave this as it is or change it to something more appropriate to your system.

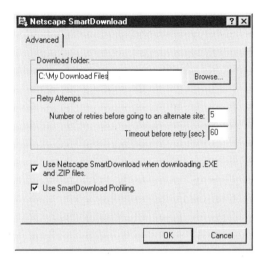

Use Other Smart Downloaders

There are other smart download programs to be found on the Internet; the TUCOWS site, which calls them download managers, is a good source. A commonly used one is GetRight, which comes in both shareware and freeware versions, and another is ReGet, which is freeware. These are much more elaborate than SmartDownload, allowing for batch downloading, scheduled downloads, and other advanced features. If you do a lot of long downloads they're worth looking into.

Where to Find It

Web Site	Address	What's There
GetRight	www.getright.com	Smart downloader
Microsoft download page	www.microsoft.com/downloads	Many Windows and application updates
Microsoft Office updates	www.officeupdate.microsoft.com	Office updates
Netscape download page	www.netscape.com/computing/download/	Updates and other downloads
ReGet	www.reget.com	Smart downloader
TUCOWS	www.tucows.com	Download managers, smart downloaders

Chapter 9

Using FTP

How To . . .

- Understand FTP and FTP sites
- Install WS_FTP, an FTP program
- Use WS_FTP to download files
- Upload files to FTP sites
- Use your browser to get files from FTP sites

Just to warn you up front, this chapter is about something called FTP, or File Transfer Protocol, and it's fairly technical. In fact, a close friend of mine who likes using the Web, but isn't very interested in the nuts and bolts of it, told me that FTP was such a horrible subject that it shouldn't even be allowed into the book. My friend said that any beginner who looked at this chapter first would promptly despair of ever understanding the Internet, and would put the book down and forget about it.

FTP's not quite that bad, actually. But in any case, you may never need to know anything much about it, at least not in your everyday use of the Internet. So you can skip this chapter if you like, and go on to something more comfortable, like multimedia or e-mail. And if learning about FTP does become unavoidable at some later time, you can always sidle back to it.

Understand FTP and FTP Sites

FTP, as said before, stands for File Transfer Protocol. It's a communication method for transferring files from a remote computer to your own machine. FTP sites, which are analogous to Web sites and, like them, are part of the Internet, have one chief function: to provide publicly accessible repositories of files that can be downloaded using the File Transfer Protocol method. FTP sites are, in a sense, file libraries, and because there are a lot of them, the number of files available runs in the millions at least.

But, you say, I can already download files perfectly easily from Web sites, so what would I need FTP for?

One reason is that your browser uses a communication method called HTTP (Hypertext Transfer Protocol), which was designed for transferring the small files that are characteristic of Web pages and their contents. HTTP is good at what it does, but it wasn't designed for handling large files, and some of the files on the Internet are very large indeed, in the order of 50 or 100 megabytes. FTP, which has actually been in use longer than HTTP, was intended specifically to handle large files. To make life even easier, there are also specialized FTP programs designed to work efficiently with FTP sites.

Another reason is that FTP programs are good at batch downloads. *Batch downloading* enables you to use your FTP program to select several files at a time from an FTP site, and the program will download them all without further intervention.

A third reason is that full-featured FTP programs will resume interrupted downloads, if the FTP site supports this feature (most do, but for some peculiar reason, Microsoft's doesn't).

Finally, you can use FTP to upload files—that is, transfer them from your machine to an FTP site, if you need to. Also, if you use your own machine to create a Web site that is to be set up on your ISP's computers, you'll likely use FTP to upload the pages of your site to the ISP.

NOTE   *If you have a slow connection, using FTP will improve download speed only a little if at all. With high-speed connections you may notice more of a difference. Download speed is also strongly influenced by how busy the FTP site is.*

You can tell an FTP site by its Internet address, because this always starts with the letters "ftp" instead of with the "www" that indicates a World Wide Web site. For example, **ftp.netscape.com** is the Internet address of Netscape's FTP site.

Use an FTP Program: WS_FTP LE

There are plenty of FTP programs around. A very popular one is from the Ipswitch Corporation, and is called WS_FTP Pro. A freeware version is also available, named WS_FTP LE (for Light Edition). WS_FTP LE is for private or educational use only; if you need WS_FTP for business purposes, Ipswitch requires you to purchase a registration and use the Pro version.

LE has fewer features than Pro. (For example, it doesn't resume interrupted transfers caused by dropped connections.) But WS_FTP LE is easily obtained and very representative of this type of program, so we'll use it as our example. For brevity we'll refer to it just as WS_FTP, with the understanding that it's the Light Edition we're talking about.

9

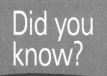
Did you know?

The technical name for an FTP program is *FTP client*. The generic word *client* is used to describe other programs as well. For example, Eudora is an e-mail client. A Web browser like IE is a Web client. Basically, *client* means that the program gets its input from another program, which is often called a *server*. Thus the Eudora e-mail client will receive its input from a *mail server* and the WS_FTP client will receive its input from an *FTP server*.

Obtain and Install WS_FTP

You can get the Light Edition of WS_FTP from the Web site of its vendor Ipswitch, at **www.ipswitch.com**, where you'll be asked to register before downloading. Alternatively, it's available from download sites like TUCOWS, which don't require registration. It comes as an EXE file, so after downloading you simply navigate to its folder and double-click the filename to install it.

There's one point to note about the installation procedure. You'll be asked for your e-mail address to serve as a password for something called "anonymous FTP sites." Most of the FTP sites that allow the general public to use them are "anonymous sites," meaning that anybody can use them provided they furnish an e-mail address. Non-anonymous sites require more rigorous user authentication, a situation that doesn't concern us here.

Installation of WS_FTP is otherwise simple; there are no major options except for choosing the installation folder and the storage folder for downloaded files. You can leave the installation folder at the default of C:\Program Files\WS_FTP. For the storage folder I generally use a temporary one like C:\Temp that I create myself. After the files have downloaded to this folder, I move them to their permanent homes.

Set Up WS_FTP and Log into FTP Sites

I admit that downloading with your browser is considerably simpler than downloading with an FTP client. To begin with, you have to know the name of the file(s) you want to download via FTP and where to find them before you can actually grab them. Unfortunately, the FTP site won't find them for you; in fact, it won't even help you look for them. If an FTP site is like a library, it's a library without any librarians.

So how do you find the file you're after, or even know if it exists on this particular site? A common situation is that you get the information about the existence of a desired file and its storage location from some other source. Suppose you're looking for a new driver for your video card, and you go to the vendor's Web site using your browser. There on the Web site you see a message like: "The file DRIVER.EXE can also be downloaded from our FTP site at ftp://ftp.wherever.com." Now you can use your FTP program to go to the FTP site and download the driver program to your computer.

Before you can connect to an FTP site, however, you must configure your FTP client to communicate with the remote computer that supports the site (*configure* means set up). As an example, let's assume you want to get something from the Netscape FTP site, and you've determined that the site's Internet address is **ftp://ftp.netscape.com**.

To get started, launch WS_FTP by choosing Start | Programs | WS_FTP | WS_FTPLE 95. The program's main window, with the Session Properties dialog overlaying it, appears as in the next illustration.

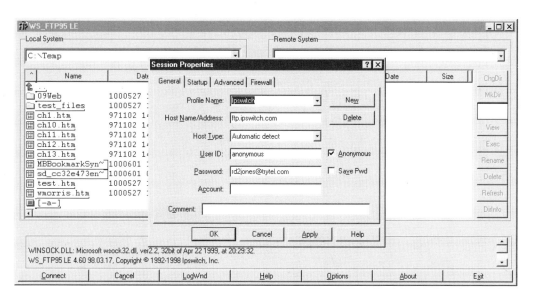

This Session Properties dialog is where you set up a "profile" of the site you want to connect to; this profile is merely a group of connection settings that you save for the next time you want to access the FTP site. You could give the program these settings every time you wanted to connect, of course, but it's much more convenient to save them as a profile. In our example, the profile we're going to create and save will be for the Netscape site.

The Profile Name box starts out by showing the profile Ipswitch. If you click the arrow button at the right of the box, you'll see a drop-down list of other pre-configured FTP sites. Netscape is already among them, but for the sake of this example we'll pretend it isn't. To create the new Netscape profile using the Session Properties dialog, do this:

1. Click the New button to clear the existing profile.

2. In the Profile Name box, type a name to identify this FTP site. In the example, I used **MyNetscape**.

3. In the Host Name/Address box, type the Internet address of the site: **ftp.netscape.com** in this case.

4. Leave the Host Type box set at its default of Automatic Detect.

5. Since Netscape's is an anonymous FTP site, mark the check box labeled Anonymous. This automatically fills in the User ID and Password boxes with "anonymous" and your e-mail address respectively (remember, you provided your e-mail address at installation time). Of course, if this weren't an anonymous site, you'd need login

information supplied by the site's administrator. In that case you'd leave the check box empty and manually fill in your user ID and password as provided by the administrator.

6. Mark the Save Password box, unless you want to be asked for your password every time you connect to the site.

7. Unless you have an account on the FTP site, leave the Account box empty. If you've been following the example, the Session Properties dialog will now look like the one in the next illustration (your e-mail address in the Password box will be different from the one shown, of course).

8. Click Apply to save the profile.

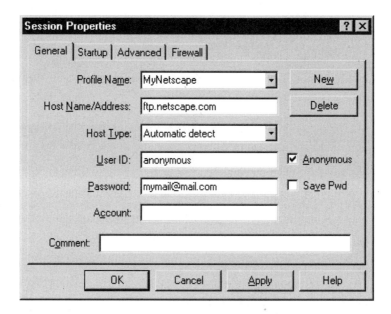

At this point, if you click OK, the Session Profile dialog vanishes and the program automatically tries to connect to the FTP site specified by the new profile. If your dial-up connection isn't active, however, you'll get an error message, because WS_FTP will not dial the connection for you. So, if you use a dial-up connection, make sure you're connected before you click OK.

Also, for future reference, note that you always use the Session Profile dialog to select the FTP site that you'll connect to. If the Session Profile dialog isn't showing, click the Connect button on the main WS_FTP window to open it. Then select the desired site from the drop-down list in the Profile Name text box, and click OK to connect.

Navigate Around an FTP Site and Download Files

Assuming you're connected, select the desired FTP site from the Session Profile dialog and click OK. WS_FTP now attempts to connect to the FTP site on the remote computer. You'll see monitoring messages at the bottom of the WS_FTP window. If something isn't working, they'll turn red and the connection may fail; if it does, check your profile settings for errors. But if all goes well, eventually the contact will be made and the WS_FTP window will resemble the illustration here. It probably won't be an exact match, because your computer will be different from mine and you may be connected to a different FTP site than the one in the example.

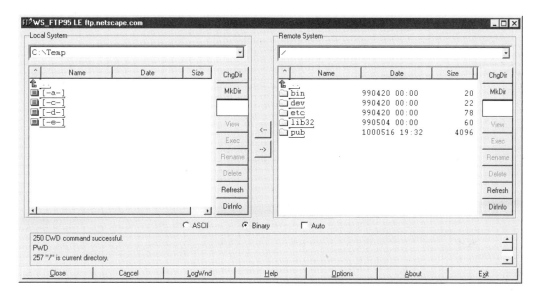

Look at the two large list boxes of the display. The left one shows the content of the download folder you specified when you installed WS_FTP, as well as icons representing the various disk drives on your system. In the illustration, the download folder is C:\Temp, as you can see in the small upper text box labeled Local System.

If you want to navigate around the drives and folders of your computer, you can do this easily in the left-hand list box. To change the display to another drive, double-click the drive icon. To open a subfolder, double-click its icon. To go from a subfolder to the folder above it, double-click the small green arrow at the top of the list box. You'll see the folder name changing in the Local System text box as you do this. Because downloaded files are stored in the folder displayed in the Local System text box, you can change the download folder easily by navigating to it in the big list box.

The large right-hand list box shows the content of the current folder of the remote system, in other words, of the FTP site. In this illustration, the name of the current folder of the FTP site appears in the text box labeled Remote System. It is simply a forward slash (/), and as you can see from the list box, it contains the subfolders bin, dev, etc, lib32, and pub. You will frequently see some of these folder names, especially pub (or sometimes only pub) on FTP sites. Pub stands for public, and this folder often will contain the most commonly desired software on the FTP site, so it's a good place to start.

You navigate the FTP site folders using the same techniques as you did before with your own system. For our example, let's assume that we want to download an older version of Communicator, specifically version 4.7. In the right-hand list box, double-click the pub folder. In a moment the box displays the subfolders of pub, among them one called communicator. We're getting warm.

Double-click the communicator folder, and its subfolders appear. None says 4.7, so try the subfolder labeled english. Bingo! There's a folder labeled 4.7. Double-click it and you get three subfolders for mac, unix, and windows. Double-click the appropriate one; windows, in this example. Still more folders appear, one labeled windows_95_or_nt. Double-click this, and when the next set of subfolders appears, double-click the one labeled complete_install.

TIP   *You can move quickly to a previously opened folder by using the drop-down lists in either the Local System text box or the Remote System text box. Just click the small arrow buttons to display the folders that you have already visited.*

Now the list box displays the content of the complete_install folder: some README files, and a single EXE file, named CC32E47.EXE, which must be the installation file for Communicator 4.7. The README.TXT file might be also useful, so we'll download it as well as the EXE file.

To select them for download, hold down the CTRL key and click on each file you want (for selecting a continuous range of files, the SHIFT-click method also works). The next illustration shows what WS_FTP will look like at this point.

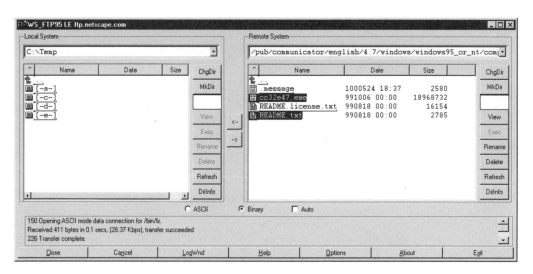

Now look at the bar dividing the two large boxes. In it are two buttons with arrows pointing left and right respectively. To begin the download of the selected files, simply click the left-pointing button. A progress indicator appears for each file as it downloads, and the name of the file being received appears in the left-hand list box. To stop the current download and prevent further downloads, if there were several selected, click the Cancel button.

When no more progress indicators appear, the download is finished and the message Transfer Complete appears at the bottom of the WS_FTP window. Click the Close button to log off the remote computer, and close down WS_FTP.

Upload Files to an FTP Site

Uploading a file means transferring it from your computer to the FTP site. There will normally be some specific reason for you to do this, such as updating your Web site on your ISP's computer. Whatever the reason, the FTP site must allow you to upload files; anonymous sites generally won't permit it. If you try to upload something to the Netscape FTP site, for example, it will issue an error message and refuse the transfer.

Uploading with WS_FTP is easy, though, once you've learned how to navigate around an FTP site. Begin by connecting to the site. Then, in the left-hand list box, which displays the content of your machine, navigate to the folder that contains the files you want to upload. Select the desired files.

Then, in the right-hand list box, which shows the folders of the FTP site, navigate to the destination folder for the files. Then go to the bar between the two list boxes, and click the button with the right-pointing arrow. This starts the upload. A progress indicator appears for each uploaded file until all uploads are complete.

There are numerous other options and techniques available with WS_FTP LE and even more with Pro. To explore these, click the Help button. Pro options are visible in the LE screens, but are grayed out and not available until you register for the full version (and pay for it).

There are also other excellent FTP clients. For alternatives, try out CuteFTP or FTPVoyager.

 TIP

Zipped archive files are a convenient way of uploading several files at a time. If you have many or large files to upload, you may want to use WinZip to create archives or compress your files. How to do this is described in Chapter 11, in the section on zipping attachments for e-mailing.

Use Your Browser with FTP

While an FTP client is a very effective tool for downloading files from an FTP site, you can also use your browser to do it, as long as the browser version is IE 4 or later, or Navigator 4 or later. This works seamlessly with anonymous FTP sites; however, if you try to access a restricted ftp site, the browser will ask for your name and password.

As before, you have to know the Internet address of the FTP site you want to connect to. If you're using IE, type it into the Address text box and press ENTER. For example, to connect to the Microsoft FTP site, you'd type the address **ftp.microsoft.com**. This produces a folder and file listing like the one in Figure 9-1.

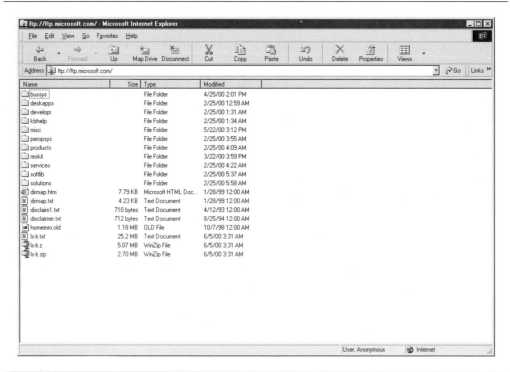

FIGURE 9-1 You can download files from an FTP site with your browser as well as with an FTP client

The folder icons behave as they do in Windows Explorer, so you have to double-click on one to display its contents. Each time you do this, a new copy of IE opens to display the folder's contents, so if you open a lot of folders you'll end up with a lot of copies of IE running. However, this apparent drawback is what makes batch downloading possible, as described a bit later. You can close the unneeded copies of IE to get them out of the way, if you want to.

To download a file, simply right-click it, and when the pop-up menu appears, choose Copy to Folder. This opens a browse dialog where you can choose your download folder. Select the folder and click the OK button to begin the download. A progress indicator appears to show you how it's going.

With IE, you can also do batch downloads from FTP sites. Select the files you need, right-click on any one of them, and the pop-up menu described in the previous paragraph appears. Use the Copy to Folder choice as before to download all the files without further intervention.

If you open an FTP site in Netscape, you get a somewhat different display (see Figure 9-2). Unlike those in IE, the folder icons are actually links, so you single-click one to open it.

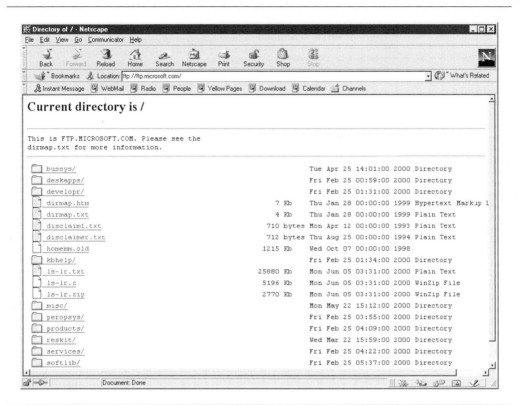

FIGURE 9-2   The Netscape FTP display uses links rather than filenames to access the desired files

The filenames are links as well. To download a file, right-click on it and from the pop-up menu choose Save Link As. You can't do multiple downloads, however, as you can with the IE display.

Note that you don't get a fresh copy of Netscape every time you open a new folder, as you do in IE. Instead, each new folder and file listing replaces the previous one in the same copy of the browser.

NOTE
IE 5.5, which should be available as an update by the time you read this, and which is installed with Millennium, can be set up to prevent multiple copies of the browser from opening. Choose Tools | Internet Options and go to the Advanced sheet. Clear the check box labeled Enable Folder View for FTP Sites, and click OK. Now the FTP screens will all display in the same copy of the browser, just as in Navigator. Also as in Navigator, the folder entries are now links (and are called directories) *so you single-click to open them. However, if IE is using this type of display, it can't do batch downloads.*

Where to Find It

Web Site	Address	What's There
CuteFTP	www.cuteftp.com	CuteFTP FTP client
FTPVoyager	www.ftpvoyager.com	FTP Voyager FTP client
Ipswitch	www.ipswitch.com.	WS_FTP FTP client
Microsoft FTP site	ftp.microsoft.com	Anonymous FTP
Netscape FTP site	ftp.netscape.com	Anonymous FTP

Chapter 10

Enjoy Multimedia

How To . . .

■ Identify the hardware you need for multimedia

■ Locate, download, and install RealPlayer

■ Locate, download, and install RealJukebox

■ Locate, download, and install Windows Media Player

■ Understand and use plug-ins and ActiveX controls

■ Listen to music and radio online

■ View video online

■ Download and play back MP3 music files and video files

When I began to write this chapter, figuring out how best to organize it perplexed me. The reason is that multimedia on the Web is really a pair of complementary subjects, and these entwine and overlap in ways that aren't particularly neat. One subject, as you might expect, covers the media resources themselves: streaming audio and downloadable audio, streaming video and downloadable video, online radio, still pictures, animations, and all the rest of the Web cornucopia of sounds and images.

The other subject is the tools people use to listen to or look at them. There's been a proliferation of media players of all sorts in the last few months, and in many cases you can use two different players with the same kind of audio file, but one of them will play video and the other won't, and while that second one doesn't do video it will handle a type of sound file that the first player won't, but a third one will, and so on.... You get the picture.

So multimedia on the Web doesn't fit easily into neat packages. What we'll try to do in this chapter, therefore, is spread out a representative part of the whole extravagant buffet, with its eight different kinds of potato salad and sixteen types of pickles, so you can assemble your own plateful. It won't likely be the same as anybody else's.

What You Need to Enjoy Multimedia

Multimedia requires some minimum hardware and software components to work satisfactorily. The hardware, obviously, is the computer itself. The software is a specialized type of program called a *media player*. There are several brands of players, some that play back both video and audio, and some that are only for audio. In the next two sections we'll examine what you need to enjoy your Internet multimedia experience, including how to obtain and install the needed players.

Understand Hardware Requirements

For audio playback at its most rudimentary, your computer must be at least a Pentium 120 or Macintosh equivalent, and obviously must have a sound card. This should be at least a 16-bit card; most recent machines come with some sort of basic 16-bit card installed. If you're an audiophile, though, you might want to replace the card at some point. The more you pay for a sound card, usually, the better sound you'll get from it.

However, a Pentium 120 machine is the very bottom of the ladder for audio, and will be no good for video. A Pentium 200 or Mac equivalent is the minimum for this, but even so you'll be stuck with a very small video window and jumpy pictures.

But the real bottleneck for video playback, assuming your computer is otherwise capable of it, is the speed of your video card. A Pentium 500 or Celeron 500 with an old, slow video card will perform no better, and perhaps worse, than an elderly Pentium 200 with a new, fast video card. So if you try playing video and get poor results, investigate replacing your video card before going out to buy a new computer. Note also that a fast video card in a reasonably fast machine may allow the video to play in full-screen mode, rather than in a small window. However, the picture quality in full-screen mode will be determined either by the nature of the playback file or by the speed of the Internet connection.

The video card itself should also be capable of displaying 16-bit color, also known as Hi Color, and should be able to do this at a minimum screen resolution of 800 × 600. The computer itself should have at least 32MB of RAM. If you're not sure whether it has all this stuff, check your manuals or get some knowledgeable assistance. You can also simply download a player and try it out. If sound or video is poor or nonfunctional, look into the hardware situation.

10

Did you know?

"Pentium" and "Celeron" are the trademark names of processor chips made by Intel Corporation. The processor, also called the CPU (central processing unit), is the "brain" of the computer and, as its name suggests, it carries out the processes that do the actual work. The number associated with the processor's name indicates how fast the processor can make calculations, which in turn largely determines how fast the computer will do things. For example, a Pentium 200 processor runs twice as fast as a Pentium 100, and the computer with the 200 will give noticeably faster responses than the one built around the 100.

Intel's processors predominate in the personal computer market, though another company, called AMD, makes the Athlon and Duron processors; these are worthy competitors for the Pentium and Celeron and tend to be a bit cheaper. As of Summer 2000, the slowest new Intel-based machines widely available were Pentium 600 and Celeron 500 computers, and the entry-level AMD-based computers were in the same range. Machines of this speed, provided they have a decent video card, will handle multimedia with ease.

TIP *In Windows you can easily check your color and resolution. Right-click on the desktop and choose Properties from the pop-up menu. In the Display Properties dialog, choose the Settings tab. The Colors box should read Hi Color (16 bit) and the Screen Area slider should show 800 by 600 pixels or greater (if it's greater, for example 1024 by 768, leave it at that setting). Use the Colors box and the slider to change the settings if necessary.*

Once you have a fast-enough computer with a sound card, you'll need speakers. Often these come with a new computer, and some monitors have speakers built into them. You can pay a lot of money, or a little, for speakers. People who like really good (or loud) audio sometimes connect the sound card to their stereo system and use that.

The speed of your Internet connection will also dictate the results you get from online playback of sound or video. Faster is better, as usual, and dial-up connections will be much less satisfactory than DSL or cable. Playing back a previously downloaded file isn't directly affected by the connection speed, of course. A slow connection just means it took you longer to download the file in the first place.

Get and Install Media Players

Several different media players, which is the generic term for these software tools, are available. Your choice will ultimately be based on a combination of personal preference and the varying capabilities of the players. The three we'll use as examples are RealPlayer 8 Basic, RealJukebox 8 Basic, and Windows Media Player 7.

Understand and Obtain RealPlayer 8 Basic

RealPlayer 8 Basic is a freeware version of the RealPlayer 8 media player, which displays video and audio either online or from files. It was in beta version at the time of writing, but the finished version will probably be the one available by the time you read this. Because the beta was used for this chapter, RealPlayer 8 Basic as described here may differ slightly from what you see on your own machine.

NOTE *As you may remember from a previous chapter, beta software is software that hasn't had all its bugs worked out yet, but is mostly usable.*

RealJukebox 2 Basic, which is discussed in the next section, is an add-on audio component for RealPlayer. You can get it as an online update to RealPlayer, or download it as part of the RealPlayer package and install both together.

However, Real Corporation's packaging of these freeware players is a bit confusing, especially when we're trying to decide the simplest download situation. Here's how you can get them:

- As the Entertainment Center Basic Complete package, including RealPlayer, RealJukebox, RealDownload, and Net2Phone.

- As the Entertainment Center Basic Standard package, including RealPlayer, RealJukebox, and RealDownload.

- As RealPlayer Basic Standalone.

- Finally, if you download RealPlayer Basic Standalone, you can then obtain RealJukebox Basic as an online update to RealPlayer. Since this is, in fact, the simplest approach (because it doesn't involve coping with the RealDownload program during install), this is the option we'll choose.

If you have installed Netscape Communicator, you may have an earlier version of RealPlayer already on your system. Even if you do, however, you still might want to download version 8, since Communicator 4.73 provides only the somewhat elderly version 6.

To download RealPlayer, navigate to the RealPlayer Web site at **www.real.com**. Somewhere on that page you'll find a link to a download page; see if you can find a box labeled "Top Free Downloads" and look for it there. Click the link, and you'll find yourself on another page where you can select the purchased version or stick with the freeware one. Unless you want to buy the player right now, make sure you click the link that says RealPlayer 8 Basic or something like it, because "Basic" refers to the freeware version. You may have to look around for the link, because the Real Corporation would obviously prefer you to go for the purchased version. Next comes a registration page. As well as providing your name and e-mail address (which do not have to be your real ones), you need to make a number of other choices:

- **Select OS**   This asks for the operating system of your computer. From the drop-down list, select the correct version, which for most people will be one of the Windows or Mac choices.

- **Select CPU**   If you're using Windows, the correct choice is Pentium-class system. If you have a Mac, consult your documentation to determine which CPU you have.

- **Select Language**   This is self-explanatory.

- **Select Connection**   If you have a dial-up connection, it will be either 14.4, 28.8, or 56. If you have a high-speed connection, use the choice that matches the one you have. If you can't figure it out, use Other/Don't Know and the software will try to determine it for you.

10

Click the big Download Free RealPlayer button to move to the next page, the Download Options page. There you'll find a table where you can choose to download either the standalone RealPlayer or two different versions of the Real Entertainment Center. Since we want the standalone player, make your selection by clicking the round option button below the RealPlayer Basic Standalone column. Then click the Download button.

Next you see a screen giving choices of download locations. Pick a link that is geographically near you (or at least on the same continent!). From that point the download is just like the others you've done; choose or create a destination folder, and save the RealPlayer installation file to it. You should see a progress meter in a download info box. It will take about 30 minutes with a 28.8K dial-up connection.

To begin installing the package, double-click on the installation file, which is named RP8-SETUP.EXE. You can accept all the defaults and keep clicking Next until you reach the final screen, where you click Finish.

The actual installation begins at this point, and you'll see some progress indicators. Then the RealPlayer configuration dialog automatically opens (see the next illustration). Follow the configuration procedure as outlined here.

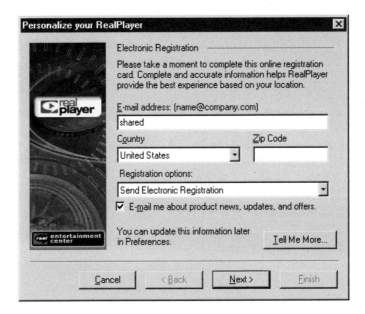

1. Fill out the registration card and, if you don't want e-mail about the product, clear that check box. You can also put in a false name and address if you like. Click Next.

2. In the next dialog you get to choose your connection speed. It defaults to a likely choice, but verify it anyway. Click Next.

3. If you're installing on a machine that has no version of RealPlayer on it, you'll see a dialog where you specify the media files for which RealPlayer will be the default player. (If an earlier RealPlayer version is installed, you won't see this dialog; skip to step 4.) If you think you'd like to use RealPlayer for most media, leave both check boxes filled in and click Next.

4. In the next dialog you can add channels to the pre-set ones in the player. Channels give you one-click access to categories of resources. Check off any you want and click Next.

5. In the next screen you get to personalize the player to play back headlines of interest. Check off any you want and click Next.

6. The next screen offers tips and tricks and special offer options. Clear or select them as you prefer and click Next.

7. The next screen allows you to send and receive certain kinds of information. As a security measure, I'd clear all of the check boxes. Click Next.

8. In the final screen, you review your choices. If you like them, click Finish. RealPlayer is now fully installed and configured and will appear as in the following illustration.

10

If you remain connected to the Internet while installing, or if you connect after installing, the player will automatically download the channels you specified in step 4.

To reconfigure the player at a later time, choose View | Preferences and use the dialogs provided. Note that an icon for RealPlayer is placed both on the desktop and in the System Tray.

Obtain RealJukebox Basic

RealJukebox Basic is a freeware audio player developed to handle most types of audio and particularly MP3 files. It has more sophisticated capabilities for dealing with audio than RealPlayer does, and requires a Pentium 200 machine or better, not the Pentium 120 that RealPlayer can get away with. Also, unlike RealPlayer, it is available only for Windows.

To do an online update of RealPlayer to install RealJukebox, go to the Real download page and click the link for RealJukebox 2 Basic, which takes you to the registration page. Fill in the form and click the big Download button to go to the page where you choose the download version. Since we just want to update RealPlayer, select the RealJukebox Basic Standalone option button and again click the big Download button. You have to negotiate one more screen to confirm your selection, and then the update begins with an AutoUpdate dialog box. Click the OK button and the update begins. A progress meter shows how it's going; it will take about 20 minutes with a 28.8K dial-up connection.

Once the files have downloaded, the program begins its installation procedure with the Setup dialog, as follows:

1. In its first screen, click the Accept button to agree to the legalese. In the next screen, leave the install folder at the default and click Finish.

2. A progress meter appears, and tracks the installation. A dialog may appear that asks if you want to restart your computer. Click Yes.

3. The computer restarts, if that was selected in step 2. If this is the first RealJukebox installation on the machine, a registration dialog will appear. However, if an earlier version of RealJukebox was installed and registered, there will be no registration dialog and you'll move directly to step 4. If a registration dialog does appear, fill it out and click Next to go to step 4.

4. In the next dialog, click Next again to go to the Setup Options dialog. Select the Express Setup option button and click Next.

5. In the final screen, click Finish and RealJukebox has been fully installed.

When the Setup dialog closes, you may see a Reclaim dialog that says "Another application is the default player for one or more music file types supported by RealJukebox." Then it asks if you want the program to be the default player for those types. Click Details if you want to see which types they are. But unless you have definite reasons for doing so, you can leave them as they are and close the Reclaim dialog. Then click Yes to make RealJukebox the default player. When you open RealJukebox, it will look like the next illustration.

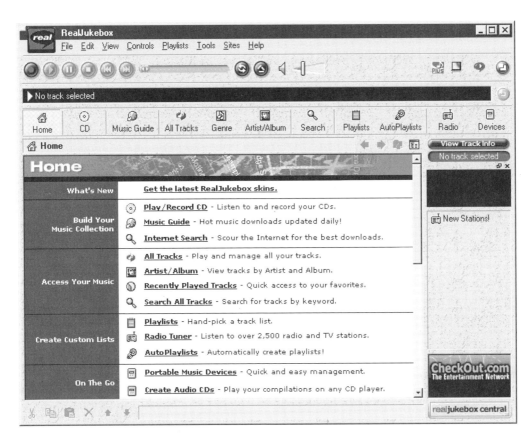

NOTE   *Around the time the Reclaim dialog opens, RealJukebox may attempt to connect to the Real Web site. If you're not connected, you'll get an error page. Just close it and proceed as described perviously. If it does connect, you can close that page too, or read it and then close it. It's just informational.*

If you want to change its setup options later, choose Tools | Preferences or, for configuration assistance, choose Tools | Configuration Wizard. Note that an icon for RealJukebox is placed both on the desktop and in the System Tray.

At this point, if you want to experiment with multimedia right away, you can skip ahead to the sections about RealPlayer and RealJukebox in the section called "Listen to Music and Radio Online." If you want to learn about and perhaps install the new Windows Media Player 7, go on to the next section.

Obtain Windows Media Player

Some version of the Windows Media Player (WMP) is installed automatically when you install Windows. It is a player for both video and sound and the latest version is Media Player 7, which is the one that comes with Windows Millennium. The beta of version 7 was used in writing this chapter, and because it is a beta, what's described here may be slightly different from what you see in the finished product.

Windows Media Player version 7 cannot be used with Windows NT 4 or Windows 95. If you are using either of these operating systems you'll have to stick with the older version, which is 6.4. Version 6.4 can be obtained from the Microsoft Download Center if you need it.

If you don't have Windows Millennium but want Windows Media Player 7, you can download it from the Microsoft Download Center at **www.microsoft.com/downloads**. This is the same download page you learned about in Chapter 8. Use the Product name box to scroll down to the Windows Media Player entry and select it. Then use the Operating System box to select your operating system, which will have to be Windows 98, 2000, or Millennium. With this done, click the Find It button, and you'll get a link to the installation file. Click on that to start the download, saving the file to a new or existing folder. It will take about 40 minutes to download on a 28.8K dial-up connection.

Once you have the file, installation is straightforward; double-click the filename and the installation dialogs begin.

Click Yes twice to get to the Windows Media Component Setup dialog. In this dialog, click Next to get to the Privacy Statement dialog. This has a lot of information in it about what information the player will and will not send from your machine to other computers on the Internet. It's worth reading, because some of the player's components are there to allow future Internet options like pay-per-view services and music licensing, and the use of a media rights monitoring system called the Windows Rights Manager System. This technology is still in development, and whether it will ever see the light of day is a good question.

For the moment, however, you can't install the player without accepting the policy, so select the acceptance option button and click Next. Then go on as follows:

1. The next screen presents a list of components for the player. Leave them all selected and click Next.

2. The next screen is a customization screen. Leave all the check boxes checked and click Next, then Next again in the next screen.

3. A set of progress indicators appears. If prompted to do so, click the Finish button to restart your computer and complete the installation. After the computer restarts (if that was necessary) you'll find a Windows media player icon on your desktop.

4. Connect to the Internet and launch the player. It will automatically connect to the Windows Media site and will resemble the next illustration, although you'll see different content in the player window itself. It's now ready to use.

If you install WMP after installing RealPlayer and RealJukebox, you may find that both these later complain about not being the default player for certain files. This is because WMP has taken them over.

What to do? Well, if you're just getting into Web media, it doesn't really matter which players you leave as the defaults. So, when RealPlayer asks if you want to correct the situation, click Yes if you want it to be the default, and No if you prefer the look of WMP and want it to be the default. When RealJukebox asks a similar question, click Yes if you want it to be the default, and No if you prefer WMP.

Once you get used to working with the players you can mess around with the options if necessary, and set the defaults the way you want them.

Actually, even RealPlayer and RealJukebox will sometimes argue between themselves over the ownership of an audio file type. If this happens, click No in the RealPlayer dialog to let RealJukebox have it, since this program is optimized for audio.

 *You can alter the appearance of both WMP and RealJukebox by means of skins. A skin modifies the look of a program in some thematic way. To use skins in RealJukebox, choose View | Skins. To do so in WMP, click the Skin Chooser button at the left of the player window. To change RealJukebox back to its original appearance, right-click on its display and choose Full Mode from the pop-up menu. To change WMP back, right-click on its display and choose Return to Full Mode from the pop-up menu.*

Other Players

The players from Real and from Microsoft aren't the only ones you can try out. Apple QuickTime, a video player, is available both for Windows and for the Mac at **www.apple.com**. A widely used MP3 music player, Winamp, can be had from **www.winamp.com**. There are also multipurpose, all-in-one players you can purchase, such as Media Wizard from CDH Productions (**www.cdhnow.com**) that will handle most video or audio file formats.

 *You may already have Winamp on your machine, since a version gets installed automatically with later versions of Communicator. Go to Start | Programs | Netscape Communicator and see if there's a Winamp icon in the program menu there.*

Understand and Use Plug-Ins

Plug-ins are programs that you download and install so that you can use your browser to view certain types of multimedia. In some cases, the plug-in becomes part of the browser and can't be used on its own. In other cases, the plug-in is actually a normal program that you can use without the browser's participation, but which also integrates itself into the browser so that you can use its services while browsing the Web; this is usually referred to as a "helper application." RealPlayer is an example of this helper type of plug-in, one that can either work by itself or be launched by your browser as required.

Navigator and IE use different software methods for plug-ins. Strictly speaking, *plug-in* refers to the software used with Navigator; while IE employs tools called ActiveX controls. Generically, though, they've all come to be called plug-ins.

Use Netscape Navigator Plug-Ins

You'll know you need a Navigator plug-in when you click on a link, and the next thing you see is an Unknown File Type message from Navigator. The message resembles the one in the following illustration:

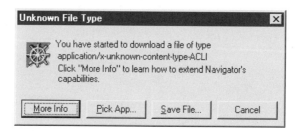

These plug-ins are usually of the type that won't run by themselves but require Navigator to function. To obtain one, click the More Info button, which will take you to the Netscape plug-in page. Here you'll need to locate the plug-in file required by the item you were trying to link to. Download the plug-in file to a temporary folder and then close Navigator. Then use Windows Explorer to navigate to the download folder, and double-click the filename to install the plug-in.

Sometimes a plug-in offers itself automatically from the Web page being viewed, so that you don't have to rummage around the Netscape site. For example, many multimedia-oriented Web sites are designed with Macromedia Shockwave, and to view them as intended you need the Shockwave and Flash players. Such sites will tell you that you don't have the plug-ins and need them, and will offer a link to the Macromedia site where you can download the software.

If you want to use Windows Media Player 7 with Navigator, a plug-in is available from the Microsoft Download Center; it's on the same page you used earlier to download the WMP itself. Note that you must install the full version of WMP, however, before you can install the Navigator plug-in.

Use Internet Explorer Controls

IE's version of the plug-in is the ActiveX control. If you go to a page that requires such a control to view its content, you'll get a message like the one in the next illustration. In this particular example, IE is trying to open a Web page that uses the Flash control, which hasn't yet been installed. The green certificate appears to tell you that the control is legitimate and doesn't harbor viruses. To install the control, click Yes. If you click No, the page will open but you won't see the Flash-based animations.

10

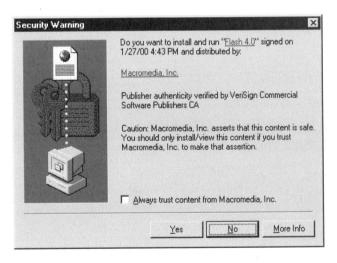

Shockwave and Flash sites can be painfully slow on dial-up connections. They're much better if you have a high-speed Internet service. In fact, most multimedia, including the radio and sound aspects of it discussed next, are far more satisfactory on a high-speed service. And for online video, a slow connection is almost impossible to use.

Your Internet Multimedia Experience

Music, both online and downloaded, is the big draw on the Internet at the moment, and there is a *lot* of music available out on the Web. Online video isn't as popular yet, because of its need for broadband (high-speed) connections, but it's coming on strong. The following sections of this chapter will give you a sense of what's out there and how to experience it.

Listen to Music and Radio Online

You can use the Web as a source of music in two basic ways: You can either listen to it online, or download it as a file and play it back later. Listening to radio overlaps listening to music, because radio stations are also present on the Web, carrying not only music but everything else that radio stations offer. We'll start off our exploration of Internet multimedia by looking at online audio resources and how you can use them.

Listen Online with RealPlayer

Online audio depends on a technology called *streaming audio*. This means that you don't have to download and save a file and then play it back; instead, the information "streams" from the remote site, through your Web connection to your computer and is played as it arrives.

A good place to start with streaming audio is the Real Guide Web site. Start either IE or Navigator and go to **www.realguide.real.com**. When the home page of the site opens, it will resemble the one in Figure 10-1.

On the menu at the left of the window, you can choose from many categories, including Music and Radio. Let's try the Music one first (you may see a smaller advertising window floating around, which you can close if you want to). Click the link to go to the page, and you'll be presented with links to current music, music archives, music videos, and a lot more.

Click one of these links and a copy of RealPlayer will open on top of the browser. After a few moments (or almost immediately if you have a high-speed connection) the linked music file will begin to play. The player has controls for pause, stop, play, volume, and other functions; you can experiment with them as you listen.

NOTE   *When you listen online with RealPlayer, it's functioning as a kind of plug-in to the browser. You can use it as a standalone program too, as explained a little later.*

When you've explored the Music page a while, go back to the home page and click the Radio Tuner link. On the Radio Tuner page, there's a drop-down list box at the left of the window, labeled My Presets. From this list you can choose among over a dozen types of music. Select one, and a list of available radio stations appears below the list box. Click one of these stations and a copy of RealPlayer opens on top of the browser, connects to the station, and begins playing (though you may have to listen to a brief commercial before the music starts).

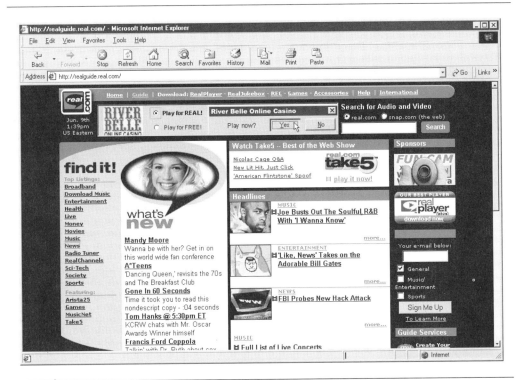

FIGURE 10-1   The Real site offers a selection of streaming audio sources

The stations in the preset list may not be ones you care for, so RealPlayer allows you to add to them or delete them. To add more stations to your preset list, go to the Radio Tuner page. You'll see a menu with the choices "Featured," "Find," and "Customize." Choose Find, which opens a window with a list box labeled Choose a Format. Click the box's arrow button to display the list of formats, and select one. Then click the large blue Find button (*not* the "Find" on the menu). A list of available radio stations in this category appears (see Figure 10-2).

To connect to a station, click on the small loudspeaker icon next to its name or on the name itself. To add it to your preset list, select the proper category using the My Presets list box, and click the small + icon in the second line of the station listing. Now you can connect to it directly from the My Preset list.

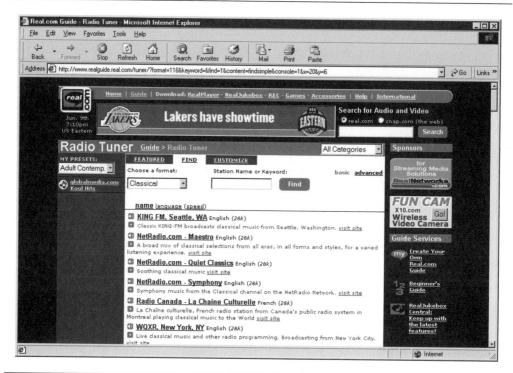

FIGURE 10-2   You can locate lists of available radio stations in RealPlayer

To delete a station, open the Radio Tuner page and choose the required category from the My Presets list box. Then choose Customize on the menu to open a customization window for that category (see Figure 10-3). In the Preset Stations list box, select the one you want to delete and click the blue Delete button. Then click Save All Changes to complete the operation and update the My Presets list.

In the preceding procedures, make sure to let the pages load completely before going from one step to the next. If you don't, you may end up with the wrong customization choices displayed, for example.

That's a very brief look at how you can use RealPlayer with your browser. RealPlayer has a multitude of options and menus; unfortunately, space limitations prevent us from examining them all. Experimenting and using the online Help are the best ways to figure out how everything works.

While it may not be immediately obvious, you actually don't have to go through your browser to use RealPlayer. If you close the browser, leaving RealPlayer running by itself, you'll see a row of icons at the bottom of the player, two of them being labeled Radio Tuner and Guide.

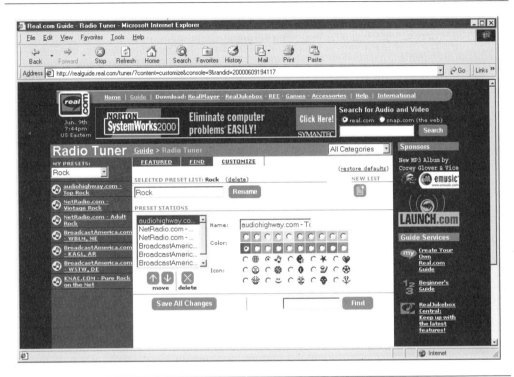

FIGURE 10-3   RealPlayer allows you to customize your list of preferred radio stations

Clicking on Guide opens a version of the Real Guide Web site in the player window. It provides fewer categories than the browser-oriented page, however.

If you click the Radio Tuner icon, you open the same Radio Tuner page we were exploring earlier. Choose a station category and station to tune in, or use the Find and Customize menus to locate more stations and add them to your Presets list. You can also use the Radio menu choice on RealPlayer's menu bar to select categories of stations.

> **TIP**   *The Take 5 icon that appeared on your desktop when you installed RealPlayer is actually a link to a daily updated page of entertainment information. (A similar link appears in RealPlayer itself.) Click it to find out about the latest in music, comedy, and movies.*

You will also have noticed the various channel icons on the left of the main player window. These are for both audio and video, and the best way to find out about them is to experiment.

10

How to ... Control the Volume

The media players discussed here have their own volume controls, but you can use Windows' own control as well. To do so, right-click the speaker icon in the System Tray, and choose Volume Control. A Volume Control window opens. To adjust the master volume, move the leftmost slider up and down. The other sliders control volume for specific sources such as MIDI devices.

NOTE   *In both RealPlayer and Windows Media Player, you'll see links to a Broadband category. This category contains material that is specifically designed to be viewed or heard over a high-speed Internet connection.*

Listen Online with Windows Media Player

Like RealPlayer, WMP can be used as a plug-in through IE (and through Navigator, if you've installed the plug-in as described in the earlier section on the subject). The main resource for WMP sound and video is the Media Guide home page at Microsoft's multimedia Web site at **www.windowsmedia.com**. Navigate to that address, and you'll get a page resembling the one in Figure 10-4.

Click the Music tab and you'll go to a page where, at the time of writing, a rather limited supply of online music and music videos were available. Clicking a music link opens WMP, which plays the music. The video links also play in WMP; this is examined later, in the section on online video.

Clicking the Radio tab opens a page where you'll find a panel labeled Find Radio Stations. This provides a list of preset radio stations; you can see more lists by choosing from the drop-down list box at the top of the panel. To connect to a station, you click on it. This may open a subsidiary window for the station's Web page, or it may simply start playing the station. Once the station is playing, you can close the subsidiary window, if there is one. There is a Start/Stop button on the toolbar, along with a volume control and a drop-down list of recently visited stations.

NOTE   *On a slow connection the radio signal may "drop out" intermittently and you'll get moments of silence—another reason to invest in high-speed service if you can get it.*

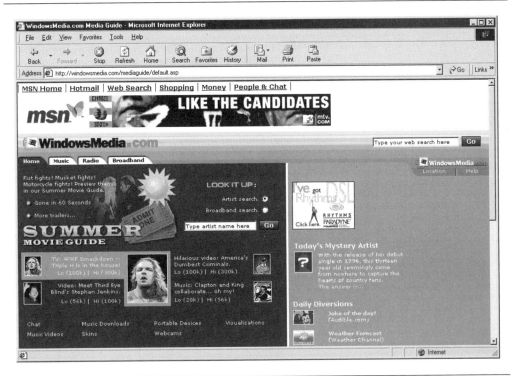

FIGURE 10-4   The Windows Media site offers a selection of online resources

You can also use the Windows Media Radio Tuner to search for stations, and customize a list of preset stations for yourself. Click the Radio Tuner button in the left panel, and the tuner opens in a new browser window. Next, open the Find By list box and select from the categories available. If you select Format, for example, you'll get another list box where you can choose classical, rock, and so on. Pick one of these and you'll get a display like the one shown in Figure 10-5 (I picked the News Radio format).

To connect to a station, double-click its name in the displayed list. To add it to your custom list of preset stations, go to the Presets drop-down list box and choose My Presets. Then click the Add button on the bar between the two tuner windows. You connect to a station in your Presets list by double-clicking on it.

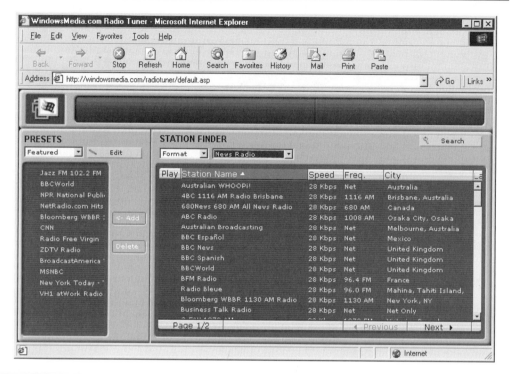

FIGURE 10-5   WMP allows you to customize a list of radio stations for yourself

> **TIP**   *A very good general source of Internet radio stations is NetRadio at **www.netradio.com**. In Music, for example, you'll find everything from mediaeval and baroque to the most current offerings.*

Just as with RealPlayer, you can run WMP by itself without using a browser. Start the player and the Windows multimedia Web site's home page opens in the player window (see the next illustration).

You'll see a row of buttons down the left side of the player. These manage its main functions:

- **Now Playing**   Switches to controls for a music CD, if one is playing in the CD player, or to the display for a downloaded file that is being played.
- **Media Guide**   Connects to the Windows Media Web site.
- **CD Audio**   Allows you to copy music from a CD to your hard disk.
- **Media Library**   Helps you identify and organize the multimedia files stored on your machine.
- **Radio Tuner**   Opens the radio tuner, examined earlier.
- **Portable Device**   Copies files to devices like Palm PCs or micro drives.
- **Skin Chooser**   Allows you to modify the appearance of the player.

Again, the best way to get used to WMP is to spend some time playing with it. It has many more features than we can explore here.

View Video Online

As suggested earlier, trying to use video online with a dial-up connection is an exercise in frustration. Even if you have a fast computer and a fast display card, it won't help, because the bottleneck is the slow speed with which a dial-up connection delivers the video itself. What you'll get is a very small picture of poor quality, which does not move smoothly but instead looks like a series of blurry slides.

If you do have a fast connection, however, you can get quite good results. Some enterprising movie people are even now beginning to offer movies over the Internet. However, watching a movie over the Net means, for most of us, watching it on our computer monitors, in other words on a 15″ or 17″ screen. Even with a DSL or cable service, this is hardly competition for a 27″ TV with a good VCR or a DVD player. Internet video's time may come, but it isn't here yet.

That said, it can still be mild fun with a fast connection. Both RealPlayer and WMP will show you streaming video, which works like streaming audio; the file is played as it's downloaded.

View Online Video with RealPlayer

As an example of what can be viewed, I went to the Real Guide Web site and chose Movies from the list at the left of the window. Then I found a link to a clip from a newly released film and clicked it. The next illustration shows the result as delivered by a 28.8K dial-up connection. As you can see, the picture is very small (it's under the title "The Clip of the Day") and, as you can't see, the motion was quite jerky.

View Online Video with Windows Media Player

To see how WMP handles streaming video, launch the player and click the Media Guide button to go to the Windows Media Web site. There should be a video or two available; click a link and see what you get. I looked under the Trailers link for movie trailers, and found several. Note that if you have less than a 56K connection, you can only play the trailers' soundtracks; WMP will not display the video from the Windows Media site at less than 56K speed.

Download Music and Video

The other way to enjoy music and video is to download them in the form of files and play them back on your computer or portable device. Which device is used depends on the *file format*, which refers to the method used to structure the sound or picture information within the file.

Many different file formats exist for both video and sound. In Windows systems, these formats are identifiable by the filename extension. For example, the file SOMESONG.MP3 has the extension .MP3, which tells both you and Windows that this is an MP3 music file. Similarly, SOMEVIDEO.RM is a RealPlayer video file, indicated by the .RM extension.

You download these files in exactly the same way you download any file. Once it's saved on your machine, you can then play it back with the appropriate player. If it's MP3 format, you can also transfer the file to a portable device so you can take the music with you.

Download and Play MP3 Music with RealJukebox

If you have any interest in Web-based music at all (and probably even if you haven't) you will have heard about something called MP3. But why has it become so important, notorious even, in such a brief time?

Shorn of all but the essentials, MP3 is simply a file format for storing music. What makes it different is that it's *much* better than the other formats at squeezing a lot of music into a very small file. MP3, in fact, provides near-CD quality sound, in files that are small enough to download even over a slow Internet connection.

This apparently inoffensive talent has caused enormous uproar in the music recording industry, for the following reasons. A person can now take any CD and transfer music from it to his hard disk, at the same time turning the music into an MP3 file. This file can then be made available on a Web site for other people to download and play back, or even re-record to their own CDs with a CD-R machine. Because the file is digital, like all computer files, there is no loss of quality in the downloaded or re-recorded copy.

Since music is copyrighted, making recordings of it by any means is technically a violation of copyright laws. But soon after MP3 became available, Web sites like MP3.com, and a great many others, began making vast quantities of music available for free download. This upset the recording industry a great deal, as well as annoying many of the composers and groups who felt they were losing sales, and the lawyers moved in. As of late Spring 2000, lawsuits were flying thick and fast, especially against Web sites that made the music available, and the future of freely downloadable copyrighted music was murky, to say the least.

10

NOTE   *At the time of writing, MP3.com had settled some of its legal problems with the recording companies and was providing music for legal download. However, the Napster site (an exchange site for music files) came under heavy legal assault from battalions of record company lawyers. What the ultimate result will be for Web-distributed music is anybody's guess.*

So that's why MP3 has the high profile it does. There's more to the story, and it's nowhere near over yet, but that's all the space we need to devote to it. The more interesting question is, of course, how you can obtain MP3 music and play it back.

A good place to begin is the MP3.com Web site at (where else?) **www.mp3.com**. On its opening page you'll see a long list of categories. Pick one to go to another page, where you can narrow down among subcategories. Eventually you'll end up on a page that has the songs you want; in the example in Figure 10-6 it's a page for the Celtic group called Slainte.

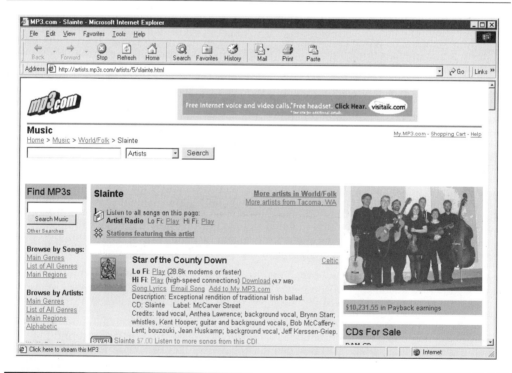

FIGURE 10-6   The MP3 Web site now offers a wide selection of music for legal download

On this page find the song you want to download, and look for the Download link. In IE, left-click on this link to open the Save As dialog. Specify a download folder and filename in the usual manner, and click Save to save the file.

CAUTION *In IE, the Save As dialog may not appear and the browser will begin downloading the file to a temporary folder. You'll see an info box telling you that this is going on. If it happens, click Cancel to stop the download. Then right-click the Download link, and choose Save Target As from the pop-up menu. This will open the Save As dialog, which you can then use normally to save the file.*

To download using Navigator, hold the SHIFT key down and left-click the Download link to open the Save As dialog, then proceed as usual.

TIP *You can also listen to the songs online by choosing the Lo Fi or Hi Fi link, depending on your connection speed.*

To play the song back, open RealJukebox. If a dialog appears that says RealJukebox isn't the default player for some file types, click the Details button to open the Reclaim dialog. To make it the default MP3 player without affecting other file formats, clear all the boxes except the one for MP3 and click OK. When you return to the first dialog, click Yes. RealJukebox is now the default MP3 player. (If it asks this question again the next time you open it, click No to make your changes permanent.)

To play the file, launch RealJukebox. Choose File | Open and navigate to the folder where the file is saved. Select the desired file and click Open to begin playback.

TIP *You can play any media file in its default player simply by double-clicking the filename in a Windows Explorer display.*

As you've likely already guessed, there's a lot more you can do with RealJukebox: You can make up playlists, record music, play CDs, and transfer downloaded music to portable devices, among other things. Experiment and enjoy yourself.

TIP *MP3.com isn't the only source for MP3 music, by a long way. Just a few others are Tunes.com (**www.tunes.com**), Emusic.com (**www.emusic.com**) and Checkout.com (**www.checkout.com/music**). The Real Guide Web site (**www.realguide.real.com**) has links to many more.*

Use MP3 with Other Players

You can, of course, play back MP3 files with several other players. WMP is a possibility and so is Winamp. Try them out and see which you prefer.

NOTE *Other sound file types, such as WAV and MIDI, are still around. For listening to music, though, they have been overwhelmed by the tidal wave of MP3. You'll find them here and there on the Web, and they're useful for sound effects and some other non-musical purposes. But for music, MP3 is the only file in town.*

10

Play Videos with Media Players

The only way to get remotely decent Internet video on your computer, if you have a dial-up connection, is to download it first, then play it back. Even then you can spend hours downloading enough video for a clip a few minutes long, so you'll have to *really* want it. High-speed connections will make this a lot faster, of course.

Video files are commonly of the types called AVI, MPG, MOV, and RM. RM files are RealPlayer files, MOV are Apple QuickTime files, and AVI and MPG files can be played back by Windows Media Player. There's nothing special about downloading them or playing them. Once you've got them onto your computer, open the file in the appropriate player to play it back. If you're not sure which player to use, double-click the filename in Windows Explorer and see which player opens. If you don't have a player for the file type, you'll need to download it from the supplier's Web site.

Another Multimedia Method: WebTV

WebTV is a combination, or *convergence* as the buzzword has it, of television and the Web. You start off with a TV set, then add a small box that is the WebTV Internet receiver, and a keyboard. You also need a specialized WebTV service provider for the signal, which runs through your phone line; Microsoft is one of the few around. It is a possible solution for people who want the Web but don't want to get mixed up with computers, but its functionality is very limited. Since it isn't run through a computer, for example, you can't save anything. If you're interested, however, you can obtain more information at the WebTV Network at **www.webtv.net**.

Where to Find It

Web Site	Address	What's There
Apple	www.apple.com	QuickTime media player
CDH Productions	www.cdhnow.com	Media Wizard all-in-one player
Microsoft Download Center	www.microsoft.com/downloads	Windows Media Player
MP3.com	www.mp3.com	MP3 music downloads
NetRadio	www.netradio.com	Online radio
Real	www.real.com	RealPlayer, RealJukebox
Winamp	www.winamp.com	Winamp MP3 player
Windows Media Center	www.windowsmedia.com	Multimedia resources

Part III

Communicate on the Internet

Chapter 11

Basic E-mail with Outlook, Outlook Express, Eudora, and Netscape Messenger

How To . . .

- Install and set up the Outlook, Outlook Express, Eudora, and Netscape Messenger e-mail programs
- Compose, send, and read e-mail
- Send and read e-mail attachments
- Create, maintain, and set up an address book

In spite of the hoopla surrounding the World Wide Web, the most-used service of the Internet is e-mail. It's the single most important reason that individuals get an Internet connection and, of course, it's an absolutely essential means of communication for business and government.

If you've never used e-mail, rest assured that it's not difficult to do so. The only complicating factor is that there are several major e-mail clients in widespread use.

NOTE *Remember the word "client"? As was said in an earlier chapter, a* client *is a program that gets its input from another program, which is often called a* server. *Thus the Outlook e-mail client (a.k.a. the Outlook e-mail program) receives its input from a* mail *server. I wouldn't bother you with this bit of technical vocabulary, except that the term "client" is used so often that you do need to know about it.*

Which client, if any, you have on your machine at the moment depends on what your ISP or online service has provided for you, or which one you've acquired on your own initiative. Or, if you're in an office, there's probably one you're expected to use. This chapter, naturally, has no way of knowing which client you may have. Consequently, it will deal with four of the major ones: Outlook, Outlook Express, Eudora, and Netscape Messenger.

However, rather than work through all the essentials of Outlook, and then go on to do the same thing with Outlook Express, et cetera, the chapter takes a more task-oriented approach. In the next major section, for example, you'll see how to set up each of the e-mail programs. In the section following that, you'll find out how to compose, send, and read e-mail for each client. We'll go on like that until all the topics have been covered.

So, once you've used the next section to set up whichever client you prefer, you may want to skip directly to the major section that tells you how to do the actual e-mailing. Each of the major sections has a brief introductory part that provides some general information about the topic, and you may find it useful to read this before you go on to the subsection that deals with your specific e-mail client.

One other point needs to be made here. These four programs have many more functions and tools than we can explore in a couple of chapters. Consequently, we'll have to restrict ourselves to the essentials of each of them. To learn about the more advanced subjects, try the programs' Help systems and your own knack for experimentation, or acquire one of the specialized books that deal with the particular client.

Install and Set Up Your E-mail Program

In what follows I'm going to assume that you haven't set up your machine to do any e-mailing, or indeed that it has ever been set up to do it. We're beginning from square one, in other words.

The first thing you need to do is figure out which client or clients may already be on your computer. Here's a pair of clues:

■ If you have installed Communicator, you already have Netscape Messenger.

■ If you have installed Windows, you probably already have Outlook Express.

However, you aren't bound to use either just because they're there. You can leave them installed and ignore them, and go with some other client. An excellent alternative is Eudora, a standalone program that your ISP may have provided in some version, though you can also download the latest Eudora version free from the Web.

If you're on a corporate network, Outlook may have been installed on your machine by the network administration. If you're not sure about this, check with your network administrator. Or, if you already own the Microsoft Office suite or a standalone copy of Outlook, you may want to install the program and try it out. Since Outlook is so widely used, both in the home and in the business environment, we'll examine it first.

 Despite the misleading similarity in names, Outlook is not *the same program as Outlook Express. You have to buy Outlook as a separate program, while Outlook Express is part of the tools set that come with Internet Explorer and is therefore free. Both programs provide similar basic functions, but Outlook is more powerful and has more features than Outlook Express.*

11

Outlook 2000

Microsoft Office (both Office 97 and Office 2000) can be had in several different packages, depending on what programs are included, but all the packages have Outlook. Outlook is not only a mail client, it is also a Personal Information Manager (PIM) with an address book, task list, calendar, and so on. Large books can be written about both Outlook 97 and Outlook 2000, so we'll have to restrict ourselves here to the program's e-mail aspects. The version we'll be working with is Outlook 2000. If you have Outlook 97 there will be some differences, but the basics will be the same.

Install Outlook 2000

Here we assume you're on a computer that has an Internet connection but is not part of a network. Installation of Outlook proceeds as for any other Office program, from the CD. Once it's completed, you'll need to restart the computer, after which you'll see an Outlook icon on the desktop.

Set Up Outlook 2000

Double-click the Outlook icon to launch the program. Outlook's configuration is done through the Outlook 2000 Startup Wizard, which appears when you run the software for the first time. The wizard's first screen is introductory, so click Next. Then go on as in the following steps:

1. The second screen is E-mail Upgrade Options. The list box shows the other e-mail clients installed on your computer. If you were already using one of these you could import (copy) its settings, and the e-mails stored in it, into Outlook. But since we're assuming a from-the-ground-up installation here, select None of the Above. Then click Next.

2. In the next screen you have three options. Since we're assuming the machine isn't on a corporate or workgroup system, the one you want is the first one: Internet Only. Select that option button and click Next. You may get a message telling you that you won't be able to use Exchange Server and asking if you want to continue. You do, so click Yes.

3. In the Your Name screen, type your name into the Display Name text box, just as you want it to appear in the "From" line of an e-mail. Note that this is not your e-mail name as assigned by your ISP, such as cdickens. For example, if you regularly sign your name Charles Dickens, you'd type that, or maybe C. Dickens. Then click Next.

4. In the next screen, type your actual e-mail address into the text box, as in cdickens@someisp.com. Click Next.

5. For the next screen you'll need some information as supplied by your ISP. They should have given you the name of the POP3 or IMAP server (POP3 is more common, so assume it unless specified otherwise) that you use for incoming mail, and the name of the SMTP server for outgoing mail. Often the incoming and outgoing servers have the same name. Select POP3 or IMAP in the list box and type the two server names into their respective text boxes. Then click Next.

6. In the next screen, type your username, as given by your ISP, into the Account Name text box. Type your password into the Password text box, and click OK. If you don't want to type your password in each time you check your e-mail, check the check box labeled Remember Password. (But note that it is *very* inadvisable to do this if other people have access to your machine—unless you don't care who reads your mail.) Then, unless you have been told that your ISP requires SPA security, leave that check box blank and click Next.

7. In the next screen, we assume you connect to the Net over a phone line instead of through a network, so select the top option button and click Next.

8. In the next screen, you can choose to create a new connection to the Net or use an existing one. We'll assume the second option, so select the connection name in the list box and make sure the lower option button is selected. Then click Next.

9. In the last screen, click Finish.

As the installation completes, you are asked if you want to make Outlook your default manager for mail, news, and contacts. If you're just experimenting and haven't made up your mind yet, click No; otherwise, click Yes. You should see the Outlook window, open to the Inbox, as shown in Figure 11-1.

You can do extensive customization of Outlook, but for our purposes it can be left as it is. The one thing you may want to do is remove the "Welcome to Microsoft Outlook 2000" message in the lower section of the window. To do so, look at the upper section of the Inbox window, where you'll see a subject line that also says "Welcome to Microsoft Outlook 2000." Click it to select it, and press the DELETE key. The message vanishes from both sections of the Inbox.

Now that you've set up the program, you can proceed directly to the section entitled, "Compose, Send, and Read E-mail with Outlook 2000."

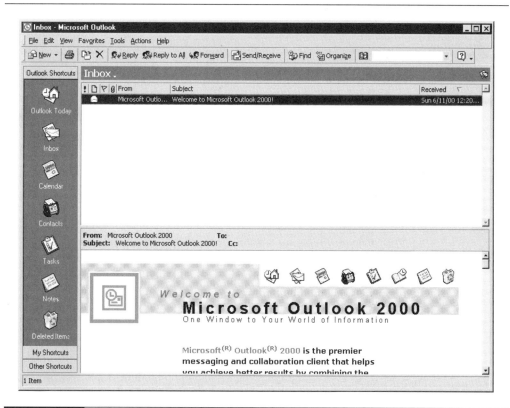

FIGURE 11-1   The Inbox is the default window of a new Outlook 2000 installation

11

Outlook Express

Outlook Express is installed automatically with Windows. It is not, I should repeat here, the same program as Microsoft Outlook, having fewer features. But it is a competent e-mail program in its own right. Outlook Express version 5 installs with Windows 98 Second Edition, and is the one used in this chapter.

Set Up Outlook Express Version 5

Since Outlook Express installs with Windows, all you need do to use it as your e-mail client is set it up. Launch it from its desktop icon or use Start | Programs | Outlook Express to do so. You may see a dialog asking if you want it to be your default mail client. If you're experimenting and haven't made up your mind, click No; otherwise, click Yes. The Outlook Express opening screen appears (see Figure 11-2).

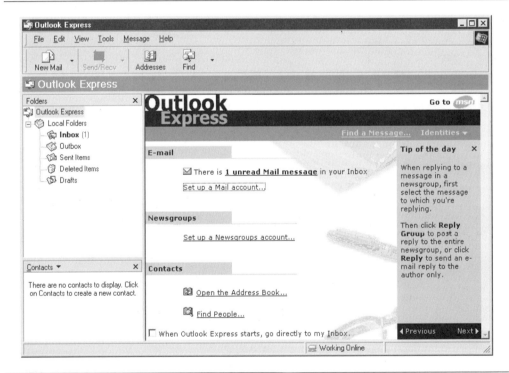

FIGURE 11-2   Outlook Express's main screen gives you tools for both e-mail and reading newsgroups

The Internet Connection Wizard may start automatically when you launch the program. If it doesn't, click the Set Up a Mail Account link from the opening screen and the wizard will open. Then work through the following procedure:

1. In the Your Name screen, type your name into the Display Name text box, just as you want it to appear in the "From" line of an e-mail. Note that this is not your e-mail name as assigned by your ISP, such as cdickens. For example, if you regularly sign your name Charles Dickens, you'd type that, or maybe C. Dickens. Then click Next.

2. In the next screen, you could sign up for a Hotmail account, but we'll assume you already have an account from your ISP. Type your e-mail address into the text box labeled E-mail Address. Click Next.

3. For the next screen you'll need some information as supplied by your ISP. They should have given you the name of the POP3 or IMAP server (POP3 is more common, so assume it unless specified otherwise) for incoming mail, and the name of the SMTP server for outgoing mail. Often the incoming and outgoing servers have the same name. Select POP3 or IMAP in the list box and type the two server names into their respective text boxes. Then click Next.

4. In the next screen, type your username, as given by your ISP, into the Account Name text box. Type your password into the Password text box, and click OK. If you don't want to type your password in each time you check your e-mail, check the box labeled Remember Password. (But note that it is *very* inadvisable to do this if other people have access to your machine—unless you don't care who reads your mail.) Then, unless you have been told that your ISP requires SPA security, leave that check box blank and click Next.

5. Depending on your installation, you may now have to tell Outlook Express whether you access the Net through a dial-up connection or a local area network, and whether you want to create a new connection or use an existing one. Select the applicable responses and click Next. If this information is not requested, you'll go to the final installation screen.

6. In the last screen, click Finish.

Outlook Express is now set up, and you can go on to the section titled "Compose, Send, and Read E-mail with Outlook Express."

Eudora

You may have received a "Light" version of Eudora with your ISP signup package. If so, it's worth experimenting with it, because Eudora is an excellent mail program, one of the best around. If you don't have a copy, you can download a complete version for free from the Eudora site at **www.eudora.com**. It's worth doing, because the complete version is very powerful, and you might want to do this even if you have the Light version. At the time of writing, the current

11

full-download version was Eudora 4.3.1, with a maintenance update to bring it to 4.3.2, which is the one used in this chapter.

Install Eudora

Assuming you'd like to try out Eudora, go to the Eudora Web site and download the installation file; you'll have to register before you can do this. If there is a maintenance update, you might as well download it at this time so you can get the latest version of the software.

Once you've downloaded the installation file to its own folder, double-click it in Windows Explorer or use the Start | Run dialog to start the installation. Accept all the defaults and follow the instructions on the screen until the installation reaches the Installing Eudora Accessories dialog. Clear the check box that will take you to the accessories download page. Depending on whether you want to look at the README file (which gives up-to-date information about the version installed), leave that check box selected or unselected, and click Finish. If you chose to read the README file, it will appear. Have a look at it, and close the window. Eudora is now installed.

If you downloaded a maintenance update program, also called a *patch*, run that program at this point to update your installation. Follow the screen instructions until the update is complete.

Set Up Eudora

Once Eudora is installed, you have to set it up. Launch the program by double-clicking its desktop icon or choosing it from the Start | Programs | Eudora menu. You may get a message asking if you want it to be your default mail program. If you're just experimenting, click No; otherwise, click Yes.

Now you see an introduction box telling you there are three licensing modes. You can use Eudora in sponsored mode, in which case it's free and full-featured, but with this mode you see small ads in one corner. Second, you can pay for it, giving you the full version without the ads. Third, you can use it in a "Light" mode (which is still very powerful) that is free but has no ads.

To keep it simple, we'll accept the default, which is the full-featured, sponsored version. Close the introduction window and the New Account Wizard opens. Then follow this procedure:

1. Select the Create a Brand New Email Account option and click Next.

2. Type your name into the Your Name box as it will appear in your e-mails. Click Next.

3. Type your e-mail address into the E-mail address text box. Click Next.

4. Type your login name (that is, your username as supplied by your ISP) into the Login name text box. Click Next.

5. In the next screen you'll need some information as supplied by your ISP. They should have given you the name of the POP3 or IMAP server (POP3 is more common, so assume it unless specified otherwise) that you'll use for incoming mail. Select POP unless instructed otherwise and type the server name into the Incoming Server text box. Click Next.

6. In the next screen you have to supply the name of your outgoing (SMTP) server as given by your ISP. It may be the same as the incoming server. Leave the authentication check box checked and click Next.

7. In the final screen, click Finish to create the new account, and you'll see the main Eudora window as shown in Figure 11-3.

Eudora is now set up, and you can go on to the section titled "Compose, Send, and Read E-mail with Eudora."

    To change the licensing mode of Eudora, choose Help | Payment & Registration from the menu bar.

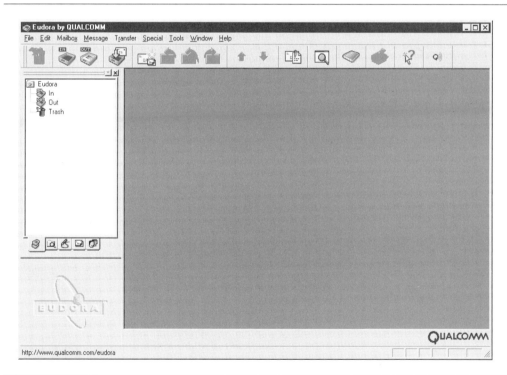

11

FIGURE 11-3   Eudora's main window includes a mailbox display as well as a large window where you compose and read messages

Netscape Messenger

Netscape messenger is the e-mail client that installs automatically with Communicator, so if you've got one, you've got the other. Messenger is a capable e-mail program, though less elaborate than the other three examined here.

Install Messenger

If you have already installed Communicator and you want to try Messenger as an e-mail client, you can go directly to the next section.

   If you haven't installed Communicator, just install it exactly as was described back in Chapter 2. That method skipped over e-mail configuration, but follow it anyway, because in the next section you'll find out how to set up Messenger from a fresh start, even when Communicator is already installed.

Set Up Messenger

To set up Messenger, do this:

1. Launch Communicator and choose Communicator | Messenger from the menu. This opens the Mail and Newsgroup Setup dialog. The first screen is introductory, so click Next.

2. In the next screen, type your name (for example, Charles Dickens) and your e-mail address (for example, cdickens@someisp.com) into the corresponding text boxes. Your ISP should have given you the name of your outgoing (SMTP) mail server, so type it into the bottom box and click Next.

3. In the next screen you type your username, as assigned by your ISP, into the Mail Server User Name text box. Type the name of your incoming mail server, as provided by your ISP, into the second text box. Then select whether it is a POP or IMAP server, depending on what your ISP told you. Click Next.

4. The next screen asks about news server accounts, so we'll ignore it. Click Finish to complete the setup of the e-mail account.

5. You may get a dialog asking if you want to make Messenger your default e-mail application. If you're just experimenting and aren't sure which client you'll end up using, click No. Otherwise, click Yes.

   That completes the setup. When all the dialogs are gone, you see the main Messenger window as shown in Figure 11-4.

   You can now go on to the next section about composing, sending, and reading e-mail.

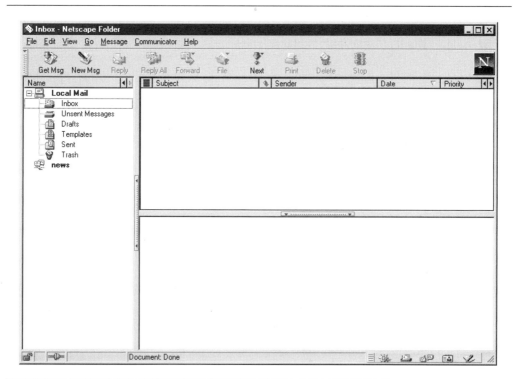

FIGURE 11-4   The Messenger window has three main panels where you manage, read, and compose messages

Compose, Send, and Read E-mail

This, of course, is what e-mail is all about: communication. But it's no different in principle from the traditional, paper-based mail system. You write a letter, address it (maybe from memory, maybe from an address book) and send it. Going the other way, you look in your mailbox, take out the letter, and read it. That, essentially, is all there is to it.

You'll probably want to test your e-mail setup before using it to send messages to other people. To do so without bothering anybody, you can use your own e-mail address as the recipient's address, so as to send the message to yourself. If you can receive it, everything is working as it should.

Compose, Send, and Read E-mail with Outlook 2000

Begin by launching Outlook. As you saw in Figure 11-1, its main controls are in a vertical bar at the left of the window, in the form of icons. You'll also see a button at the top of the bar that says Outlook Shortcuts, and for convenience we'll call this bar the Outlook bar. Two more buttons sit below the Outlook bar, and these are labeled My Shortcuts and Other Shortcuts. When clicked, these switch to the My Shortcuts bar and the Other Shortcuts bar respectively, which give you access to other groups of icons.

For now, remain with the Outlook bar. If you don't see the Inbox window, click the Inbox icon, second from the top, although if you haven't done any customization to the program, it will open to the Inbox automatically. This is where we'll start.

Compose and Send an E-mail Message with Outlook 2000

To compose a message, do this:

1. On the toolbar, click the New button, or chose File | New | Mail Message. A message window opens where you will write the e-mail text, give it a subject, and address it (see the next illustration).

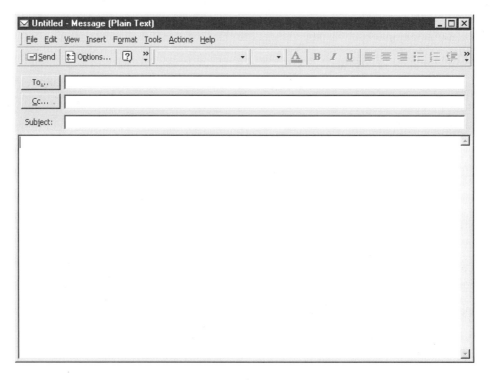

2. The top text box has a To button beside it. This is the To box, but don't click the To button at this point. That would open the Contacts (address) book, but we're assuming you have no contacts stored on your machine yet. (Using the address book will be covered later.) At this point, simply click in the To box to put the insertion point there, and type the e-mail address of the recipient.

3. Press the TAB key twice or click in the Subject box to place the insertion point there. Then type the subject of your e-mail, so the recipient will have an idea of what the message is about.

4. Press the TAB key once or click in the large box to place the insertion point there. This is where you type the text of your message. Do so, and when you're finished, you're ready to send it.

5. You have to be connected, obviously, in order to send the e-mail (you don't have to be connected to compose it, of course). Assuming you are, click the Send button. This closes the message composition window and transfers the message to the Outbox.

6. Now click the Send/Receive button on the Outlook toolbar. An info box appears informing you that the message is being sent. The message is also copied from the Outbox to the Sent Items folder so that you'll have your own copy of it. At the same time, Outlook checks for any incoming mail, as discussed a bit later.

> **NOTE** *If you're on a network, Outlook may send the message automatically from the Outbox, so you won't need to use the Send/Receive button.*

If you want to see what's in your Outbox, refer to the Outlook bar (see Figure 11-1). At the bottom of the bar is a button labeled My Shortcuts. Click it to reveal the My Shortcuts bar with another set of icons, including an Outbox icon. Click this to view its contents.

To return to the Inbox, go to the top of the My Shortcuts bar and find the button labeled Outlook Shortcuts. Click it to redisplay the Outlook bar. Then click the Inbox icon, if necessary, to open the Inbox display again.

That's basic e-mail. Nothing to it, is there?

> **NOTE** *Of course, you probably have a collection of people to whom you regularly send e-mail, and it's inefficient to type their addresses into the To box every time you want to communicate with them. Outlook, like all the other e-mail clients discussed in this chapter, has an address book where you can store such addresses and use them with a click of the mouse. How you use the various address books is examined later in this chapter, in the section titled "Create, Maintain, and Back Up an Address Book."*

Here are two other essential sending options you may need from time to time:

■ To send the message to several people at once, type all their e-mail addresses into the To text box, separating the addresses with semicolons.

■ To send a copy of a message to someone besides the chief recipient, type his/her address into the Cc text box. If there's more than one address, separate them with semicolons.

■ To send a blind copy of a message to someone other than the chief recipient, choose View | Bcc Field to make the Bcc text box appear. (A *blind copy* means that the person in the To field is not notified that a copy was sent to someone else.) Type the person's address into the text box. If there's more than one address, separate them with semicolons.

Before you send any e-mail, always, always, *always* check the recipient's address in the To box. It is easy, with a powerful e-mail program, to send a message to a person or persons who weren't meant to get it. At best, this is mildly embarrassing. At worst, and if the message says the wrong things, it can lead to job loss, libel suits, divorce, disinheritance, and other such misfortunes. This may sound like exaggeration, but it's not.

To see what messages you've sent, go to the My Shortcuts bar and click the Sent Items icon. To see if there are any items waiting to be sent but not yet sent, go to the My Shortcuts bar and click the Outbox icon.

Check and Read Mail with Outlook 2000

To check for incoming mail, simply click the Send/Receive button. (You may be asked for your e-mail password.) If you have new mail, an entry for each message appears in the upper section of your Inbox. An open-envelope icon denotes that the message has been read; a closed one, that it hasn't. You can read the message by clicking on its entry in the upper section, in which case its text appears in the lower section. Alternatively, double-click on the entry and the text appears in its own window.

To delete a message, select it and press the DELETE key. You'll note a Deleted Items icon in the Outlook bar; the number in parentheses indicates how many items it contains. Click the icon to open the Deleted items window and view them. To delete an item permanently, select it in the Deleted Items list and press the DELETE key. A confirmation dialog appears. Click Yes to delete the item for good.

Reply To and Forward Messages with Outlook 2000

Often you will want to reply to an incoming message. You could compose a new message from scratch but there's a simpler way. Do this:

1. In the Inbox, select the message you want to reply to. Click Reply on the toolbar to open a new message window.

2. The text of the sender's message appears in the new message body, and you'll see that the new message is addressed to the original sender, now the recipient. Change the subject line if necessary and add Ccs or Bccs if you want, and then type the text of your reply. You can leave the sender's text intact, delete bits of it, or remove it entirely.

3. When finished, click the Send button to put the message in the Outbox, and if necessary click Send/Receive from the toolbar to transmit the message (remember, if you're on a network the message may get sent from the Outbox automatically).

To reply to all the recipients listed in the To, Bcc, and Cc boxes, click the Reply to All button instead of Reply.

Forwarding a message means sending it on to a third party. Select the message to be forwarded and click the Forward button. Fill in the address of the forwardee, add any text desired to the body of the message, and send it as you just learned.

Compose, Send, and Read E-mail with Outlook Express

Begin by launching Outlook Express. The main e-mail tools are up on the menu bar and toolbar. There are also Folder and Contacts windows at the left of the main window. These can be closed by clicking the X icons, but we'll leave them open.

Compose and Send an E-mail Message with Outlook Express

Begin by choosing File | New | Mail Message, or click the New Mail button on the toolbar. A New Message window opens, as shown in the next illustration.

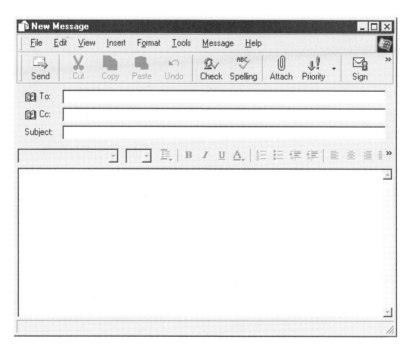

To create the message, do this:

1. The top text box has a To button beside it, but don't click the button at this point. That would open the Contacts (address) book, but we're assuming you have no contacts stored on your machine yet. (Using the address book will be covered later.) For now, simply click in the To box to put the insertion point there, and type the e-mail address of the recipient.

2. Press the TAB key twice or click in the Subject box to place the insertion point there. Then type the subject of your e-mail, so the recipient will have an idea of what the message is about.

3. Press the TAB key once or click in the large box to place the insertion point there. This is where you type the text of your message. Do so, and when you're finished, you're ready to send it.

4. Assuming you're connected, click the Send button. This closes the message composition window and immediately sends the message to the recipient. At the same time a copy is placed in the Sent Items folder so that you'll have your own copy. If you're not connected, the message is put in the Outbox for later transmission.

Here are three other sending options you may need from time to time:

- To send the message to several people at once, type all their e-mail addresses into the To text box, separating them with semicolons.

- To send a copy of a message to someone besides the chief recipient, type his/her address into the Cc text box. If there's more than one, separate them with semicolons.

- To send a blind copy of a message to someone other than the chief recipient, choose View | All Headers to make the Bcc text box appear. (A blind copy means that the person in the To box is not notified that a copy was sent to someone else.) Type the person's address into the text box. If there is more than one address, separate them with semicolons.

To see what messages you've sent out, click the Sent Items icon in the Folders window. To see if there are any items waiting to be sent, click the Outbox icon in the Folders window.

Creating an address book, so you won't have to type commonly used e-mail addresses, is covered in a later section of this chapter.

Check and Read Mail with Outlook Express

To check for incoming mail, click the Send/Recv button on the toolbar. (You may be asked for your e-mail password.) If you have new mail, an entry for it appears in the upper section of your Inbox. An open-envelope icon denotes that the message has been read; a closed one, that it hasn't.

You can read it by clicking on its entry in the upper section, in which case its text appears in the lower section. Alternatively, double-click on the entry and the text appears in its own window.

To delete a message, click it and press the DELETE key. You'll see a Deleted Items icon in the Folders window, and you can view a list of deleted items by clicking this icon. To delete an item permanently, select it in this Deleted Items list and press the DELETE key. A confirmation dialog appears. Click Yes to delete the item for good.

Reply To and Forward Messages with Outlook Express

You can compose a new message to reply to an incoming one, but there's a better way. Do this:

1. In the upper section of the Inbox, select the message you want to reply to. Click Reply on the toolbar to open the message window.

2. The text of the sender's message appears in the new message body, and you'll see that the new message is addressed to the original sender, now the recipient. Change the subject line if necessary, add Ccs or Bccs if you want, and then type the text of your reply. You can leave the sender's text intact, delete bits of it, or remove it entirely, just as you prefer.

3. When finished, click the Send button to send the reply back to the original sender.

To reply to all the recipients listed in the To, Bcc, and Cc boxes, click the Reply to All button instead of Reply.

Forwarding a message means sending it on to a third party. Select the message to be forwarded and click the Forward button. Fill in the address of the forwardee, add any text desired to the body of the message, and send it as just described.

Compose, Send, and Read E-mail with Eudora

Begin by launching Eudora. The large main window is where you will compose and read messages. The upper window at its left can be switched to display mailboxes and other tools (see Figure 11-3 for the Eudora display). In sponsored mode, the lower window to the main window's left is where the ads appear. The e-mail controls are on the menus and the toolbars across the top of the Eudora window.

If you can't see the mailboxes in the upper-left window (there should be an In, an Out, and a Trash) click the leftmost tab at the bottom of that window.

Compose and Send an E-mail Message with Eudora

To create a new message, choose Message | New Message or click the New Message button on the toolbar (the envelope with the star on it). The message composition window opens as shown in Figure 11-5. It has two sections, the upper one for the addressing information and the lower for the message itself. Note that your name is already in the From line.

11

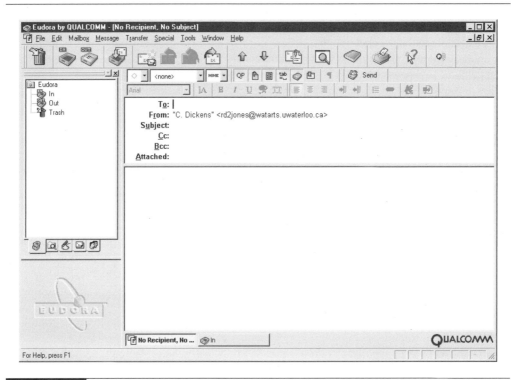

FIGURE 11-5   The Eudora main screen has an upper window for addresses and a lower one for the message

Type the recipient's name into the To line; if there is more than one, separate the addresses with semicolons. You can copy the message to other people using the Cc line and the Bcc line; again, if there is more than one, separate the addresses with semicolons. Type a subject into the Subject line. You can move among the lines with the TAB key, or just click in them.

Tab down to or click in the lower window, and type your message there. When you've finished, click the Send button and the message goes on its way. Eudora, as you've just seen, is very streamlined and easy to use.

Creating a Eudora address book, so that you won't have to type commonly used e-mail addresses, is covered in a later section of this chapter.

Check and Read Mail with Eudora

To begin, go to the upper-left window of the main Eudora display and click the In icon. This will open the incoming mail display in the main window. This In window has an upper and a lower section. The upper section shows a one-line entry for all messages received to date, and the lower shows the content of whatever message has been selected in the upper section.

To check your mail, choose File | Check Mail or click the Check Mail button on the toolbar (the envelope with an arrow pointing into a box). You may be asked for your e-mail password, whereupon Eudora will retrieve your mail from the server and display an entry for it in the upper section of the In window. To view the content, click the message line and the text appears in the lower window. You can also use the entire In window to display a message by double-clicking its entry. To close this message, click the X button in its upper-right corner.

As a general method, you close any window in the Eudora display by clicking the X button in its top-right corner. To close the In window, for example, click the X button as just described. If you happen to lose the display of mailbox icons, choose Tools | Mailboxes to redisplay it.

To delete a message, click its entry in the upper section of the In window and press the DELETE key. This sends it to the Trash. You'll see a Trash icon in the upper-left window of the Eudora display (it's shown along with the mailbox icons) and you can view a list of deleted items by double-clicking this icon. To delete an item permanently, select it in the Trash display and press the DELETE key.

Reply To and Forward Messages with Eudora

To reply to a received message without creating a brand new message, do this:

1. Display the In window by double-clicking its icon in the mailboxes window. From the upper section, select the message you want to reply to. Click the Reply button on the toolbar (the envelope with the single left-pointing arrow) or choose Message | Reply.

2. The message composition window appears with the text of the original sender's message present and with the original sender's address filled in as the recipient. Change the subject line if necessary, add Ccs or Bccs if you want, and then type the text of your reply. You can leave the sender's text intact, delete bits of it, or remove it entirely, just as you prefer.

3. When finished, click the Send button to send the reply back to the original sender.

To reply to all the recipients listed in the To and Cc boxes, click the Reply to All button (the envelope with the two left-pointing arrows) or choose Message | Reply to All.

All windows and messages currently open in Eudora are represented by labeled buttons along the bottom margin of the large message window. Click a button to display the corresponding item.

Forwarding a message means sending it on to a third party. Select the message to be forwarded and click the Forward button on the toolbar (the envelope with the right-pointing arrow) or choose Message | Forward. Fill in the address of the forwardee, add any text desired to the body of the message, and send it as just described.

11

With Eudora you can also redirect e-mails. The difference between forwarding and redirecting is this: A forwarded e-mail has the e-mail address of the forwarding person in the From line. A redirected e-mail has the e-mail address of the *original sender* (not the forwarder) in the From line. However, it also says "by way of" so you can see who redirected it.

Compose, Send, and Read E-mail with Netscape Messenger

Begin by launching Communicator. Then choose Communicator | Messenger to open the e-mail client. When it opens, it defaults to displaying the contents of the Inbox. The main e-mail tools are up on the Messenger menu bar and toolbar. There is also a left-hand panel where icons for the various e-mail storage locations, such as the Inbox and Trash, are displayed (see Figure 11-4 earlier in the chapter).

Compose and Send an E-mail Message with Messenger

Begin by choosing File | New | Message, or click the New Msg button on the toolbar. A Composition window opens as shown in the next illustration.

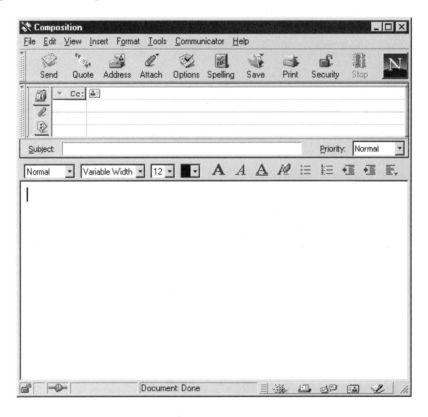

To create the message, do this:

1. The top section of the Composition window has three buttons at its left edge. The top button is the Address Message button. Click it, and a button appears at its right. This button should be labeled To. If it isn't, click the button and choose To from the pop-up menu that appears.

2. When the To button is displayed, this line is the recipient's address line. Click in the text line to the right of the To button to put the insertion point there. Type the recipient's e-mail address.

3. Click in the Subject text box to place the insertion point there. Then type the subject of your e-mail, so the recipient will have an idea of what the message is about.

4. Press the TAB key once, or click in the large box, to place the insertion point there. This is where you type the text of your message. Do so, and when you're finished, you're ready to send it.

5. Assuming you're connected, click the Send button. This closes the message composition window and immediately sends the message to the recipient. At the same time a copy is placed in the Sent Items folder so that you'll have your own copy.

Here are three other sending options you may need from time to time:

- To send the message to several people at once, type all their e-mail addresses into the To text box, separating them with commas.

- To send a copy of a message to someone besides the chief recipient, click the To button and choose Cc from the pop-up menu. The button will now be labeled Cc. Type the copy-recipient's address into the text line next to the button. If there's more than one address, separate them with commas.

- To send a blind copy of a message to someone other than the chief recipient, click the To button and choose Bcc from the pop-up menu. The button will now be labeled Bcc. Type the copy-recipient's address into the text line next to it. If there's more than one address, separate them with commas.

To see what messages you've sent, click the Sent Items icon in the left-hand window of the Messenger display. To see if there are any items waiting to be sent, click the Unsent icon in the left-hand window.

Creating an address book, so that you won't have to type commonly used e-mail addresses, is covered in a later section of this chapter.

Check and Read Mail with Messenger

To check for incoming mail, simply click the Get Msg button on the toolbar. (You may be asked for your e-mail password before you can connect.) If you have new mail, an entry for it appears in

11

the upper section of your Inbox. An icon of an envelope with an arrow denotes that the message has not yet been read; an envelope without an arrow, that it has. You can read it by clicking on its entry in the upper section, in which case its text appears in the lower section. Alternatively, double-click on the entry and the text appears in its own window.

To delete a message, click it and press the DELETE key. You'll see a Trash icon in the left-hand window of the Messenger display, and you can view a list of deleted items by clicking this icon. To delete an item permanently, select it in the Deleted Items window and press the DELETE key.

Reply To and Forward Messages with Messenger

To reply to a received message without creating a brand new message, do this:

1. In the upper section of the Inbox, select the message you want to reply to. Click Reply from the toolbar to open the Composition window.

2. The text of the sender's message is already there, with the sender's address filled in as the recipient. There is a second To button under the first, which you can use for Ccs or Bccs if you want. Change the subject line if necessary, and then type the text of your reply. You can leave the sender's text intact, delete bits of it, or remove it entirely, just as you prefer.

3. When finished, click the Send button to send the reply back to the original sender.

To reply to all the recipients listed in the To, Bcc, and Cc lines, click the Reply All button instead of Reply.

Forwarding a message means sending it on to a third party. Messenger handles forwarding differently from the other three clients, however. With them, when you forward a message, it is treated as a normal e-mail with the original message quoted in the body of the forwarded one. With Messenger, the original message is turned into an attachment and sent with the forwarding message.

If you don't want Messenger to do this, and want it to behave like the other e-mail clients, do this:

1. Choose Edit | Preferences.

2. In the Preferences window, choose Mail & Newsgroups | Messages.

3. In the Messages window, locate the list box labeled By Default, Forward Messages. Click the list box's arrow button and change the As Attachment entry to Quoted.

4. Then click OK to establish this as the default forwarding behavior.

To forward a message, whichever forwarding mode you use, first select the message and then click the Forward button. Fill in the address of the forwardee, add any text desired to the body of the message, and send it as described earlier.

Send and Read Attachments

Attachments are exactly what they sound like: something that is attached to the e-mail message and goes along for the ride when you send it. At the other end, the recipient can open the attachment and see what's inside it.

Attachments are always files, but they can be any kind of file: word processor documents, archive files, image files, text files, programs, and so on. They are widely used because they allow you to send information, such as documents with complex formatting, that can't be put into the e-mail message itself.

The trick with attachments isn't sending them, because doing that is quite simple. The potential problem is the recipient's ability to open the file and look at its contents. For example, if the attachment you send is a document prepared in Microsoft Word 2000, the recipient must have installed some program that can open a Word 2000 file. If the recipient only has WordPerfect 7, he or she probably won't be able to read what you've sent.

In other areas the problem can be less acute. If you send someone an image taken from the Web, for example, his browser will open it without difficulty. And any plain text file can be read on just about any computer. However, sometimes it's a good idea to check with the recipient before you send an attachment, to make sure he or she has software that's compatible with it.

A common technique used with attachments is to compress them into ZIP files or ZIP archives before sending them. This will be covered in Chapter 12.

CAUTION *When you attempt to open a received attachment, you will likely get a security dialog warning that the attachment file may contain viruses. The dialog gives you two options for dealing with this: either go ahead and open the file, or save it to disk. If you are absolutely sure that the attachment is safe, open it by choosing the Open It option and clicking OK. If you have any doubts at all about its safety (for example, if it comes from somebody you've never heard of), choose the Save It to Disk option and click OK. Then check the attachment with a virus-checking program before opening it. The details of such checks are examined in Chapter 18.*

Send and Read Attachments with Outlook 2000

To do this, carry out the following steps:

1. Create a new message, just as you would normally. It can have text in the body and Ccs and Bccs as required.

11

2. Make sure the insertion point is in the body of the message.

3. Choose Insert | File from the message window's menu bar. An Insert File dialog appears (see the next illustration).

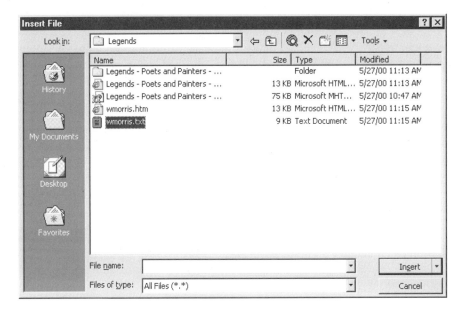

4. Use the dialog to locate and select the file to be attached. To attach multiple files from the same folder, select all the required ones (if they're in different folders you'll have to repeat this procedure instead). Then click the Insert button. The dialog closes and you see an icon or icons in the message window labeled with the filename(s) of the attachment(s).

5. Click Send to close the message box, then Send/Receive, if necessary, to send both message and attachment.

When you receive an attachment, you'll know it because there will be a paperclip icon beside the message entry in the upper Inbox pane. Furthermore, when you open the message to read it, an icon denoting the attachment file will appear in the message body. To read the attachment, double-click it.

You may get a security warning when you do this. For information about what to do, refer to the Caution at the end of the previous section, "Send and Read Attachments."

Send and Read Attachments with Outlook Express

Sending and reading attachments in Outlook Express is done the same way as it is in Outlook, with some minor variations. Do this:

1. Create a new message, just as you would normally. It can have text in the body and Ccs and Bccs as required.

2. Make sure the insertion point is in the body of the message.

3. Choose Insert | File Attachment from the message window's menu bar. An Insert Attachment dialog appears.

4. Use the dialog to locate and select the file to be attached. To attach multiple files from the same folder, select all the required ones (if they're in different folders you'll have to repeat this procedure instead). Then click the Attach button. The dialog closes and a small text box appears above the message window, containing the filename(s) of the attachment(s).

5. Click Send to close the message window and send both the message and its attachment.

When you receive an attachment, you'll know it because there will be a small paperclip icon beside the message entry in the upper Inbox pane. Click once on the message entry to display its content in the lower pane, and you'll see a large paperclip icon appear on the top margin of the lower pane. To open the attachment, click the paperclip. A small pop-up menu appears, giving the filename and a Save Attachments entry. To open the attachment, choose the filename. To save it in a folder other than the e-mail folder, choose Save Attachments.

You may get a security warning when you attempt to open the attachment. For information about what to do, refer to the Caution at the end of the introduction to the "Send and Read Attachments" section, earlier in this chapter.

Send and Read Attachments with Eudora

Sending and reading attachments is easy in Eudora. Do this:

1. Create a new message, just as you would normally. It can have text in the body and Ccs and Bccs as required.

2. Choose Message | Attach or click the Attach File button (the one with the paperclip). An Attach File dialog appears.

3. Usc the dialog to locate and select the file to be attached. To attach multiple files from the same folder, select all the required ones (if they're in different folders you'll have to repeat this procedure instead). Then click the Open button. The dialog closes and you'll see the name(s) of the desired file(s) in the Attached line.

4. Click Send to send both the message and its attachment.

When you receive an attachment, you'll know it because there will be a small icon of a paperclip and sheet of paper next to the message entry in the In window. Click the entry to make the message text appear in the lower section, and you'll see a large icon for the attachment below the message body. To open the attachment, double-click this icon.

11

You may get a security warning when you attempt to open the attachment. For information about what to do, refer to the Caution at the end of the introduction to the "Send and Read Attachments" section, earlier in this chapter.

Send and Read Attachments with Netscape Messenger

To send and read attachments with Messenger, do this:

1. Create a new message, just as you would normally. It can have text in the body and Ccs and Bccs as required.

2. Choose File | Attach or click the Attach button, then choose File from the pop-up menu. An Enter File to Attach dialog appears.

3. Use the dialog to locate and select the file to be attached. To attach multiple files from the same folder, select all the required ones (if they're in different folders you'll have to repeat this procedure instead). Then click the Open button. The dialog closes.

4. In the upper section of the Composition window, an Attach Files button (a red paperclip on a white rectangle) pops up. The name(s) of the attached file(s) appears in the section's top line. To redisplay the To line if necessary, click the Address Message button, which is immediately above the Attach Files button.

5. Click Send to send both the message and its attachment.

When you receive an attachment, you'll know it because there will be a small green icon in the message entry in the In window. Click the entry to make the message text appear in the lower section, and you'll see a rectangle denoting the attachment, below the message body. To open the attachment, click the filename link within the rectangle.

You may get a security warning when you attempt to open the attachment. For information about what to do, refer to the Caution at the end of the introduction to the "Send and Read Attachments" section, earlier in the chapter.

Create, Maintain, and Back Up an Address Book

Just about everybody has a contact list or address list of people with whom they regularly communicate, and e-mail users are no exception. Each of the four programs discussed in this chapter have such a tool, and we'll examine them in turn in the following sections.

Outlook 2000

Outlook refers to its address book as a Contacts list. It's easy to create such a list, add to it, and maintain it. Backing up is more complex, but is an essential task.

Create and Maintain a Contacts List in Outlook 2000

To start adding people to your Contacts list, launch Outlook and click the Contacts icon in the Outlook Express bar. This opens the Contacts window, but if this is a new installation, the window will, of course, be empty. To add a contact to the list, choose File | New | Contact or click the New button. The General sheet of the Contact dialog opens (see the next illustration). You will fill in one of these for each person you add to your Contacts list.

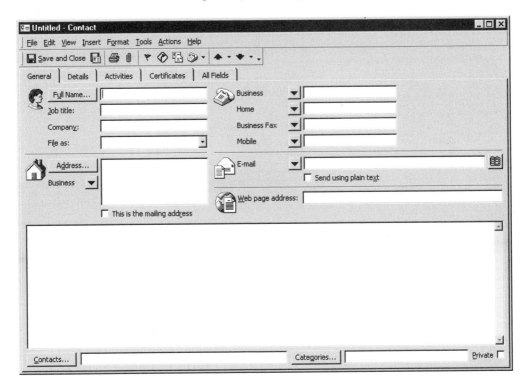

The form is pretty obvious. Fill in the information for each text box, or for as many of them as you see fit. The only required data is the Full Name, although you'll require the e-mail address, naturally, if you want quick addressing for your messages. You can give the contact as many as three e-mail addresses, but for our examination we'll stick to one.

Once you've filled in the name and e-mail, and anything else relevant, click the Save and Close button. The contact's name will now be visible in the Contacts list.

If you want to delete a contact, click on the line with the Full Name, then press the DELETE key. The entry vanishes from the Contacts list.

To change the contact information, display the Contacts list and double-click the desired entry. The General sheet of the Contacts window appears, displaying the information for that person. Make the desired changes and click the Save and Close button.

Suppose now that you want to send an e-mail to that person. Open the Inbox and click the New button to open a new message window. Click the To button and a Select Names dialog opens as in the next illustration.

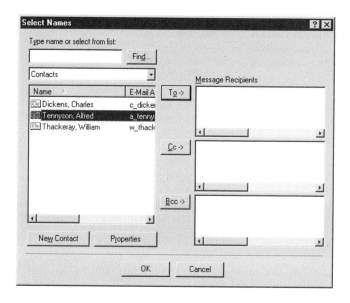

Select the name of the desired recipient or recipients, and click the To button to copy the address (or their addresses) into the topmost Message Recipient box. You can also select other recipients to go into the To, Cc, or Bcc boxes and move them there with the corresponding buttons.

When you've done this, click OK. The dialog vanishes and the addresses have been inserted into the message window in their proper places. Now you can compose the rest of the message and send it.

Back Up Your Outlook 2000 Contacts List

It can be extremely awkward to lose your address book through computer failure or accidental erasure. Using the Import/Export tool, you can save it in a file that you can later restore in case of disaster.

1. Open Outlook and choose File | Import and Export. The Import and Export Wizard opens.

2. From the list box, choose Export to a File and click Next.

3. In the next screen you see the Create a File of Type list box. Select Comma Separated Values (Windows) and click Next.

 If the Import/Export tool isn't installed, you'll be prompted to insert the Office CD and do so. When the installation is finished, you can proceed with the wizard.

4. In the next window you select the folder to export from. Choose Contacts and click Next.

5. In the next window use the text box labeled Save Exported File As to give the file a name, such as Contact Backup. Then use the Browse button to select a destination folder, preferably on some removable backup media such as a floppy. Click Next.

6. Now you see a confirmation window. Click Finish to export the file. It will be saved as a file with a .CSV extension.

Using the backup is essentially reversing the procedure. Let's suppose you accidentally erased part of the content of your Contacts list. Here's how to get it back:

1. Launch Outlook and choose File | Import and Export. From the list box, select Import From Another Program or File. Click Next.

2. In the next window's list box, select Comma Separated Values (Windows). The principle here is that you use the same kind of file for import that you did for export. Click Next.

3. In the next dialog, use the Browse button to locate the backup file. To be sure you get all your backed-up contacts restored, leave the Allow Duplicates to Be Created button selected. You can edit the list later to remove unwanted duplicates, if necessary. Click Next.

4. In the next window, select Contacts from the list and click Next.

5. The next window shows a confirmation dialog. Click Finish to do the import. If you now switch to your Contacts list you should see the restored entries.

Outlook Express

Like its big brother Outlook, Outlook Express lets you use an address book to streamline your e-mail work. The next two sections tell you how to create one and back it up.

Create and Maintain an Address Book in Outlook Express

Begin by clicking the Addresses button on the toolbar, to open the Address Book window. Then, from the Address Book window's menu bar, choose New | New Contact. This opens a Properties window for the new contact, as in the next illustration.

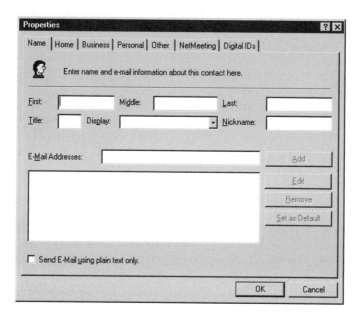

Type at least the first name, last name, and e-mail address of the contact into the respective text boxes. When you're finished, click Add, then OK. The Properties dialog vanishes and you'll see that the contact has been added to your address book. Add any other contacts you wish, then close the address book.

To delete a contact, open the address book, select the desired contact, and click the Delete button on the toolbar.

To change the information for a contact, open the address book, then double-click the contact entry to open his/her Properties sheet. Click the Name tab to modify the name and e-mail entries, or the other tabs to add or change other kinds of information about the contact.

To use the address book for e-mail, click New Mail from the Outlook Express toolbar to open a New Message window. Click the To button and the Select Recipients dialog opens (see the next illustration).

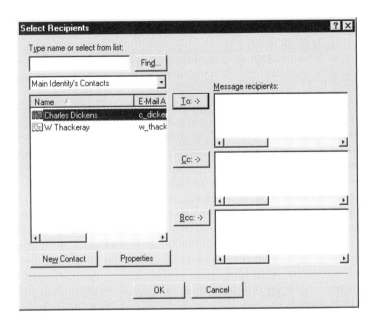

Select the name of the desired recipient or recipients, then click the To button to copy the address (or their addresses) into the topmost Message Recipients box. You can also select other recipients for the To, Cc, or Bcc boxes and move them there with the corresponding buttons.

When you've done this, click OK. The dialog vanishes and the addresses are inserted into the message window in their proper places. Now you can compose the rest of the message and send it.

Back Up Your Outlook Express Address Book

To make a backup copy of your address book, open Outlook Express and click the Address button on the toolbar. Then, in the Address Book dialog, choose File | Export | Address Book (WAB). This opens the dialog labeled Select Address Book File to Export To.

Don't use the File | Export choice on the menu bar of Outlook Express itself. This creates a CSV file format, which you don't want. Also, if Outlook 2000 is installed, the Outlook Express import and export tools choices will be grayed out and unavailable. To use them, you'll have to uninstall Outlook 2000.

This dialog is just an ordinary Save As dialog. Type a name for the backup file and specify a folder for it in the Save In box, and then click Save. The file is saved as a Windows Address Book file, with a .WAB filename extension.

To restore the address book from the backup, first open the address book by clicking Addresses on the Outlook Express toolbar. Choose File | Import | Address Book (WAB) to open the Select Address Book File to Import From dialog. Navigate to the desired file and select it. Then click Open to restore the address book.

Eudora

Eudora's address book is less elaborate than the ones provided by Outlook and Outlook Express, since it is specialized for e-mail rather than being a general-purpose contact manager. But it is very capable at what it does.

Create and Maintain an Address Book in Eudora

Begin by launching Eudora, then click the blue Address Book button or choose Tools | Address Book to open the address book (see Figure 11-6). If the Address Book window isn't visible, click the Address Book tab to display it.

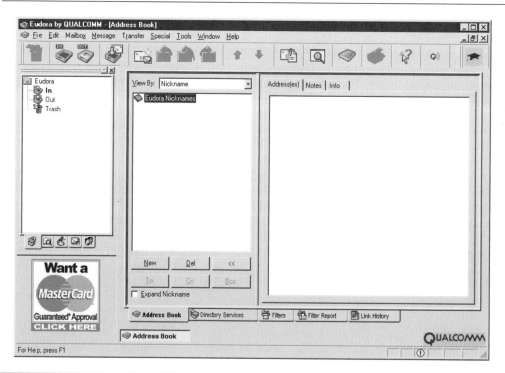

FIGURE 11-6 The Eudora address book provides tools for keeping a contact list

To create a new e-mail contact, do this:

1. Click the New button. A small New Nickname dialog appears, which is a bit misleading because you don't use a real nickname here but the person's actual name, such as C. Dickens (or Dickens, C. if you want the list to be sorted by surname). So, in the text box labeled What Do You Wish to Call It, type the actual name of the contact.

2. Check the check box labeled Put It On the Recipient List and click OK.

3. The nickname dialog disappears and you're back at the Address Book window. You'll now see the contact's name in its left panel, under the Eudora Nicknames icon.

4. Look at the large right-hand panel. It should be displaying the Address(es) sheet; if it isn't, click the Address(es) sheet tab. Click on the sheet to place the insertion point there, and type the e-mail address.

5. Close the Address Book by clicking the X button at its upper-right corner (don't click the X button above that one, or you'll close Eudora). When asked if you want to save changes to the Address Book, click Yes.

> **TIP** *If you want to add the contact's postal address and phone numbers to the record, click the Info tab and fill in the information form.*

The contact is now in the Address Book. To create a message for this person and address it automatically, choose Message | New Message To. A submenu will appear, listing all the contacts you've put in the address book. If the contact isn't on the submenu, you probably forgot to select the Put It On the Recipient List check box in the address book.

Assuming it is, click the one you want and the composition window opens with a blank e-mail and the recipient's name already inserted.

To place addresses in the Cc and Bcc lines, click in the line to place the insertion point there. Then choose Edit | Insert Recipient and a submenu of the address book appears. Click the desired contact and the e-mail address is inserted into the line.

To delete a contact, open the address book, select the contact, and click the Del button. Note that you don't get a confirmation dialog; the entry is simple deleted.

> **TIP** *In the address book, clicking the To, Cc, and Bcc buttons will place the selected contact's address in the appropriate line of the currently displayed message. If there is no current message, a new one will be created when you click one of these buttons. Also, when you type within any of these lines, a list of contacts matching your address book and people that you have recently sent mail to automatically appears.*

Back Up Your Eudora Address Book

The address information is stored in two files, NNDBASE.TOC and NNDBASE.TXT. You will find them in the main Eudora folder, which in a default installation will be C:\Program Files\Qualcomm\Eudora. Copy these files to a safe place as a backup. If you need to restore your address book from them, simply copy them back to the main Eudora folder. If you make additional

11

address books, you must also back up the folder C:\Program Files\Qualcomm\Eudora\Nickname to secure them.

Netscape Messenger

Messenger's address book is a good basic one with all the tools you're likely to need in everyday use. Like the others, you can use it not only for e-mail addresses but also for postal addresses and phone numbers.

Create and Maintain an Address Book in Messenger

Begin by launching Communicator, then choose Communicator | Address Book to open the address book (see the next illustration). If the Address Book window isn't visible, click the Address Book tab to display it. Then make sure the Personal Address Book entry is selected in the left window.

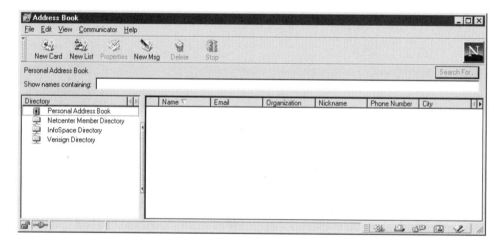

Click the New Card button to open the New Card dialog. If the Name sheet isn't visible, click the Name tab to display it. Then fill in the contact's name and e-mail address, and any other appropriate information. When you're finished, click OK. The dialog vanishes and you'll see that the contact has been added to your address book. Add any other contacts you wish, then close the address book. Note that the names are sorted alphabetically, not by surname.

To delete a contact, open the address book, select the desired contact, and press the DELETE key.

To change the information for a contact, open the address book, then double-click the contact entry to open his/her card. Change the information as needed, then click OK to update the address book.

To use the address book with e-mail, first click New Msg to open the Composition window. To specify the recipient's address, click Addresses to open the Select Addresses dialog (see the next illustration).

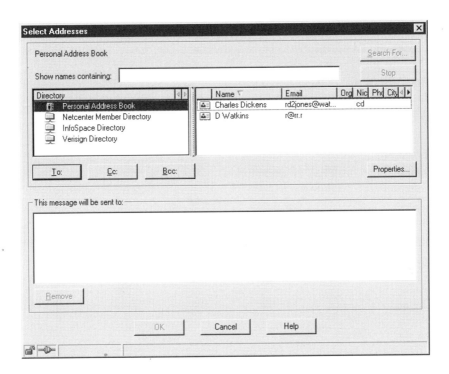

Make sure the Personal Address Book entry is selected in the left window, so that the contacts are visible in the right window. Click the recipient, then the To button, and the recipient's name and e-mail address appears in the large lower box. If there are multiple recipients, select them and click the To button. All the names will appear in the lower box.

If there are people for Cc or Bcc, select them and click the corresponding buttons. Their names and addresses also appear in the lower box.

When all the recipients are selected, click OK. The dialog vanishes and you will see that the various recipients are now listed in the upper section of the Composition window. Compose the rest of the e-mail and send it as usual.

Back Up Your Messenger Address Book

To make a backup copy of your address book, choose Communicator | Address Book to open it. Then, in the Address Book window, choose File | Export. This opens an Export As window, which is identical to a Save As window. Specify a filename and use the Save In box to navigate to the desired file folder. Then, in the Save As Type box, select the desired file format for export; you can leave it as LDIF, in fact. Then click Save to save the backup file.

To restore the address book from the file, go to the Address Book window again and choose File | Import. This opens the Import Utility dialog. Select a file format from the displayed list;

this must be the same file format in which you originally saved the backup file. So, if you saved it in LDIF, select the LDIF File entry. Then click Next.

An Import LDIF File dialog opens. Use it to navigate to the location of the backup file, select the file, and click Open. The file is automatically imported and the address book is restored.

Where to Find It

Web Site	Address	What's There
Eudora	www.eudora.com	Eudora mail program

Chapter 12

More About E-mail

How To . . .

- Use multiple e-mail addresses
- Organize mail with mailboxes and folders
- Automate mail organization with filters and rules
- Back up your messages
- Use e-mail on the road
- Zip e-mail attachments for fast transmission
- Use free e-mail accounts
- Understand LISTSERV mailing lists
- Learn e-mail etiquette
- Understand and prevent junk e-mail (spam)

The previous chapter presented the basics of sending and reading e-mail and using an address book. However, there's more to e-mail than that. In what follows, we'll examine some of the other tools that will enhance your use of it.

Use Multiple E-mail Addresses

It's not uncommon for people to have more than one e-mail account and therefore more than one e-mail address. For example, you may have two accounts set up with the same ISP. One might be for personal correspondence, such as cdickens@someisp.com, and the second for your home office, such as charlesdickens@someisp.com. You might also have a third account with a free e-mail provider such as Hotmail, for instance, an account called cd@somefreemail.com.

Outlook 2000, Outlook Express, and Eudora (in paid or sponsored mode) all allow you to use such multiple addresses. Netscape Messenger, however, does not allow multiple accounts with POP servers, only with IMAP servers. Most ISPs provide e-mail services through POP servers, so if you need multiple accounts you should use one of the other three clients, or some other program that permits using POP-based multiple e-mail accounts.

Use Multiple E-mail Addresses with Outlook 2000

To set up a new e-mail account, choose Tools | Accounts to open the Internet Accounts dialog. In this dialog, choose Add | Mail. This opens the Internet Connection wizard. To add the new account, refer to the procedure in the section titled "Set Up Outlook 2000" in Chapter 11, and follow steps 3 through 9. After you return to the Internet Accounts dialog at the end of that procedure, click Close and the new account will be ready for use.

To check for incoming e-mail on all accounts at once, click the Send/Receive button on the toolbar and all the accounts you have will be checked. To check just one account, use the menu bar (not the toolbar) to choose Send/Receive. This opens a submenu that lists the accounts separately. Click the account to be checked and the action will be carried out.

Note that automatic checking, which is done when you open Outlook and have an active Internet connection, is only applied to the default account. To change the default, choose Tools | Accounts to open the Internet Accounts dialog. Click the Mail tab and select the account you want as the default. Then click the Default button to make the change, and close the dialog.

To remove an account, choose Tools | Accounts to open the Internet Accounts dialog. Click the Mail tab and select the account you want to remove. Then click the Remove button to make the change, and close the dialog.

Use Multiple E-mail Addresses with Outlook Express

To set up an additional e-mail account on Outlook Express, begin by going to its opening screen and clicking the link labeled Set Up a Mail Account. The setup is exactly the same as it was for the setup of the initial account, so for details refer to the section entitled "Set Up Outlook Express Version 5" in Chapter 11, steps 1–6.

To check for mail on all accounts at once, and also send any mail that is waiting in your Outbox, first select the Inbox icon. Then choose Tools | Send and Receive | Send and Receive All. To receive mail only, choose Receive All. To receive mail from a specific account, choose Tools | Send and Receive and select the name of the desired account from the menu.

As a shortcut, clicking the Send/Rcv button on the toolbar checks all accounts and also sends any unsent mail in the Outbox.

Use Multiple E-mail Addresses with Eudora

In Eudora, e-mail accounts are referred to as "Personalities." The "dominant personality" in Eudora is another name for the default account, which is the term used by the other three programs.

12

NOTE

You can have multiple e-mail accounts only if Eudora is in sponsored or paid mode. The unpaid, unsponsored mode is restricted to one account.

To set up more personalities once the dominant personality has been created during the Eudora installation, do this:

1. Choose Tools | Personalities to make the Personalities window appear at the left of the main Eudora window.

2. Right-click inside the Personalities window and choose New from the pop-up menu. The New Account Wizard appears.

3. Follow the procedure to set up a new account as described in the section entitled "Set Up Eudora" in Chapter 11, steps 1–7.

When you've finished, the new account will appear in the Personalities window.

To check for mail on all your accounts at once, click the Check Mail button on the toolbar. To check a specific account, first make sure that the Personalities window is visible. (If it isn't, choose Tools | Personalities to make it appear.) Then right-click on the desired account and choose Check Mail from the pop-up menu.

Organize Mail with Mailboxes and Folders

If you receive and send a lot of e-mail, keeping it organized can be a problem. One way to deal with the flood is to create multiple folders or mailboxes, so that you can pigeonhole your mail in categories after you receive it.

Organize Mail with Folders in Outlook 2000

You can set up as many folders as you need to classify and store your e-mail. To create a folder, do this:

1. Launch Outlook and display the Inbox, if necessary, by clicking the Inbox icon in the Outlook Shortcuts bar.

2. For your convenience in seeing what happens next, display the Folder List by choosing View | Folder List. This opens a Folder List window next to the Outlook bar, in which you can see the Inbox folder, the Outbox folder, and so on.

3. Choose File | New | Folder. The Create New Folder dialog appears (see the next illustration).

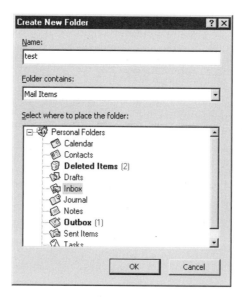

4. In the Name box, type a name for the folder. Ensure that the list box labeled Folder Contains is displaying the selection "Mail Items."

5. Click OK. The dialog vanishes and another one appears, asking if you want a shortcut to the folder added to the Outlook bar. If you click Yes, you'll create a shortcut icon on the My Shortcuts bar (not on the Outlook Shortcuts bar). If you click No, you won't get the icon.

6. Whichever you chose, though, the new folder appears as a subfolder of the Inbox folder. You can create subfolders of this folder as well, just as you can in the Windows Explorer file manager.

To move an e-mail message from the Inbox folder to another folder, first click on the Inbox icon to display the e-mail window. Select the desired message entry in the upper section of the Inbox, and drag it to the destination folder. To copy it to the folder instead of moving it there, hold down the CTRL key while dragging.

Finally, to display the contents of a subfolder of the Inbox folder, first make the Folder List visible (if necessary) as in step 2. Then locate the desired folder under the Inbox folder, click on it, and its contents are displayed. Alternatively, if you created a shortcut icon as in step 5, open the My Shortcuts bar and click the icon to display the folder content.

Organize Mail with Folders in Outlook Express

Just as with Outlook 2000, Outlook Express lets you create as many storage folders as you need. To do so, follow this procedure:

1. Launch Outlook and display the Inbox, if necessary, by clicking the Inbox icon in the Folders window.

2. Choose File | New | Folder. The Create Folder dialog appears.

3. In the dialog list box, ensure that you've selected the Inbox folder under Local folders. In the Name box, type a name for the folder. Click OK.

4. The dialog vanishes and the new folder appears as a subfolder of the Inbox folder. You can create subfolders of this folder as well, just as you can in the Windows Explorer file manager.

> TIP
>
> *If you close the smaller windows in Outlook Express (the Contacts window, for example), it isn't obvious how to get them back. To do so, choose View | Layout to open the Window Layout Properties dialog. Then select the window you want to restore and click OK.*

To move a message from the Inbox to the desired folder, simply drag its entry from the upper section of the Inbox to the desired folder in the Folders window. To copy it into the folder, hold the CTRL key down while dragging.

12

Organize Mail with Folders and Mailboxes in Eudora

In Eudora, you can use mailboxes alone to organize your messages, or a combination of folders and mailboxes. Mailboxes can be created at the top level of the Eudora folder structure, or placed in subfolders within that structure.

To create a mailbox at the same level as the basic In, Out, and Trash mailboxes, choose Tools | Mailboxes to make sure the mailboxes window is visible. Then choose Mailbox | New to open the New Mailbox dialog, as shown in the next illustration. You'll see that it says "Creating a Mailbox in the Top Level," which means that this is the level of the In mailbox and the other two primary mailboxes. Type a name for the mailbox into the text box and click OK. An icon for the new mailbox appears in the mailbox window.

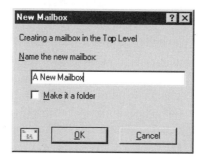

To move a message from the In mailbox to another location, double-click the In icon, so that the messages in the In mailbox appear in the upper section of the main Eudora window. Locate the desired message entry, then drag it over to the mailbox window, and onto the icon for the desired storage mailbox. Release the mouse button, and the message is moved. To copy it, hold down the CTRL key while dragging.

To create a folder in which to store mailboxes, open the New Mailbox dialog as described earlier, but select the check box labeled Make It a Folder. The folder is created at the top level of the Eudora mailbox structure.

To create a mailbox within a folder, first select the folder in the mailbox window. Then follow the normal procedure to create a mailbox, and the new mailbox will end up contained in the selected folder.

You can also create folders within folders. First select the folder in the mailbox window. Then follow the procedure for creating a mailbox, but this time select the check box labeled Make It a Folder. The new folder will end up contained in the selected folder.

To delete a mailbox or folder, select it and press the DELETE key. Note, however, that you cannot delete the In, Out, or Trash mailboxes.

Organize Mail with Folders in Netscape Messenger

This is very simple. Launch Communicator and choose Communicator | Messenger to open Messenger at the Inbox window. Then choose File | New Folder to open the New Folder dialog (see the next illustration).

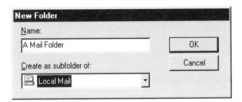

Type a name for the folder into the Name text box, and use the lower text box to specify the location of the new folder. When you've done that, click OK. An icon for the new folder appears in the left section of the Messenger window.

To move a message from the Inbox into a folder, select the message entry in the upper section of the window and drag it to the desired folder. To copy it, hold the CTRL key down while dragging.

Automate Your Mail Organization

If most of your mail falls into some definable set of categories, you can avoid at least some of the need for manually sorting it into folders after it's received. Simply put, you tell the e-mail client to automatically route incoming messages to specified folders, depending on some characteristic of the e-mail.

12

Organize Mail with Rules in Outlook 2000

The automation technique in Outlook 2000 is referred to as Rules. The example given here is a simple one, but there are many others you can experiment with. Here's how this one works:

Suppose you have a folder called Family, which you've been using to store correspondence from your closer relatives. You know most of these people's e-mail addresses, and we'll assume that you've put them in your Outlook Contacts list. Now you decide you want to automate your e-mail a bit, and have Outlook move all incoming messages from these individuals to the Family folder as they arrive. To set this up, carry out the following procedure:

1. Open Outlook to the Inbox, and choose Tools | Rules Wizard to open the wizard's first dialog. Then click the New button to actually start the wizard. This displays a dialog with a set of rules in the upper list box, and a description of the selected rule in the lower list box (see the next illustration).

2. We want to deal with messages from specific people as the messages arrive, so select the rule that says Move New Messages from Someone. The lower list box now displays two links: People or Distribution List, and Specified Folder.

3. Click the People or Distribution List link. This opens the Rule Address dialog, which shows the people in your Contacts list, as in the next illustration.

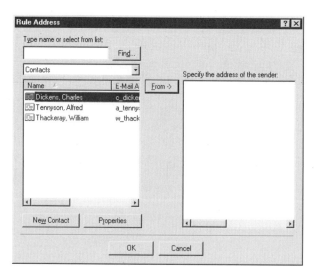

4. In the Name list box, select the people who are to be subject to this rule, in other words, the people whose e-mail you want in the Family folder. For each one you select, click the From button to transfer the contact to the right-hand list box labeled Specify the Address of the Sender.

5. When all the contacts are transferred, click OK to return to the wizard. Now click the Specified Folder link in the wizard's lower box to display a dialog where you will locate and select the Family folder.

6. With the Family folder selected, click OK. You return to the wizard, and the lower box will display your rule specifications. Click Next, then keep clicking Next until you end at the screen where you get to specify a name for the rule (the default name will likely be unwieldy). Type a rule name into the upper text box and click Finish.

7. The wizard dialog will now be displaying the new rule you have created. Click OK to close the wizard. From now on, your family's messages will automatically be moved to the Family folder as soon as they are received.

Organize Mail with Rules in Outlook Express

For Outlook Express we'll use the same example as we did in Outlook 2000: You have several family members who send you e-mail, and you want to route the messages automatically to a Family folder as they arrive. We also assume that you've put these family members into your Outlook Express address book, and that you've created the required folder. Do this:

1. Launch Outlook Express and choose Tools | Message Rules | Mail to open the New Mail Rule dialog (see the next illustration).

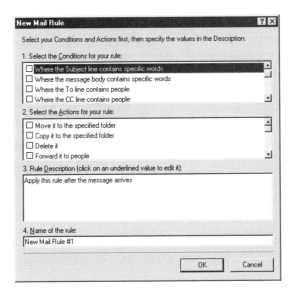

2. Go to the top list box, which is labeled Select the Conditions for Your Rule. Select the check box for the line that says Where the From Line Contains People.

3. Go to the second list box, labeled Select the Actions for Your Rule. Select the check box for the line that says Move It to the Specified Folder.

4. In the third list box, labeled Rule Description, click on the link that says Contains People. This opens the Select People dialog. Click the Address Book button to open the Rule Addresses dialog, as in the next illustration.

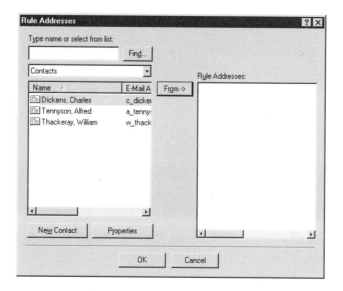

5. In the Name list box, select the people who are to be subject to this rule, in other words, the people whose e-mail you want in the Family folder. For each one you select, click the From button to transfer the contact to the right-hand list box, labeled Rule Addresses. When finished, click OK, then OK again to close the Select People dialog.

6. Now you're back in the New Mail Rule dialog. In the third list box, click the Specified Folder link to display a dialog where you will locate and select the Family folder.

7. With the Family folder selected, click OK. The third list box will now display your rule specifications.

8. Type a descriptive name for the rule into the bottom list box. Then click OK. The Message Rules dialog will now be displaying the new rule you have created. Click OK to close the dialog. From now on, your family's messages will automatically be moved to the Family folder as soon as they are received.

Organize Mail with Filters in Eudora

Eudora calls its automation tools "filters" rather than "rules" but they work much the same way. As in the preceding two sections, we use the example of routing messages from family members into a mailbox named Family, which you've already created.

However, automating message reception in Eudora is a slightly more cumbersome process than with Outlook or Outlook Express. In the case of our example, you can't use the Eudora address book to select a whole bunch of such people at once. Consequently, you have to create a separate filter for each family member who will be sending you mail.

With this limitation in mind, do this:

1. Launch Eudora and open the In mailbox. In the upper section, select any message that was sent by one of the desired individuals.

2. Choose Special | Make Filter from the menu bar. The Make Filter dialog appears (see the next illustration).

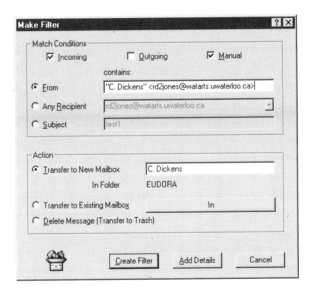

3. Since you selected an incoming mail message, the Incoming check box at the top of this dialog is selected. To ensure that the messages are routed automatically, clear the check box labeled Manual.

4. There are three text boxes in the Contains section. The topmost, the From box, should already be selected, and will have the sender's name and e-mail address in it. Leave this as it is.

5. In the Action section, select the Transfer to Existing Mailbox option and click the In button. A menu appears showing the top level of the Eudora mailbox structure. Use it to navigate to the desired mailbox, and select that mailbox.

6. Choose Create Filter and the filter is created.

7. Repeat steps 1 to 6 for each desired sender. When you're finished, incoming mail from those addresses will automatically transfer to the Family folder on receipt.

Organize Mail with Filters in Netscape Messenger

Like Eudora, Messenger calls its automation tool "filters." In this section, we'll assume again that you want to automatically route messages from family members into an already-created mailbox named Family. As in Eudora, you can't use the Messenger address book to select several people at once for the filter, but unlike Eudora, Messenger allows you to create a single filter that will do the job. Follow this procedure:

1. Launch Communicator and choose Communicator | Messenger to open the Messenger window.

2. Choose Edit | Message Filters to open the Message Filters dialog. In the list box labeled Filters For, make sure the Inbox is selected.

3. Click New to open the Filter Rules dialog (see the next illustration).

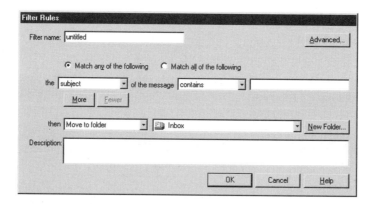

4. In the Filter Name text box, type a name for the filter.

5. Select the Match Any of the Following radio button.

6. Look at the list box beneath that button. This is where you specify the item to which the filter rule will apply. In our case, we want it to apply to senders, so use the drop-down list in this box to select Sender.

7. You will want the Sender item to contain the sender's e-mail address. So, in the next list box across, use the drop-down list to select Contains.

8. In the third list box across, type the e-mail address of the desired sender.

9. Assuming you have more people you want to filter, click the More button. This opens a new set of three boxes, exactly like the three you just filled out. Repeat steps 6 to 8 to fill out this set. Click the More button again if there are more people to be filtered, and so on until your list is complete.

10. Now, in the list box labeled Then, use the drop-down list to select Move to Folder.

11. In the next list box across, use the drop-down list to select the Family folder. (We assume you've already created this folder, but if you didn't, you can click the New Folder button and create it on the fly.)

12. Fill in a brief description for the rule in the Description box. Then click OK.

13. You're back at the Message Filter dialog, where you see the new filter listed in the main list box. Click OK again to complete the process. Incoming mail from the addresses you specified will now automatically transfer to the Family folder on receipt.

Back Up Your E-mail

If you get a lot of e-mail, you likely do some housecleaning occasionally and toss out the messages you'll never need again. However, you don't want some other factor, like a bad hard drive or a mistaken series of keystrokes, to erase *all* your correspondence. This is bad enough for personal mail, but with business e-mail it can be a disaster. So, as with all the other important data stored on your machine, you should back up your mail.

12

Back Up Messages in Outlook 2000

You back up your mail in Outlook 2000 in the same manner you back up your Contacts list, by exporting it to a file. Do this:

1. Open Outlook and choose File | Import and Export. The Import and Export Wizard opens.

2. From the list box, choose Export to a File and click Next.

3. In the next screen you see the Create a File of Type list box. Select Comma Separated Values (Windows) and click Next.

NOTE   *If the Import/Export tool isn't installed, you'll be prompted to insert the Office CD and install it. When the installation is finished, you can proceed with the wizard.*

4. In the next window you select the folder to export from. Choose Inbox and click Next.

5. In the next window use the text box labeled Save Exported File As to give the file a name, such as Messages Backup. Then click the Browse button to select a destination folder, preferably on some removable backup media such as a floppy. Click Next.

6. Now you see a confirmation window. Click Finish to export the file. It will be saved as a file with a .CSV extension.

 If you have folders in your Inbox, they are not backed up along with the content of the Inbox itself. Also, a folder's subfolders are not backed up along with that folder. You must back up each folder individually in order to back up its contents.

To use the backup, you essentially reverse the procedure to restore the deleted messages. Let's suppose you accidentally erased the contents of your Inbox. Here's how to restore it:

1. Launch Outlook and choose File | Import and Export. From the list box, select Import From Another Program or File. Click Next.

2. In the next window's list box, select Comma Separated Values (Windows). The principle here is that you use the same kind of file for import that you did for export. Click Next.

3. In the next dialog, click the Browse button to locate the backup file. To be sure you get all your backed-up messages restored, leave the Allow Duplicates to Be Created button selected. You can edit the collection later to remove unwanted duplicates, if necessary. Click Next.

4. In the next window, select Inbox from the list and click Next.

5. The next window shows a confirmation dialog. Click Finish to do the import. If you now switch to your Inbox you should see the restored entries.

Note, however, that restoring a deleted folder's content does *not* re-create the deleted folder. In fact, the restore procedure simply puts the restored files into whatever folder or location you select in step 4 of the restore procedure.

So, if you *do* delete a subfolder and its content from the Inbox, and you want to restore both the folder and its content, then you must re-create the folder *before* beginning the restore procedure. Then, in step 4, select the re-created folder and proceed with the restore.

Back Up Messages in Outlook Express

Backing up your messages in Outlook Express is simply a matter of making copies of the Inbox, Outbox, and Sent Messages files, plus the files in any other folders you may have created to store your messages.

What isn't so simple is locating these files. To do so, navigate to the C:\Windows\Application Data\Identities folder. In the Identities folder you'll see a subfolder that has a very long name with no resemblance to English. Open this weirdly named folder, and you'll see a subfolder named

Microsoft. Open the Microsoft folder, and you'll see yet another folder named Outlook Express. And when you at last open *this* folder, you'll find your mail files. They all have .DBX extensions, so the Inbox filename, for example, will be INBOX.DBX.

To back up all your messages, simply copy INBOX.DBX, OUTBOX.DBX, and SENTITEMS.DBX, to a backup location. If you created other storage folders, such as Family, you'll see .DBX files for these too; for example, FAMILY.DBX. Copy these files also to complete your backup.

Restoring them can be a bit tricky. If you accidentally deleted all the files in your Inbox, for example, and want to restore them from the backup, do this:

1. Open Windows Explorer and navigate to the folder containing the .DBX files, as just described.

2. Delete the INBOX.DBX file (note that you can't delete the Inbox if you're in Outlook, only if you're in Windows Explorer).

3. Copy the backup INBOX.DBX file to the folder.

4. Launch Outlook, and you'll see that your messages have been restored.

Use the same procedure for any of the other .DBX files that you need to restore.

Note that if you delete the entire Inbox using Windows Explorer, and launch Outlook without restoring the Inbox, Outlook will automatically re-create an empty Inbox.

Back Up Messages in Eudora

To back up messages in Eudora, open Windows Explorer and navigate to C:\Program Files\Qualcomm\Eudora (assuming a default installation). Then copy the following files to a backup location:

- IN.MBX
- IN.TOC
- OUT.MBX
- OUT.TOC
- TRASH.MBX
- TRASH.TOC

Copy the files back to their original location to restore them. If you created more mailboxes, you have to locate them and copy their .MBX and .TOC files as well to secure them.

Back Up Messages in Netscape Messenger

Open Windows Explorer and navigate to C:\Program Files\Netscape\Users. If Communicator has been set up with multiple Personalities, there will be a folder for each Personality.

Open the desired Personality folder then open the Mail folder contained within it. To make a full backup, copy the entire content of this folder to a storage location. To restore it, copy the backed-up data back to the original location.

E-mail on the Road

It's sometimes necessary (essential, if you're on business) to get at your e-mail via a dial-up connection while you're travelling. You'll find yourself in one of two situations:

- You have your own computer with you (a laptop, for example).
- You have access to somebody else's computer.

NOTE *If you have cable, satellite, or DSL service, check with your provider to see what provisions they make for remote e-mail access.*

Let's consider the first case first, where you're lugging your own computer around. Before you leave on your travels, check with your ISP to see if they have a local access dial-up number in the location where you'll be staying. If they do, life is simple. All you do to receive your e-mail is type that phone number into your machine's dial-up dialog when you want to connect to the dial-up service, then proceed as you normally do.

TIP *If you have a desktop computer at home which you use most of the time, and a laptop that you only use on the road, see if your laptop's e-mail program has a setting to leave e-mail on the server even after you've downloaded it. This way, when you get home you'll be able to download all the mail onto your main machine, even though you read it while you were away.*

If your ISP doesn't have a local access number, and if you're in a friend's home or in a hotel, you can of course use your laptop to connect using long distance. Use your ISP's regular dial-up number, but retype it into the connection dialog to make it a long-distance call. You'll get long-distance charges on your hotel bill, naturally (or you'll have to offer to reimburse your friends!).

Another possibility, if you're going to have Internet access through a friend's computer, is to open a free Web-based e-mail account with a provider like Hotmail. These Web e-mail accounts are accessible from any Internet-enabled computer; all you need is the Web address of the service, along with your username and password. Once you have the account, get your ISP to forward your e-mail automatically to it for the duration of your travels. To check your mail, set up your laptop to use your friend's dial-up account and phone line. Then connect to the Internet through his account, log onto your Web-based e-mail account, and download your mail to your laptop.

If you're entirely computerless, you'll have to throw yourself on the mercy of friends or acquaintances who have a dial-up connection. First open their e-mail program and write down the various server and account settings they use. Then change these to your own settings, using either your ISP's local access number, or the long-distance number if necessary. Better yet, if their e-mail client allows multiple accounts, as described in Chapter 11, set up a temporary account for yourself and leave the other one undisturbed. Also try to leave your mail on the server, as described in the previous Tip. If you can't, copy the text of any important messages to a floppy disk and take it home with you.

When you're finished using the friend's machine, put the e-mail settings back to their original values (and make sure they work!). Or delete the temporary account you set up, as the case may be.

Another alternative is to use one of the Web-based free e-mail services and have your ISP forward your mail to it, as described earlier. You can then use a friend's machine to access your mail, and copy the text of any important messages to a floppy disk that you can take home with you.

Use Zipped Attachments for Faster Sending

In Chapter 11 you learned how useful e-mail attachments can be. At the time, we noted that sending two or three medium-sized files as attachments is no major problem, even with a dial-up connection. However, there may be times when you need to send a lot of files or, as other examples, a very large text document or a big graphics file. In such cases you'll find WinZip to be an indispensable tool. The basics of downloading, installing, and using WinZip were covered, if you remember, in Chapters 6 and 7.

There are two basic tasks you'll want to do with WinZip:

- Zip a single file into an archive file to decrease its size.
- Zip several files into one multifile archive.

The first is the simplest. To compress a single file into an archive file, do this:

1. Launch WinZip. Choose File | New Archive to open the New Archive dialog.

2. Use the Create box, if necessary, to navigate to the folder in which the archive file (also called a ZIP file) will be created.

3. In the File Name box, type a name for the archive file. It will automatically be given the .ZIP extension, so you don't need to do this. Click OK.

4. The Add dialog appears (see the next illustration). You use this dialog to add files (or one file, in this case) to the archive file. Note that the original file is left intact; it's a copy of it that gets compressed and put into the archive file.

12

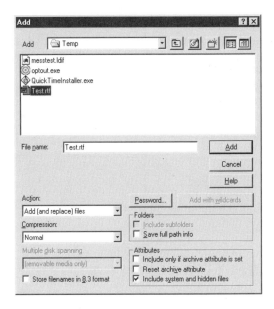

5. Use the Add box to navigate to the folder containing the file to be archived. In the large list box beneath it, select the desired file.

6. Click the Add button. WinZip copies the file, and then compresses the copy into an archive file with the name you gave it in step 3. Now the copy of the original file, still with its original name, is "inside" the archive (or ZIP) file.

7. You can now close WinZip and use the archive file as an attachment in an e-mail.

We covered the unzipping or decompressing process in Chapter 7, but we'll have a brief refresher on the subject after we examine archiving multiple files. By the way, in case you were wondering, files in an archive don't all have to be of the same type. They can be any assortment you like; WinZip will compress them all without blinking.

To create a multifile archive, follow steps 1 to 3 in the previous procedure, until you're looking at the Add dialog. Then do this:

1. Navigate to the folder that contains one or more of the files you want to archive.

2. In the large list box, select the desired file or files, using the usual Windows methods.

3. Click the Add button. The selected files are copied and then compressed into the archive file. The Add dialog vanishes, leaving you at the main WinZip dialog. Copies of the selected files, still with their original names, are now "inside" the archive file.

4. If you want to add more files to the archive, choose Action | Add or click the Add button on the WinZip toolbar, and repeat steps 1 to 3.

5. When you have archived all the files you want, close WinZip.

Now you can attach the archive file to an e-mail, and send all the contained files to the recipient in one neat package. Note, however, that the recipient has to have WinZip installed on his/her machine in order to get at them.

Here's the refresher I mentioned before on getting a file or files out of an archive. This process is referred to as *extracting* a file. Here's how you do it:

1. Launch WinZip and choose File | Open Archive to display the Open Archive dialog.

2. In the dialog, use the Look In box to navigate to the folder containing the desired archive file. Select the archive file from the list box and click Open to display its content.

As you learned in Chapter 7, you can get to the point described in step 2 of this procedure by using Windows Explorer to navigate to the archive file, and then double-clicking it.

3. You're now back in the main WinZip dialog. Select the file(s) you want to extract. Then click the Extract button on the toolbar. The Extract dialog appears (see the next illustration).

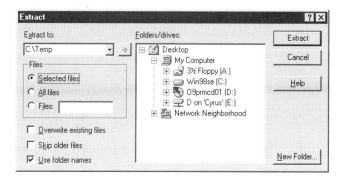

4. Use the Folders/Drives list box to navigate to the folder where the extracted files will be placed, and select that folder. The name of the folder will then appear in the Extract To text box.

5. Once the folder name is correctly displayed, click the Extract button, and WinZip will extract and decompress the files to the folder. When the green light appears at the bottom-right corner of the WinZip dialog, the process is complete and you can close WinZip.

Send a Web Page as an E-mail Attachment

This is a very handy technique if you want to send somebody a Web page in its entirety. However, you start out not with your e-mail client, but with your browser.

To send a Web page with IE, do this:

1. Launch IE and open the desired Web page.

12

2. Choose File | Send, and from the pop-up menu choose Page By E-mail.

3. If this is the first time you've carried out this procedure, and depending on the e-mail client you've installed, you may get a configuration dialog. Follow the screen instructions to set up the browser's mailing software.

4. Once the software is set up, an e-mail message window appears with the Web page displayed in it. Type the recipient's name into the To box of the window, then click Send. When the person you sent it to opens the e-mail, the Web page will appear in his or her default e-mail client.

However, a word of caution is needed about using IE to mail Web pages. After you set up IE for this function, then the next time you open Outlook Express, it will automatically try to receive your e-mail. If you always use Express for e-mail this is fine, but it's not at all what you want if you normally use a different e-mail client, such as Eudora.

However, you can stop this unruly behavior. Do this:

1. Launch Outlook Express, and when the connection dialog appears, click its Cancel button to get rid of it.

2. Choose Tools | Accounts and when the Internet Accounts dialog opens, click the Mail tab.

3. Select the name of the mail account that Express is trying to connect to, then click Properties.

4. On the Properties sheet, clear the check box labeled Include This Account When Receiving Mail or Synchronizing. Then close all the dialogs and close Outlook Express. When you launch it again, it won't try to check the e-mail account.

You can also send a Web page via e-mail with Navigator. Here's how:

1. Launch Navigator and open the desired Web page.

2. Choose File | New | Message to open a Messenger composition window.

3. In the To line, type the recipient's name, and type a subject into the Subject line.

4. In the composition window (not the Navigator window) choose File | Attach | Web Page. A dialog containing the address of the open Web page appears. Click OK to close the dialog.

5. Click Send. When the person you sent it to opens the e-mail, the Web page will appear in his or her default e-mail client.

Use Free E-mail Accounts

You can get free Web-based e-mail from lots of places, one of the best known being Hotmail at **www.hotmail.com** (it's now part of MSN, the Microsoft Network). Web-based e-mail doesn't require an e-mail client; you just need IE4 or later, or Communicator 4 or later.

All you have to do to get one of these accounts is go to the service's Web page and sign up, providing your own password and username. After that, you can get at your e-mail from any Internet-connected computer anywhere, provided it has recent enough browser software.

However, because there's really no such thing as a free lunch, you do pay indirectly for the service. Usually you're required to receive advertising e-mail from the service's sponsors, and at the very least, you'll see a lot of ads while you're using it. Nevertheless, it does have some advantages. Apart from its near-universal accessibility, you can change ISPs or jobs without having to tell everybody about a new e-mail address.

You can find a directory of free e-mail services at **www.emailaddresses.com**. This site also provides much other useful material about such services.

Use LISTSERV

LISTSERV is actually a program for managing mailing lists, but it is so widely used that the word LISTSERV has become somewhat synonymous with Internet-based mailing lists.

What is a mailing list? Briefly, it's a discussion group in which subscribers send e-mails concerning some subject or other to the group's e-mail address, and a program at that address (called a *reflector*) redistributes it to all the other subscribers in the group. There are tens of thousands of LISTSERV groups; to help you locate ones of interest, you can refer to the Liszt directory site at **www.liszt.com**. It also has good background information on the niceties of obtaining list information and subscribing.

Once you've found a list of interest, you have to see if you can join it. Not all discussion groups are open to the public. You also must distinguish carefully between the list address itself and the administrative address of the list. The administrative address is where you get information about who can join, how you subscribe, and how you unsubscribe if you eventually decide to drop out. The list address is where you actually send your e-mails, but only after you've subscribed. Do not, under any circumstances (including by accident), send subscription requests or information requests to the list address instead of the administrative address; your missive will be copied to every member of the group, and people find this intensely annoying.

12

About E-mail Etiquette

There are some basic dos and don'ts of using e-mail. Here are a few that may help you avoid those embarrassing moments:

- Don't type messages all in capitals. It is considered shouting.

- Use appropriate subject lines to give the recipient a clue about the content.

- Write clearly, spell properly, and use good grammar. E-mail may be informal compared to paper communication, but informal does not mean sloppy or careless.

- Before you send an attachment, ask the intended recipient if his software can handle it. And don't send huge attachments (over about 60K in file size) to somebody who has a dial-up connection, unless you clear it with them first.

- Be careful what you say in an e-mail. E-mails can be construed as legal documents, and have been used as evidence in lawsuits and criminal cases.

- Do not become involved in "flames," that is, abusive exchanges. If somebody flames you, don't reply unless you have a very good reason to do so (apart from your emotional reaction). Don't send e-mail you wrote while you were mad or upset, at least until you have calmed down and reread it objectively.

- Don't forward somebody's e-mail unless you know they won't mind your doing so. If in any doubt, check with the person concerned before you forward the message.

- Read all your e-mail over before sending it, and always, always, *always* check the address to make sure it's going to the right person.

Did you know?

Is somebody reading your mail? They might be. Ordinary e-mail is not secure, and that's another reason to be judicious in what you write, especially in a business environment. Furthermore, employers have established a right to examine the e-mails you send and receive at your place of work, and they may be looking at your mail without your knowledge. Being aware of this may spare you some unpleasant experiences.

E-mail encryption can secure your communications from casual prying, but it involves some extra work. We'll examine encryption in Chapter 17.

Understand Spam

Spam is unsolicited, junk e-mail. If you become a spam target, you may end up receiving floods of such e-mails every day, most of it sleazy get-rich-quick schemes, "free" offers, or invitations to pornographic sites. A few are outright scams. The next sections will tell you how this can happen to you and how you can (hopefully) prevent it from happening in the first place.

How You Get on a Spammer's List

Spam exists because some people, inevitably, respond to junk e-mail and send in their money for whatever is being peddled, and the spammers make a profit. Not only this, spammers can also make money from providing lists of spam targets. To both these ends, they send software programs called *robots* or *spiders* out onto the Internet to search for and record items that resemble e-mail addresses. Many of these items are, unfortunately, legitimate addresses. Then the spammers compile these collections into mailing lists, which they both use themselves and sell to other spammers.

The most common cause of ending up on a spam list is having posted a message to a newsgroup or to a LISTSERV group with your e-mail address in the posting. The Web can also be a problem, though. As you know, you sometimes have to register with a site to get some item or other, and some of these sites may not be above selling your address to a junk mail artist. From there, your address may get passed on to others.

How You Can Avoid Spam

The first line of defense is protecting your e-mail address. If you post to a newsgroup, modify your Reply To address before doing so, and indicate in the body of your posting how it can be changed back to your real one. For example, if your real address is me@someisp.com, change it to me@at-someisp.com and tell people to delete the at-.

Another technique is to get a free e-mail account and use that one in circumstances when you have to provide an e-mail address to persons unknown. This way you can preserve your regular ISP-based e-mail accounts from interference.

If you receive spam, you may be tempted to click the Reply button on your e-mail client and send a furious protest to the spammer. *Don't do it!* This tells him the address is a real one (his search software can't determine that, yet) and you'll get even more junk in your mailbox.

Getting off a spammer's list is tricky. If a spam e-mail includes a "remove" procedure for getting off the list, don't use it; this is just another way for the spammer to verify that your address is real. Your best defense is to try not to get on such a list in the first place, using the techniques described earlier. You will probably get some junk in your mailbox from time to time, though, no matter what you do.

If you're having a lot of spam trouble, go to **www.spam.abuse.net** for more information about dealing with it. There is also **www.abuse.net**, where you can find out who to complain to about the problem.

12

If you're wondering why we haven't discussed viruses that are spread by e-mail yet, we will do so at length in Chapter 18.

Where to Find It

Web Site	Address	What's There
Fight Spam	www.spam.abuse.net	Info on spam fighting
Free E-mail Directory	www.emailaddresses.com	List of free e-mail services
Hotmail	www.hotmail.com	Free e-mail service
Liszt	www.liszt.com	Mailing list directory
Network Abuse Clearinghouse	www.abuse.net	A complaint forwarding bureau

Chapter 13

Newsgroups and How to Use Them

How To . . .

- ■ Understand newsgroups
- ■ Understand newsgroup etiquette
- ■ Set up a newsreader program
- ■ Read and respond to newsgroup messages with Outlook Express
- ■ Read and respond to newsgroup messages with Netscape Messenger
- ■ Save newsgroup messages
- ■ Deal with news message attachments

Newsgroups are yet another communications service provided by the Internet. They were, in fact, in widespread use before the World Wide Web, in a system called Usenet. An incredible amount of information (not all of it accurate) gets swapped around on newsgroups. It's like a vast global conversation that goes on all the time.

Most of these conversations are innocuous and often even constructive, but you should be aware also of the less positive stratum of newsgroups. The truth is that some groups concentrate on subjects that many people would find distasteful or alarming, or worse. A few promote hatreds of various brands, or are posted to by people with particularly virulent opinions and tempers to match. A substantial number of newsgroups deal with erotica and pornography, and even people who are not easily shocked may be repelled by some of the content.

It should be emphasized, though, that the number of non-offensive newsgroups is far larger than the number of offensive ones, and you can spend a long time reading newsgroups without coming across anything worse than bad language from an irritated participant. If you have children, however, you should definitely keep a close eye on their newsgroup activity, since they are more trusting than adults and therefore more vulnerable. This issue will be discussed at more length in Chapter 19.

Understand Newsgroups

A newsgroup is an Internet-based collection of messages generated by people with common interests and concerns. Tens of thousands of newsgroups, available both locally and globally, exist on computers worldwide, and span a range of topics from international politics to rose gardening.

The Internet service that provides people with newsgroup access is called Usenet, and because of this, newsgroups are sometimes called Usenet groups. To get at these groups and their messages, you need two things: a program called a *newsreader*, so you can read and respond to the messages, and an Internet connection to a *news server*, where the newsgroup itself is maintained. Your ISP almost certainly has given you access to their own news server, while newsreaders (also called *newsgroup clients*) are readily available. In fact, you probably already have one, since Outlook Express is a news client as well as an e-mail client, and so is Netscape Messenger.

Kinds of Newsgroups

Every news server "hosts" anywhere from a few dozen newsgroups to tens of thousands of them (for an explanation of *hosting*, see the following "Did you know?" section). The news server's administration makes a selection from among the groups carried by Usenet, and feeds these selected groups through to their own server. As a result, not all Usenet newsgroups will be available on all servers.

There are also *moderated* and *unmoderated* newsgroups. With moderated groups, somebody looks at the incoming messages and decides whether to post them to the newsgroup (*posting to a newsgroup* means putting a message into it). Conversely, messages in unmoderated groups have been posted there with no prior scrutiny whatsoever.

Since newsgroups can be created by anybody with a computer and an Internet connection, not all are available through Usenet. Your ISP's system administrator, for example, may have created newsgroups of local interest that are hosted only on its server, and are thus not accessible to the world at large. For example, there may be a newsgroup of local "for sale" messages, or a group to discuss local entertainment. In fact, an ISP-supplied news server is probably not available to people who don't subscribe to that ISP, though there are public news servers that anyone can use, at least to read messages.

Each newsgroup has a name, but newsgroups are not randomly named. The whole collection is divided into categories and then into subcategories, so a newsgroup name might be rec.arts.books.reviews, with each category designation divided from the next by a period. Examples of the main top-level categories are alt (alternative, which covers a lot of ground), comp (computers), and rec (recreation), but there are plenty more. The subcategories define narrower and narrower ranges of interest, so that rec.arts.sf.movies is a newsgroup about science fiction movies.

Did you know?

13

Host is a common Internet technical term and is often used in conjunction with the concept of servers. A server, you remember, is the software that provides services to a client; for example, a *Web server* provides its services to a *Web client* (another name for a browser, such as IE). It's common to say that Web sites are *hosted* on Web servers, and that newsgroups are *hosted* on newsgroup servers. Sometimes, as well, the computer itself is referred to as the host, in the sense that it is the machine that "hosts" the server software.

Newsgroup Etiquette

Before going on, we should have a word about manners pertaining to newsgroups. You can get yourself scolded (or *flamed*, in newsgroup jargon) if you violate some generally accepted convention of behavior. Unfortunately, and probably because of the relative anonymity of newsgroups, some people are much more abusive and unforgiving than they would probably be in a face-to-face conversation. This can be very unnerving for a newcomer. Indeed, a few such people may be abusive even if you *haven't* done anything wrong, just because they dislike something you said. The best thing to do is ignore such messages and not become upset because of them. Most especially, do not respond in kind, and start what's called a *flame war*.

To reduce the likelihood of unpleasant exchange, here are some guidelines:

- Lurk first, before you venture to post messages of your own. "Lurking" is simply reading the messages without participating in the discussion. By doing this you'll pick up the tone of the group and get a feel for what's acceptable and what isn't. Also, you'll find out if you're in the right group, in case the name was misleading.

- Check for a FAQ, a list of Frequently Asked Questions. If there is one, it will give you pointers about the makeup and customs of the group.

- When you do post a message, write clearly and to the point. And if you're purveying information, make sure it's correct. Somebody may take some action based on what you said.

- As for the information that you yourself find in a newsgroup, don't assume it's correct. People in newsgroups can be just as wrong about things as people who are carrying on face-to-face conversations.

- Be polite and civil. The messages you read are from human beings, who can be hurt and upset in exactly the same way that you can. No discussion was ever improved by insults and abuse. Swearing is also frowned on.

- If someone flames you, don't respond. It's very tempting to do so, because of the anonymity factor, but flame wars are ultimately pointless and a waste of energy, as well as being bad for the digestion. Avoiding confrontation is especially important if you are, for some reason, posting under your regular e-mail address (more on this a bit later in the chapter).

Setting Up Your Newsreader

The simplest way to get started with newsgroups is to use the news server provided by your ISP. This may not provide all the newsgroups you may want, but you can look for others later; how to do this will be explained further on in the chapter.

Newsreaders, or newsgroup clients, are not hard to find. Some richly featured ones are available for purchase, but if you have either Windows with Outlook Express, or a Windows machine or Mac with Netscape Messenger, you already have a newsreader. Express and Messenger both function as news clients, as well as e-mail programs.

Before setting up your newsreader, though, you should think about how you want your messages to be answered. While it's true that many messages get answered publicly in the group itself, the whole newsgroup system is arranged so that a respondent can also communicate with you via an e-mail address. Consequently, you can't set up your reader without providing such an address.

However, as you learned in the previous chapter, spammers troll though newsgroups to find e-mail addresses. When you set up your newsreader, therefore, you may want to modify your e-mail address, as described in the section entitled "How You Can Avoid Spam" in Chapter 12. Better yet, you might get a free e-mail account with one of the Web-based mail services, and use that account for posting messages to newsgroups. Or you can furnish a false e-mail address, though out of consideration it must be one that is extremely unlikely to belong to anybody. As long as you're only lurking, of course, you don't need to worry about revealing your e-mail address to spammers, because it will be accessible to them only if you post a message.

Once you decide how you'll manage the e-mail question, you can go ahead and set up the newsreader, as described in the next section. However, before you do, you may find it helpful to know a bit about what's going to happen. Basically, it's this:

- ■ You tell your newsreader the Internet address of the news server (such as news.myisp.com).

- ■ Your newsreader downloads the names of the newsgroups on that server, and stores these names on your machine. It does not actually download any of the *messages* within the newsgroups, only the newsgroup names. You only need to do this once, as the names are retained on your computer until you remove them.

- ■ Once the newsgroup names are on your machine, you use the reader to select one of them. The reader will then download the messages contained in the named newsgroup, so you can read and respond to them.

Set Up Outlook Express to Read News

We'll assume here that your Internet connection is active, and that you have determined from your ISP sign-up package what the name of the news server is. To set up Outlook Express as a newsreader, do this:

1. Launch Express. From the menu bar, choose Tools | Accounts to open the Internet Accounts dialog, which will resemble the next illustration.

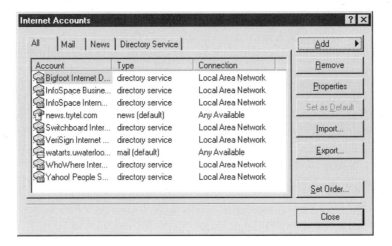

2. In the Internet Accounts dialog, click the Add button. Then choose News from the menu to start the Internet Connection Wizard. Note that if you have set up Outlook Express as your mail client, several of the boxes in the ensuing screens will already be filled in, and you may be able to leave them as is. However, we'll assume here that this is a fresh installation.

3. In the Display Name box, type the name that you want to appear in the From line of messages you send. It can be any name you like (such as John Doe, Darth Vader, Bltfxp99, or even your real one). Click Next.

4. In the next screen, type the e-mail address you're going to use with newsgroups, and click Next.

5. In the next screen, type the name of the news server your ISP gave you. Leave a blank in the check box labeled My New Server Requires Me to Log On, and click Next.

6. Click Finish to complete the setup process and return to the Internet Accounts dialog. Click Close.

7. Outlook Express now asks if you want to download the newsgroups from the news account you just added. Answer Yes, and an info box will appear, counting the number of newsgroups downloaded. If you have a slow connection and the collection is large, this may take some time.

NOTE   *This download only needs to be done once. If the server adds new newsgroups, as sometimes happens, Outlook Express will notify you and automatically add them to the complete list.*

8. Once the download is complete, a Newsgroup Subscriptions dialog appears. You will use this dialog to actually download and read news messages.

At this point, if you're going to use Outlook Express, you can skip ahead to the section titled "Use Express or Messenger to Read News."

Set Up Netscape Messenger to Read News

Begin by launching Communicator. Then choose Edit | Preferences to open the Preferences dialog. Then do this:

1. Click the plus sign next to the Mail & Newsgroup entry. When the menu expands, choose Newsgroup Servers to open the Newsgroup Servers dialog (see the next illustration).

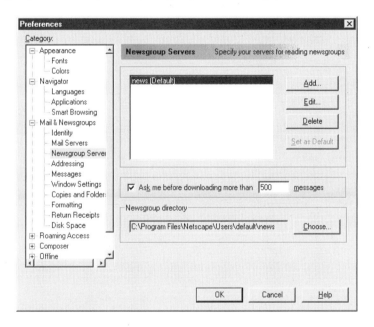

2. Click Add to open the Newsgroup Server Properties dialog. In the text box labeled Server, type the name of the news server as provided by your ISP. Leave the other entries in this dialog as they are, and click OK.

3. Now you'll see the new server's name in the large window. There will also be a listing for a server named news (Default) server. This is a dummy entry and can't be removed. Make your new server the default by selecting it and clicking the Set As Default button.

4. Click OK to close the Preferences dialog and return to the Navigator window. Now you have to download the newsgroup names from the ISP's news server to your own machine.

5. On the menu bar, choose Communicator | Newsgroups to open the News window. In the left-hand section of the News window, you'll see the name of the news server you just added. Click on it to select it.

6. From the News window menu, choose File | Subscribe. This opens the Subscribe to Newsgroups dialog, and the process of downloading the newsgroup names begins. You can tell it's going on because a status message "Receiving Newsgroups" appears at the bottom of the dialog.

7. When it finishes, the status message disappears and you can close both the News window and Communicator if you wish. Now you can move on to the section titled "Use Express or Messenger to Read News" to get started with actually using the newsgroups.

Use Express or Messenger to Read News

The process of reading messages is quite simple, and is based on the fact that each message in a newsgroup consists of a header and a message body. The header contains the subject line and other information, rather like the entries you see in your e-mail program, and the message body, of course, contains the message text. Unlike e-mail, however, you don't download both header and body at the same time. A group of headers is downloaded instead, and you decide from reading a header whether you want to read the message or not. If you do, you download the message body and it appears in the reader.

Note that you don't necessarily download all the headers in a newsgroup at once, since there might be thousands of them. Outlook Express downloads 300 at a time, and Messenger does 100, but these numbers can be customized.

Also, because some newsgroups receive very large numbers of messages, the servers remove earlier ones as later ones come in. Consequently, messages may be retained only for a couple of days, or even a few hours, before they vanish. The message header always includes a posting date (the day the news server received the message) so you can tell how old it is.

In what follows, we can examine only the essentials of Outlook Express and Netscape Messenger in their newsreader application. You can refer to their Help systems for more information about customizing them.

Read News with Outlook Express

Begin by launching Outlook Express, then choose Tools | Newsgroups to open the Newsgroup Subscriptions dialog (see the next illustration).

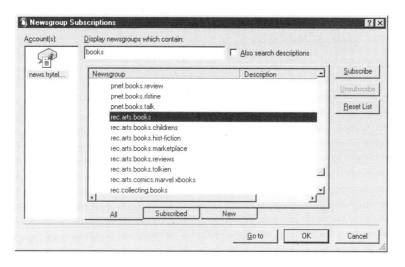

This dialog provides you with several tools:

■ In the Accounts section, you select the news server you want to use (if you have installed more than one).

■ You have three views of the selected server's contents, which you can change using the sheets labeled All, Subscribed, and New.

■ By using the search box labeled Display Newsgroups Which Contain, you can search the All, Subscribed, or New sheets for keywords. Doing so will display only the newsgroups that include the keyword.

■ If the search box is blank, and the All tab is selected, then all the newsgroups on the server are listed. If it's blank and the Subscribed tab is selected, then all the groups you subscribe to are listed. If it's blank and the New tab is selected, then all the new groups since the last update are listed.

■ The Reset List button downloads all the newsgroup's names over again, repeating the download that was done in the initial setup. Use this if something seems wrong with your list.

■ The Subscribe button tells Outlook Express that you want to make a selected group into a subscribed group, which adds it to your Folders display for easy access.

13

Begin by clicking the All tab and finding a group that may interest you by typing a keyword into the search box. In the previous illustration, the keyword was "books;" that displayed a list of possibly related groups, from which I selected the group rec.arts.books. Of course, you can simply browse through the groups to find what you want, but if there are 15,000 of them, you may be in for a long search.

With the desired group selected, click Subscribe (this automatically copies the group name to the Subscribed sheet, by the way). A subscription icon appears next to the name. Now click the Go To button, and the reader begins downloading the most recent message headers of that group. With the default setting, it will download 300 of them. Once the headers have downloaded, you'll see a display like that in Figure 13-1.

NOTE   *In Outlook Express, you don't actually have to subscribe to a group to download the headers. You can simply select it and click Go To. However, if you don't subscribe to it, you'll have to find it again the next time you launch Outlook Express.*

FIGURE 13-1   Outlook Express displays downloaded message headers in its upper window; the text of any selected message will appear in the lower window

You will now see the subscribed newsgroup listed in the Folders display, under the news server name. More importantly, the upper-right section of the newsreader window displays the message headers. You can sort them by subject, by who they were from, by the date sent, and by size by clicking the respective column buttons.

The lower section of the window is the preview pane, which allows you to see the message quickly. To open a message in the preview pane, click its header once in the upper section, and the text appears. It will remain in the preview pane until you click a different header. If you double-click a header, the message opens in its own message window.

Remove a Newsgroup from Outlook Express

To remove a group, you unsubscribe from it. Right-click it in the Folders display and choose Unsubscribe from the pop-up menu.

Understand and Follow Threads in Outlook Express

You will notice that many of the headers have a plus sign beside them. These icons indicate that at least one person has replied to this particular message. To view the replies, click the plus icon and their message headers appear. Such a collection of messages and responses is usually called a *thread*. (Outlook Express sometimes refers to threads as *conversations*, but they mean the same thing.) Revealing all the messages in such a conversation is called *expanding the thread*; hiding them again is called *collapsing the thread*. A thread is like a small discussion taking place within the context of a larger discussion, the larger one being the newsgroup as a whole. Or you can think of the newsgroup as a big talkative party, with bunches of people having their own mini-conversations here and there, and flitting from one conversation to another as the mood takes them. Read as much as you like; then, to collapse the thread, click the minus-sign icon beside the original header.

If you leave a message header selected for a few seconds, the torn-page icon beside it will turn to a complete-page icon. This is to help you remember which messages you've read.

If there are no plus signs that indicate threads, then threading may be turned off. In this case all the messages are displayed, and it's hard to tell which other messages they are responding to. To ensure that threading is turned on, choose Views | Current View and make sure that the Group Messages By Conversation menu entry has a check mark beside it. If it doesn't, click the entry to turn threading on.

You can change your header display to help keep track of what you've looked at. In the Views list box of the Outlook Explorer window, you can choose Show All Messages, Hide Read Messages, Hide Read or Ignored Messages, or Show Downloaded Messages, as the case requires.

Get More Messages or Newsgroups in Outlook Express

You'll probably want to examine more messages than the 300 that have been downloaded by default. These 300 are always the most recent postings as of the time of download, but there may well be earlier ones, and more may have come in while you were reading the others. To download another batch, which will also include the most recent messages, click the Headers button on the Outlook Express toolbar.

13

If you want to increase the number of messages that Outlook Express downloads at a time, choose Tools | Options | Read and on the Read sheet, change the number in the News section to the number you want (up to 1,000) and click OK. If you clear the Get check box, you will download all of them. In a large newsgroup, with a slow connection, this could take a long time.

At some point, too, you will want to add other newsgroups to your subscription list. On the Outlook Express toolbar, click the Newsgroups button or choose Tools | Newsgroups. This opens the Newsgroup Subscriptions dialog you used earlier, and you can simply repeat the earlier procedure to add the newsgroup.

Save Messages for Future Reference in Outlook Express

If you want to save a message for future reference (remember that messages don't stay on the server indefinitely) choose File | Save As. You can then save the message as a news file with an .NWS extension, or as a text file. Save it as a news file if you want to view it later in the Outlook Express message window (the default, and a good choice) or as a text file, if you prefer a plain-vanilla version that will appear in Windows Notepad or another text editor.

Use the Subscription List in Outlook Express

When you open Outlook Express for a new session of news reading, the groups to which you've subscribed will be listed in the Folders display (they may be collapsed into the server listing; click the plus sign next to the server name to reveal them). Click once on the name of the newsgroup and all previously downloaded messages will appear. At the same time, Outlook Express checks for messages posted to the group since your last session and downloads them as well. Alternatively, if you select the server name, the subscribed groups will appear in the upper-right section of the window. Double-click an entry to open the group, to display previous messages, and to download new ones.

Clear Old Messages from a Newsgroup in Outlook Express

From time to time, you may want to clear all the newsgroup messages and start afresh. Do this:

1. Right-click the newsgroup name (not the server name) and choose Properties to open the newsgroup Properties dialog.

2. Click the Local File tab to display the Local File sheet.

3. Choose one of the four buttons to clean up the newsgroup entries as desired, then click OK.

Deal with Attachments in Outlook Express

Just like e-mail messages, news messages can carry attachments with them. You can sometimes tell if there's an attachment from the reported size of the message; most text messages are less than 4K long, so if the size is reported as more than that, there may well be an attachment. Of course, the message body may inform you of what's riding along with it, or there may be a filename in the subject line that will give it away. For example a file with a .JPG extension is an attached JPG image file.

When you click on the message, both it and the attachment will download. If the attachment is a Web-type image, like a JPG or GIF file, it will also appear in the preview pane, along with any text in the message itself. If it's something else, like a text file, you will have to open it to see what it contains.

At this point you should be careful. While the risk of virus infection from a reputable Web site is small, this is *not* true of attached files from newsgroups. With newsgroups, you really don't know where a file has been. The person who posted it may have gotten the file anywhere, and may be quite unaware that it carries a virus (though there's always a chance that he or she is the perpetrator). It's safe to *read* messages, as you've already learned to do, but you must be very careful of any attachment that requires you to open it.

When you do attempt to open an attachment, you will normally get a security dialog warning from Windows that the attachment file may contain viruses. The dialog gives you two options for dealing with this: either go ahead and open the file, or save it to disk. If you are absolutely sure that the attachment is safe, open it by choosing the Open It option and clicking OK. If you have any doubts at all about its safety (which should be just about all the time) choose the Save It to Disk option and click OK. Then check the attachment with a virus-checking program before opening it. The use of a virus scanner is examined in Chapter 18.

Read News with Netscape Messenger

Launch Communicator and choose Communicator | Newsgroups to open Messenger. In the left section of the Messenger window, select the news server you added when you set up the newsreader.

A news server named "news" will also appear in this section of the window. Ignore it; if you delete the entry it will just reappear.

Next, choose File | Subscribe to open the Subscribe to Newsgroups dialog. It has three sheets:

- ■ All, which shows all the groups on the server, displayed in folders and subfolders.
- ■ New, which shows groups added since your last access to the server.
- ■ Search, which is where you look for relevant groups.

As with Outlook Express, you can use the All window to browse for interesting groups, using the Expand and Collapse buttons to reveal and conceal sets of subgroups within the higher-level ones. However, with a large server, you might wander for a long time before you found what you wanted. So, to begin with, click the Search tab to switch to the Search sheet, and then use the Server box to select the desired server. Then type a keyword into the Search For text box and click the Search Now button. As with the earlier Outlook Express example, I typed in **books** and got a list of newsgroups containing the word, then scrolled down until I could see and select rec.arts.books (see the next illustration).

13

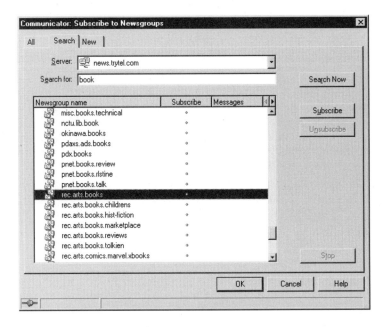

After you select the desired newsgroup, click the Subscribe button to subscribe to it. (Unlike Outlook Express, Messenger will download a newsgroup's messages only after you subscribe). Then click OK. The dialog vanishes and the newsgroup now appears in the left section of the window, under the server name.

To download a newsgroup's messages, begin by selecting its name. A Download Headers dialog then appears; if it doesn't, choose File | Get New Message. This dialog tells you how many messages there are in the group, and lets you determine whether to download all of them, or a specified number, beginning with the most recently posted. If there are several thousand messages, you may want to set the download to a manageable size. Make your selection, click Download, and a progress meter appears while the message headers are downloading.

After the download completes, the upper-right section of the newsreader window displays the message headers. You can sort them by subject, by sender, by the date sent, by size, and by several other values by clicking the respective column buttons. To reveal or hide columns in the header display, click the small arrow buttons at the right end of the bar that has the various column buttons on it.

The lower section of the window is the preview pane, which allows you to see the message quickly. To open a message in the preview pane, click its header once in the upper section, and the text appears. It will remain in the preview pane until you click a different header. If you double-click a header, the message opens in its own message window.

Remove a Newsgroup from Messenger

To remove a newsgroup, you need only unsubscribe from it. Select the group, and choose Edit |
Unsubscribe.

Understand and Follow Threads in Messenger

For a general explanation of threads, refer to the earlier section "Understand and Follow Threads
in Outlook Express." Netscape uses the same threading principle to organize messages, grouping
replies to a message under the original message. To see all the replies in a thread, click the plus
sign next to the header entry. To hide them again, click the minus sign next to the header entry.

*The very left column of the header display has a button with an icon of four black
horizontal lines. This is the threaded/unthreaded button, and clicking this button
switches the threaded display on and off. If you use any of the other column buttons
to sort the headers, threading will be turned off, and you'll have to click the
threading/unthreading button to turn it back on.*

You can specify your view of the headers by choosing View | Messages and selecting
whether to see all messages, unread messages, threads with unread messages, watched threads
with unread messages, or ignored messages.

Get More Messages or Newsgroups in Messenger

To download another set of messages from the newsgroup, which will include any new ones
posted since you last did this, select the group. Then choose File | Get New Messages (or the
Download Headers dialog may have appeared automatically when you selected the group) and
use the dialog as you did before.

When you want to add other newsgroups to your subscription list, choose File | Subscribe to
open the Subscribe to Newsgroups dialog. Then follow the same procedure you used to add the
first newsgroup.

Save Messages for Future Reference in Messenger

To save a message for future reference (remember that messages don't stay on the server
indefinitely), choose File | Save As | File. This saves the message as a text file, using a normal
Save As dialog. You can later read the file in any text editor, such as Windows Notepad.

Use the Subscription List in Messenger

When you open Messenger for a new session of news reading, the groups to which you've
subscribed will be accessible under the servers to which they belong. On opening, they will be

13

collapsed into the server listing, so you have to click the plus sign next to the server name to reveal them. Click once on the name of the newsgroup and all previously downloaded messages will appear. At the same time, Messenger checks for new messages posted since your last session and downloads them as well. Use the technique described earlier in the "Get More Messages or Newsgroups in Messenger" section to download another batch of messages, if desired.

Clear Old Messages from a Newsgroup in Messenger

To manage Messenger's retention of messages, choose Edit | Preferences and expand the Mail & Newsgroups entry. Then select Disk Space to open the Disk Space dialog. Here you can specify how long your newsgroup messages should be kept on your disk before they are erased.

Deal with Attachments in Messenger

In Messenger, an attachment shows up as a link within the message body. If it's a Web-type image, normally a JPG or a GIF file, you can view it by clicking the link, which will display the image in the preview window. To remove the image, you need to click on another header.

If the file isn't of these two types, you can't open it directly. When you click on the link, you instead get a Save As dialog, which you then use to save the attachment as a file. After it's saved, *do no*t under any circumstances open it, or run it if it's an EXE file, until you have checked it for viruses as described in Chapter 18.

Use Express or Messenger to Post Newsgroup Messages

When you decide to post a reply to a newsgroup, both Outlook Express and Messenger will provide you with a message form with the destination address(es) already filled in. When the message reaches its destination, it will be listed as coming from the name and e-mail address you used when you set up the news server.

With the desired newsgroup open in the news reader, all you do is type in your message and click the Send (or equivalent) button. However, you have several options in how you post the message:

- You can start a new discussion thread by posting a new message, to which others may respond. In Outlook Express, click the New Post button. In Messenger, click the New Msg button.

- You can reply to an existing message in the group, thus participating in an existing thread. First click the desired message header to display the message in the preview pane. Then, in Outlook Express, click the Reply Group button. In Messenger, click the Reply button.

- You can reply to the sender only, in which case your answer will go by e-mail to that person and will not appear in the newsgroup. Select the desired message header, displaying the message in the preview pane. Then, in Outlook Express, choose Message | Reply to Sender. In Messenger, choose Message | Reply | To Sender Only. Before replying, remember to check the person's message to see if there's an anti-spam measure in his/her e-mail address.

- ■ You can reply to both sender and the group, sending an e-mail to him or her and simultaneously posting your reply to the group. Select the desired message header, displaying the message in the preview pane. In Outlook Express, choose Message | Reply to All. In Messenger, choose Message | Reply All | To Sender and Newsgroup.

- ■ You can forward a newsgroup message to somebody. Select the desired message header, displaying the message in the preview pane. In Outlook Express, choose Message | Forward. In Messenger, choose Message | Forward As | Quoted.

Install Additional News Server Accounts

As noted earlier, the easiest way to access groups is to set up your news account using the news server provided by your ISP. However, you may not find all the groups you need on that particular server.

Fortunately, you can create multiple news accounts in Express or Messenger, and select whichever one has the groups you want. The problem is finding an open or public news server that you can access, and determining whether it has the desired newsgroups. The best way to do this is to locate an open server, download its newsgroup listing, and see if the one you need is there. To look for the addresses of publicly available servers, check the Serverseekers Web site at **www.serverseekers.com**, or go to Yahoo! at **www.yahoo.com**, and work down through Computers and Internet > Internet > Chats and Forums > Usenet > Public Access Usenet Sites.

Companies also sometimes set up specialized news servers to provide people with a place to discuss (or complain about) their products. An example is Microsoft, which has a public server at **msnews.microsoft.com**. If you're looking for such focused newsgroups, check the Web site of the company in question to see if it has a news server available.

Once you have the address of the news server, follow the procedure in the earlier section on setting up your newsreader, and let the reader download the list of groups. Once that's done, all you need do to access one of the newsgroups on that server is select it in your reader, and then follow the normal reading and posting procedures as described previously.

13

NOTE   *Sometimes a public server will have become private by the time you attempt to access it, and won't let you in without authorization. Sometimes, too, news servers vanish completely; in fact they tend to come and go, springing up on the Net like toadstools after a rain and vanishing some time later. Note also that some public servers allow posting by the world at large, but others don't.*

Where to Find It

Web Site	Address	What's There
Microsoft News	msnews.microsoft.com	Microsoft news server
Serverseekers	www.serverseekers.com	Lists of public news servers

Chapter 14

The Internet as a Meeting Place

How To . . .

- ■ Understand chat
- ■ Learn chat etiquette and safety
- ■ Use Web-based chat
- ■ Use Internet Relay Chat (IRC)
- ■ Use ICQ
- ■ Visit an online community

Besides e-mail and newsgroups, the Internet provides other forms of two-way communication. The chief examples of these are Web chat, Internet Relay Chat (IRC), ICQ, and virtual communities. In this chapter we'll have a look at these types of meeting places.

Understand Chat

Chat, both Web-based chat and IRC, differs from e-mail and newsgroup communication in that the chat goes on in what's called *real time*. Chatting in real time means that you get a response to your messages almost immediately. You don't, as with newsgroups and e-mail, send a message and receive an answer hours or days later.

To join a chat, you locate a *chat room,* a place on the Internet where people carry on these conversations. These "rooms" are maintained within *chat systems*, of which there are plenty, dedicated to all sorts of interests. Many chat systems are free, though others have member areas that you must pay to enter. The major online services, AOL and MSN, provide chat services for their subscribers, so if you belong to either service you can use these; they closely resemble the Web-based chat systems we examine in a later section.

To enter a room, you first register with the chat system, so as to obtain a username (usually called a *nickname* in the context of chat) and password. Don't use your real name (there's more about personal security in the next section). Then you can join the conversation going on in any of the system's rooms. While you're in the chat room, you'll be known by your nickname.

Once people have entered the room, they chat by typing their comments into a chat window and then sending them. The chat window on each user's computer displays everybody's text messages, one after another, as people "talk." Essentially, chat is like a conversation, except that people type their words instead of saying them aloud.

Lots of different kinds of chat rooms exist. Many are inhabited by people discussing everyday subjects that interest them, such as science fiction novels or bird-watching. A number of rooms, though, are dedicated to the discussion of sex in all its forms. Whether you find this unsavory or not depends on your personal attitudes, but you should be aware that it is out there.

Etiquette and Safety with Chat

A generally accepted code of conduct exists in chat rooms. Ordinary civility will keep you from committing most gaffes, but here's a general outline of how to behave.

- Before leaping into a conversation, observe it for a while to get a feel for it and the people involved. This is called "lurking" and it's not considered at all improper.

- As with e-mail, typing a message in full capitals is considered shouting, and is rude.

- As with newsgroups, don't become involved in abusive exchanges, or begin one (this is called *flaming*).

- Avoid sending long messages all in one chunk. Break them up into brief sentences, perhaps using the three dots (ellipsis) to indicate that there's more to come: for example, "My uncle Henry was out hunting bear one day and fell in the river..." Send that line, and then another installment of the anecdote.

- Generally, conduct yourself as you would in a real-world conversation in someone's living room. Respond when spoken to, don't do all the talking, and keep the feelings of the other participants in mind. They may be anonymous, but they are real people.

The other factor to consider is personal security. You may be behaving as you would if you were in someone's living room, but always remember that you don't know *anything* about these other people, except what they've told you, and that might not be the truth. Furthermore, the cues about a person's character that you pick up in a real conversation, from his or her appearance, voice, and body language, are completely absent, and this makes deceptive behavior very easy. So here are some ground rules for keeping safe:

- Never, under any circumstances, give out your real name, street address, workplace location, school name, work or home telephone numbers, or e-mail addresses.

- Do not provide personal information just because somebody asks for it. And be very wary of what you do reveal. Ask yourself: Would I tell this to a perfect stranger, on an unknown street, in the dark?

- Choose a bland nickname when you log onto the chat, unless you want to risk provoking comments on the name (for example, "World Dominator" is probably a bad idea unless you're in a chat room dedicated to fantasy games). Females should choose nicknames that do not suggest their gender, unless they want to make a point of it.

- When using Internet Relay Chat (IRC) do not type something because another user asks you to. It may be a software command (such as DO followed by some other words) that allows the person to transfer control of your computer to his own machine. (For more information on this and other aspects of IRC security, go to **www.newircusers.com/security.html**.)

14

■ Remember, always, that a person who says she is a 22-year-old unmarried actress from New York, or the person who says he is a talent scout for an international modeling agency, may be nothing of the sort. Chat gives people a chance to present fantasy versions of themselves, and many take the opportunity.

■ Most chat environments have a means of shutting out messages sent by a particular person (the ignore switch). Don't be afraid to use it.

■ If you have children, monitor their chat, if you even allow it, *very* carefully. Make sure they understand that they must remain completely anonymous at all times, no matter what a person says to them, nor how friendly that person appears to be.

Web-Based Chat

Web-based chat is chat that doesn't need any special software to display the conversation in the chat room. Instead, you go to a Web page that provides the real-time, interactive discussion. This section uses a representative site, Yahoo! Chat, to teach you the essentials.

Join a Web Chat Site: Yahoo! Chat

How and where do you find chat rooms? A good place to begin, as suggested just above, is Yahoo! Chat at **chat.yahoo.com**. Navigate to the site and you'll see a login section, but before you can actually log in, you'll need to register. You begin this procedure by clicking the link labeled "Sign Up For Yahoo! Chat" and filling out the registration form. When you finish, click the link labeled "Continue to Yahoo! Chat" and you'll go to a page where you can find out what chat rooms are available.

A section in the middle of this page is intended to hold a list of your favorite chat rooms, but when you first arrive you won't see any, since you haven't yet selected any rooms. To do so, click the small Edit button in the bar labeled "Favorite Chat Rooms."

This opens a page listing major categories such as "Cultures and Community," "Health and Wellness," and "Science." Suppose, for example, you want to chat about books. There's a link called "Entertainment and Arts," which seems likely, so click it. This opens another page, where you use check boxes to select the chat rooms you want to add to your personalized list. Select "Books and Literature" and any others you like, then click the Finished button in the top-right corner of the page.

TIP *To see all the rooms available, click the link labeled "Complete Room List." Each link appearing on the page is a link to a chat room, and you can use these to go directly to the room.*

Now you return to the general categories page where, if you wish, you can select another category and pick rooms from it. When you've made all such selections and have returned to the categories page, click its Finished button. This takes you to your original sign-in page, where you now see your selected chat room(s) listed, as links, in the section labeled "Favorite Rooms."

Click the link to one of the chat rooms. A new page will appear and you'll be informed that the computer is downloading something called a *chat applet*. This is the small software program that allows your browser to function as a chat client, and it will be downloaded each time you go to a new chat room.

If your computer is a late model Windows machine with a sound card, and if you're using IE, then in a few more moments at least one security certificate will appear, asking if you want to install voice and sound controls. This allows you to hear voice chat. If you're using Navigator, you'll get some information about installing the voice software; just follow the screen instructions to do this. However, voice chat isn't very widely used yet, so this chapter will concentrate on the text method.

Once the chat applet has installed, you'll see a display like that in Figure 14-1.

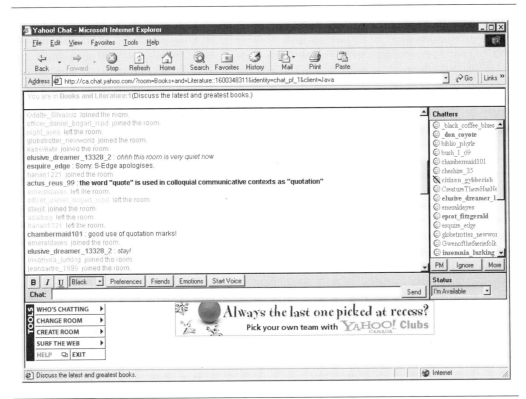

FIGURE 14-1   The Yahoo! Chat screen has two main windows: a large one where the chat text appears, and a smaller one to its right that shows the nicknames of the people chatting

Use Yahoo! Chat

From here on, the basics are simple. The next sections will explore how you contribute to the chat, as well as show you some other features such as ignoring people, and creating your own temporary chat rooms.

Basic Conversation

To add your comments to a conversation, type your message into the box labeled Chat, then click the Send button at its other end. In moments, your message appears in the chat window.

If you want to emphasize the text you send, or change its color, use the small bold, italic, and underline buttons, or pick a color from the drop-down list. If you're hearing voice transmissions from other users and don't want this, click the Stop Voice button. That's all there is to the essentials.

> **TIP**   *Help for Yahoo! Chat is readily available. You find Voice Chat help by clicking the ? button under the Send button, but for a general help window, refer to the Tools section at the bottom-left of the page. Click the Help link there to open a help window, and in that window click the link that says "Java Chat Guide." This provides links to further help subjects.*

Ignore People

Sometimes you may want to avoid seeing the messages from a particular person or persons; to do this, go to the Chatters box at the right of the window. Select the name of the person you want to ignore, and click the Ignore button at the bottom of the Chatters box. Now that person's chat will not show up on your screen. To de-ignore them, select the name and click the button again (it will now be saying Ignore Off).

Exchange Private Messages

If you want to exchange private messages with someone, so that the text doesn't show up in everybody else's chat window, select that person in the Chatters window and click the PM (private message) button at the bottom of the window. This opens a small dialog where you can exchange messages with the person. However, they might not have their chat session set to allow private messages, and if this is the case, you'll get a message to that effect. If you yourself don't want to receive private messages, click the Preferences button to open the Preferences dialog. Select the check box labeled Ignore Private Messages from Strangers and close the dialog, and attempts at private communications will be disregarded (more about strangers in the next section).

Create and Modify a Friends List

"Strangers" are specified in the Ignore dialog because you can have a list of privileged people, referred to as Friends, and Ignore does not shut out private messages from Friends. (In some chat systems they are called Buddies.) Even more useful, once you have a Friends list, you can use it to tell you when these people are online so that you can join them in their current chat room.

The simplest way to add someone to a Friends list is to right-click the name in the Chatters box to open the Select Action dialog. Then click the Add as Friend button to add the person to your Friends list. This will start a default group of names called Chat Friends, with this person in it.

When you next log into Yahoo! Chat, the nicknames of any people in your Friends list, if they are online at the moment, will appear in the Friends in Chat section, next to your Favorite Rooms list. To go to the room where they are, select the nickname and click the Go to Friend button.

To modify your Friends list, including adding new people to it, open the page that displays the list, and click the small Edit button in the section labeled Friends in Chat. This opens a window where you can add people to the list, or remove them from it.

Change Chat Rooms

You don't have to log off and then log back on to go from one room to another. Simply click the Change Room link in the Tools section in the lower-left of the chat window, and two lists will open: Categories and Rooms. If you click an entry in the Categories section, both the subcategories and rooms in that category appear in the Yahoo! Rooms section to its right. Click a room name to enter it, or a subcategory name to reveal the rooms within the subcategory.

Create a User Room

You will also see a list of User Rooms next to the Yahoo! Rooms. These are rooms created by ordinary users, like yourself, within the currently selected category. This ability to create additional rooms is another general characteristic of chat systems. In Yahoo! Chat, these User Rooms come in three flavors:

- ■ Public rooms, which function just as the regular ones do. These appear in the list of User Rooms so people can find them.

- ■ Private rooms, which don't appear in the User Rooms list. However, anyone who goes to a person already in the room—by means of their Friends list, for example—will be allowed into the room.

- ■ Secure rooms are not on the User Rooms list; furthermore, no one can get into yours unless you invite them.

Created rooms aren't permanent. They persist as long as at least one person (not necessarily the creator) is inside them, but as soon as the last person leaves, they vanish. To create one, click the User Rooms link; below the list of User Rooms, you'll see a link labeled Create a Room Here. Click this link and you get a dialog where you specify the room's name, a welcome message for it, and whether it is to be public, private, or secure. Make sure your selections are what you want and click the Create My Room button.

14

To invite people to your room, click the More button under the Chatters list. In the Select Action dialog, type the person's nickname into the User box and click Invite. The person gets a message asking if he or she wants to come to your room, but it's up to the invitee to accept or decline the invitation.

Yahoo! Chat is a good example of a Web-based chat service. With these basics, and a little working on terminology differences (such as referring to private messages as *whispers*) you should be able to negotiate any of the others you visit, including those provided by AOL and MSN.

Internet Relay Chat (IRC)

IRC is a form of chat that preceded Web-based chat. It is based on a network called the IRC network which, like the World Wide Web, is yet another part of the Internet.

The basic principle of IRC is that you use a program called an *IRC client* to connect to an *IRC server* (you remember our earlier discussions of clients and servers; the latter "serve" information to the former). A large number of IRC servers are combined to create the IRC network just referred to, and each server provides you with access to a number of *channels*. These channels are essentially the same environments as the chat rooms you learned about in the section on Yahoo! Chat. Once you've selected a server and connected to it, you can join one of these channels and begin chatting.

Several IRC clients exist, but the single most commonly used one is likely mIRC, which you can get from TUCOWS (**www.tucows.com**) or from its creator, mIRC Company at **www.mirc.co.uk**. This is the example program that we'll use in the next few sections.

After you download mIRC, installation is straightforward. Just navigate to the folder where you stored the downloaded EXE file, and double-click the file to begin the installation. When it's done you can proceed to set up the program.

Set Up mIRC

Begin by making sure you're connected to the Internet. Then launch the program by choosing Start | Programs | mIRC | mIRC32 and carry out the following procedure. Note that mIRC is shareware, and that you can evaluate it for free for 30 days. If you go on using it longer than that, you must register and pay the $20 (U.S.) registration fee.

1. The first time you start mIRC, you get a connection dialog. Since you're evaluating the software, close the small "About mIRC" splash screen.

2. The mIRC Options dialog appears (see the next illustration). In the Full Name box, enter a name, but be aware that people on IRC will be able to see this name. Very few people use their real names in chat, and you may prefer to imitate them.

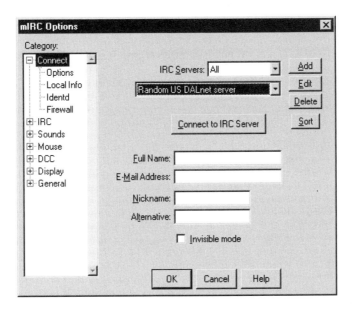

3. In the E-mail Address box, enter an e-mail address that you want to use if other people send you e-mail. If you don't want e-mail, just fill in the name you used in step 2.

4. Enter a nickname and an alternative for it. Your nickname is the one that will appear in the chat window during chat.

5. If you select the check box labeled Invisible Mode, people will not be able to find you on IRC unless they know your nickname, you join a chat, or you use private messaging.

6. At the top of the dialog are two boxes. The upper one, labeled IRC Servers, provides lists of server groups. It defaults to All, so you can use the lower box to select any IRC server. If you use the upper box to select a server group other than All, then the lower box will display the servers within that group. Some will have only one choice, such as "Acestar: Random Server." It's a good idea to connect to a server geographically near you, though this may be difficult to figure out. If the server is slow, try another one.

7. When you've selected a server, click the OK button, and mIRC is set up in its basic configuration.

Use mIRC

mIRC is a program with a lot of tools and options, far more than we can cover in part of a chapter. In the sections that follow, we'll necessarily have to restrict ourselves to the basics.

14

Connect to a Server

Launch the program and choose Tools | Connect to see if you can get through to the server you selected during setup. If you can't, choose File | Cancel Connect. Then connect to a different server by choosing File | Options. This opens the connection dialog you saw earlier, where you select a new server and click OK. Then choose Tools | Connect to try again.

Once you've connected, you see an introduction in the window, and over the top of it a smaller window containing a partial list of the channels available from the server. This smaller window is the mIRC Channels Folder, and the channels in it are chosen by the server administration as a sample (see the next illustration).

Join a Channel, Issue Commands, and Chat

To join one of these sample channels, you can select it and click the Join button, or simply double-click it. This takes you to a window like the one you explored with Yahoo! Chat, where the conversation appears in lines of text with the "speakers" identified by their nicknames. Go ahead and try it, and watch the conversation in the selected channel flow by for a while.

As you do, you'll notice a text box across the bottom of the chat window, with a blinking cursor in it. This is the box where you create your messages before sending them. To contribute to the conversation, simply type your message and press the ENTER key. You'll see it appear in the chat window a few instants later.

The text box is also where you enter commands to do things like leave the channel, log off IRC, and so on. All commands are prefixed by a forward slash, so if you want help, you would type **/help** into the box and press ENTER.

The other essential command is **/quit**. This disconnects you from the current IRC server completely. Many of the basic commands are also available from the Commands menu. For example, to leave a channel, you can type either **/leave** or **/part**, or choose Commands | Part Channel. If you use the menu commands, you'll have to fill in an IRC input request dialog to make it work, so you may prefer to memorize the commands and type them in.

 If you issue some commands, their results appear not in the chat window but in the Status window, the window you see when you first open mIRC. Click the Status button above the chat window to reveal the Status window.

Change Channels

Suppose you've been watching a channel for a while but want to explore others. Type **/part** (or **/leave**) and press the ENTER key, and the chat window disappears. To display the Channels Folder you saw earlier, click the Channels Folder button up on the mIRC toolbar (it's third from the left). Double-click another channel to open its chat window. You do not, however, have to leave one channel in order to join another. Simply leave the current chat window as it is and use the Channels Folder to connect to another one.

List Additional Channels

The Channels Folder by no means displays all of the channels available. To get a full list, type **/list** in the text box, in either the main mIRC window or the current chat window. The list is displayed as it downloads, but this may take a long time—there may be hundreds of channels, so be patient. However, if you want to stop the listing, right-click in the listing window and select Stop Listing Channels from the pop-up menu. You can't close the listing window, by the way, until you've used the Stop Listing Channels command.

If you now see a channel that you want to join, select it, then right-click it, and choose Join Channel from the pop-up menu. The chat window for that channel will open.

 If you don't send any messages for a period of time, you may be automatically disconnected from the server.

To filter out channels that have only a few people on them, type **/list -min** and a number; for example, **/list -min 12** will display only channels with more than 11 people in them. Note, however, that the entire list of channels will still be downloaded. The "hits" are displayed as they are found, while the download proceeds.

Exchange Private Messages

There are three ways of talking to someone without alerting the other people on the channel (except the person you're talking to, of course!). Here are the possibilities:

■ To send a message privately to another person in the channel, double-click his or her nickname in the Nickname list box. A private message window opens where you can type in the message. If you receive an unsolicited private message from someone, a button appears above the chat window with the sender's nickname on it. Click this button to read the message and respond if desired.

14

■ If you're not on a channel, you can type **/query** *nickname*, where *nickname* is the nickname of the person to whom you want to talk. If they're on IRC, they'll get the message. To see if a person's on IRC before trying to send a message, type **/whois** *nickname*.

■ You can use DCC, or Direct Client Communications, to correspond. This is a more secure and faster way of communicating since it connects the two IRC clients directly together. Type **/dcc chat** *nickname*, and a message window opens where, if the person agrees to chat, you can exchange messages. If you receive such an invitation, you get a confirmation box asking if you will chat with the sender. Click Yes or No as you wish. To end the DCC session, simply close the private message window.

Ignore People

To ignore a person who is sending you private messages, type **/ignore** *nickname*. Any such messages will be rejected. To remove the ignore, type **/ignore -x** *nickname*.

Create a Private Channel

Creating a private channel, which is just like a private chat room in Yahoo! Chat, is pretty easy. Type **/join** *#channelname* where channelname is the name of some unused channel (the # sign is required). These channels can be of three types:

■ **Public**   There are no restrictions on visitors. This is the default.

■ **Private**   The channel is visible in the channels list, but people can join only if invited. Once you've created a channel, make it private with the command **/mode** *#channelname* **+p**. To remove its private status, type **/mode** *#channelname* **-p**. To invite someone into it, type **/invite** *nickname #channelname*.

■ **Secret**   The channel does not appear in the channels list, and people can join only if invited. Once you've created a channel, make it secret with the command **/mode** *#channelname* **+s**. To remove its secret status, type **/mode** *#channelname* **-s**. To invite someone into it, type **/invite** *nickname #channelname*.

As the creator of the new channel, you are the channel operator. You can tell an operator by the @ sign prefixed to the nickname. Operators have certain privileges, among them banning people from the channel. Refer to the mIRC Help files for more information.

As was said earlier, mIRC isn't the only IRC client available, but once you've learned to cope with it, the others will come quite easily.

ICQ ("I Seek You")

ICQ is technically what's called a "talk" program, a program that allows people to exchange text messages privately online, in real time. Nowadays it and programs like it are more often referred to as messenger programs or "instant messengers," as reflected in the names of two other such clients in widespread use, Yahoo! Messenger and AOL Instant Messenger. The key characteristic of instant messengers is that if you're online, your computer alerts you when a message arrives from one of the people on your correspondent list.

ICQ is one of the most widely used and capable of the instant messenger clients. Once you install ICQ and register, you get an ID number by which you'll henceforth be known to the system. Any other ICQ user who can determine your ID can then send you messages; unfortunately, however, AOL and Yahoo! users can't do so, because the various instant messaging systems don't interact. They can coexist on the same computer, though, so once AOL and Yahoo! users install ICQ, they too can exchange messages with you.

In the next sections, we'll use the example of ICQ to learn the basic use of an instant messaging program.

Obtain, Install, and Set Up ICQ

You can get ICQ from download sites like TUCOWS (**www.tucows.com**) or from its maker at **www.icq.com**.

After you've downloaded the program, installation is simple. Make sure you're connected to the Internet, then navigate to the folder containing the EXE program and double-click it. Follow the onscreen instructions until the program is installed.

CAUTION   *The version of ICQ used here was a beta version, version 99B. If you have a full release of the program, it may differ slightly from what is described. If you use the beta version, remember that betas are not fully finished and may have significant bugs.*

To set up ICQ, do the following:

1. Launch ICQ by choosing Start | Programs | ICQ | ICQ. The first screen of the Registration Wizard appears. Select the New ICQ option button and click Next.

2. In the next screen, select the option button for your connection type (Modem and dial-up, Permanent or high-speed) and click Next. An info box appears explaining the information you'll be asked for during registration. Click OK.

3. In the next screen, fill in the identification boxes. The nickname is what you'll be known as to people sending you messages. Click Next.

4. A dialog appears where you can fill in additional details about yourself. Until you get a better feel for ICQ, leave these blank; in fact you probably should leave them blank for good. Click Next.

5. The next screen asks if you'll participate in market research. Unless you like doing this sort of thing, select the option labeled I Don't Think I Will Participate, and click Next.

6. The next screen is where you can determine your privacy level. Type a password and confirm it. Leave the other options at their defaults; you can change them later if you wish, to tighten access to your ICQ address. Click Next.

14

7. The next screen provides you with your ICQ number. Click Next.

8. In the next screen you verify your SMTP or Outgoing Mail server name. This will have been provided by your ISP (you used it in setting up your e-mail client, remember?). If you don't have e-mail, leave it blank. Click Next.

9. The final screen gives you some information about using ICQ. Read it over and Click Done.

10. The Contact List Wizard appears. You could use it to set up a contact list, but we'll start fresh with that in the next section. The client has now been set up, so for now, close all the ICQ dialogs.

Communicate with ICQ

The basics of using ICQ are simple. The essential thing to have, of course, is somebody to talk to. To set up a list of such people, you add contacts, or what ICQ calls "chat partners" to a contact list.

Begin by connecting to the Internet and launching the program. This opens a small ICQ window on your desktop, resembling the one in the following illustration. (It also opens an ICQ Web site announcements page, which will close in ten seconds, so you can ignore it.) This window can be gotten out of the way by clicking its Minimize button; note that if you click the window's Close button, it will shut the program down. While the program is running and you're on the Internet, a small green flower appears in the System Tray; if the program is running but you're not connected and therefore offline, the flower is orange.

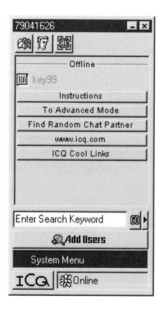

You can only add contacts to your contact list if they are also ICQ subscribers. The best thing to have in order to do this is the person's ICQ number. Alternatively, an e-mail address will do, or nickname and first and last name.

Assuming you know some items of the information, click the Add Users bar in the ICQ dialog. This opens a Find/Add dialog. Fill in the appropriate box(es) and click the Search button next to the ones you filled in. After a period of time, assuming the person is listed in the ICQ records according to that information, a dialog will be displayed showing the person's information. Double-click the listing to add that person to your contact list.

You'll note that this person's nickname now appears in the upper part of the ICQ dialog, above the Instructions button. If the name is in red, the person is offline at the moment. If it's blue, the person is online and ICQ is running on his/her computer.

To remove a person from your contact list, click his name in the ICQ dialog to open a menu. Choose Delete, and answer Yes to the confirmation dialog. If you want another name there instead of the nickname, choose Rename instead from the menu and change the name.

To send a message, click the person's nickname in the ICQ window and choose Send from the pop-up menu; alternatively, double-click the nickname. This opens a message window (see the next illustration). Type your message into the text area and click Send, and the text goes on its way. If the person is offline, ICQ will offer to save the message and send it when the person comes online.

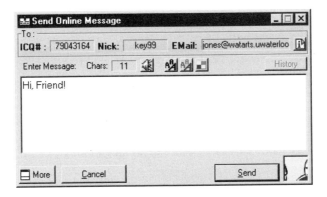

At the other end, the ICQ user will get an audible alert from the ICQ client, and the flower in the System Tray will change to a blinking message icon (if the ICQ window is open, a message icon will blink there, as well).

To read a message, double-click on the message icon and the message window appears with the sender's text in it. If you want to reply to it on the spot, click the Reply button, which closes the incoming message window and opens an outgoing one. Type your reply, and click Send.

One kind of message you will likely see is the one that arrives when another ICQ user adds you to his or her contact list. The alert appears in the System Tray as a flashing red and yellow icon. Double-click it and you'll see the dialog box in the next illustration. To find out more about this person, or at least as much as they registered with, click the Get User Info button. If you want to add this person to your own contact list, click the Add to Contact List button.

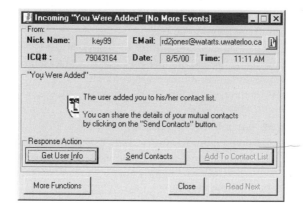

You can also use ICQ as a chat client as well as a messaging client. Suppose someone sends you a message, and you want to have a further conversation about the subject. You both could go on sending messages back and forth, but switching to chat mode is more convenient.

To set it up, click the Request Chat button in the incoming message dialog. This opens the Send Online Chat Request dialog, as in the next illustration. Enter a subject for the chat and click the Chat button.

The recipient now sees a blinking text balloon icon in the System Tray, which is the request for the chat. Assuming you received it, double-click the icon to open the Incoming Chat request dialog. You can read the subject, to decide if you want to participate; if you do, just click the Accept button.

Now life gets interesting. A chat window opens where you type your end of the conversation and receive replies. You can arrange the window in one of four ways, the two most likely being these:

■ In IRC mode, with a single window where all the conversation appears. Below the window is a text box where you type your message, just as you learned to do with mIRC. To send it, you press the ENTER key. To select this mode, choose Layout | IRC.

■ In split mode, which has two panes in the window (see the next illustration). You type in the upper pane and the other person's typing appears in the lower pane. In split mode, the recipient sees your text appear as you're typing it. (If you're a bad typist, this can be humiliating.) However, if you like split mode, choose Layout | Split to get to it. Note that each person in the chat can be using a different mode.

Whichever layout you choose, you simply begin typing to carry on the conversation. Just remember that in IRC mode, you have to press ENTER to send the message, while in split mode it appears in the recipient's window as you type it.

There are other things you can do with IRC, such as participate in topic-oriented chat groups and send files. Refer to the Help system for more information. The ICQ site itself (**www.icq.com**) has a good online user manual you can look at.

Exploring a Virtual Community: Cybertown

Among the interesting places developing on the Web are what are called virtual communities. They're rather hard to describe; in effect, they're towns or cities (or countries, even) that lead a kind of virtual existence on the World Wide Web. They're imaginary places, sort of, except that unlike the ones that exist in your head or in books, they're inhabited by real people with whom you can interact.

Representative of these places is the virtual community called Cybertown. Since it's easier to show it by example than describe it, connect to the Internet and go to **www.cybertown.com**. It's a science-fiction sort of place (the year is 2088) where you can build a home (with a mailbox and a personal chat space), go shopping, visit clubs, play games, have a virtual pet, and even get a job. Be aware, however, that you won't get the real feel of it unless you have a high-speed connection; it's very heavy on animation, and a fast 3D video card is needed as well for best results.

You need to register, a simple process, before you can enter. Click the Login/Join link, and fill in a nickname and a password in the registration page. Once you're in, you'll be asked if you want to install a plug-in; answer yes, and you're in business. You'll find yourself in the Cybertown Plaza, with a lot of people chatting in a green-tinted window at the bottom of the screen (see Figure 14-2).

From here you can start exploring by means of the control panel at the right of the screen (the City Tour is a good place to start) and later, when you've got a sense of the place, come back to City Plaza and see what the other Cybertown citizens are saying in the chat window. For deeper explorations, the How Do I link will give you information about getting around the city and using its facilities. It's an interesting place, and if you've never spent any time in a virtual world, you may find that being in one is an engaging experience.

Where to Find It

Web Site	Address	What's There
Cybertown	www.cybertown.com	Virtual community
ICQ Company	www.icq.com	Messaging client
mIRC Company	www.mirc.co.uk	IRC client software
NewIRCusers.com	www.newircusers.com/security.html	IRC security information
TUCOWS	www.tucows.com	IRC clients

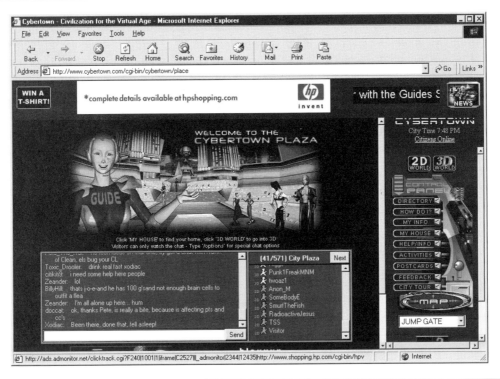

FIGURE 14-2   The Cybertown Plaza is the central meeting place of the Cybertown virtual community

14

Chapter 15

Online and E-mail Gaming

How To . . .

■ Play adventure, action, and role-playing games

■ Play strategy, military, and simulation games

■ Play sports games

■ Play board, card, and other traditional games

■ Play trivia and word games

■ Play casino games

■ Find games for your children

Computer games have been around for a long time, but widespread online gaming is a comparatively recent phenomenon, one that owes its existence to the Internet. It's a big phenomenon and getting bigger, just as the games themselves are. You can play online games not only alone, but also in virtual worlds inhabited, at any given moment, by literally thousands of other players.

Unfortunately, the majority of the online role-playing, adventure, and action games, especially the really big ones, are oriented to the combative tastes of younger male players. Few of these games, as far as I've discovered, are of much interest to women in particular, or to the older population in general. However, people who aren't interested in adventure-sorcery-military-strategy games do have other sources of online entertainment. There are lots of sites on the Internet where you can, for free, play traditional games like euchre, backgammon, chess, and bridge, and have a chat with the other players while you're at it.

Games for Grownups

If you're new to online gaming, locating places to play them may be a bit of a puzzle. The best approach at the beginning is likely to use one of the "gateway" sites that lead to a selection of online titles. Four major gateway sites are the following:

■ CNet GameCenter at **www.gamecenter.com/Play**

■ MSN Gaming Zone at **http://zone.msn.com**

■ The Station at **www.station.sony.com**

■ Yahoo! Games at **http://games.yahoo.com/**

Given the large number of online games available on the Internet, we can only examine a representative sample here. There are plenty of others, which you can explore through the gateway sites just mentioned.

Role Playing, Adventure, and Action Games

The divisions among role-playing games (RPGs), adventure, and action games tend to be rather blurry. Loosely speaking, RPGs are adventure games in which the characters gain experience and skill as the game proceeds, while in pure adventure games the characters have much the same abilities from beginning to end. Adventure-action games are RPGs that focus mainly on fast-paced, real-time action, often combat-oriented. In what you might call "pure action" games, there is virtually nothing but combat.

One thing you should be aware of before becoming involved in these games is that they do have technical glitches, such as servers being down, and occasional long lag times between issuing a command and actually getting the result. However, a lot of people find them a great deal of fun.

EverQuest

One of the most popular RPGs at present is EverQuest. This is a commercial game, in other words you register and then pay a set monthly fee of about $10 (U.S.) in order to play. In addition, you have to buy the game software itself, which you can locate in computer gaming retail stores, or online, for about $40 (U.S.).

Before buying it, however, be aware that the hardware requirements are not insignificant. A *minimum* install of the game requires half a gigabyte (500MB) of disk space, and a fast 3D graphics card and a fast Pentium-class processor are essential for enjoying the game.

Did you know?

The very first computerized adventure game was named Colossal Cave (though most players simply called it Adventure) and was written in 1977 by Will Crowther and Don Woods. It ran on the large mainframe computers of the period and was a text-based game; you used a Teletype machine to type in commands like **e** (for "go east") and got printed feedback like "You see a small opening in the rock ahead of you." Over the years, other programmers made versions of the game to run on other types of mainframes, and it turned out to be the great-grandfather of all modern computer adventure games. Versions still exist for the Mac and the PC as well as other computers; you can get them at **http://ifarchive.org/indexes/if-archiveXgames.html**.

15

A high-speed connection will also make the game move more quickly. Check the box or the game site for exact system specifications.

To look over the game information, navigate to **www.station.sony.com**. Click the EverQuest link, then bypass the advertising screen by clicking the Continue On to EverQuest link. Now you're in the EverQuest "foyer," from which you link to the EverQuest page itself. Click the EverQuest Site link to go there and have a look at it (see Figure 15-1). The Support section gives some valuable background on the game, including hardware needs, so if you're deciding whether to join in, its links are worth following.

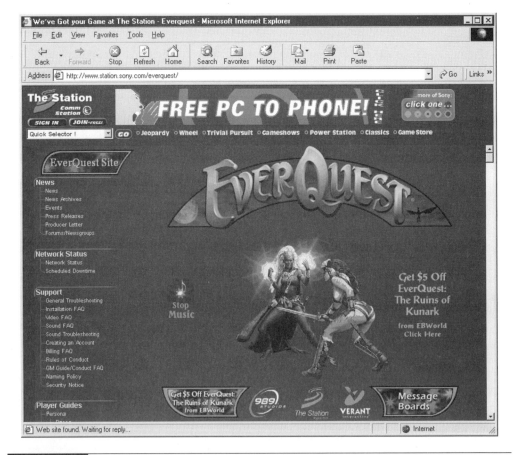

FIGURE 15-1   You begin your EverQuest adventure at the home page of the EverQuest site

The world of EverQuest is what's called a persistent world. It exists whether you're connected to it or not, and if you come back after a while, things will have changed. It's the classic medieval sorcery-ridden world with various sentient races, but it is a very large one, with three continents and a variety of political and economic systems. As usual with role-playing games, you select a character to represent you (anything from a dwarf to a wizard) and set off on your quest for knowledge, power, and excitement. There's plenty of magic, and you can adventure either alone or in company. You *can* get killed, but if you decline what's called "player killing," the other players won't be able to murder you (and you won't be able to do *them* in, either). You're still vulnerable to the game-based perils, of course. The game tends to reward cooperative play.

Assuming you have the hardware you need, you begin by purchasing the game and installing it on your machine. The next step is to go to the EverQuest Web site and set up an account under which you will play. The registration procedure will ask for an account key, which is supplied with the retail package you purchased. The documentation that comes with the game tells you how to get connected, and you can get additional help under the Support section of the EverQuest home page, as well as in the EverQuest foyer.

Rainbow Six: Rogue Spear

An enhancement of the earlier Rainbow Six, Rainbow Six: Rogue Spear is an RPG with very strong action elements, in a modern setting. You select a team of Special Forces soldiers, of which you are the leader, and lead them in a series of tactical anti-terrorist actions. These actions are the meat of the game, and provide its main excitement. However, Rainbow Six is more than a shoot-em-up; as you progress through the various missions, a background plot of world-threatening proportions develops.

The MSN Gaming Zone offers multiplayer online play of both Rainbow Six and Rainbow Six: Rogue Spear. To join a Rogue Spear game, you first have to own the game itself, which is available from most computer gaming retail outlets, or can be purchased online. Before you buy it, though, check the system requirements listed on the box to see if your hardware is capable of running the game.

> NOTE
>
> *On the MSN Gaming Zone, you have to pay only for the games that are listed in the Premium category. All the others (including Rogue Spear) are free, barring the purchase price of the original game, of course.*

Assuming you buy it, install the game on your machine, and you're ready for online play. Go to the MSN Gaming Zone page at **http://zone.msn.com**, and look for a link to the game. If you can't see one, click the Game Index link from the menu at the top-left of the page, and you'll get a list of all the games on the Zone (see Figure 15-2). Note that this menu also allows you to display games according to category.

When you reach the Rogue Spear start page, you'll see that the gaming environment is laid out in about 30 rooms, which represent various ways of playing the game. Before you can get involved, though, you'll have to get a Zone membership. To do so, select Getting Started from the menu, and when the Getting Started page appears, click the Sign Up link. Follow the instructions for signing up, and a set of core files, which allow your machine to play online,

15

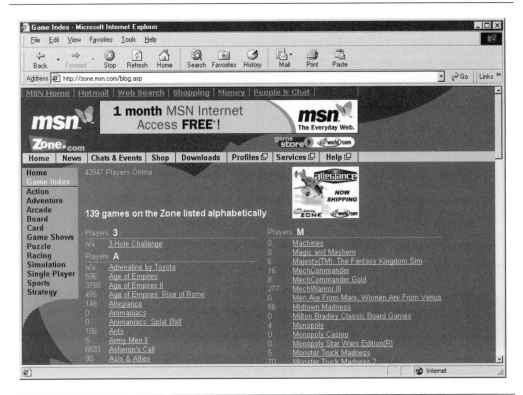

FIGURE 15-2   The MSN Gaming Zone home page provides links to the Microsoft online games collection

will be downloaded. When you see the dialog asking if you want to download and install the Essential Zone Files (or an equivalent plug-in, if you're using Navigator) click Yes, and proceed with the instructions.

When this process completes, you're offered a short tutorial about the way the Zone works. Read through it, and when it's finished you will return to the Rogue Spear start page (see Figure 15-3). If you're a novice at the game you probably should check out the links labeled Tips and Strategies, and the Game Help link. Then click the Play Tom Clancy's Rainbow Six: Rogue Spear link, and you're on your way. Note that you must have the CD of the game in your CD-ROM drive in order to play.

On the MSN Zone, you can host a new game as well as simply join an existing one. Refer to the tutorial, available from every game's Getting Started page, to find out how to do this.

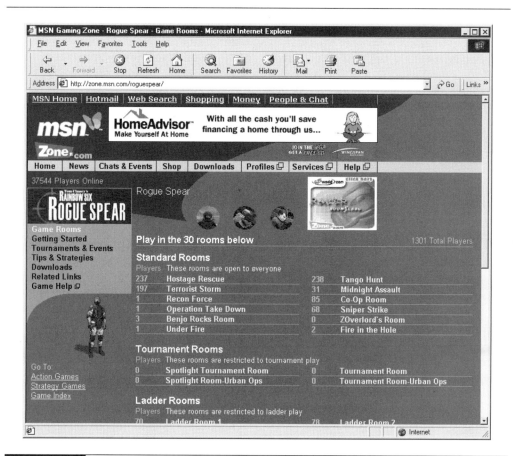

Quake II

The MSN Zone also offers Quake II. This is a pure action "shooter" game, in which you have a first-person view of events, normally through the sights of some exotic weapon. Your basic aim is to kill the other inhabitants of the game's alien environments before they kill you. The other inhabitants, of course, are the other players.

As with Rogue Spear, you must have purchased and installed the retail version before you can play. Put the Quake II CD in your drive, navigate to the Zone home page, and locate the Quake II link and click it. If you haven't got a Zone name and password, use the Getting Started link to get one (see the Rogue Spear section for information on this). If you do have one, click the Game Rooms link to see what games are available, and join one.

15

Strategy, Military, and Simulation Games

These games somewhat overlap the types discussed in the previous sections. The strategy and military games tend to be on a large scale, but many of the simulation games are at a tactical level. Even within this group the boundaries are somewhat uncertain; for example, the strategy games usually have a major military component.

Age of Empires II

Another offering from the MSN Gaming Zone, Age of Empires II has the same basic getting-started requirements as Rogue Spear and Quake II: You have to own the game and install it, and you have to possess a Zone name and password.

Once you've got these, you can play Age of Empires II. This involves selecting a civilization to run, building its economic power, translating that into military might, and conquering the world (or at least avoiding being conquered yourself). The other players run other civilizations, and with over a dozen civilizations available for play, the game can become very complex indeed.

Some of the games on the MSN Gaming Zone, such as Age of Empires II, have free trial versions that you can download and play online. Check the game's main page to see if there's a Download link, and follow that to find out what's available.

Allegiance

Allegiance, available on the MSN Zone, is a large multiplayer space warfare game set in the distant future, when Earth has been destroyed and the survivors fight over the remnants. It has both tactical and strategic aspects, in that you can either participate directly in combat or manage your interstellar combat forces from a starbase.

You have to purchase the game, install it, and then log onto the MSN Zone and navigate to the Allegiance start page. This is one of the Zone's premium games; you can play it for free for the first month, but after that the subscription is $9.95 (U.S.) per month.

Fighter Ace

Fighter Ace is a simulation of WWII air combat provided by the MSN Gaming Zone. It differs from the previous games mentioned in that you don't need to purchase a retail version. Instead, you download the software from the Zone and use that to play the game. However, it's a premium game; after a three-day free trial, a subscription costs $1.95 (U.S.) per day or $9.95 (U.S.) per month.

The game puts you into the cockpit of one of 34 German or allied fighters, which you fly against your opponents in environments called Arenas. These come in several flavors. Arcade Arenas are the ones where flying is easy, while in the Realistic Arenas, your plane may be damaged if you stress it too far. There are also Territorial Combat Arenas, where you can carry out ground attacks.

Sports Fantasy Games and Sports Games

Sports games are not generally as popular as the games discussed, but they do have a following. One main type is the "sports fantasy game" in which you construct your ideal team or league and manage it through a season.

One good site for this is available at **http://fantasysports.yahoo.com** (see Figure 15-4). The players on the Yahoo! teams are analogues of real-life players, and the performance of your team is based on how well the real-life players perform in actual games. The Yahoo! site collects these

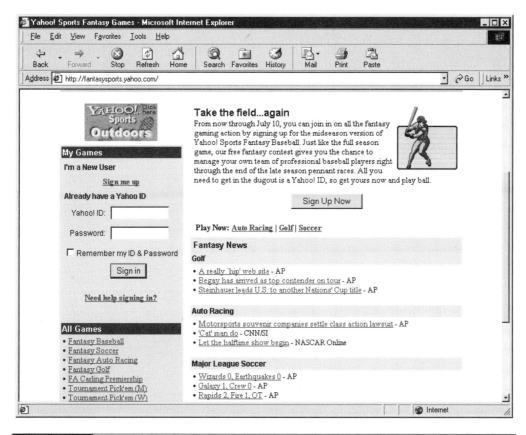

15

FIGURE 15-4   The Yahoo! Games site lets you participate in several types of sports games

statistics and updates the various team standings. As for the sports available, you can "play" baseball, soccer, auto racing, golf, basketball, football, hockey, and others.

The other main type of sports game is the simulation sports game. A representative example is the MSN Zone's Links LS 2000. To play this golf game, you purchase the retail version, install it, go to the MSN Gaming Zone and obtain a Zone name and password, and then play the game (see the section earlier on Rainbow Six: Rogue Spear, for more details on this procedure). There are several game rooms available, including several tournament rooms.

Card, Board, and Other Traditional Games

For a wide selection of multiplayer card, board, and other games, as well as some single-player ones, check out the Yahoo! Games site at **http://games.yahoo.com** (see Figure 15-5).

To play chess, for example, you click the chess link under Board Games. A registration screen appears where you register a username and a password. Note that if you have already registered anywhere on Yahoo! (in Yahoo! Chat, for example), you can use that identification;

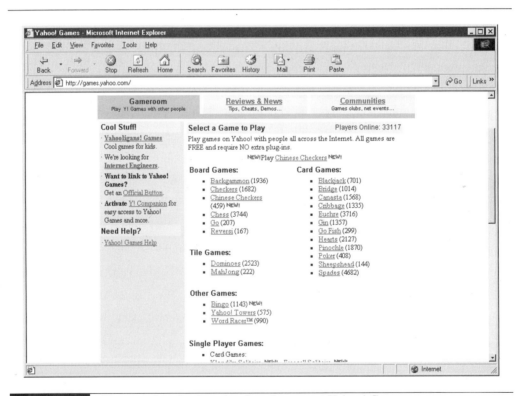

FIGURE 15-5   You can also play board and card games at Yahoo! Games

you don't have to register over again. A list of game rooms appears, showing which ones are full, and you can choose to play at various levels from Social to Advanced.

Click one of the rooms with space available, and after a few moments you'll be asked to install a plug-in that allows you to play the game. Answer Yes. After the plug-in installs you'll see a new window listing the various "tables" that are in use (see Figure 15-6). If you see a Join button, you can click it to join that particular game. Alternatively, you can click the Watch button to observe one in progress, although if somebody doesn't want you watching, you may get "booted" and the observation window will close. There is also a chat window in the lower part of the tables window screen, where you can chat with other players.

The other multiplayer games on Yahoo! Games get set up in much the same way as chess, including the download of the plug-in, so once you've managed that, the others won't be very mysterious.

Several single-player board and card games are also available at the MSN Gaming Zone.

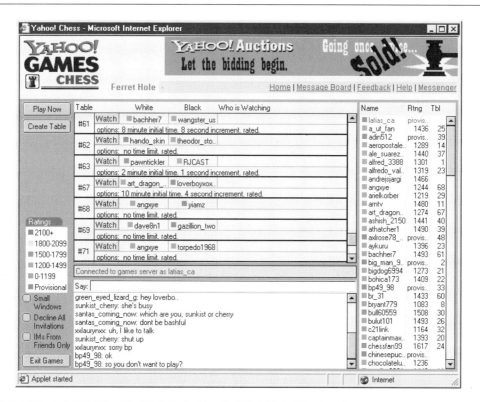

FIGURE 15-6   You can select different chess games to observe, or play a game yourself

15

Trivia and Word Games

If you like playing trivia games, you can find some at **www.station.sony.com**. The classic example is Trivial Pursuit Online at **www.station.sony.com/trivialpursuit/genus**. To play, navigate to the Web site and click the Sign In button; from here you'll be asked to register (it's free). Once you've registered and clicked the Accept button, you'll have to download and install a plug-in, just as you did with the Yahoo! games. The plug-in then downloads the game software and installs it, and you're ready to begin. Click the Play button and wait a few seconds, and you'll find yourself at a table and automatically matched with your opponents. From there the game progresses as does the traditional one.

The classic word game, of course, is crosswords. While it's a single-player game, you can still play it online at the MSN Gaming Zone; an example appears in Figure 15-7.

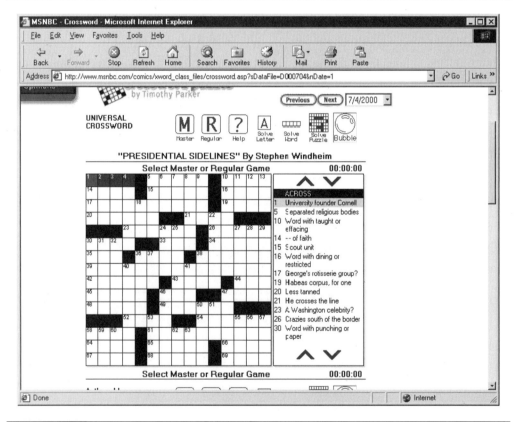

FIGURE 15-7   Crossword addicts will find what they need on the MSN Gaming Zone

Casino/Gambling Games

There are two kinds of casino games on the Internet: those where your money is safe and you can't lose anything but pride, and the others, where you're in the game for real money and, just as in real life, you can lose a lot of it. You can sometimes win in some of those games, of course, but remember that the odds *always* favor the house.

Non-Monetary Gambling Games

You can find some of these, where you play without money, at the World Opponent Network at **www.won.net**. Click the Card/Casino link and choose from blackjack, craps, roulette, and poker. There are a number of social rooms; choose one and you'll have to download a plug-in to play the game you selected. Then you have to register, if you haven't already done so, and wait for a further download. Once it's present and installed, you enter the room and can play the game (see Figure 15-8).

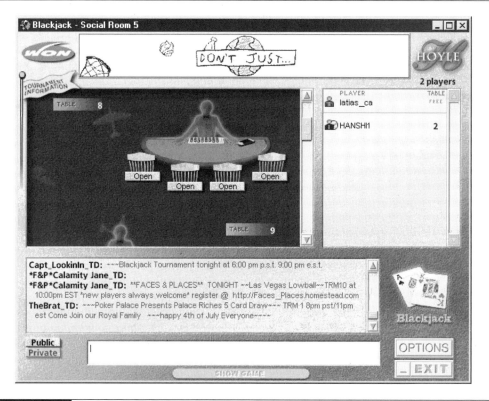

FIGURE 15-8   Casino games such as blackjack are a feature of the World Opponent Network

15

Did you know?

When you buy a game, check its documentation to see if it's enabled for PBEM (Play By E-Mail). You can use e-mail to play such games against a human opponent, the limitation being that your opponent must also have the game installed on his/her computer. You play in this mode by saving the game at the end of each turn, and then e-mailing a save-game file, as an attachment, to your opponent. He loads the attached save-game file into his copy of the game, and the software displays the state of the game as it was when you ended your turn. Your opponent then counters your moves, saves the game at the end of *his* turn, and e-mails that file back to you.

Real Gambling Games

Before you even think of getting involved in the kind of Internet gaming where you play for real money, be aware that not all the online gaming establishments are licensed. There is no regulation at all of such unlicensed establishments, and their management can do as it pleases, including rigging the odds. So if you lose your shirt in a dishonest game in one of these places, you will have no legal recourse at all, and you can kiss your money good-bye. Furthermore, the whole question of the legality of cross-border Internet gambling is unresolved, and the U.S. Congress is still scratching its collective head over it.

To find out more about online gambling before visiting an Internet gaming site, you would be well advised to visit the Internet Gaming Commission's Web site at **www.internetcommission.com**. They have lists of accredited and licensed sites, and other useful information. Note that the Commission is *not* a U.S. government organization.

Games for Kids

There are also online games for children. A place to begin looking is the Kid's Domain at **www.kidsdomain.com**. Navigate to the site, then click the Kids link, then the Online Games link (see Figure 15-9). Most of these are single-player games but there are a few multiplayer ones as well.

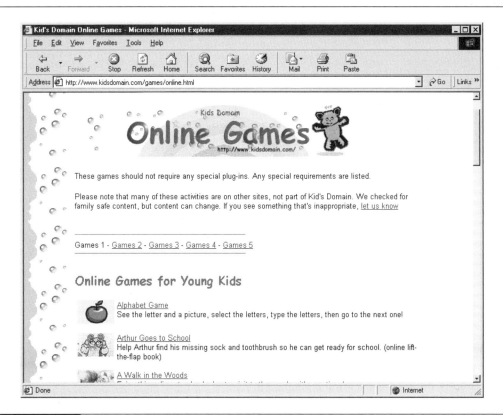

FIGURE 15-9   The Kids' Domain offers online and other types of games for children

Some other sites with children's games and related resources are:

- Cyberkids (**www.cyberkids.com**)
- Kidscom (**www.kidscom.com**)
- Headbone Zone (**www.headbone.com**)
- Yahooligans (**www.yahooligans.com**)

15

Where to Find It

Web Site	Address	What's There
Cyberkids	www.cyberkids.com	Children's online games
Headbone Zone	www.headbone.com	Children's online games
Kidscom	www.kidscom.com	Children's online games
MSN Gaming Zone	http://zone.msn.com	Online games
Sony Station	www.station.sony.com	Online games
Yahoo! Games	games.yahoo.com	Online games
Yahoo! Sports	fantasysports.yahoo.com	Fantasy sport games
Yahooligans	www.yahooligans.com	Children's online games

Chapter 16

Buy, Sell, and Obtain Services on the Internet

How To . . .

- ◼ Understand online privacy and security when buying online
- ◼ Learn how to research online vendors
- ◼ Safeguard your personal information and your privacy
- ◼ Safeguard your credit card information
- ◼ Buy online at retail Web stores
- ◼ Buy at online auctions
- ◼ Understand the complexities of selling on the Web

You can buy just about anything on the Internet nowadays, from automobiles to clothing. However, while online shopping is certainly significant and is growing steadily, it hasn't yet produced the explosion of electronic purchasing that some enthusiasts predicted. Part of this is because people aren't really in the habit (yet) of looking for goods and services online, but a lot of their reluctance can be traced to consumer distrust about the safety and privacy of online transactions. Added to this is the normal anxiety of many novice computer owners about using their machines. Finally, there is the sheer awkwardness of actually buying something on many vendors' Web sites. So, in this chapter, we'll try to demystify the issue of online commerce, mostly from the consumer's point of view.

Buy Goods and Services

Much of the following will be related to privacy and security considerations in online purchasing, because the process of actually *buying* something is fairly simple (assuming the designer of the e-commerce Web site did a decent job). While Chapter 17 also treats security questions, I put the issues related to e-commerce into this one, since dealing with them in the later chapter would fragment the subject unnecessarily. *E-commerce,* by the way, is a current buzzword that refers to business carried out by electronic means, in other words, through the Internet.

What About Privacy and Security?

The question of security is probably uppermost in people's minds when they contemplate online shopping. Not only do you have to send your credit card information out into the wilds of the Internet, a lot of Web sites also ask you for information above and beyond the legitimate basics of "What do you want and what's your shipping address?" The next sections will help you understand how to cope with these issues.

Research the Company

How do you know if a Web-based vendor is legitimate or fly-by-night? You can protect yourself, to a large degree, by researching the company before you buy anything from it. If it's a well-known

Web-based outfit like Amazon.com, or the Web site of a traditional brick-and-mortar store like Sears, you can be pretty confident that you're dealing with reputable people (you still may not want to tell them things you don't have to, though).

If you don't know anything about the company, however, you should do at least a little snooping before you undertake a purchase. Do a search on the company name or Web address, and see what comes up. Also, see if anybody you know has dealt with the company. You can also check the Better Business Bureau at **www.bbbonline.com** to see if the company is registered with their Privacy Program or Reliability Program. Note that as of Summer 2000 this service was new, and only a tiny fraction of the Web-based companies were listed.

 Some fly-by-night vendors put up Web sites intentionally designed to look like those of other, major Web companies. These deceptive sites may also have Web addresses that closely resemble those of the sites they imitate. Be sure you're in the right place before you order anything.

Some Web sites are registered with independent consumer-protection organizations (for example, those that are part of the BBB programs), and will display a logo to this effect. This is a good sign, but remember that it is not an absolute guarantee of good service. The independent agency may simply be attesting that the vendor does in fact comply with his privacy policy, for example, but that does not necessarily mean that the privacy policy is one you will accept. Also, to ensure that the logo is legitimate, click it and see if it takes you to its organization's Web site, and then ensure that the vendor is indeed listed there.

There are also Web sites that specialize in rating Web-based vendors. Two of these are FeedbackDirect at **www.feedbackdirect.com**, and another is BizRate at **www.bizrate.com**. The information on such sites should be treated judiciously, though, since they are supported by paid advertising.

Finally, and this may be stating the obvious, remember that you can check out companies through the non-Web services of the BBB and similar organizations. You're not restricted to online investigations just because you're looking into an online company.

Safeguard Non-Credit Card Personal Information

Assuming you've determined that the business is legitimate, you may eventually find yourself at their Web site, planning to buy something. To do this you are going to have to give them some information, so the first thing to look for is a link to their privacy policy. Follow the link and read the policy, and if there's something you don't like about it, don't do business with these people. And if there's no privacy policy, don't do business with them, either.

If you can accept the privacy policy, you should then inspect the purchasing form and see exactly what the vendor wants to know about you. This information is usually gathered during the process of setting up an account with the vendor, as shown in the representative sign-up page in Figure 16-1.

The usual first step in account setup is to provide a username and password. If you order from the vendor at a later time, this password-username combination will be used to retrieve your account information, so you won't have to re-enter the data every time you shop.

16

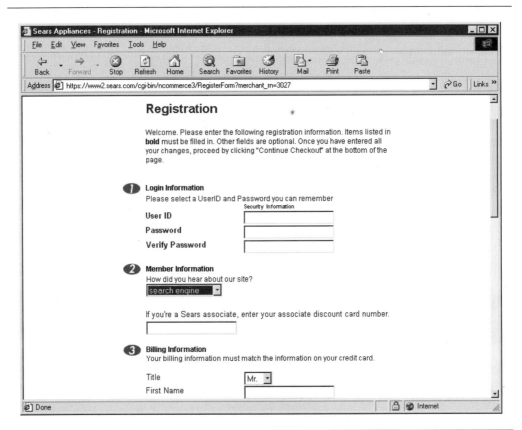

FIGURE 16-1   To make an online purchase, you usually have to register with the e-commerce
Web site

Sometimes you will also have to supply an item of verification information that the vendor can
use, if circumstances require it later, to ensure that you are really you. This verification is a piece
of personal data that is not likely to be known to anyone who has stolen your username and
password, and is frequently your mother's maiden name (you don't have to supply her real one,
of course; this is just a device to help you remember the verification information).

The information requested by an e-commerce site request falls into two categories:
information they require before they'll process the order, and information that's optional for you
to provide. A reputable Web company will indicate the items that are required, often with bold
type or asterisks next to the text boxes. Some of the required information is innocuous and would
be required by any mail-order company, which is basically what these outfits are. In addition to
your credit card number, they need your name and shipping address, and a phone number where
you can be reached. Except for the card number, anybody could get these from a phone book, so
providing them is not really an issue.

They also invariably want your e-mail address. To reduce the risk of constantly finding spam in your regular mailbox, you should consider setting up a free, Web-based e-mail account, perhaps from Yahoo! Mail or Hotmail, and giving them that address instead of the one you use on a daily basis.

Be wary of a vendor who wants your Social Security Number (Social Insurance Number, in Canada). No commercial, non-government purchase should require this. If the purchasing form insists on having it, you should do your shopping elsewhere.

The optional information that vendors ask for is stuff like your income level, gender, age group and so on. They use this demographic data to determine what other products you might be interested in, and if you give it to them they will likely send you e-mail about such products, unless you specifically tell them not to. However, before you provide this data, be aware that you certainly don't *have* to give them anything other than the information required to make the purchase. So, as a general rule, give a vendor only this required information and no more.

Also look for check boxes on the form that ask if the vendor may e-mail you about other products, and whether you will permit your personal data to be shared with other vendors. Unless you want your privacy compromised, answer no to these and similar questions. These boxes are often unobtrusively placed at the bottom of the form, so you may have to search for them.

Also search for information about the vendor's return/refund policy. If he doesn't seem to have one, or makes it very hard to determine, you should do business somewhere else. Alternatively, e-mail them and ask for the information. Read the return policy carefully. You don't want nasty surprises later on if the goods turn out to be unsatisfactory or defective.

Finally, check for warranty information, if applicable. Be sure you know what is covered by the warranty, and what isn't, *before* you buy.

Protect Your Credit Card

Along with unease about privacy, people's concern over sending credit card information across the Web is probably their topmost worry about online shopping.

In fact, your card number is at risk no matter how you use it. For example, the restaurant server who takes your card and bill away has an opportunity to swipe the data into an illegal reader, and ordering over the phone gives out the information just as openly. In fact, however, there is not much danger of your card number being stolen simply by the act of transmitting it over the Internet.

This is partly because no reputable vendor will manage purchases on an insecure Web site. Secure sites depend on a technology called SSL (Secure Sockets Layer), which protects the whole transaction from prying eyes. Furthermore, your credit card number is encrypted (turned into apparent gibberish) before it's transmitted from your browser to the site, and even if someone managed to snag it off the Internet, the number would be meaningless.

You can tell if you're on a secure site in a couple of ways. First, the vendor will likely tell you, and if he doesn't, you can often find out more about his security levels by reading his privacy policy. Second, your browser will clue you in. IE and Navigator 4 show you a locked

16

padlock in their status bars while you're connected to a secure site, and Navigator 3 shows an icon of an unbroken key.

Alternatively, some vendors allow you to order by telephone, and you may prefer to use this approach.

 Never send your password, credit card information, or other sensitive personal data, in an e-mail message or other unsecured form of Internet communication, no matter who has asked for it. Doing so makes stealing your identity easy, and having a felon pretend to be you is a very, very serious problem.

The real issue with a credit card number is what happens to it after the order is placed. Does the vendor retain it for use in future orders, or is it thrown away so that you have to enter it each time you order something? The second option is more secure, so if it's offered, take it. There have been cases of vendors whose files of credit card numbers were not properly secured, and hackers managed to get at least some of the numbers that were in storage. The amount of loss involved in these thefts, however, is minuscule compared to the more traditional forms of credit card stealing.

To protect yourself further against credit card abuse, whether you use your cards on the Internet or not, check your monthly statement carefully for charges you didn't make. Let the card company know immediately, by phone and in writing, if you don't recognize a charge.

How to Buy on the Web

Once you've decided you want to buy something, you've got two main Internet possibilities: ordinary online retail buying, and buying by auction. Since the former is the most widely practiced, we'll examine it first.

Online Retail Buying

Actually, buying online isn't all that different from any buying behavior. If you think of it as closely resembling catalog mail-order by phone, it takes a lot of the mystery out of it. The difference is that the Internet is your catalog, and to make the purchase you fill out a secure Web form, instead of giving your order verbally over the telephone.

The first step, of course, is to find the best price for the item or service you want (this concept comes as a surprise, doesn't it?). Search engines will come in handy here. The bottom line, so to speak, is that you have to do just as much comparison shopping with the Internet as you do with traditional shopping. There are some Internet tools to help you do this; one is mySimon at **www.mysimon.com**, which will search out a set of prices on an item you specify. Figure 16-2 shows the mySimon results for a search of prices on a Kodak digital camera.

Other useful sites, like Productopia (**www.productopia.com**) and Epinions (**www.epinions.com**) offer consumer reviews; check these out as well before making a decision. If you're looking for computer equipment, C|net's reviews at **www.cnet.com** offer

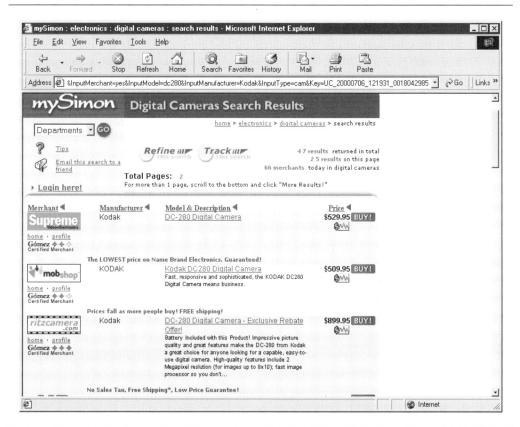

FIGURE 16-2 You can use specialized search engines to look for the best prices on an item

not only the hardware review itself, but plenty of user opinions about the item. C|net also hosts **www.shopper.com**, another source of comparative prices.

Once you've settled on a vendor and satisfied yourself as to his privacy and security policies, go ahead and set up the account, and purchase the item or service. If your native currency is different from that of the Web site's (most Web sites can quote you a price in U.S. dollars), see if there's a conversion table so you can figure out how much you'll actually be spending, and don't forget that the final price will have to include shipping charges. Most larger Web sites use the shopping basket concept, so that you can put several items into your virtual basket and order them all at once when you "check out." Since there's normally a minimum shipping charge, you may be able to get the most out of that charge by buying several items at a time.

When you check out with your basket, your credit card number will be verified on the spot and the billing will be made to the card, so be sure your order is correct before you check out.

16

The process can take up to two or three minutes, depending on how busy things are, so be patient. Once the order has been processed, the company will usually send you an e-mail confirming the order and, depending on the shipping method used, the item(s) will eventually turn up. After processing is completed, it's a good idea to print out the Web page(s) describing what you ordered; some Web sites will suggest this and even provide a printer-friendly version you can use.

If this item is coming by courier or express mail, you may be able to track its progress. All the major courier companies have Web sites where you can see what's happening to the shipment, if you have a means of identifying your package. The waybill number is best for this purpose, if you can get it. For example, if you know the item is coming by UPS, go to **www.ups.com** and follow the links to their tracking page.

But once the item arrives, what if it's unsatisfactory and you want to return it? As indicated before, the Web site should have a return policy posted somewhere, and you should have read it before you placed your order. Return policies vary a lot, but most Web companies require you to contact them for an RMA (Return Merchandise Authorization), and there is often a 30-day return policy. Also, you should hang onto the packing materials, at least for those 30 days, since many vendors require that the item be returned in the original packaging. And retain the packing slip, because it has a lot of the information you'll need if something goes wrong.

After you send the item back, watch for an e-mail indicating that the company received it. If you don't get a message to this effect, follow up to make sure the thing arrived.

TIP *There's another source of merchandise you can tap into: Don't forget to check the ads posted in local newsgroups. Check your ISP's news server for groups with names containing keywords like "for-sale" or "forsale."*

Auction Buying

This is a recent Internet phenomenon: Web sites where you can actually bid against other people to acquire an item. Just as with real-life auctions, however, you can get caught in a bidding war and end up paying more for an item than you needed to. Check retail prices or newsgroup ads to find out the range you should expect, and keep it in mind if and when you bid.

Yahoo!, Amazon, and Excite all host auction "houses," but the best known is probably eBay at **www.ebay.com**. So, if you want to try buying at auction, the eBay home page (see Figure 16-3) is an obvious place to start. Before you attempt a bid, however, you should click the Help link to open the Help page. On this page there is a New to eBay link, which provides a tutorial about using this system. This is a useful guide, so read through it before you try bidding in earnest.

Note that you will have to register before you can put in a bid. If you are using an anonymous e-mail address when you register (such as a Hotmail or Yahoo! Mail address) you will be asked for a credit card number as well. This seems to be an attempt by eBay to ensure that bidders are legitimate; your card will not be charged for your registration, since registration is free. Use your normal e-mail address if you don't want to supply the credit card number.

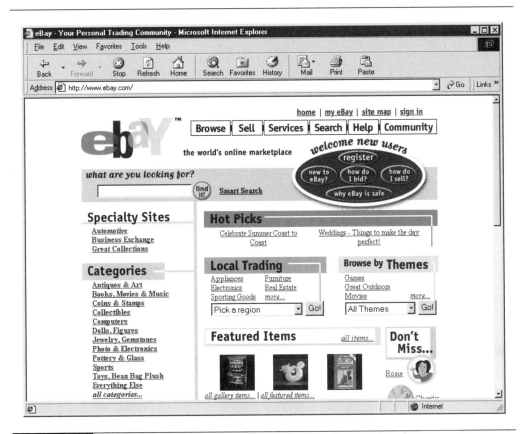

FIGURE 16-3 The eBay home page is representative of online auction sites

This, admittedly, is a choice you may not like; you have to give away either your normal e-mail address or your card number. There is a way around it, though. Your ISP may provide more than one mailbox with your account, or you may be able to set up a new one for a nominal fee. You can dedicate such a secondary account to online purchasing, since it won't matter so much if it gets spammed. That's better than revealing your card number.

After you've registered, go ahead and locate an item that interests you, and put in a bid. To find an item, you can either drill down through the category links or, more efficiently, use the Search box to look for it. In the example shown in Figure 16-4, I looked for an Epson inkjet printer and got several listings.

To place the bid, select the specific item and a new window opens giving information about that item. It's worth looking around within this window, because there are links that tell you

16

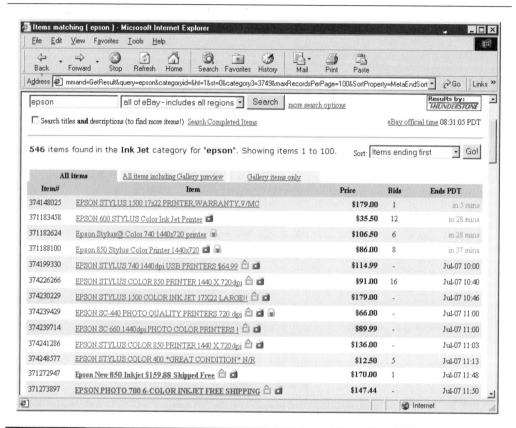

FIGURE 16-4   The eBay search tool is useful for locating items of interest

about the current state of the auction and even about the record of the seller, if he/she has sold things on eBay before. At the bottom is a text box where you enter your bid, and it obviously must be higher than the current bid (see Figure 16-5). If the current bid is $200.00, and you enter $250.00 (the maximum you're willing to pay, presumably), then the eBay software will bid on your behalf up to this maximum, using the increments listed. You confirm your bid by entering your username and ID.

If you win the auction for the item, you are committed to buying it, so be sure you mean it before you confirm. Normally, the seller contacts the winning bidder and arrangements are made for shipping and payment. Arranging shipping is usually the responsibility of the seller,

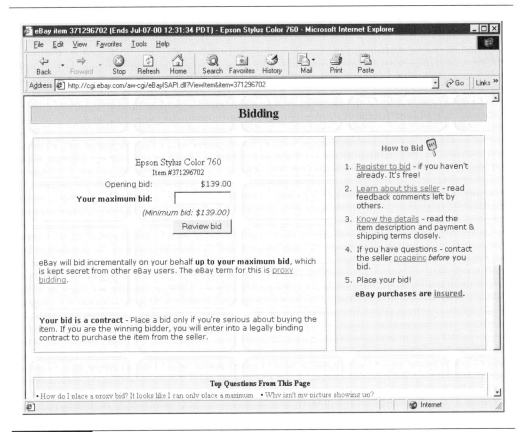

FIGURE 16-5 The eBay bidding window is where you post your bids on an item

though the buyer should expect to pay for it. Note that eBay and the other auction houses are merely places for buyers and sellers to meet and bid. The auction houses have no legal authority to enforce transactions, so all legal obligations concerning a transaction are between the buyer and the seller.

TIP *If you like getting freebies, take a look at Freeshop.com (**www.freeshop.com**). Most of its offers are free or trial ones that are tied closely to marketing projects, but some of them might repay investigation. Be sure to give an e-mail address where you're willing to accept direct-mail advertising.*

16

Sell on the Web

You may have considered setting up your own Web site to sell your goods and services directly to potential customers. After all, creating a Web site is *supposed* to be simple, isn't it? After all, lots of very ordinary people have their very own sites.

Well, yes, lots of ordinary people do. But they don't usually sell things through them. The truth is that a basic personal Web site is fairly easy to establish, but creating an e-commerce Web site is another kettle of fish altogether. As you've already probably figured out from the first parts of this chapter, most Web purchasing is done by credit card, and that brings in all sorts of complications about becoming a vendor who can accept cards, as well as the very complex issue of security. In short, if you want to have your very own e-commerce site, you'll have to hire an expert or experts to set it up for you, and that's going to cost you money.

However, there are alternatives to having your own site. One is to find a site that acts as a broker or gallery for the kinds of items you produce, and join one of them as a client (to see how this has been done for artisans' work, check out the Novica site at **www.novica.com**). For a commission, they will add your product to their catalog and deal with the billing and your payment. Policies of such sites vary, but in most cases you will be responsible for setting up the shipping. But investigate the company very thoroughly before you commit your product to it. If it gives bad service, your reputation will suffer. Try ordering a couple of things from it to see how well it handles e-commerce.

Another alternative is to hook up with what are called "Web storefronts." These companies will host a Web site for you, and give you the basic Web tools to create the site itself, plus a shopping cart feature, and an ordering system that customers can use easily. They also, by various means, handle the billing and the remittance of payments to your account. Some of the Web storefront companies have no monthly charge for their setup or for maintaining the site,

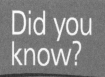

Did you know?

Of those who try to buy something online, many give up before completing the transaction because the relevant Web pages were so slow to load, or because the site was so badly designed they couldn't figure out what they were supposed to do. Moreover, if people do get close to completing their purchase, but the site seems to stop responding, or if they're suddenly informed that the item is out of stock and not available, they don't usually bother to try again. So, if you get somebody to set up an e-commerce site for you, these are factors they should keep very much in mind. Also, be aware that those e-commerce sites that turn people off, as described earlier, are probably designed by professionals, or by people who are supposed to be professionals. Look closely at real-world samples of their work before you hire them.

but instead make their money by levying a charge on every purchase a buyer makes from you. Two representative storefront services are Bigstep (**www.bigstep.com**) and Freemerchant (**www.freemerchant.com**); you can check these out to get a feel for how these systems work.

Finally, you can also sell stuff by putting it up for auction through an auction venue like eBay. The process of doing this is becoming easier and more sophisticated. For example, using its Billpoint system, eBay now makes it possible for people to buy items from you with a credit card, even though you have no vendor account with the card company. This is a great convenience for everybody (not to mention reducing the risk of bounced checks!).

There may, however, be a reason to have a humble, non-e-commerce, business Web site, one such as you might create yourself. This is to use it as an advertising medium. If you run a catering business, for example, you could create a Web site listing the services you offer, the menus available, your pricing structure, and all your contact information. Then, when you list your business in the Yellow Pages or other such directories, add your Web site address to the listing. Many people now look for such an address automatically, and it may very well help drum up some business from customers who wouldn't otherwise have contacted you. You'll find out more about creating your own Web site later in the book, in Chapters 20 and 21.

Where to Find It

Web Site	Address	What's There
Better Business Bureau	www.bbbonline.com	Vendor reputations
Bigstep	www.bigstep.com	Web storefront services
BizRate	www.bizrate.com	Vendor ratings
eBay	www.ebay.com	Online auctions
Epinions	www.epinions.com	Product reviews
FeedbackDirect	www.feedbackdirect.com	Vendor ratings
Freemerchant	www.freemerchant.com	Web storefront services
mySimon	www.mysimon.com	Comparison shopping
Productopia	www.productopia.com	Product reviews

16

Part IV

Your Security and the Internet

Chapter 17

Personal Privacy on the Internet

How To . . .

- Understand why there are threats to your privacy
- Understand the basics of privacy protection
- Understand the principles of e-mail encryption
- Understand and deal with cookies

Personal privacy and security on the Internet are major issues, as you can tell from the number of times I've mentioned them in the preceding 16 chapters. In this chapter we'll examine some further aspects of the matter, and re-emphasize the more important aspects of it that appeared earlier.

Understand the Privacy Threat

All of us have personal information about our lifestyles, habits, and relationships that we don't, as a matter of reticence and good manners, share with strangers. Doing so would make us uncomfortable, and a stranger who asked for such information out of the blue would likely get a very fast brush-off. But there are strangers who routinely make such queries, and these aren't just oddball characters you might encounter on the street. They may work for companies about whom we know little or nothing, and they ask for the data because they want to make money from it, or through it.

How do they make money? Well, the data they collect is, essentially, the raw material for marketing research. Once accumulated, it can be processed in various ways and then sold to companies that want to target certain people for a particular product. Moreover, this information can be used, though usually it isn't, to identify you *while* you browse the Internet. In such circumstances a vendor could, quite possibly, target specific ads to you personally and send them to you while you're online.

These ads would appear, in case you were wondering, in the banner advertising that is present on almost every Web site you run across. Mostly, of course, the ones you see are not targeted to you personally. But the collection of large amounts of information, plus information about you specifically, is a good start toward a subtle monitoring system of you and other Internet users. Conceivably, with your e-mail address and a good profile of your Web browsing and online purchasing behavior, a company could e-mail you ads concocted specifically to appeal to your tastes—or weaknesses. This is called *direct-mail advertising,* and is favored by marketers over spam because most people hate spam so much.

Well, this is all very unpleasant, but you don't actually *have* to buy the stuff they're peddling, do you? No, of course you don't. But do you really want total strangers to know your marital status, your Web browsing habits, the things you download or buy or listen to, your e-mail address, your income and age range, your profession? And do you want somebody's tracking software *following you around* on the Internet, even if it's only to try to sell you something?

Probably you don't. Admittedly, it's very hard to keep your privacy completely inviolate if you spend much time on the Internet, but at least you can make it a lot more difficult to breach.

Basic Rules for Maintaining Your Privacy

Many of the following recommendations have appeared earlier in the book, but here we have them under one roof, so to speak, for your convenience. If you stick to them, your privacy will be less at risk than it might otherwise be.

Passwords

Passwords are your first line of defense against breaches of privacy and security. Here are some guidelines for them:

- Create passwords from random or apparently random letter and number combinations. Don't use a word that can be found in the dictionary, or family or pet names, or other easily discovered items of personal information. A useful technique is to think of a phrase you can remember easily, and create the password from the first letter of each word. Then, for added security, tack a number on at the beginning and end.

- Create different passwords for different purposes. If you have a password for online banking, use a different one for a free e-mail account. That way, the loss of one password won't compromise other aspects of your privacy.

- Never tell anyone your passwords. (Your spouse might be an exception!)

- Do not write down your passwords. If you have several and can't remember which one belongs to which account, consider a protected storage program like Qwallet (**www.qwallet.com**) in which you can store your passwords and other personal data, in an encrypted and unreadable form, and get at them by using just one password.

- Do not send passwords by e-mail or by other unsecured means, no matter who asks you to do so. No reputable organization will ever ask you to do that, and the person asking either (a) is incompetent or (b) is targeting you for some unpleasant purpose.

- Some password-protected Web sites, and Windows itself, will offer to "remember" your password so that you don't have to type it in every time you log on. If your computer is physically secure from tampering, such as a home machine might be, you might consider doing this. Otherwise don't, unless you don't care who reads your e-mail or looks up your Web browsing history.

Anonymous E-mail Accounts

You can use free Web-based e-mail accounts to provide both a sort of "junk" mailbox and an alternative e-mail address to divert spam from your regular mail service. This is especially useful if you post to newsgroups, which are regularly trolled by spam-collection software looking for e-mail addresses. If you do use your regular e-mail account in newsgroups and similar places, you should spam-proof it to a degree by changing the return address slightly and telling the people receiving the message how to restore the correct address. For example, when you tell Outlook Express what return e-mail address to use for a newsgroup account, type myaddress@at-myisp.com instead of

17

myaddress@myisp.com. Some people use myaddress@nospam-myisp.com, but spammer software is getting smarter and sometimes looks for the words "nospam" or "no-spam" on purpose.

Keep Information to Yourself

Registering on a Web site can also expose personal information you may prefer to keep private. For example, sites that provide free software downloads may ask for optional income and professional information. If you don't want to give this data to them, don't. You can also use an anonymous e-mail account, as just described, to satisfy their address requirements.

In general, don't tell anybody anything that they don't absolutely require. If you feel they require too much, look for a site that provides similar services with less snooping. For example, TUCOWS doesn't ask you to register before downloading a program, whereas if you download that same program from the vendor's Web site, you'll often have to provide some registration information.

If you buy online, as you know, you do so with a credit card number. Ensure that the site is secure before buying anything, by looking for the locked-padlock icon in the status bar of both IE 4 and later and Navigator 4 and later. Navigator 3 displays an intact-key icon.

If you *must* give a Web site information in order to get something, find and read its privacy policy first. If you don't like it, go elsewhere.

"Anonymizing" Services

If you want your Web browsing patterns to be almost untraceable, you can subscribe to a service that provides anonymous browsing. Two representative services are Anonymizer at **www.anonymizer.com**, and Freedom at **www.freedom.net**. These use combinations of encryption and software called *proxy servers* to conceal where you've been and what you did while you were there. Most of the services cost money ($15 per quarter is typical) but the best ones will conceal all evidence of your browsing, e-mail messages, IRC activity, and news reading.

Did you know?

If you dig very far under the surface of Internet technology, you'll come across references to *proxy servers*. These servers are software programs that sit between your computer and the server that is actually providing the information, such as a Web server. If you're on a network in a business environment, for example, a proxy server can temporarily store Web pages in a cache, and when you or other network users need the page, the proxy server provides it. This speeds up the response time, since the page does not have to be retrieved from the Internet whenever somebody needs it. System administrators can also set up proxy servers to prevent users from retrieving data from undesirable Internet sites.

E-mail Encryption

Encryption is a way of concealing information by changing it into apparent gibberish, and only legitimate users have the key to changing the gibberish back into a comprehensible form. Data is encrypted by means of mathematical formulae, and the most powerful forms of encryption, called *strong encryption,* are extremely difficult to break. The very strongest forms would, theoretically, take a very large number of computers many billions of years to solve. By that time the Earth will be gone, anyway, so the information would be rather out of date.

There are several methods of encrypting e-mail, but the most common consumer method is to use a system called PGP (Pretty Good Privacy). PGP is a public/private key system, and in principle it works like this:

You use the PGP software to create a pair of related keys, which are really just small computer programs. One is a public key, which you give to people who are going to send you e-mail. The matching complement to the public key is a private key, which you keep for yourself and give to no one. Here's how the system works:

1. Jane creates a public key and a private key, using her encryption program. She sends her public key to Mary and Bill.

2. Mary writes Jane an e-mail, then uses Jane's public key to encrypt it into gibberish. Bill does the same thing.

3. Mary sends the encrypted e-mail to Jane. Bill sends his e-mail to her, too.

4. Jane receives the two encrypted messages, and then uses her private key to decrypt them both into *plaintext,* text that she can read. Since no one else has Jane's private key, no one else (including Mary or Bill) could read the encrypted messages even if they intercepted them. In other words, the public key encrypts a message in such a way that only the matching private key can decipher it.

The whole system, of course, depends on the condition that people who want to correspond all have each other's public keys. One source for PGP software is the McAfee corporation; you'll find its product list, including two PGP programs, at **http://software.mcafee.com/products**. For another version of PGP software, go to the original PGP Web site itself, at **www.pgp.com**, and follow the PGP Freeware link. There's a free version of the PGP software there, for noncommercial use only, which includes plug-ins for Eudora and Microsoft Outlook.

The great virtue of e-mail encryption is its high security, but as usual there's no free lunch. The tradeoff for the security, once the software is installed and working, is having to distribute the public key to all your correspondents, plus the extra steps of encrypting and decrypting the messages on a day-to-day basis. Furthermore, some versions of PGP can be difficult for novice users to manage. Finally, there is no standard encryption scheme yet, so if you use PGP and a friend uses something else, the two systems won't be compatible with each other. Consequently, one or both of you will have to change your software. Whether the added security is worth the extra work is a decision you'll have to make in light of your specific circumstances.

17

Deal with Cookies

You may or may not have heard of *cookies*. These are small snippets of software that a Web site sends to your computer when you access that site. Some cookies are what's called *per-session* cookies, because they vanish from your hard drive when you shut down your browser. Persistent cookies, by contrast, remain until they hit their expiry date, which may not occur for a couple of years.

How do cookies work and what are they for? Here's a thumbnail explanation:

1. You open your browser and go to a Web site. When the Web server gets a request for a Web page from your browser, it sends not only the page but also a cookie. Your browser then stores the cookie on your hard drive in the folder C:\Windows\Cookies. You can look at this folder with Windows Explorer to see what's there.

2. When you visit the site again, the Web server checks your hard drive for a cookie bearing its unique site identification, and reads the information stored in the cookie. This information varies; with an e-commerce site, it may be data about things you've already purchased. Or it may be as simple as counting how many times you've turned up at the site.

3. The Web server now has some information about your visits to its site. Using this information it could, if the site administration were inclined to do so, send you information keyed to your visiting patterns. The marketing implications are obvious.

All this explains how a Web site sometimes seems to "know" you've been there before, and "know" what you ordered, downloaded, or looked at.

Even persistent cookies have expiration dates, although they may be a considerable time in the future. Your browser will automatically clean out the cookie collection if it gets too big, so it won't clog up your hard drive. And as a rule, cookies are pretty innocuous, so you can safely ignore them.

But what if you don't *want* Web sites to leave cookies all over your hard drive, even if they are harmless? They do leave a record on your drive of where you've been, and you may not like that.

The trouble is that cookies are extremely common. You can set your browser to alert you whenever a cookie is about to be stored on your machine, but you'll always be clicking the mouse to accept or deny it if you do this, and in any case, some Web sites don't work properly if they can't store a cookie on your computer.

There are, however, some anti-cookie measures you can take if you're determined to. In IE 5, you can choose Tools | Internet Options | Security Settings and click the Custom Level button to change the browser's cookie behavior (see the next illustration).

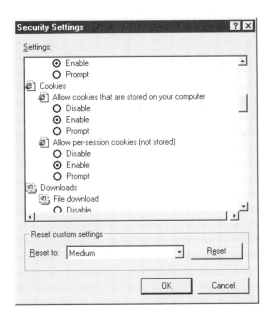

In the Cookies section there are two subsections, one for per-session cookies and one for persistent ones. You can prevent all cookies from being downloaded by marking both the Disable options. To force a prompt before downloading, mark one or both Prompt options. Or you can experiment with the browser's behavior by disabling the per-session cookies and enabling the persistent ones. Click OK when you're done, and accept the message saying you've created a custom security level. IE is now set up to handle cookies the way you want.

TIP *If you're trying to do online updates through the Windows Update site and it isn't working, check to make sure you have cookies enabled. The site will not be able to update your software if they aren't.*

In Navigator, choose Edit | Preferences and select the Advanced option. In the Cookie section of the Advanced dialog, you can decide to accept all cookies, accept only a cookie that communicates with the server that sent it, disable cookies entirely, or prompt before accepting a cookie.

If you want to clean out the cookies yourself periodically, you can navigate to the C:\Windows\Cookies folder and delete the entire contents.

Finally, for more precise cookie management, you can obtain one of the anti-cookie utilities available on the Web. Try Cookie Crusher (**www.thelimitsoft.com**) or Cache and Cookie Washer (**www.webroot.com**). They're shareware so you can evaluate them before buying.

17

Where to Find It

Web Site	Address	What's There
Anonymizer	www.anonymizer.com	Anonymous Web browsing
Cache and Cookie Washer	www.webroot.com	Anti-cookie software
Cookie Crusher	www.thelimitsoft.com	Anti-cookie software
Freedom	www.freedom.net	Anonymous Web browsing
McAfee.com	http://software.mcafee.com/products	PGP encryption software
PGP Corporation	www.pgp.com	PGP encryption software
Qwallet	www.qwallet.com	Password wallet

Chapter 18

Viruses and Other Nasties

How To . . .

- Understand viruses and how they work
- Understand how anti-virus programs work
- Install and configure an anti-virus program
- Learn how to update an anti-virus program
- Defend against viruses in e-mail attachments
- Defend your computer against intruders
- Use Internet Explorer security settings

Viruses have become a fact of life on the Internet. The appearance and spread of the ILoveYou virus and its relations across the Internet in the Spring of 2000 was a shock to many who hadn't taken the danger seriously. Unfortunately, the threat is definitely worse than it used to be, and is probably here to stay.

This said, you shouldn't lead your online life in a state of constant apprehensiveness. We have been using personal computers for almost 20 years, and have encountered only two real viruses in all that time. However, our house has not burned down in the last 20 years, either, but that doesn't mean we don't carry fire insurance. Virus protection is like fire insurance in one very real respect: You may never need it, but when you do, you need it badly, and there's no substitute.

There is no 100 percent defense against the risk of virus infection through the Internet or by other means, such as infected programs on a floppy disk. You can, however, protect yourself to a great extent by taking some fairly straightforward protective measures.

Understand Viruses

Anti-virus researchers have identified tens of thousands of the little brutes. Most are harmless, and even if one is lurking in your computer you may never know it unless you run a virus scanner. Some, however, are very dangerous indeed, gleefully erasing or changing critical files in your machine, and the worst are capable of erasing all the information on your hard drive.

 Despite what you may have heard, there is no clear evidence that any virus has ever succeeded in damaging a computer's hardware. This doesn't mean it will never happen, but to date the damage has been exclusively to data and software.

The term "virus" is applied broadly these days to almost any malignant computer infection, but viruses are not all the same. They fall into several broad classes; admittedly, they overlap somewhat and there are arguments over exact nomenclature.

■ **"True" Viruses**   These are small computer programs that link to a legitimate program and run when it does. When the virus program runs, it reproduces itself and may also cause the computer running it to misbehave in inconvenient or damaging ways. These viruses used to be spread mostly by floppy disks containing infected software. Now, unfortunately, such virus-laden programs can also be downloaded from the Internet. Often there is a built-in delay between the actual infection and the destructive actions of the virus, so that it has a chance to infect other machines before it is detected. These viruses tend to attack the operating system itself, rather than the applications and data stored in the computer.

■ **Trojans**   Named for the Trojan Horse, these are also computer programs that ride on the coattails of a legitimate one, but they don't usually reproduce themselves. When a Trojan sneaks into your computer, it changes some of the settings without your knowledge. One use for a Trojan is to put a "back door" into your operating system so that another user can get into your computer without your knowledge (hence the name).

■ **Worms**   These programs don't attach themselves to other programs, but run all by themselves, reproducing at a great rate until they clog the system they're on. They tend to show up on networks, of which the Internet is, of course, the biggest example. Some 12 years ago, a worm jammed a substantial proportion of the Internet for hours until it was finally cleared out, at great expense and effort. It didn't damage data or programs but it did use up huge amounts of computer resources.

■ **Macro Viruses**   Modern application programs like Microsoft Word allow you to attach small programs, called *macros*, to data files, in order to do something useful. Unfortunately, macros can also be malignant, and these are referred to as macro viruses. Such viruses can and do infect data files, damaging them in the process. For example, if you open an infected Word document file, perhaps one you received as an e-mail attachment, the macro virus runs and infects your system. Thereafter, whenever you create or open an *uninfected* document, the macro detects this and immediately infects the file. Macro viruses can raise havoc with your data, for example, by changing its formatting. The recent ILoveYou virus was in a sense a hybrid infection of macro virus and worm. It was a worm in that it was a standalone program that reproduced across the Internet network, but it did its work by means of a macro virus.

■ **E-mail Viruses**   This is actually a misnomer. There are, as yet, no viruses, worms, Trojans, or other infections that are spread by the text of the e-mail message itself. Viruses, so far, have always been carried by the e-mail *attachments*, and do their dirty work when the recipient opens the attachment. So rest assured that just opening and reading the e-mail itself isn't dangerous. But opening an attachment may be quite a different matter.

18

Another form of attack on computer systems is the virus hoax. This actually does no concrete damage to anything, but it is very costly in wasted worker time, the time that system administrators spend in dealing with the hoax, and the extra load it inflicts on communications systems. It works like this.

The hoax perpetrator sends an official-looking e-mail to several people, often in business offices, alerting them to a sudden, severe virus threat, and telling them to immediately forward the warning e-mail to several more people. These people are then supposed to forward it to several more, creating a chain letter effect, increasing the number of messages in a geometric progression. If the people involved fall for the hoax, thousands of warnings spread over the e-mail system, wasting bandwidth and time and causing administrators no end of trouble to defuse the situation. So, if you get such a warning by business e-mail, check with your management before accepting its warning. If you see one in a home environment, you can go to the VMyths site at **www.vmyths.com** to see if they have information on the "threat."

Defend Your System Against Infection

Your first line of defense is an anti-virus program. There are several on the market, and you can download evaluation versions of most of them. None is very expensive (in the region of US$60) and, as with fire insurance, if you have a disaster you'll be very happy you spent the money. Three you might consider are:

- **Norton AntiVirus 2000 (www.symantec.com)**   For a trial copy, go to the Web site and click the Trialware link. On the Trialware page, click the Try Before You Buy link.

- **McAfee VirusScan (www.mcafee.com)**   For an evaluation copy, go to **software. mcafee.com** and click the Downloads link.

- **Trend Micro PC-cillin (www.antivirus.com/pc-cillin)**   Click the Download Free Trial link to get an evaluation copy.

These are for Windows machines. For a Mac anti-virus program, try Dr. Solomon's Virex for Macintosh. This is also available from McAfee at **software.mcafee.com**.

How Anti-Virus Programs Work

Basic anti-virus measures rely on the fact that viruses each have a characteristic "signature." This signature is the pattern of the numbers that make up the program code of the virus. Such signatures are referred to as virus definitions, and each anti-virus program contains a definition for every virus against which it defends.

When the anti-virus program is working, it scans through the code of a suspect piece of software or data, looking for a match to one of these definitions. If it finds one, it prevents the software from being run or the data file from being opened, and sounds or displays an alarm (and yes, false alarms are possible). On the other side of the battle, the writers of virus programs try to find ways to prevent these signatures from being detected, and the anti-virus people try to write virus definitions that detect them anyway. It's a kind of arms race.

If the virus is detected before it does any damage, it is isolated so the user can delete or otherwise deal with the file containing it. However, modern anti-virus programs do more than this. If the machine is already infected, they can remove the virus software from its various lurking places, and hopefully return the computer to a clean and uninfected state.

These programs have two main modes of operation. In one, they run "in the background," which means that they run all the time, though you're not aware of them doing so. As they run, they scan the data flowing between your machine and the Internet, looking for the patterns that match one of their virus definitions. If they detect one, they sound an alarm. This mode is often referred to as *online scanning*, and is an excellent way of preventing most virus infections before they start. As well, the programs can also be used to scan files already stored on your machine, on demand, either in batches or singly. In this second mode, the current content of the computer's memory (the RAM) is also checked, in case a virus may be hiding out there but has not yet copied itself to disk.

In both modes, the programs check not only program files but also e-mail attachments and other potential sources of trouble. The two modes give a pretty comprehensive defense against infection from known viruses.

 Since running any program takes some of your machine's resources, there will be a small performance penalty to operate an online scanner. However, you're not likely to notice the hit, and anyway it's worth it for the added protection.

Install an Anti-Virus Program

While you can download evaluation copies of several anti-virus programs, most have 30-day expiry dates and cannot be reinstalled. There is no real point in not buying one, and as they are quite large, you'll free yourself from a long download if you're on dial-up by just skipping the evaluation copy and buying the full version right off.

The example used here is Norton AntiVirus 2000, a widely used, full-featured representative of modern anti-virus software. To install it, insert the CD in your CD-ROM drive and wait until the opening screen appears; if it doesn't, choose Start | Run to locate the CDSTART.EXE file on the CD and launch that.

Install Norton AntiVirus

Installing the program is somewhat complicated because of the many options. The following steps will help guide you through the procedure.

18

1. In the opening screen, click the Install Norton AntiVirus button to open the selection dialog, which gives you several choices of what to do next (see the next illustration). One of them is to install the Adobe Acrobat Reader version 4. If you don't already have this program or an earlier version of it on your system, you will need to install it in order to view the online documentation, which is in PDF format. Installation is optional, and you can do it at a later time if you like.

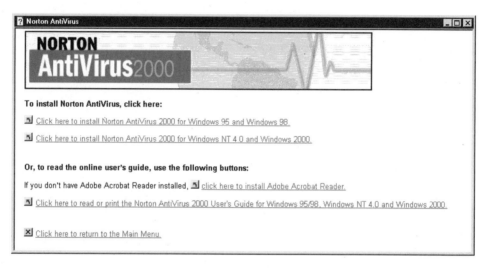

CAUTION *If you decide to install Acrobat Reader 4, and if you have an earlier version of the software already on your machine, you should uninstall the earlier version before proceeding. Exit from the Norton AntiVirus installation program, uninstall the earlier version of the Reader, and start over again.*

2. If you decide to install it, click the button labeled Click Here to Install Adobe, and follow the onscreen instructions. When Acrobat Reader has completed its installation, you'll return to the Norton dialog.

3. Choose the option you need for your particular version of Windows; in the example, it's Windows 98.

4. Follow the instructions on the screen, accepting the defaults and clicking Next until you reach the dialog that has two check boxes, the upper one labeled Enable Auto-protect at Startup (see the next illustration). Make sure this box is checked, because it's the one

that enables the online scanner. Note that the online scanner checks files when they are run, opened, created or downloaded, not just as they are downloaded.

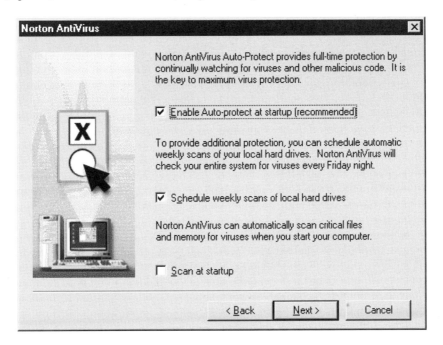

5. If you want regular Friday-night virus checks of your hard drive as well as running the online scanner, mark the second check box as well.

6. For maximum protection, also mark the bottom check box. This makes Norton run a virus scan of critical files and the computer's memory each time you start the machine. In a home environment, though, if you're running the online scanner and carry out weekly virus checks, this option is likely unnecessary. When you've made your selections, click Next to move on.

7. In this dialog, decide whether to have Norton check incoming e-mail attachments for viruses, and select which of your e-mail clients should be so protected (see the next illustration). Make the desired choices, then use the bottom list box to decide how detected infections should be handled. For maximum flexibility, leave it at the default of Ask Me What To Do. Then click Next to move on to a confirmation dialog, then Next again to begin the actual installation.

18

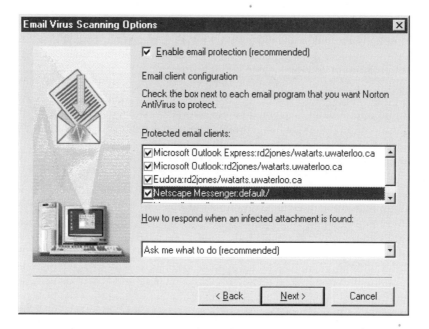

8. The installation proceeds, being tracked by a progress meter. Eventually, an info box appears to tell you that a rescue disk setup is being carried out. Wait till this completes, and when it does, a registration screen appears.

9. You can register later, so to keep our installation process simple, click the Cancel button. Answer Yes to the confirmation dialog, then click Next again. A dialog appears warning you to run LiveUpdate at the end of installation (this will be explained later). Click Next.

10. Check or uncheck the boxes for the desktop shortcut and the README file. Click Next to go to the last set of setup options.

The final setup options require some explanation. There are three of them (see next illustration).

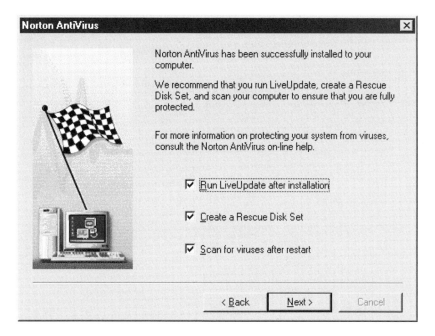

■ **Run LiveUpdate After Installation**   As you may know, new viruses are appearing all the time. To keep your protection current, Norton needs to obtain a regular update of new virus definitions. LiveUpdate is a convenient method of downloading and installing these definitions. We'll cover how to use it a little later. Since you may prefer to learn the manual method of running LiveUpdate, uncheck this box.

■ **Create a Rescue Disk Set**   This is a set of floppies or a floppy/zip disk combination that allows you to start your computer and (we hope) make repairs if your hard disk has crashed. Since some viruses can't be removed from a hard disk unless the machine starts from a clean floppy disk, and since other infections prevent the machine from starting from the hard disk at all, having a rescue disk set is important. Leave this option selected.

■ **Scan for Viruses After Restart**   To complete the installation procedure, you will shortly have to restart your computer. This option will force Norton to do a full scan of your drives after it's restarted. Leave this option selected.

18

When you've made these selections, click Next. You will be asked to restart your computer, so do so.

The computer restarts. If you opted to read the README file, it now appears. Look through it if you wish, then close it.

At this point, if you're running Navigator, you'll get a dialog for installing Norton AntiVirus as a Netscape plug-in. This allows Norton to check for viruses in files while Navigator is downloading them (in IE this happens without the need for a plug-in). Leave all the check boxes selected and click OK, then OK again to close the confirmation dialog.

Now the Rescue Disk dialog appears (see the next illustration). We'll assume you're going to use floppies for the rescue disks, so select the A: drive. The dialog also tells you how many floppies you'll need. Click the Create button to begin the process. When you are asked to turn off the virus scanner temporarily, click Yes. Then follow the dialog prompts to create the set.

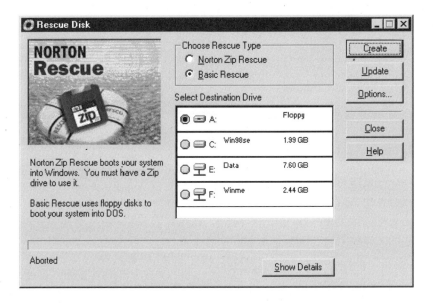

To make sure it works, follow the instructions in the final screen of the creation procedure and restart the machine from the first disk of the set. If all is well, you'll see a Rescue Disk screen. However, don't test the set any farther than this, because doing so can cause difficulties in a clean system. Instead, press ESCAPE to leave the Rescue Disk screen, remove the floppy, and restart your computer normally. Norton AntiVirus is now protecting your system.

Assuming you set Auto-protect (the online scanner) to start automatically when your computer starts, you will see a small monitor icon in the System Tray. It can be either enabled or disabled while it is still running. Occasionally, you may want to disable it temporarily; to do so, right-click the icon and choose Disable Auto-protect from the pop-up menu. A red X appears on top of the icon to remind you it's disabled. Remember to re-enable it when appropriate.

Use Norton LiveUpdate

When you start your computer, you may see a Norton AntiVirus Alert to the effect that your virus protection is out of date. The alert dialog gives three options: run LiveUpdate immediately, remind you later, or don't notify you of the issue. If updating at that time is inconvenient, choose the second or third option and close the dialog. (If you have a bad memory, choose the second!) Run LiveUpdate manually when it's convenient.

 All virus scanners, not just Norton, must have their virus definitions updated regularly. If you don't, you are throwing away much of the protection these programs provide. Remember to update regularly, and set the program to remind you if you forget.

To run it manually, begin by connecting to the Internet. Then launch Norton AntiVirus from the desktop icon or the Start menu. The main screen appears (see the next illustration).

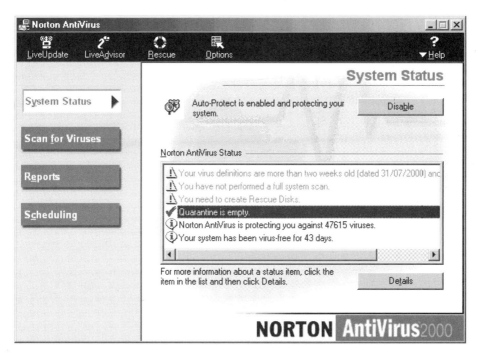

Entries in red indicate conditions you should check into; because you got the virus definitions alert, one will resemble "Your virus definitions are more than one month old."

 To get more information on an item in the program list box, select it and click the Details button.

In the top-left corner of the window is an icon labeled LiveUpdate. Click it, and the LiveUpdate dialog opens. Leave the list box set at Find Device Automatically, and click Next. The program connects to the Symantec Web site and begins the process by checking to see what updates your particular installation needs. On a 28.8K connection, this takes about a minute.

When the update check finishes, you see a dialog resembling the one in the next illustration. To make sure you get everything, check all the boxes and click Next. The download starts. Once all the updates are downloaded, Norton automatically installs them and informs you that the virus definitions are now current.

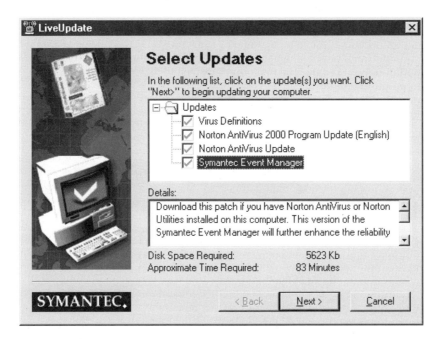

Norton's other options and features are also accessible from the main Norton AntiVirus screen. The buttons on the left of the screen allow you to do manual scans of various types, examine reports, and schedule automatic scans. The Options button in the toolbar provides configuration options. Refer to the documentation for details on how to use these tools, and for the measures you should take if the scanner detects a virus.

 *After you run LiveUpdate, you should also update your rescue disk set to update its definitions as well. To do so, click the Rescue Disk icon in the toolbar of the Norton AntiVirus window.*

Test Your Virus Scanner

Your virus scanner does its work quietly in the background, so you may wonder from time to time if it's actually working. To find out if it is, go to the Web site for the European Institute for Computer Anti-Virus Research (EICAR) at **www.eicar.com**. They provide a test file that works for all major virus scanners. On the EICAR page, click the link labeled "The AntiVirus Test File eicar.com." This takes you to a page that describes the test file; you should read it over before you go on. However, be assured that this file is absolutely harmless.

As a brief test and familiarization with the Norton scanner, or with whatever scanner you're using, click one of the links labeled "test file" (in Norton, make sure Auto-protect is enabled). As soon as it begins to download, you get a warning that displays, among other things, the type of virus detected. In the case of the test file, the virus is listed as "EICAR Test String 68." At this point the computer has been temporarily halted, for its protection. The only thing you can do with it is select one of the options from the drop-down list box. After that, a wizard will help you through the process of dealing with the virus. Only after the virus is cleaned up can you begin using your machine again. If you really want to be prepared, consult the program's documentation on virus removal and try out its various options using the test file.

If you get a real virus warning, the important thing is: *don't panic*. Nothing bad will happen to your computer while it's just sitting there displaying the virus alert.

Defend Against E-mail Attachment Viruses

Running a good virus scanner and keeping it up to date will go a long way toward keeping your system free of infection from e-mail borne viruses. However, this defense depends on the scanner having a definition of the virus, so that it can recognize the threat. If a completely new and fast-spreading virus gets loose, the anti-virus makers may not have time to identify its patterns and get a new definition out before an infected attachment reaches you, and you open it. Here are some precautions you can take to reduce that threat, until the needed definition becomes available.

- Make regular, comprehensive backups of important data files so you can restore them if the originals get infected.

- Keep your anti-virus program up to date.

- Do not open an e-mail attachment if you don't recognize the sender.

- Do not open an e-mail attachment if you know the sender but there's something odd about the message. Would a work colleague send you an e-mail saying he (she) loves you? In other words, if you have the slightest suspicion regarding an attachment that has been sent to you by someone you know, check with that person *before* you open it.

- Do not open an e-mail attachment if the covering e-mail asks you to forward it to other people. And even if you believe it's legitimate, don't forward it until you find out what's in it.

- Do not open an e-mail attachment if it is a file that can be run as a program. Such files may have filename extensions such as .EXE, .VBS, .JS, and .BAT. Animated greeting cards often have such extensions. I wouldn't open such a card myself, no matter who it came from.

- Be suspicious of forwarded attachments. They may be propagated by a virus that is using somebody's e-mail address book to forward itself to unsuspecting victims.

18

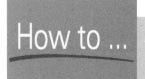 **Scan Attachments for Viruses**

You may remember that back in the mail and newsgroup chapters, you were told that you should save attachments without opening them, and open them only after they've been checked with a virus scanner. Here's how to do it:

1. Save the attachment under the desired filename in a folder.

2. Open Windows Explorer and navigate to that folder.

3. Right-click on the attachment file to open the pop-up menu. Assuming you have a full-featured scanner installed, one of the menu choices will be to check the file for viruses. For example, with Norton AntiVirus 2000, the menu item is Scan With Norton AntiVirus. Select that item to scan the attachment file. If the file has a virus, the scanner will detect it and you can decide what remedies to take.

You should also make sure that the Windows Scripting Host (WSH) is not installed on your computer, unless you have a very good reason for it to be present. The Scripting Host is software that allows Visual Basic scripts, which are a form of computer program, to run on your machine. These, in fact, are the files mentioned earlier that end in .VBS.

If the WSH is not installed, you can't run the script by double-clicking its filename, which is how many attachments are opened. To see if it's present in Windows 98, use the My Computer icon to open the Control Panel. Then choose the Add/Remove Programs icon and click the Windows Setup tab. Select Accessories, then click the Details button. Scroll down till you find the Windows Scripting Host entry, and clear its check box if it is marked. Then click OK twice to back out of the dialog, and the Scripting Host has been removed from your computer.

NOTE   *Windows Millennium does not include the Scripting Host, so you won't find it in the Add/Remove dialog.*

Microsoft's Outlook 2000 and Outlook 98 both have certain security vulnerabilities that the writer of the ILoveYou virus used to propagate the virus far and wide. When an innocent recipient of the ILoveYou e-mail opened the attachment, this activated the virus, which was inside the attachment. The virus then looked for e-mail addresses in the Outlook Contacts list of the machine it had infected, and sent an e-mail with the virus-laden attachment to everybody in the list. When one of these people opened the attachment, his Outlook Contacts list (if he had one) was used to send it to all *his* contacts, and so on. Since Outlook is a widely used mail client, especially in business, this explains why the virus spread so fast. Microsoft has now posted a security fix for Outlook to keep this from happening, but it is rather complex. For more information about how to secure Outlook, go to the Office Update site at **officeupdate.microsoft.com** and follow the Outlook 2000 or Outlook 98 link as appropriate for your software.

Defend Your System Against Intrusion

It may not have occurred to you that people might be poking around inside your computer while you're online. In fact they could be, because it is not particularly difficult to get into an unsecured computer when it is connected to the Internet. "Get into" at its worst means that the intruder can read, view, copy, move, or delete any file on your machine, run programs on it, or store his or her own files on your hard drive. You can imagine for yourself how much damage this might do.

How much of a concern should the intrusion threat be? To answer this, you need a bit of technical background (a very small bit, though).

Understand IP Addresses

Remember that we talked earlier about Internet addresses, an example of such an address being **www.microsoft.com**? In fact, computers don't understand words like "microsoft," so these

18

addresses are actually changed into numbers before they are used. These numbers are the real Internet addresses, and they are made up of four smaller numbers separated by periods. A couple of examples would be 212.5.66.121 or 191.164.089.2. Every computer that is connected to the Internet is assigned one of these numbers. They are called *IP addresses*, the "IP" being short for "Internet Protocol."

IP addresses can be fixed (that is, permanent) or temporary. If you are on a high-speed connection that is always on, such as cable, then you probably have a fixed IP address that was assigned to you through your ISP. When you turn your computer off and later turn it on again, you still have the same address. If you are on dial-up, on the other hand, you are assigned a temporary IP address when you log on, and the number is released for someone else to use when you log off. Consequently your IP address, in a dial-up situation, will not likely be the same one from one session to the next.

In order to get into a computer, an intruder needs to determine the IP address of that machine. However, if its address keeps changing, as it does with dial-up, he can't be sure that he's always looking at the same computer. Intruders tend to prefer stationary targets to moving ones, so fixed IP addresses are the more tempting prey. So, if you're on dial-up, the chances of getting unwelcome outside attention are low.

The situation is quite different if you're on a high-speed connection and have a fixed IP address. Hackers use software programs to wander around the Internet, looking for machines with open software "ports," or connections, which are like unlocked doors of a house. Once an intruder has found the address of such a machine and decided to take an interest in it, he or she can keep coming back to it, getting into it through the open ports and poking around at leisure. Even if the person doesn't actually do any harm, this is a profound invasion of your privacy.

The corporate and governmental worlds are very worried about this sort of thing (or should be) but the subject of large-network security lies far outside the bounds of this book. However, if you're a home user with a single computer, or perhaps with a small home network using a fixed IP address, there are some things you can do to see how vulnerable you are. There are also defenses you can put into place, if you feel that intrusion could be a danger.

Test and Improve Your System Security

Conveniently, there's a way to see if your computer can be gotten at by unauthorized users. The Gibson Research Web site provides an easy-to-use tool that will tell you how vulnerable your system is. It also has a great deal of useful technical data about preserving system security, which you can read up on if you're inclined to that sort of thing.

To test your system, go to the Gibson Research Web address at **http://grc.com** (the absence of the "www" in this address isn't a typo, by the way). Click the Shields Up link, which takes you to the main test page. Find the Test My Shields button and click it. After an interval (up to a minute, possibly) you'll get a report about your system's vulnerability. You can see an example result in Figure 18-1. The example computer is open to intrusion on port 139, a serious flaw, since port 139 gives access to just about every piece of data in the machine. For information about the security of other ports on your computer, click the Probe My Ports button.

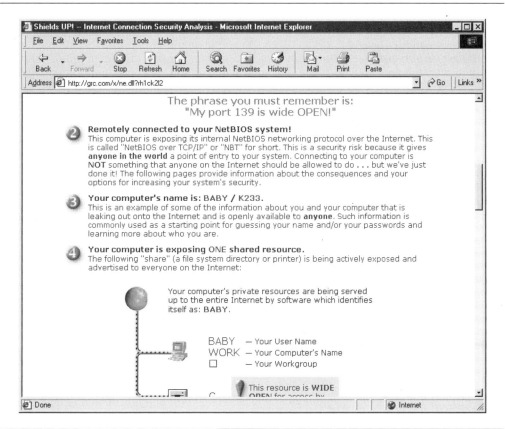

FIGURE 18-1 This computer is extremely vulnerable to intrusion by people elsewhere on the Internet

The Gibson Research site will tell you more than you likely want to know about this sort of thing, but most people just want to find out how to make their home system secure. You can do so with either hardware or software barriers; such barriers, of both types, are usually referred to as *firewalls*. One firewall-type program that is free for personal use is called ZoneAlarm; you can find out more about it at **www.zonelabs.com**. In the case of the vulnerable computer referred to earlier, ZoneAlarm secured all the ports on the machine, including those that were previously open, by making them effectively invisible to outside probes.

NOTE *Firewalls, even home-use types like ZoneAlarm, can be somewhat tricky for novices to use. ZoneAlarm, for example, must be carefully set up if it is to work properly on a home network that uses Internet Connection Sharing. Be prepared to spend a certain amount of time experimenting.*

18

Another protection system is Norton Internet Security 2000, which you can buy from Symantec and which also includes the Norton AntiVirus 2000 software. There are also hardware solutions to the problem; D-Link Systems (**www.dlink.com**) and Linksys Corporation (**www.linksys.com**) both have hardware firewalls designed for home or small office use.

Note that these defenses do not make your system invulnerable; they can be penetrated by a determined individual with the right skills. However, since there are lots of unprotected machines on the Internet, such people will likely pass yours by in favor of softer targets.

Use IE 5 Browser Security Settings

IE 5 has user-specified settings with which you can tighten or loosen the browser's security measures. To get at them, open IE and choose Tools | Internet Options. Then select the Security tab to display the Security sheet (see the next illustration).

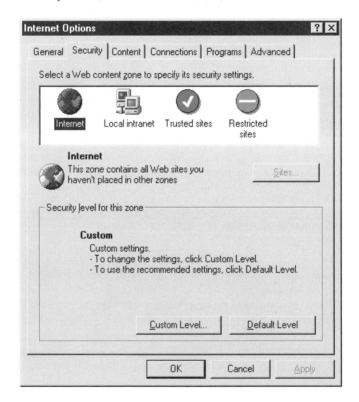

The four icons (Internet, Local Intranet, Trusted Sites, and Restricted Sites) are actually shortcuts to setting four security levels, which can also be set by the vertical slider. These levels represent various selections of safeguards that are designed to restrict the downloading of dangerous or unwanted content to your browser, and through it, to your computer.

"Dangerous" content is software like ActiveX controls or plug-ins that can, if badly or maliciously designed, affect your computer's operation. This type of content is referred to by Microsoft as *active content*, because it is in fact small program modules that can run on your computer without your intervention. As well as active content, dangerous content can also be programs and files downloaded by the user, a very common operation. Finally, an example of "unwanted" content is cookies.

You can get at the individual settings controlling these types of content by clicking the Custom button, and using the list of options to set your own custom security levels. Alternatively, you can select among the four predefined levels that are represented by the icons. You can also move the slider control up and down to change the predefined level associated with a selected icon.

The four security levels and their corresponding icons are:

- ■ **Low/Trusted Sites** "Trusted sites" are ones that you know have absolutely no dangerous content. If you're visiting one of these sites, you can switch to this level so that the active content, or most of it, will run automatically. When you return to normal browsing, *don't* forget to switch back to the Medium/Internet setting.

- ■ **Medium Low/Local Intranet** Use this if you're only using your browser in your local network.

- ■ **Medium/Internet** Use this setting for most of your browsing activity. It is the default.

- ■ **High/Restricted Sites** Use this if you're visiting sites that may have dangerous active software on them.

As a general rule, you can leave the security setting at its default level of Medium. This is adequate protection for almost all your browsing.

Where to Find It

Web Site	Address	What's There
D-Link Systems	www.dlink.com	Firewall hardware
European Institute for Computer Anti-Virus Research	www.eicar.com	Virus test file
Linksys Corporation	www.linksys.com	Firewall hardware
McAfee VirusScan	www.mcafee.com	McAfee anti-virus software
Symantec Corp.	www.symantec.com	Norton anti-virus software
Trend Micro	www.antivirus.com	PC-cillin anti-virus software
VMyths	www.vmyths.com	Virus hoax information
Zonelabs	www.zonelabs.com	ZoneAlarm firewall software

18

Chapter 19

The Net Has Slums, Too

How To . . .

- Understand issues of personal security
- Use IE and Navigator filtering tools to keep children out of objectionable Web sites
- Use blocking software to keep children out of objectionable Web sites
- Understand the danger of Internet scams

Just like a big city, the Internet has not only libraries and art galleries and places where like-minded people can meet and converse, it also has slums. They are not very big, but they do exist, and wandering into one can get a person into uncomfortable situations. Fortunately, common sense and responsible behavior go a very long way toward staying safe. In the next pages we'll examine some of the issues concerning the safety of both adults and children.

Personal Security Issues

Some of the material accessible on the Internet is, without a doubt, unsavory. A small proportion is illegal in many countries and jurisdictions, the most frequently publicized example being child pornography. Leaving such obvious barbarism aside, though, even the legal stuff may be extremely repellent to many people. However, if you are careful not to reveal your actual identity online, and guard your main e-mail address from spammers, you're very unlikely to have distasteful content inflicted on you.

NOTE
*Or you're usually unlikely to have it inflicted on you. A few pornography sites have acquired Web addresses very like those of legitimate ones. The most blatant example is **www.whitehouse.com** (a porn site), which is intended to snare people looking for the real White House site, which is **www.whitehouse.gov**.*

But this is not to say you can't get into unpleasant or even dangerous situations by unwise or careless actions you take online. Your computer and the Internet can't hurt you by themselves (unless you get Net-addicted) but if you undertake to meet with someone you only know from online encounters, you may be putting yourself in real, physical danger. People have been badly hurt and even killed by Internet acquaintances they agreed to see face to face. (On the other hand, they have also ended up marrying them.) The Internet is in many ways a microcosm of the real world; most people there are ordinary and harmless. Sadly, a small number, which seems larger because of the publicity they get when something dreadful happens, are very bad company indeed.

The basic rule, which cannot be repeated too often, is this: *Preserve your anonymity.* As long as people don't know your telephone number, your real name, where you live, or where you work, they can't easily find you. And if they can't find you, they can't injure you. Remember, too, that physical harm isn't the only possible threat that accompanies loss of anonymity. A carelessly revealed phone number may lead to disturbing calls, and a known street address can subject you to stalking or other forms of harassment. Of course, such hazards aren't restricted to

It is a common practice for organizations to monitor the Internet sites visited by their employees, while the employees are at work and are using the corporation's Net connections. People have been fired for going to Web sites that their company deems inappropriate. This may or may not be fair, but while you're at work, be aware that somebody may be electronically looking over your shoulder, and govern yourself accordingly. Remember, too, that your e-mail may be monitored, so keep it businesslike. Don't put anything in an e-mail that you wouldn't put on paper.

the online world. Unwise behavior in everyday life can lead to equally nasty consequences, without any help from the Internet.

Never forget that the person you're talking to, in a chat environment, for example, may be lying about his/her gender, age, and a lot of other things. Also, the people you meet on the Internet may, if you meet them in real life, be quite different from what their online personality led you to expect. Even if you do feel comfortable enough with an online acquaintance to meet him or her in reality, use common sense precautions when you do. Make sure the meeting occurs in a public place, during daytime hours, with lots of people around. You should also consider taking a friend. If you don't, make sure that someone knows where you're going and why, and when you'll be back in touch.

However, if you're new to the Internet, please don't get frightened away from it by the foregoing warnings. With reasonable care, such as anybody takes in real life when dealing with strangers, you are in very little danger at all, apart perhaps from receiving the occasional flame from an irate newsgroup member. Millions upon millions of people use the Net every day, and never have the least problem with it. You will almost certainly be among them.

Block Objectionable Sites

If you have children and are worried about what they may encounter while surfing, you can use specialized blocking software, or alternatively IE 5 and Navigator content filtering, to keep them away from undesirable places.

Most of these tools, including the two browsers, work with the Web site rating system developed by the RSACi (Recreational Safety Advisory Council on the Internet). This rating system is managed by ICRA (Internet Content Rating Association), whose Web site is at **www.icra.org**. To find out more about the rating system and how to use it, go to the ICRA Web site and click the Support button in the site's home page.

19

CAUTION   *Children are more at risk on the Internet than adults because they are less experienced and often more trusting. If you have children, monitor their Web surfing, and also be very aware of their access to newsgroups, if you permit such access at all. The major protection for children on the Internet, just as it is for adults, is anonymity. Impress on them that they must never, for any reason, tell any person on the Internet what their real name is, how old they are, what school they go to, their home address, their telephone number, their parents' or siblings' names, or any other identifying information.*

Use IE 5 Content Settings

IE 5 can be set to block out objectionable sites. To do this, choose Tools | Internet Options and click the Content tab to open the Content sheet. In the Content Advisor section, click the Settings button to open the Content Advisor dialog.

IE 5's filtering operation depends on a site having an RSACi rating, which IE can read to determine whether to block the site or not. Of course, non-rated sites have to be dealt with somehow, which is done by the simple expedient of blocking any site that is not rated.

Choose the Ratings sheet to specify how much filtering you want done in the four categories of language, nudity, sex, and violence. As you move the respective sliders, information appears as to what will be blocked (see the next illustration).

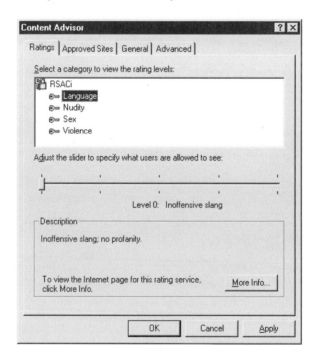

Now switch to the Approved Sites sheet. Here you can specify sites that are always allowed or never allowed, regardless of whether or not they have a RSACi rating. If a you want a non-rated site to be accessible, enter it here and make it an approved site by clicking the Always button. To make a specific site inaccessible despite an RSACi rating, enter it here and click the Never button.

Once you have the filters set as you want them, click OK. You will then be asked for a password. This password is necessary to enable or disable IE 5's filtering, or to change the filter settings.

Use Navigator Content Settings

You must have Navigator 4.5 or a later version for this to work. While online, launch the browser and choose Help | NetWatch. This opens an introductory screen; read it over and then click the link near the top of the page.

On the succeeding page, follow the instructions to specify filtering; you can use either the RSACi ratings or the somewhat more elaborate SafeSurf rating system (see Figure 19-1). As

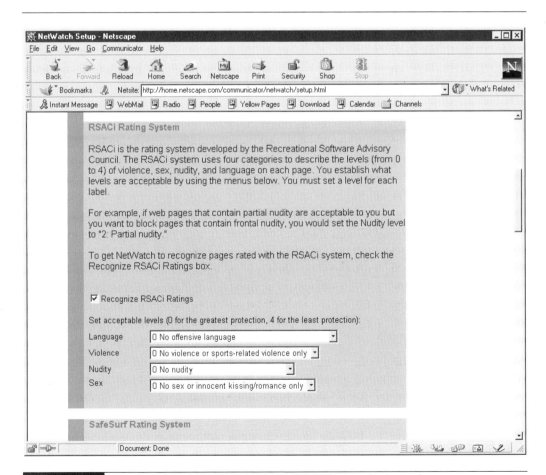

FIGURE 19-1   NetWatch lets you set up content filters for the Navigator browser

with IE 5, you must supply a password to allow the filtering to be turned on and off, or to change its settings. To prevent any access to sites that have not been rated, clear the check box labeled Allow Users to See Unrated Sites. Make sure the option labeled NetWatch ON is selected, then click the Save Changes button at the bottom of the page. Filtering is now turned on and can be turned off or modified only by a person who knows the NetWatch password.

Use Blocking Software

Several blocking software programs exist. After they're installed, you configure them to prevent access to undesirable sites. To restore unrestricted browsing, as an adult would presumably wish to do, the user must supply a password. The programs aren't foolproof but they can help control your children's Web travels to a considerable degree; just remember that no software can replace the supervision of a parent. By all means use a blocker, but check regularly on what your kids are doing.

Examples of this software are NetNanny (**www.netnanny.com**), SurfWatch (**www. surfwatch.com**), CyberPatrol (**www.cyberpatrol**), and CYBERSitter (**www.cybersitter.com**).

Avoid Internet Scams

Just as in other areas of life, there are scam artists on the Internet. The amount of money being lost to Internet fraud pales beside the sums thieved in the traditional ways, but you should still be aware that such fraud exists.

The basic rule for avoiding being scammed or defrauded is an old one: If it sounds too good to be true, it is. So if you get e-mail messages or happen on Web sites that promise prizes, free merchandise, free holidays, quick and effortless ways to get rich, or things of that nature, ignore them. Here are some other tips:

- Do not call anybody on a 900-number you see on a Web site, in a newsgroup, or in an e-mail; you are charged for such calls.
- Remember that people who approach you on the Net may not be who or what they say they are. Masquerading is very easy on the Internet.
- Be suspicious of communications requesting donations for charity.
- Do not send cash to anybody under any circumstances.
- Preserve your anonymity so that scam artists cannot get to you in person.

A useful resource for finding out about frauds in general is the U.S. Postal Service. These are not necessarily Internet frauds, but you can be sure that somebody will figure out how to use the Net to perpetrate some of them. Go to the U.S. Postal Inspection Service main page at **www.usps.gov/websites/depart/inspect** and click the Consumer Fraud link.

Where to Find It

Web Site	Address	What's There
CyberPatrol	www.cyberpatrol	Content filtering software
CYBERSitter	www.cybersitter.com	Content filtering software
Internet Content Rating Association	www.icra.org	Content rating information
NetNanny	www.netnanny.com	Content filtering software
SurfWatch	www.surfwatch.com	Content filtering software
U.S. Postal Inspection Service	www.usps.gov/websites/depart/inspect/	USPS site for consumer fraud information

19

Part V

Your Own Web Site

Chapter 20

Get Started on Your Own Web Site

How To . . .

- Understand the structure of Web sites
- Understand Web page editors
- Obtain and install a Web page editor
- Preview a Web page you're working on
- Create basic Web pages with text and text formatting
- Learn simple text layout with alignment, centering, and indents
- Work with bulleted and numbered lists
- Understand and create hyperlinks

Why would you bother to have a Web site, unless you were planning to get into e-commerce of some kind? Well, lots of people do, and never think of selling anything at all; they just do it for the pleasure. In fact, if you have a creative streak, putting a Web site together and tinkering with it can be a lot of fun and very satisfying. Not only that, if you possess a talent of some kind, for example in writing, art, or music, a Web site can be a way to present your work to a potential audience of millions (millions may not like it, but that's another matter).

So there are a few good reasons already, and no doubt you can think of more. Now that we know why we might do this, let's look at how it would actually be done.

Three Ways of Setting Up a Web Site

There are three main ways to set yourself up with a simple Web site: hire somebody to create it from start to finish; use one of the sites that provide free Web hosting, such as GeoCities; or create it yourself and have your own ISP host it. This chapter and the next assume you want to do it yourself, so we'll drop the idea of hiring somebody to do the work. The second choice, using a free Web hosting service, is a possibility, at least if you prefer a fast and easy method with some limitations; we'll examine this alternative briefly at the end of the chapter.

The third choice, creating the site yourself with a Web page editor and having your ISP host it, is the one we'll spend most of our time on, because it is the most flexible and gives free rein to your creativity.

NOTE   *Remember the term* hosting? *It's common to say that Web sites are* hosted *on Web servers, meaning that the server software controls the Web site and sends (serves) the site's content to users via the Internet. Web hosting services are companies that provide heavy-duty Web servers that are capable of hosting many independent Web sites at once.*

Understand Web Site Structure

A Web site, at its most fundamental level, is no more than a collection of files. To turn this collection into a functioning site, you need a second element: a Web server. A *Web server* is a specialized computer program that organizes the files, manages the links among the pages and makes the links work, sends the pages out over the Internet on request from a browser, and does all the other housekeeping involved in running a Web site.

You, fortunately, do not have to worry about the Web server; that end of things is taken care of by the company that hosts your Web. The most obvious organization to furnish hosting is your ISP, and most ISPs offer this service for small personal Web sites as part of their package. For additional fees you can get more advanced options, such as your own domain name (a permanent Internet address); such options will be discussed in the next chapter.

What all this boils down to is this: To set up your own basic personal Web site, you create one or more Web pages and send them to your ISP, who will then host them and make them accessible to everybody on the Internet.

The question you're likely now asking is, "Okay, but what tools do I use to create Web pages?" The next section will give you some background.

Understand Web Page Editors

To begin with, an "editor" in the software sense refers to a program for creating, editing, and saving text or document files. Microsoft Word is, in fact, an editor, a very powerful one that is specialized for the production of long, complex documents. Similarly, Web page editors are programs specialized for the task of creating Web pages.

But, in fact, you don't actually need a Web page editor to create a Web page. Believe it or not, a humble, plain-vanilla text editor will do, for example, Windows Notepad.

But how can you use such a simple tool as Notepad to create complex Web pages? Well, it's because a Web page is merely a text file, and the text itself is no more than a list of instructions that tells your browser what to display and how to display it. When you click a link to a Web page, the Web server on the remote computer sends this instruction list, in the form of a Web page, to your machine. Once the page is in your machine's memory, your browser reads the instructions in it and uses them to display the page on your monitor.

The instructions themselves are fundamentally very simple, too. They are written in a language called Hypertext Markup Language, or HTML. Here is what the list of HTML instructions looks like for a very basic Web page, as they would appear in a text editor:

```
<HTML>
<HEAD>
<TITLE>A Very Simple Web Page</TITLE>
</HEAD>
<BODY>
<P>Hi! I'm a Web page!</P>
</BODY>
</HTML>
```

If you type this into a text editor like Notepad, then save the file with an .HTM extension instead of a .TXT extension, and open it in a browser (using the File | Open command) you will see a display that says "Hi! I'm a Web page!" And that, essentially, is the foundation of all Web pages.

However, if you're feeling uneasy at the thought of learning HTML before you can create a page, you don't need to worry. You can make perfectly good pages without writing a line of HTML, and this chapter and the next one will show you how to get started doing so.

Needless to say, most Web pages have a much longer list of instructions than the example shown previously. That is why not many people use Notepad to write Web pages, and why Web page editors have appeared to make the task of creating pages easier. These editors fall into two main groups:

- **HTML Editors**   These tend to be used by professionals who want ultra-precise control over their pages, and by people who are comfortable writing code. You need to know HTML to use them effectively.

- **WYSIWYG Web Page Editors**   These editors give you a What You See Is What You Get (WYSIWYG) display so that you can concentrate on the page's content rather than on HTML coding. They behave rather like page publishing software or high-end word processors. You type text and place images on a page, and the program converts your work into the corresponding HTML code. This is the type of editor used in this chapter and the next one.

Obtain a Web Page Editor

There are lots of Web page editors, but most are HTML-oriented, so if you want a good WYSIWYG editor for a modest price your choices are somewhat restricted. Until recently, Adobe Pagemill or FrontPage Express would have been at the top of the list for this book, but at the time of writing, Pagemill was no longer available for trial download. Likewise, FrontPage Express, which was formerly offered as an optional free component of Internet Explorer, was dropped from the new IE version, IE 5.5.

As an alternative, you could use Netscape Composer, the free Web page editor that is part of the Communicator suite. You certainly can produce good basic Web pages with Composer, but unfortunately this editor is showing its vintage, and is less flexible and capable than the newer tools available. I mention Composer so you know it's there, but there are more advanced editors around that you can download and experiment with.

One you might consider, which is the example editor used in this book, is the HotDog PageWiz editor from Sausage Software, at **www.sausage.com**. PageWiz is the medium-strength version of the editor; it also comes in a simplified form suitable for children's use, and there is a heavy-duty professional version called HotDog Professional. You can download PageWiz for a 30-day trial, after which you must purchase it to go on using the program. At US$69.95, it's a bargain if you're just getting started.

Three other WYSIWYG editors you might want to investigate are, in no particular order of merit:

- **SoftQuad HotMetal Pro Version 6 (www.hotmetalpro.com)** A 30-day evaluation version can be downloaded from the HotMetal Web site. Purchase price is US$129.

- **Microsoft FrontPage 2000 (www.microsoft.com/frontpage)** A 45-day evaluation version is available on CD (no download is offered) for $6.95. Purchase price is US$149.

- **Macromedia DreamWeaver 3 (www.macromedia.com/software/dreamweaver)** This high-end package (purchase price US$299) is intended for professionals. However, a 30-day trial version is available from the Web site, so you might want to check it out to see what an advanced editor can do. Versions are available for both Windows and Macintosh.

After you download PageWiz, install it by double-clicking the name of the download file. Follow the instructions on the screen; you will have to supply an e-mail address and be online for the installation process to complete itself.

Unfortunately, we can't work with all the features of PageWiz in the space of this chapter and the next, so you'll need to explore the editor by yourself to understand some of its tools. However, we'll cover enough of them to give you a solid start in Web page construction.

Create Basic Web Pages

The first page you create is usually the home page of your Web site. This is where your visitors will arrive first, so it should be clear, attractive, and well laid out. The main links to other pages of your site will normally appear on your home page, so it should give the visitor a pretty good idea of what the site is all about.

However, you shouldn't just leap into creating a site without some planning. Before you begin the actual page layout work, you should figure out what the site's objectives are, what pages and other resources (such as images) you'll need, and how the site should be organized and its components linked together. There are lots of books that will tell you how to do these things, so I won't attempt it in a couple of short chapters. Instead, we'll concentrate on learning the essential nuts and bolts of PageWiz, so that you'll know how a Web page editor works and what it's capable of, when you come to designing a real Web site.

In the spirit of being organized, though, you should first set up a folder in which the Web pages for your site will be stored. Once you've created the storage folder, you can launch PageWiz and get down to work.

If you're using an evaluation version of PageWiz, you'll get an intro screen with several option buttons as soon as you start the program. Click the one labeled "I want to try this software" to get to the program itself. On opening, it will resemble Figure 20-1.

20

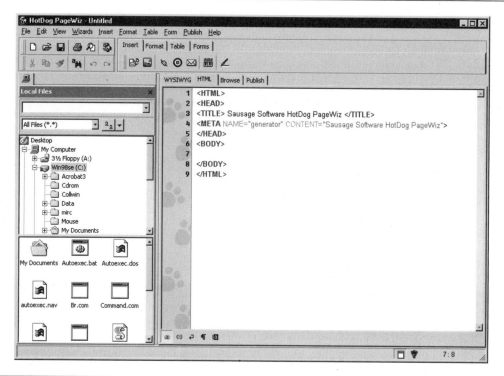

FIGURE 20-1   The opening window of PageWiz displays a basic HTML template

The Local Files box at the left of the screen is a file manager for PageWiz; you can close it by clicking the X button to give yourself more working space. You'll also notice that the workspace itself is displaying some HTML code, which, in fact, is the code for a basic page with no content. This is because PageWiz can double as an HTML editor; however, we want it to be a WYSIWYG editor, so click the WYSIWYG tab at the top of the workspace.

TIP   *To get the Local Files display back again, choose View | Resources | Local Files.*

PageWiz now displays a blank page ready for editing. To open an existing page, you can either choose File | Open and navigate to it using the Open dialog, or restore the Local Files window and use that.

Did you know?

The *mechanics* of creating a basic Web page are simple enough, but good Web page *design* is trickier than it seems. There are multitudes of badly designed sites out on the Web, and many of them are that way because of faults like these:

- The pages do not have enough white space. White space is essential to readability, so don't crowd masses of text and dozens of images onto your page.

- The site has very long pages that require a lot of scrolling.

- The author designed his pages to be viewed on a large monitor. Remember that although *you* may have a 19" monitor, most of your viewers won't. Design for a 15" monitor set at 800 × 600 resolution in 256 colors.

- The author wrote carelessly and did not check for grammatical and spelling errors. Nothing undermines a page's authority like sloppy writing.

- The author did not test her pages to make sure they worked properly. For example, broken links (ones that don't lead anywhere) are a serious flaw.

- The author did not test his pages in both the major browsers. Sometimes Web pages don't look the same in Navigator as they do in IE.

Title a Page and Save It

Just to be on the safe side, you ought to save a page almost as soon as you begin editing it. However, there is one other essential task you should do when starting a new page, and that is to give the page a suitable title. Titles are important because they appear in the title bar of a viewer's browser, and are therefore a clue as to what the page is about. They also are used by Web search engines to identify the content of a page.

The default title, which you can see in the editor's title bar, is "Sausage Software HotDog PageWiz." Obviously, you don't want that to appear at the top of all the pages in your Web site, so here's how to change it:

1. Choose Format | Page Info. The Document Information dialog appears (see the next illustration). The dialog defaults to the Title sheet, which has some useful information about the function of page titles. Read it over if you like.

20

2. In the upper text box, delete the default title and type in a new one. You can use any characters you want, since the page title is not a filename. It can also be as long as you want, but it's best to keep it to about 60 characters maximum, for people who use low screen resolutions.

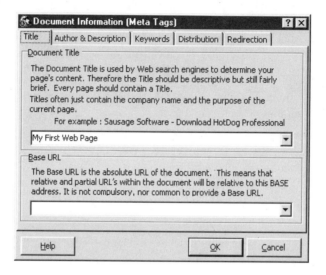

3. Click OK. The dialog vanishes and the new title appears in the editor's title box. Now that the page has an informative title, you should save it under a suitable filename. Remember that the page title and the filename are not the same things, so it's quite normal for the two to be different.

4. Choose File | Save As to open the standard Save As dialog. Navigate to the storage folder, give the page its filename, and click OK to complete the save.

The home page of a Web site usually has the filename INDEX.HTM. Sometimes it is DEFAULT.HTM. Check with the hosting service you intend to use to determine what the home page filename should be.

Preview Your Page in a Browser

Testing a page is essential to make sure it works properly, and the best way to do this is to look at it in a browser. Unfortunately, the two chief browsers, IE and Navigator, sometimes display the same HTML code in slightly different ways. You therefore must test your pages with both of them, which implies that you must have both browsers installed on your machine. PageWiz provides previewing tools that let you examine your page in any of the browsers you have on your computer.

One tool is the Browse tab above the PageWiz workspace. If you click this, you will see a preview of how the page will look in IE. That's useful, but what if you want to test the page in other browsers, for example Navigator or Opera?

If you already had these browsers on your machine before you installed PageWiz, you're in business, because PageWiz automatically senses them during installation. To preview the page in one of them, choose File | Preview to pop up a browser menu, and select the one you want to see.

If, however, you install a browser after you install PageWiz, you have to tell PageWiz to make it available. To do this:

1. Choose Edit | Preferences to open the Preferences window.

2. Click the Browsers entry to display the Preview Browsers dialog (see the next illustration).

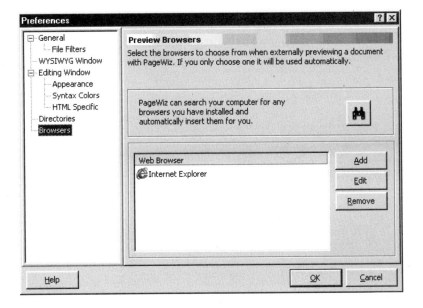

3. Click the binocular icon button to have PageWiz search for the browser. Answer Yes when it asks if it can clear the browser list, and in moments the new list with all the installed browsers appears in the list box. The search utility sometimes finds two versions of Navigator, one with the proper version number and one that says Netscape(). If this happens, you can click the Remove button to delete the one labeled Netscape().

4. Click OK to leave the dialog. The browsers will all now be available in the File | Preview menu.

When you use the Browse tab as described earlier, PageWiz doesn't actually open a copy of IE to preview the page, but rather emulates IE's behavior. To make sure you're seeing the page exactly as it will appear in your installed version of IE, use the File | Preview method, which does open the browser.

Create and Format Text

Now that you know how to title a page, save it, and look at it in a selection of browsers, we can get down to some serious work. We'll begin with that old standby, the printed word, because the fundamental element of most Web pages is text. Carefully employed images and multimedia are certainly essential for adding interest, flair, and character to a page, but most of the information people get from a Web site is textual information.

Use Headings

Headings come in six levels (sizes), and are used to set off sections of text. They help you organize your page, just as newspaper headlines or the section headings in this book assist in organizing the content. To see what all these headings look like on a page, do this:

1. Click the Format tab on the menu bar to open the Format toolbar (see the next illustration).

2. Look at the leftmost text box of this toolbar; the entry in it probably says Normal. This is the Styles box, which is used for selecting text styles. Click the small button at its right end to reveal a drop-down list of styles, and select Heading 1.

 All the tools on the Format toolbar are also available from the Format menu on the menu bar.

3. Type some text. It will be quite large. Press ENTER. You will see an info box telling you about the difference between new paragraphs and new lines. I'll explain this shortly, so mark the check box labeled Don't Show Me This Screen Again and click OK.

4. Repeat step 2, but choose Heading 2.

5. Type some more text, which will be a bit smaller. Press ENTER.

6. Repeat this process until you have put examples of all the heading levels on the page. Your page might now resemble the one in Figure 20-2.

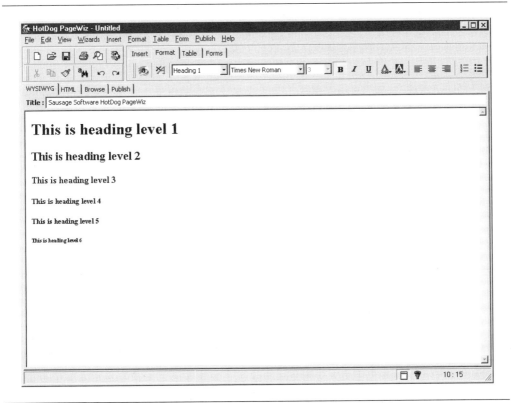

FIGURE 20-2 A display of all six sizes of heading text

What if you want to change an existing heading to a different size? To do this, click anywhere in the text. Then use the Styles box to select the desired heading level. All the text of that heading will change to the new size.

> **TIP** *To undo your most recent action, click the Undo Your Last Action button (the leftmost of the two arrow buttons above the Browse button). Repeated clicks will "back up" further. The right-hand button redoes the most recently undone action.*

Delete Text

This is so basic you've probably already assumed it. To delete text, select it and press the DELETE key. Or use the BACKSPACE and DELETE keys to remove single characters as needed.

20

Add Normal Text

By "normal text" we mean the default text of a Web page; for Windows machines, this has been arbitrarily established by the HTML language specifications to be the Times New Roman font at size 3.

Web page fonts are not sized according to the point scale you may be familiar with from other text-oriented programs. Unless you are using Cascading Style Sheet technology (a subject too complex for this book, I'm afraid), Web text comes in seven sizes only. Size 3, the default size for normal Web page text, corresponds to 12 points.

To put normal text on a page, use the Styles box to select Normal, and then begin typing. Notice that as you reach the right margin of the page, the insertion point automatically jumps to a new line, just as it does in a word processor. The difference here is that if you change the width of the editor window, the text reformats to stay within the window, no matter how narrow you make it.

After you type several lines, press the ENTER key to start a new paragraph, and type another line or two. You'll see that a blank line is inserted between the paragraphs. This may be handy sometimes, but what if you want to break a line and have the text continue immediately under it, without the space you get between paragraphs?

It's quite easy. When you come to the spot where you want to end the line, hold the SHIFT key down and press ENTER once. The insertion point moves down one line and you can begin typing again. In Figure 20-3 you can see examples of both paragraph breaks and short lines standing together.

Format Text for Size and Emphasis

You are not restricted to Normal text, however; there are numerous other formatting possibilities. For one thing, you can change the size of the text, using one of two methods.

To resize existing text, first select it, then click the arrow button at the right of the Size box on the Format toolbar. You see a drop-down list of the seven font sizes. Click the one you want, and the selected text changes.

To type new text in a selected size, first place the insertion point where you want the text to begin. Then use the Size box to specify the size you want, and begin typing. The selected size persists across paragraph breaks.

As well, you can emphasize a section of text by applying bold, italic, or underlining formatting to it, or all three effects together. You do this using the three buttons to the right of the Size box on the Format toolbar. You modify existing text by selecting it and clicking the desired button(s). To format new text, click the desired button(s) and start typing.

Finally, you can use color for text emphasis. To color existing text, select it and click the "A" button immediately to the right of the Underline button. This opens a color palette. Click on a desired color, and the selected text takes on that color. To type new text, select the color first and begin typing.

To restore the default text color of black, move the mouse pointer around the black selections of the palette until you find one that displays "Hex: # 000000" in the palette's bottom-right

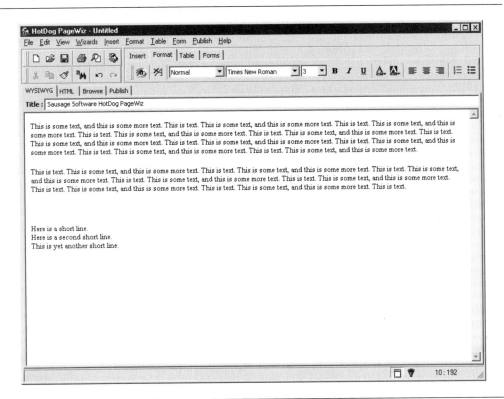

FIGURE 20-3   Paragraphs automatically have a line break between them as shown, but you can keep short lines together with the SHIFT-ENTER key combination

corner. Select this one to change the text to black. Perfectly white text in the top-left corner will display "Hex: #FFFFFF."

If you've been experimenting with text formatting and have really messed it up, it's easy to return to the default. Select the desired text and click the blue "A" icon immediately to the left of the style box. This button clears all formatting from the text selection and restores it to Normal text (Times New Roman, size 3, without any character enhancements such as italics).

Change Fonts

You no doubt have fonts other than Times New Roman installed on your computer. On a Windows machine, for example, even with a bare-bones installation, you've got Arial, Tahoma, Courier, and a few others. You can change the text of your Web page into any font on your machine.

A word of caution before you do this, however. Suppose you have a rarely used font such as Algerian installed on your computer, and you put some text in Algerian onto your Web page

20

because it gives exactly the look you want. This is fine, but a person who views the page must also have Algerian installed on her machine in order to see the text the same way. If she doesn't, her browser will substitute her default font, which will likely be Times New Roman.

Another word of caution: Don't use a dozen different fonts on your page. This is bad design because it detracts from the visual coherence of the page and also makes the text harder to read. Stick to two or three fonts that complement each other.

Now that all the warnings are out of the way, here's how to change the font of existing text:

1. Select the text you want to modify.

2. In the Format toolbar, click the button at the right-hand end of the Fonts box (it will likely be displaying Times New Roman).

3. A drop-down list of the fonts installed on your machine appears. Click the one you want, and the change is immediately applied to the selected text. You can see an example of the results in Figure 20-4.

To add new text with a particular font, place the insertion point where you want the text to begin. Then use the Fonts box to select the desired font, and begin typing.

 You can also change fonts by opening the Fonts dialog. Choose Format | Font to do this.

Align and Indent Text

From time to time you'll need to align headings or other text against the right or left margins, or center it on the page. To do this, click in the text that is to be aligned. Then, on the Format toolbar, choose one of the three buttons at its right-hand end to apply left alignment, centering, or right alignment, respectively.

To indent a paragraph from the left margin, click anywhere inside it and choose Format | Indent. To unindent it, choose Format | Outdent.

Make Bulleted or Numbered Lists

Lists are common everywhere, and the Web is no exception. As you already know, there are two basic kinds: bulleted lists (also called *unordered lists*) and numbered lists (also called *ordered lists*). Here's how to create a bulleted list from scratch:

1. Place the insertion point where you want the list to begin. From the menu bar, choose Format | List | Bulleted.

2. A bullet appears. Type the first item of the list and press ENTER.

3. Continue typing list items until finished. Press ENTER twice to end the list.

4. To add items within the list, put the insertion point at the end of the item that is to precede the new item, and press ENTER to get a new bullet.

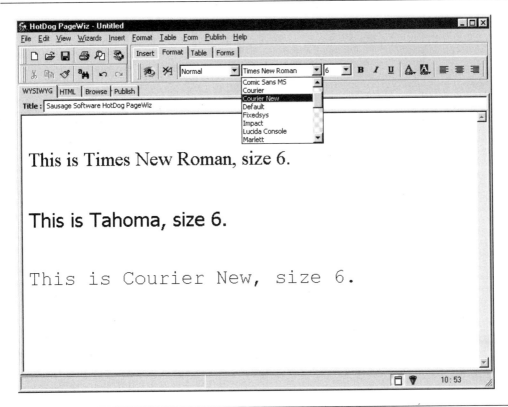

You can select a desired font quickly from the Fonts box list

To create a numbered list, choose Format | List | Numbered and proceed as you did for bulleted lists.

You can create sublists inside other lists. Let's say you have a bulleted list of four items and you want to put a sublist after the second item. Do this:

1. Place the insertion point at the end of the second item, and press ENTER.

2. A new bullet appears with nothing beside it. Choose Format | Indent. A hollow bullet shape appears, indented under the second item of the main list. This new bullet denotes the first item of the sublist.

3. Type the item, then press ENTER to get a new sublist bullet.

Continue until the list is complete. When you have entered the last item, do not press ENTER. Simply click anywhere outside the pair of lists, and you're done. The results will resemble those in Figure 20-5.

20

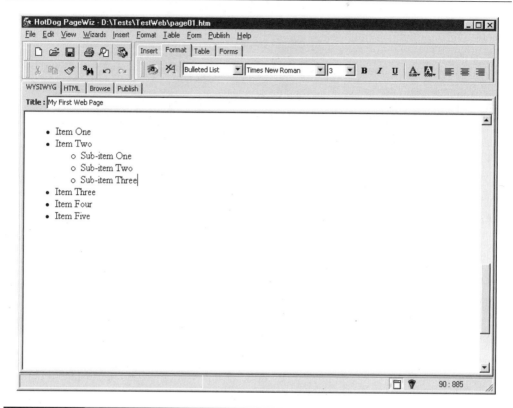

FIGURE 20-5   You can create sublists within lists

To create a list, either bulleted or numbered, from several existing paragraphs of normal text, select the desired paragraphs and choose Format | List | Bulleted, or Format | List | Numbered, respectively.

Add Horizontal Lines (Horizontal Rules)

Lines of various thickness and length are used to divide page sections from each other, and are often placed under headings to emphasize the "headline" effect. They are easy to insert; just choose Insert | Line and the following dialog appears.

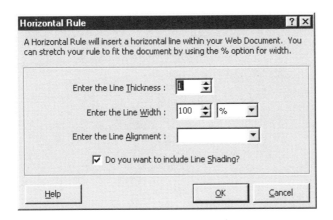

Enter the line thickness you want, and the width in percent or pixels. (*Pixel* is short for "picture element," and refers to the tiny units that make up the screen display, like pebbles in a mosaic.) The difference between percent and pixels is that a percentage line will adjust to cover the specified percentage of the user's screen, regardless of the screen's resolution setting. A line specified in pixels, however, will remain the same length independent of the monitor resolution. This means that if the line is too wide to fit on the screen, the viewer will get scroll bars in her browser. Percentage is the easiest to work with, so I'd use it unless I were being very picky about layout.

The Line Alignment list box lets you put the line against the left margin, the right margin, or centered. Obviously, the length must be less than 100% for this to have any visible effect.

Finally, you can introduce line shading by marking the bottom check box. Experimenting for a while will give you an idea of the range of effects you can get.

Work with Hyperlinks

The characteristic that really makes a Web page a Web page, of course, is the hyperlink, or more commonly, link. There are two major ways of using hyperlinks. One is to connect pages on your site to other pages on that site. The other is to connect pages on your site to sites out on the Internet.

Link to a Page Within Your Web Site

We'll start with the simplest type of link, which connects one page in your Web site to another page in it. To set this up, naturally, you'll need more than one page in the site, so make sure you create and save a second one before you begin to experiment.

Let's assume you're on the Home Page of your site and you want to make a link to another page. Images can be used as links, but we'll begin with a plain text link. Place the insertion point where you want the link to appear, and then choose Insert | Link to open the Insert Link dialog (see the next illustration).

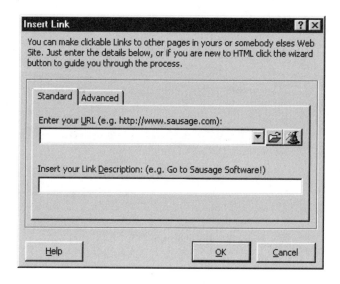

The upper text box is labeled Enter Your URL. (URL is short for Universal Address Locator, which is another name for an Internet address.) In this case, the URL is actually the filename of the link's destination page.

Click the folder button at the right end of the text box. This opens a standard Choose File dialog. Use it to navigate to the file that is the link's destination page and select the file. Click the Open button; the dialog vanishes and the filename of the destination page is now in the text box.

TIP *The small blue wizard button next to the folder button opens the Hyperlink Wizard. It will help you with setting up links, but we'll do it the old-fashioned way for now.*

The lower text box is labeled Insert Your Link Description. In this box, type the text of the link as you want it to appear on the page. Then click OK. The link appears on the page, blue and underlined as is the default for text links.

Now to test it. First, save the page. Then choose the Browse tab to display the page in IE (or you can use File | Preview and pick another browser). Click the link, and if all is well, the destination page should appear in the browser window.

Link to a Page on the Internet

Most people put external links on their Web site, that is, links to other places on the Internet that they think their visitors will find interesting or useful. To do this, first open the page that is to contain the external link. Then, as in the previous section, choose Insert | Link to open the Insert Link dialog.

In the Enter Your URL box, you must now enter the full Internet Address of the site you want to link to. This should include the http:// part preceding the www part; for example, to create a link to the Microsoft site, you would enter **http://www.microsoft.com** into the box.

However, what if you want to link to a specific page within a Web site, rather than to the home page of the site, as in the Microsoft example? You could, of course, type it in, but some addresses are long and prone to mistyping.

A way around this is to go online, launch a browser, and then navigate to the desired Web page. Then select the entire URL of the site in the browser's Location or Address box, and copy it to the Windows Clipboard by holding the CTRL key down and then pressing the C key (the CTRL-C combination).

Next, return to PageWiz's Insert Link dialog and place the insertion point in the upper text box. Hold the CTRL key down and then press the V key (the CTRL-V combination) to paste the URL into the upper text box.

Once the correct URL is in the box, fill in the lower box with the text of the link, and click OK. When you go online and test the link, the external page should appear in the browser you selected.

To delete a link, select its text and press the DELETE key.

An Alternative: Use a Free Web Hosting Service

After perusing the earlier part of this chapter, you may have decided that creating your own Web site in this way is not for you, after all. If you reach this conclusion, all is not lost, because you can use a free Web hosting service. This does indeed involve editing work, but these services do their best to make it as painless as possible. The drawback is that they pay for themselves by placing ads on your Web page. If you don't want this to happen, then these services are not for you.

The best known of the free Web hosts is probably GeoCities, now part of Yahoo!, at **http://yahoo.geocities.com**. Go to this address, and if you've already registered with Yahoo!, you can use your Yahoo! username and password to log in. If not, you must register before you can use their free hosting service.

One you've registered and logged in, you are taken to an introductory page. Click the Start Building Now link, and the process of creating your personal Web page gets under way. Follow the instructions on the screen until you reach the page where you select the tools you want to use. These range from a simple HTML text editor, to wizards that walk you through the setup of a simple page, to a WYSIWYG editor called PageBuilder.

Be aware that if you're on a dial-up connection, the process of creating, saving, and testing pages on Yahoo! will be slow to extremely slow. However, these services do provide a simple way of getting a Web page onto the Internet. But for an ad-free site that looks exactly the way you want it, you have to either hire somebody to create it to your specifications, or go the do-it-yourself route.

Having said this, let's continue along that route. In the next chapter, you'll learn about using images, tables, and a bit of multimedia, and about arranging a host for your site once you've completed it.

Where to Find It

Web Site	Address	What's There
Macromedia	www.macromedia.com	DreamWeaver Web editor
Microsoft FrontPage	www.microsoft.com/frontpage	FrontPage Web editor
Sausage Software	www.sausage.com	PageWiz Web editor
SoftQuad HotMetal	www.hotmetalpro.com	HotMetal Pro Web editor
Yahoo! GeoCities	http://yahoo.geocities.com	Free Web hosting

Chapter 21

Develop Your Web Site

How To . . .

- Understand Web image formats
- Find images you can use
- Add images to your pages
- Use images as links
- Use basic multimedia
- Use tables
- Publish your Web site to the world

Now that you've got a handle on text, it's time to go on to a more colorful subject, quite literally: putting images on your Web page. Using images is actually quite a lot simpler than using text, and often more fun, so you can look forward to enjoying yourself.

Use Images

While text is still the core of most Web pages, big chunks of such material are tiring to read on a monitor. You can reduce the text density by using lots of white space, but this makes for a bland page.

The answer, naturally, is to employ images (also called *graphics*) to enliven the page without at the same time making it hard to read or navigate. Well-chosen, well-laid-out images attract your visitor's eye and interest, and will help draw her into reading what you have to say.

Understand Web Images

Images come in all sorts of flavors: photographs, line art, icons, buttons, graphical lines, and so on. But almost all the images you see on the Web fall into one of two classes, from a technical viewpoint. They are either JPEG images or GIF images.

You may have heard of these without knowing exactly what the terms mean. They actually refer to the file format in which the image is stored; a GIF file has the filename extension .GIF, while a JPEG file has the filename extension .JPG. Here are the essential differences between the two formats:

- JPEGs can contain up to 16.7 million colors, far more than the human eye can differentiate. They are the format of choice for reproducing continuous-tone images and shading of colors, such as photographs.

- GIFs can contain up to 256 colors. They are preferred for line art with flat colors and no shading. Most of the small images on an average Web page, such as icons and buttons, are GIFs.

A word now about the best size for image files. As you already know, everything that appears on a user's screen has to be downloaded through her Internet connection, and the more information there is on a page, the longer it takes to appear. This is less of an issue for people with high-speed connections, but most people are still on dial-up. Consequently, if you put a large image (240K in size, for example) on your page, it will take so long to download even on a 56K dial-up line that your visitor will likely get tired of waiting and go elsewhere. And that, obviously, defeats the whole purpose of having a Web site.

As a rule of thumb, then, keep any graphic on your Web page to a file size of 30K or less, and remember that five such graphics will slow the page download as much as a single 150K graphic.

JPEG files can be compressed; that is, be reduced in file size at some loss in quality. Any good image processing program, such as Adobe's Photoshop or Jasc Software's PaintShop Pro, will be able to do such compression, so consider it if you have a large photographic image that you absolutely must include on your page.

Another way of giving your visitor access to large images without forcing them to wait for the download is to put links to the images on the page. Then your visitor can decide for himself whether he wants to see the picture, and the page will load a lot faster.

These links can be short bits of descriptive text, but a more common method is to use thumbnails. *Thumbnails* are small versions of the big image, typically 5K-8K in size, which you can make with an image processing program. You put the thumbnail onto the page, and then make it into a link to the large image.

Obtain Images

You can get images from all sorts of places. If you have access to a scanner, you can scan in photographs, drawings, maps, all kinds of things. If you have a digital camera, that's another obvious source. As well, you can obtain images from the Web for a wide range of purposes, from buttons to large stock photographs.

A good place to start looking for both images and general information about Web graphics is The Web Developers' Virtual Library at **http://wdvl.internet.com/Multimedia**. Open this page and find the Multimedia section, and within that section you'll see links to sources of images, graphics, and more. There is so much material here for free download that you can probably find just about anything you need.

Another good site is the IconBazaar at **www.iconbazaar.com**; you might also want to glance at Barry's Clip Art Server at **www.barrysclipart.com**. Finally, a page of links to graphics sites on the Net can be found at ClipArt.com at **www.clipart.com**.

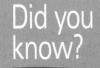

I've referred to image processing programs a couple of times. These are programs that let you manipulate graphics in all sorts of interesting ways. Quite a few different ones, of varying capabilities, are available, and some can be downloaded for trial use from sites like TUCOWS or from the vendor's site. Examples are PaintShop Pro (**www.jasc.com**, downloadable trial available), Microsoft Picture-It 2000 (purchase only), and LView Pro (**www.lview.com**, downloadable trial available).

 *Copyright exists on the Internet just as it does anywhere else. Don't assume, just because a picture is on the Web, that you can use it as if it were your own. If you do want to use such an image and you're not sure what its status is, contact the Webmaster of the site and ask. Freely usable graphical materials are usually identified as such, along with the terms under which they can be used.*

Add Images to Your Page

We'll assume you've acquired some GIFs and JPEGs and have tucked them into the same folder that contains your Web pages. Now, to insert one of these images into your page, do this:

1. Place the insertion point where you want the image to appear.

2. Choose Insert | Image to open the Insert Image dialog (see the next illustration).

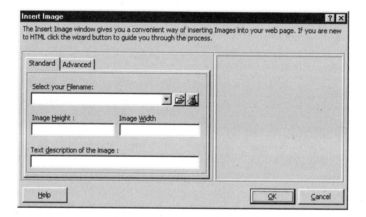

3. The top text box is labeled Select Your Filename. Click the folder icon at the right end of this box, and a standard Open File dialog will appear.

4. Use the Open File dialog to navigate to the desired image file. Select the file and click the dialog's Open button.

5. The Open File dialog disappears and a preview of the selected image appears in the Insert Image dialog.

6. The current height and width of the image, in pixels, appear in their respective text boxes. If you change the numbers, the image size on the page will change. If you do this, remember to keep the same proportion between the numbers or the image will be squashed or stretched. This allows for very precise sizing of the image.

7. Click OK. The image is inserted into the page.

 *If you have a lot of images, you should make a subfolder for them within the main Web site folder. That way they'll be easier to find and organize.*

If you want to center the image, click it to select it. You'll know it's selected when you see eight small sizing rectangles around it. Then go to the Format toolbar and click the centering button, and it will move to the page center.

To put it against the right margin, click the right-align button, and to put it back against the left margin, click the left-align button.

You can also resize an image by eye. Click it to select it, then drag one of the sizing handles to enlarge or reduce it, or change its proportions if desired.

To delete an image, select it and press the DELETE key.

> **TIP**
>
> *You can edit the properties of an already inserted image. Right-click on it and from the pop-up menu, choose Edit Image Tag. This opens the Insert Image dialog so you can modify the image's characteristics. When you close the dialog the new properties will take effect.*

Flow Text Around Images

One problem you'll soon notice if you use text and images together is that the text wants to avoid being on the same line as the image. You can see what I mean in Figure 21-1.

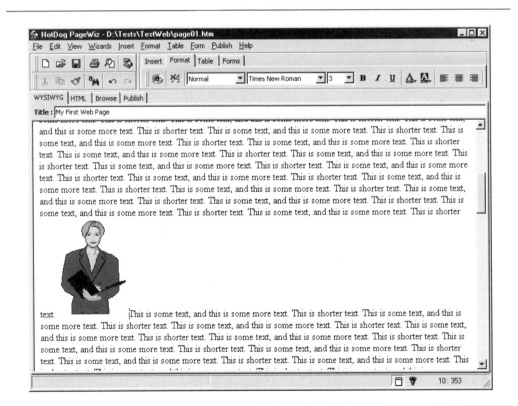

FIGURE 21-1   The text shown here breaks around the image

Often, however, you want to flow the text around the image so that the picture is better integrated with the words. Here's how to do it:

1. Place the insertion point on the line where you want the top edge of the image to be.

2. Follow steps 2 through 4, inclusive, of the previous procedure to select the desired image.

3. When you see the image preview in the Insert Image dialog, click the Advanced button to display the Advanced sheet.

4. Click the button at the right end of the Alignment list box. We'll place the image against the left margin, so select Left from the list box (see the next illustration).

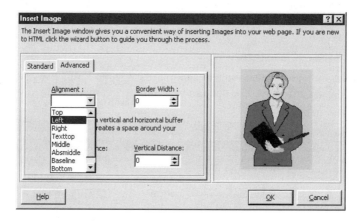

5. Click OK. The dialog vanishes and the image is placed so that the text flows around it (see Figure 21-2). To put the image against the right margin, of course, you'd choose Right in the list box.

Use Images as Links

This is a real standby on Web pages; a lot of links, perhaps most of them these days, are made from the small images called buttons or icons. The technique for turning an image into a link is simple. Do this:

1. Choose Wizards | Image Wizard.

2. In the opening wizard screen, click Next to display the next dialog.

3. In the upper text box of this dialog, use the folder button to locate and select the image file.

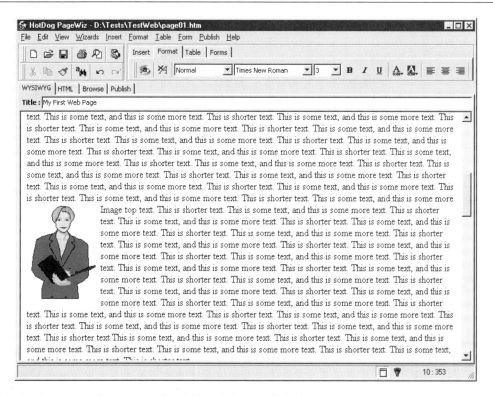

Title : My First Web Page

FIGURE 21-2   Here, with adjusted image alignment, the text flows around the picture

4. In the lower text box, use the folder button to locate and select the destination page for the link (see the next illustration).

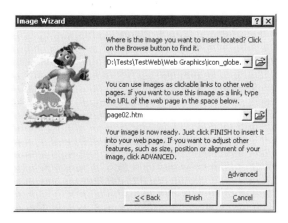

5. Click the Finish button. (If you click Next, you'll get more image options, but in the interest of simplicity we'll stop at this point.) The dialog vanishes and the image is inserted onto the page.

6. Use the Browse tab to test the image's linking behavior. The destination page should appear in the browse window when you click it.

You likely are aware of images that seem to have different links in different parts of them. Such image-based multiple links are called imagemaps. *They are tricky to create if your editor doesn't provide an imagemap tool. PageWiz doesn't have such a tool, so I'll have to leave imagemaps for you to explore on your own.*

Use Multimedia

To add video or sound to your page, you simply place a text or image link on the page, using the techniques you've already learned. Then, instead of making a Web page the link's destination, you insert the name of the sound or video file as the destination. Then, when somebody clicks the link, the file will play back in the appropriate player on his or her machine.

Be aware, though, that file download times can be very long when you use sound or video. Sound files are not too bad, but a video of any length will require an enormous file. For example, a 500K video file will take a couple of minutes to download on a 56K dial-up connection, but may give only about two seconds of playback. You don't see this delay when you're testing video in the PageWiz environment, but this is because the file is already on your machine.

As well as linking to a sound file, you can embed sound in a page so that it plays as background music as soon as somebody opens the page. To do this, choose Insert | Sound Item, and provide the filename of the sound file. I advise against doing this, however, because a lot of people become irritated at getting sound they didn't ask for. And if they don't like the music, they may immediately leave your Web page for somewhere else. Also, it only works with IE, not with Navigator.

Use Tables

Tables are often used by Web designers to organize page elements such as text, buttons, navigation bars, and images. They're also used as layout templates for whole pages, though you may not be aware of this because tables are invisible when their borders are turned off.

To insert a simple table into a page, do this:

1. Choose Wizards | Table Wizard to open the Table Wizard dialog. In the first screen, click Next.

2. In the second screen, choose the Classic option. Click Next.

3. In the third screen, specify the number of rows and columns you want in the table. Leave the other values at their defaults, and click Next.

4. In the fourth screen, specify the border thickness. If you want the table borders to be invisible, set this value to zero. Specify the colors, if any, that you want for the cell backgrounds and for the border colors themselves. Click Next.

5. In the fifth screen, specify cell spacing and padding. Click Next.

6. In the sixth screen, decide whether you want commented or plain text inserted into the table cells. Leave these boxes blank and click Finish.

The results don't look like much, do they? Just a squashed little grid at the corner of the page. However, once you start inserting data into the table cells, things will look better, since the cells will automatically size themselves to fit the content.

If you prefer to fix the minimum table dimensions yourself in step 3, specify them either in pixels or in percent. As these are minimums, the table will expand if the cell data requires it. For example, in Figure 21-3, the table size is set at 400 pixels wide by 100 pixels high, but the inserted frog image has forced the resizing of the lower row of cells.

Unfortunately, PageWiz does not give you a way to edit an existing table in WYSIWYG mode, so you'll have to begin over again if you don't like the results. Alternatively, you can learn to do table editing in HTML (not a pleasant thought—it's *very* picky work).

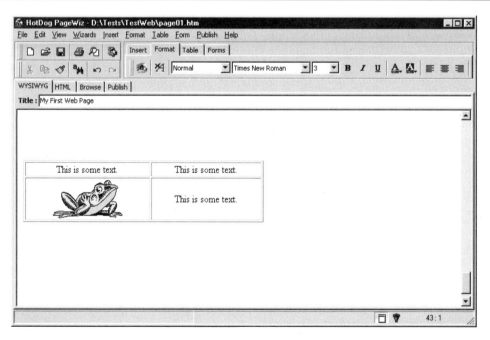

FIGURE 21-3   Tables can contain both images and/or text

The elements inside the cells can be text or images or both. You can align them within the cell boundaries by selecting them and using the controls on the Format toolbar. For example, the image and text in Figure 21-3 were aligned with the centering button.

Publish Your Web to the World

Eventually, you'll have all the bits of your Web site the way you want them, and it will be time to put the site on a Web server so the world can beat a path, figuratively speaking, to your door.

We've assumed in this chapter and the previous one that you'll be using your ISP to host your site. You have two choices as to how to do this, however:

■ Your ISP can provide server space for the site. Often this is free for small personal sites needing no more than 5-10 megabytes of storage. The Internet address of your site will be associated with your ISP's address; for example, www.myisp.com/~my_site_name.

■ You can go to a professional Web hosting service. Your ISP may provide such a service, but you can certainly use a different company if you wish. Through the hosting service you will set up a permanent Internet address, also called a domain name, such as www.myweb.com. You can choose a domain name that reflects the nature of your site (assuming nobody else has already taken the name) and the hosting service will register it for you. The domain is then yours forever, or until you de-register it. Having your own domain name is a good thing because it makes your site easier to find, and certainly sounds more professional. For registering a domain name, your hosting service should charge US$70, plus a smaller maintenance fee of about US$35 per year thereafter. On top of this fee, you will pay a monthly charge for the service, which typically includes things like multiple mailboxes, CGI scripting access, and other technical stuff.

Choosing a hosting service is not an exact science, so you should approach it in the same way that you researched your ISP. Following are some questions to ask. They are primarily applicable to the fee-for-service hosting arrangements, not to the free service your ISP may provide for personal pages.

■ Is the service capable of carrying the traffic you expect at your site?

■ How much disk space do you get, and how much does more of it cost if you need it?

■ What provisions do they have for backup servers if their main servers go down? You don't want your site to be inaccessible for hours or days.

■ Can you get tracking data to find out who visited your site and for how long, and what they did there?

■ If you want to get into multimedia, do they provide specialized audio and video servers you can use? How much will that cost?

■ Do they provide 24-hour support, seven days a week?

■ Can you find out how other clients like the support service they provide?

■ Since the service's other clients obviously have Web sites, find out which ones they are and go visit them at peak hours to see how the connection speed is.

If you get satisfactory answers to these questions, and the price is right, the service is probably one you can live with. Once you've signed up, the details of moving your Web site to the host server will vary according to the hosting service. It is quite likely that you'll be asked to use FTP to upload to files, but there's a whole chapter about that earlier in the book, so you should be just fine!

Where to Find It

Web Site	Address	What's There
Barry's Clip Art Server	www.barrysclipart.com	Web graphics
ClipArt.com	www.clipart.com	Web graphics links
IconBazaar	www.iconbazaar.com	Web graphics
JASC	www.jasc.com	PaintShop Pro image processor
LView Pro	www.lview.com	LView Pro image processor
Microsoft	www.microsoft.com	Picture-It 2000 image processor
Web Developers' Virtual Library	http://wdvl.internet.com/ Multimedia	Web graphics links

Appendix A

A Very Brief Chronology of the Internet and Web

1958   U.S. Department of Defense establishes the Advanced Research Projects Agency (ARPA). Its founding directive states that the organization is to direct and carry out "advanced projects in the field of research and development." ARPA starts out by providing funding for a number of universities as well as government establishments. (After 1958 the agency sometimes called itself DARPA (the "D" for "Defense") but DARPA and ARPA were always the same entity.)

1966   ARPA provides funding to experiment with a computer network that would connect some of its member universities together. The intention is to allow researchers to communicate their findings to each other more easily via e-mail. (The name of the network eventually became ARPANET.)

1969   ARPANET begins operation with four universities connected.

1971   Fifteen universities with 23 network sites are connected by ARPANET.

1974   The TCP design for network communications among computers is first set out. The term "Internet" is used for the first time.

1978   The basic specifications of TCP/IP, the Internet communications method, are established.

1982   TCP/IP is established by the U.S. Department of Defense as the communications standard for ARPANET and all U.S. military computer networks.

1983   ARPANET is split into military and civilian divisions. With the creation of the civilian side, the Internet proper is born.

1987   The first personal hypertext authoring system is introduced by Apple with their Hypercard.

1989   CompuServe and MCI, providers of private electronic mail services, connect to the Internet.

1989   Tim Berners-Lee at CERN (Center for European Nuclear Research) outlines a hypertext system to help researchers at CERN share information.

1990   ARPANET closes down for good, replaced by the Internet. Tim Berners-Lee writes the first versions of the software that will make the World Wide Web a possibility.

1991   Restrictions on commercial use of the Internet are dropped, essentially opening it to the public. The first text browser is developed and released.

1993   First version of the Mosaic WWW graphics-capable browser is released.

1994   Explosive growth of the number of Internet host computers. The World Wide Web Consortium (W3C), an organization to establish common standards for the Web, has its first meeting. Netscape Communications releases the Navigator Web browser, which soon displaces Mosaic.

1995   Work begins on the Apache Web server software. Apache later becomes the major Internet Web server.

1996   Nine million Internet hosts are in existence. In the summer, Microsoft hastily releases the first version of its Internet Explorer Web browser.

1997   The number of Internet hosts passes 16 million.

1998-2000   Consumer use of the Internet continues to expand rapidly, and high-speed cable, wireless, optical fiber, and DSL connections begin to replace dial-up.

Index